MIRTH OF A NATION

MIRTH
OF A
NATION
The Best Contemporary Humor

Edited by
MICHAEL J. ROSEN

Perennial
An Imprint of HarperCollinsPublishers

FIRST EDITION

Designed by Christine Weathersbee

Library of Congress Cataloging-in-Publication Data

Mirth of a nation: the best contemporary humor/edited by
Michael J. Rosen.—1st ed.
     p.   cm.
   ISBN 0-06-095321-7
     1. American wit and humor.   I. Rosen. Michael J.,
1954– .
   PN6162.M54 2000
   817'.5408—dc21   99-44293

00 01 02 03 04 ❖/RRD 10 9 8 7 6 5 4 3 2 1

Submissions Guidelines

The Thurber Biennial of American Humor welcomes submissions. Some guidelines are as follows. **GENERALLY:** All submissions should be typed, double-spaced, and printed on paper. This paper should be recycled paper, manufactured from at least 80 percent recycled post-consumer recycled fiber. If your submission is printed on unrecycled paper, it will be thrown out. **WHITENESS OF PAPER:** The paper used should be as white as possible. If the paper is not as white as The Thurber House believes it could be, you may be asked to resubmit your manuscript, on paper that is whiter. **MARGINS:** On all pages, margins should be one inch, on all sides, with the exception of the top margin, which should be one and one-half inch. However, if the submission is over eleven pages, the margins should increase by one quarter inch for every additional page. If the submission is over eleven pages, the submission should be shortened, for no submissions should be over eleven pages. **TABS:** Tabs should be between one quarter of an inch and one third of an inch deep. One third of an inch is preferred. If for whatever reason your tabs are not between one quarter and one third of an inch, please write to The Thurber House for a copy of Form 56G, on which you can explain your deviance from the tab-depth norm, and make clear exactly why you are engorging yourself on our free time simply to scribble mindlessly, meekly justifying your indulging of your unfortunate tab-making proclivities. In the unlikely event that your alternative tabbing is approved, you will then be asked to adjust your manuscript so that it is then not double-spaced, but single-spaced, and printed on paper that is less white. If, however, your manuscript is over eight pages, and has tabs less than one quarter inch, please increase your margins by one third of an inch, and place your page numbers on the left sides of the page, as opposed to the bottom. **PAGE NUMBERS:** Please place page numbers at the top of the page, unless your submission is over eight pages, in which case page numbers should be at the bottom, unless the margins are less than one half inch, or the tabs are not more than one quarter inch, in which case page numbers should be on the left-hand side of the page, and rendered in a type size no bigger than 5 point. In a departure from our last submissions guidelines, we now insist that page numbering be sequential. **FASTENING AND MAILING:** When fastening the pages of your manuscript, do not use staples, and do not use paper clips. Do not fasten the pages of your submission together at all. There is no justifiable reason to pierce the pages together, invading their individual integrity only so that they be made part of some ostensibly greater whole. We reject the notion of bound-together pages, and would greatly prefer you to let your pages stand on their own, albeit in orderly fashion. Simply stack them, neatly, making sure that all corners are precisely in accordance with one another, and then, without carelessly undoing the straightening work you have just finished, insert them in a 9" × 12" white—not manila—envelope. Important: When closing the envelope, please do not use your saliva. While the trustees of The Thurber House are passingly interested in viewing your attempts at humor, they are not at all interested, while opening your missive, in running their fingers through your dried oral discharge. **ALSO:** Before undertaking the typing, straightening, and mailing of your submission, please do us the small favor of washing your hands. Please. It should not be so much to ask for you to simply run your hands under a running faucet, with a little soap. Not much to request, correct? It should only take a second—you go into the washroom, turn on the water, wash for a minute or two, then you come back. Yes. Yes. We will wait here. We will wait here, whistling softly perhaps, thinking of Maine, the summers clear, warm, the lake, Lake Mittenoka, still, frigid in June but by August . . . Oh there you are. Great. Oh no. That won't do. If you don't mind, would you wash them again? You seem not to have done a thorough job the first time around. That's right, go on. We will wait here. We are happy to wait, if it means that your hands will be clean. We will be fine, waiting here, in

Maine, in the cabin, 4D, with the older boys, the year there was Sharon, the new counselor, with her long, tanned legs . . . Oh good, you're back. Ok, let's see them. Good, good, now let's see the backs. Oh no. No, no. Please. You have not even touched the backs of your hands! You *must* wash both sides. Oh but you must. We do not care if you think they're clean. Oh really? Can you *see* bacteria? Do you have supra-microscopic X-ray vision? Are you some kind of Bacterial Over-Man, unbound by laws of cleanliness, untethered by rules of hygiene and guidelines of decency? Did you come from a planet where the gravity or atmosphere or whatever was different, such that your appearance on this world rendered you capable of not only extraordinary feats of strength but also the ability to be self-cleaning? Well, are you? No. No, we didn't think so. Now go, wash. We will be waiting here, chewing gum and humming quietly. Oh, Sharon! **SELF-ADDRESSED STAMPED ENVELOPES:** Do not bother enclosing a self-addressed stamped envelope, as the Thurber House will only be contacting you in the highly unlikely event that we find your work at all amusing. So save your envelopes, save your self-addressing, and save your stamp. Self-addressed stamped envelopes erroneously sent to The Thurber House will be angrily disposed of, and your name will be crossed off the list. WHAT LIST? *The* list, dummy. OH. Yes. Oh. **INCLUSION OF WIT AND WHIMSY IN/ON RÉSUMÉS:** If you are including a resumé or curriculum vitae, please be sure to include on it or on your cover letter some hint that you are a funny, offbeat person. Such indications help us. Otherwise, how are we to know? We recommend: in your margins, little cartoons; instead of bold or italic type, offbeat colors; generally, whimsical changes in fonts and font sizes. This way we know that fun is in store, that you know how to "shake it up." Also, when writing your cover letter: First, skim the table of contents page of this edition of *Mirth of a Nation*. Then, pick out one essay. Turn to it—its page number will be indicated on said table of contents—and read its title and first paragraph. Then, refer to it casually in the second paragraph of your cover letter, in a way that does not betray your overall (rapacious) ignorance but instead says, "Thurber House, I am one with your sort of content and mission, having spent much time and heart devouring your product, the quality and goals of which I care about much, much more than simply the feathering-in-my-cap of my appearing within its hallowed pages." **CONTENT:** In terms of content, we are glad to say that at The Thurber House, we put no restrictions whatsoever on content, with a few exceptions. We are no longer accepting work related to or making light of humidity. Humidity, we find, is no longer funny. Also, due to an unexpected surplus, the following subject matters are no longer encouraged: boating, Alexander Graham Bell, colonial America in general, and philately. In addition, for reasons that may not be obvious to someone like yourself but which are no less valid simply because you insist on avoiding what should be searingly obvious, please try to avoid touching on World War II, World War I, the Korean War, the Vietnam War, Desert Storm, and the recent conflict in Kosovo. (Grenada, however, is still available for comment.) In a departure urged by The Thurber House's trustees, work making light of the dentistry profession will not be considered. Farming is also no longer seen as funny. Please also avoid touching on roofing, bricklaying, masonry in general, and mechanical engineering. Vacuuming is not funny. Tiling is not funny. The Hague is not funny. Also not funny are events or people taking place or living in: Africa, Asia, North America, Europe, and Australia. Other subjects best avoided: astronomy, dolphins, movies, toys, animals, families, towns, sports, people, relationships, pets, celebrities, and work. The following subject matters are encouraged, however, as they seem to always yield great humor: 1) funny things the president has done or might soon do; 2) funny things actors and actresses have done or might soon do; 3) funny things religious people have done or might do, given the chance, because they are strange religious types who always seem to do very, very funny things, often while wearing funny, funny, funny outfits. **LENGTH:** All submissions should be under 1,500 words, unless they need to be longer, in which case they will be accepted at whatever length, provided they are brief (ideally under 1,500 words). **IN CLOSING:** Thank you for reading and we look forward to reading your work.

Contents

Outside the alphabetical presentation of writers listed here, throughout *Mirth of a Nation* four other writers' words are featured:

"Millennial Maxims" by **MARK O'DONNELL** (to be known henceforth as M.O'D.) appear on pages 45, 88, 124, 145, 174, 212, 231, 274, 355, 440, 543, 554, 589, and 596. Beyond these aphorisms, his other work is listed within the contents pages.

"Zone Five: Gardening Advice from Mertensia Corydalis," by **BONNIE ABBOTT,** appears on pages 59, 102, 151, 188, 296, 335, 408, 457, 531, and 552.

"News Quiz" by **RANDY COHEN**—and a slew of guest contributors—appear on pages 39, 80, 115, 167, 209, 245, 311, 360, 432, 475, 536, and 573. His wrap-up and News Quiz Extras follow each piece.

DAVE EGGERS has supplied the book with "A Note About the Type" (page 599), "A Note About the Editor" (page 597), and "Submissions Guidelines" (page v).

MIRTH OF A NATION

Introduction: Humor Me

"... humor in a living culture must not be put away in the attic with the flag, but should be flaunted, like the flag, bravely. Every time is a time for comedy in a world of tension that would languish without it."[1] So wrote James Thurber in the foreword to the last book he published during his life. Surely, forty years later, the world is no less filled with tension, no less in need of flaunted flags. To judge from the contents of this vol-

[1] *Lanterns and Lances:* New York, Harper & Brothers (1961). Now, I cite this here both to remind readers that it's been forty years since Thurber's death, and to inform those innocents who, when I say I'm phoning from The Thurber House, ask me to spell "Thurber" as though it were an especially tricky word, like Michael ... "Is it *a-e-l* or *e-a-l?*" Anyway, Thurber was born in 1894 and died at the age of sixty-seven. This has no bearing on the present volume since it contains none of Thurber's work and we didn't, at the last, even title the book "The Thurber Biennial of American Humor," which might have lent a certain caché or literary imprimatur much as the name O. Henry lends to the American short story (which is curious, since O. Henry must be the only writer besides Stephen Crane whose readership is constituted entirely of high school students). There were a few reasons we went with *Mirth of a Nation,* even though we have no motive to play off the title of D. W. Griffith's film. First, some folks thought that some other folks wouldn't know who Thurber was, let alone know how to spell his name. And second, the word "biennial" can be confused with "biannual" (every other year versus twice a year), leaving book buyers with the unsettling feeling that this inaugural volume, even at 650-some pages, is somehow incomplete. (Is anyone still reading this tiny type? Me, I haven't been able to read anything this size since my eyes' lenses

1

ume alone, even Thurber's "life and hard times" didn't have to contend with inventing white lies so children could understand White House goings-on (see Prudence Crowther's "What We Told the Kids"), the moot (by the time you're reading this) miscalculations of our millennium-passing computer chips (see Daniel Radosh's "T.G.I.Y2K!"), or tips for teens on being conscientiously queer (see Bob Smith's "A Few Notes on Sex Education")—all of which would have made our own Jim Thurber quite tense.

The age-old bugaboo about humor writing goes like this: Comedy isn't a serious form, while tragedy is. In the scholarly words of Louis D. Rubin, Jr., "Thalia, the muse of comedy, has always been something of a wallflower in critical circles, and the attention has gone principally to Melpomene and her more glamorous celebrants of tragedy."[2] And so *Mirth of a Nation*—a new biennial series, I'm delighted to report—will make another claim: that humor writing is seriously funny. Now by "seriously," I mean, of course, "genuinely" or "honestly" funny, but I also mean also "seriously" in a way that I'd suggest only poetry rivals (being a poet rather than a humorist myself, I make this comparison advisedly): a deliberate attempt at taking something to heart or to task, a sustained effort at acknowledging a complexity that a passing comment or glance simply doesn't reveal.

OK, now bear with me. Both humor and poetry employ a nuance-splitting selection of words and an overall compression of language that encourages the repetition necessary to slow down and scrutinize the too-fine print of our omnimedia-besotted days.

hardened, along with all the other baby boomers', around the age of forty. If you're among the "some folks" too nearsighted to know Thurber, trust me: Eight-point type will not always be your friend.) So *Mirth of a Nation* it is. We're assuming "mirth" isn't too off-putting, despite the fact that, like "merriment," no one uses the word in conversation.

[2] I found this quote in a book edited by Nancy A. Walker entitled *What's So Funny*, which was, as you guessed, not so funny, and not supposed to be. It's a collection of academic essays, which as a responsible editor, I felt obliged to

And aren't these the only two forms that we consistently choose to reread, read aloud to friends, clip and save and post on the fridge or the Internet?

Surely this is, in part, due to the forms' shared brevity. But both also contain more than a cursory reading reveals. The way that humor arrives at its ideas is as interesting as the ideas themselves, and so, like poetry, it's less the revelations themselves (we hardly need either to tell us what we know or, at least, suspect) than the way such truths are surprised from us, sprung loose in fits of laughter and sighs of recognition from the otherwise inattentive nod we give most of what passes before our eyes.

I'd also have us remember that both poetry and short humor pieces used to be the province of all readers. They were the mini-features, the columnist's 600-word forum, the marginalia and boxed favorites of most every magazine. Amateurs (in the truest sense of that word) practiced both forms as simply part of family entertainment or solitary amusement. And still, when someone with no pretense of being a professional writer approaches the fields of literature, it's for reflection or deflection, for poetry or for humor (which, for the moment, leaves aside the humor of bad poetry). Toasts, tributes, retelling jokes, recounting anecdotes, regaling one another with the quirks of ancestors—it's humor that most often serves as the social currency of our nation. It's the shibboleth of kindred spirits, the decoded message of anxious allies, the high five of the Diaspora's home team.

Humor is, in fact, a sign of life, a *vital* sign. A sign that there's

---

read. Louis D. Rubin Jr.'s quote comes from his essay "The Great American Joke," which I understand, from squinting to read Walker's footnote, is from Rubin's own book, *The Comic Imagination in American Literature*. I gather that book touches on Melville, Henry James, Hawthorne, Twain (folks I haven't read for so long that I'd need to reread them before reading Rubin), along with other authors I don't think I've ever read or plan to get around to reading. At some point—probably about the time the lenses harden—a person just has to draw the line and say, "I won't have time, this life, for Dreiser." There's nothing funny about this either, and there isn't supposed to be.

one life we imagine for ourselves and another life that we end up living, and there within that discrepancy resides one form of limbo or another. Either you see it as the unfunny Catholic kind of limbo, where your hapless soul languishes between heaven and hell with only Melpomene for company . . . or you see it mirth-fully as the West Indian sort of limbo, where you say, "Oh, what the hell," grab the hand of Thalia—that bashful wallflower beside the bowl of rum punch—bend over backward and do your tourist best to dance under the bar.[3]

My hope in *Mirth of a Nation* is to preserve and perpetuate just these shorter pieces of humor most often considered the filler of magazines or airtime, but which are, in fact, essential supplements to our well-being. There are no excerpts here of book-length satires or exceptionally witty or campy novels. I've resisted narrative cartooning, redacted stand-up sketches, or jokes, as well as humorous forms that were not created specifi-cally as laughter *qua* laughter, humor for its own sake.[4] (I hesi-tated having contributors sign affidavits saying they had no motive beyond merriment and the token emolument some mag-azine coughed up.) I read a good many extremely funny per-

---

[3]Just for the record, this metaphor occurred to me since I lived in the West Indies for six months while attending school at the now famous St. George's School of Medicine, where Reagan staged Operation Lift in 1985. Alas, the first-year students—among which I counted myself, at least for one semester— were located at a different campus than the beach-side bungalow his troops managed to free from the wicked influence of Cubans and Communists and so forth. I lived there seven years before all that half-baked brouhaha, and while we didn't really have a lot of time outside of our studying and snorkeling to dance the limbo, I don't recall ever seeing anyone engaged in this giddy recre-ation, not even at the tourist hotels where the proportion of liquor to mixer in most drinks was reversed (the cost of importing things like tonic water far exceeded the cost of local liquors) and patrons might have achieved a requisite level of uninhibitedness. While martinis were not in fashion then or there, it's always good to remember Thurber's aphorism: "One martini is just right. Two is too many. Three is not enough."

[4]I thought that employing the Latin *"qua"* might lend a less impeachable authority to what is clearly nothing more dignified than my particular taste or

sonal essays and pieces of investigative journalism but had to pass them by, sensing that their humor had been eclipsed by the reporting of a particular topic. Perfectly legitimate work, I grant you, but for this biennial, I'm insisting that humor is not the spoonful of sugar that helps the medicine go down, but the medicine itself. And potent stuff it must be.[5]

Finally, I have edited this book at The Thurber House, where I've been literary director since the restoration of James Thurber's boyhood home. The house is a center for writers and readers, and, over the last sixteen years, we've featured many of the nation's most engaging authors in our readings and residencies. We've shown particular favoritism toward humorists. Since 1997, we've been awarding the Thurber Prize for American Humor, a national book award for the best volume of humor published in a given two-year period.

Which bring us to this volume, slated to be the first in a series that will establish a lasting format for the literature of short pieces of humor writing.

About writers of said pieces, Thurber himself understood the serious aspect of their work: "Afraid of losing themselves in the larger flight of the two-volume novel, or even the one-volume novel, they stick to short accounts of their misadventures because they never get too deep into writing them but that they feel they can get out. This type of writing is not a joyous form of self-expression but the manifestation of a twitchiness at once cosmic and mundane. Authors of such pieces

---

editorial bias. For the record, I do feel some comfort with Latin since I studied Latin in seventh grade—a decidedly unpopular choice, but, even then, I had my heart set on becoming a physician. Coincidentally, my teacher was one Mrs. Elaine Rubin. (Of course, this is the first time I've actually employed her first name.) I can't say if she was or wasn't related to the aforementioned scholar Louis D.

[5]Parents everywhere should take some small pleasure in knowing that the thousands of dollars spent on a child's medical school education can yet have some small pay-off such as these otherwise far-flung metaphors.

have, nobody knows why, a genius for getting into minor difficulties: they walk into the wrong apartments, they drink furniture polish for stomach bitters,[6] they drive their cars into the
prize tulip beds of haughty neighbors, they playfully slap gangsters, mistaking them for old school friends. To call such persons 'humorists,' a loose-fitting and ugly word, is to miss the
nature of their dilemma and the dilemma of their nature. The
little wheels of their invention are set in motion by the damp
hand of melancholy." I can't say that everyone here possesses
this particular genius,[7] but they have all found some means of
recalibrating the reality we receive, though frequently can't
quite believe.

   I invite readers and writers alike to share work for subsequent
volumes. While Dave Eggers has penned welcoming enough
guidelines for submissions on pages v–viii, folks may also simply
send materials with a self-stamped, self-addressed envelope to
The Thurber House, 77 Jefferson Avenue, Columbus, OH 43215.
Or stop by someday and tour the place. Information about

---

[6]Perhaps some help with the phrase "drink furniture polish for stomach bitters." No Caribbean medical school education required here. First of all, the
"for" connecting the two liquids is shorthand for "in place of." And truth be
told, if Thurber had been able to see both bottles, the brown glass beneath the
label might be identical enough to offer some confusion. But honestly. The
smell alone should have been a clue. What are stomach bitters? The quaintly
archaic packaging of any bartender's bottle of Angostura Aromatic Bitters (45
percent alcohol by volume, produced in the West Indies—coincidence again?)
states quite clearly that bitters have "long been known as a pleasant and
dependable stomachic." Just as archaic, this word "stomachic," which just
means "good for the stomach" according to the two-volume OED with the
magnifying glass in the drawer that I never imagined anyone needing to use
when I first bought the set. Oh to be able to have flexible lenses and, while
we're at it, a college student's stomach.

[7]Not anyone in this book shares the visual impairment that eventually produced Thurber's complete blindness as well as the unlucky but not unfunny
incidents he cites. But given the chance to grouse and gripe, our contributors
could certainly offer up their own inspiring hardships and handicaps. The
quote is from Thurber's essay, "Preface to a Life," My Life and Hard Times,
New York, Harper & Brothers (1933). A good vintage for bitters.

the house and its programs can be found on our Web site: www.thurberhouse.org.

Now, put on the limbo music and pour yourself some rum punch. That's it, take your medicine like a good patient. (Don't kid yourself: Your condition is serious.)

—Michael J. Rosen
The Thurber House
Columbus, Ohio

"You'll Never Groom Dogs in This Town Again!"

HENRY ALFORD

Spitting is prohibited in subway cars mainly to:

a) encourage politeness

b) prevent spread of disease

c) reduce the cost of cleaning cars

d) prevent slipping

From the Telephone Maintainer civil service test

Assume that, while a [Bridge and Tunnel] Officer is collecting a toll from a motorist, the Officer sees a child tied up in the rear of the car. Of the following, the best thing for the Officer to do is to:

a) ignore what has been seen and continue collecting tolls

b) try to delay the car and signal for assistance

c) reach into the car and untie the child

d) tell the driver that he cannot use the bridge
unless he unties the child

*From a preparation guide for the Bridge
and Tunnel Officer civil service test*

The proper technique for selling floral designs involves:

    a) ignoring customers when they are waiting for
        service
    b) being assertive, taking no nonsense from the
        customer
    c) treating the customer the way you want to be
        treated
    d) calling the customer "honey" or "dear"

From an exam given by the Rittner's School
of Floral Design in Boston, Massachusetts

In earlier, simpler times, you became established in
a trade by following a steady path from apprentice to journey-
man to master. You matured into a trusted artisan through a
natural process, and you did not need to be worried about
becoming "certified" and filling in computer-readable answer
bubbles with a number-two pencil and responding "true" or
"false" on a psychological test to the statement "I prefer tall
women." No, a blacksmith was a blacksmith because he was
a blacksmith; chandlers chandled and wheelwrights wrought
wheels. In today's superrationalized, postindustrial world, however, we trust numbers more than experience, so to qualify for
almost any money-making endeavor, from lawyer to interior
decorator to cement mason, you may be obliged to take a test.
There is a Certified Picture Framers examination. There is an
Aerobics Instructors test.

    In an attempt to identify exactly what employers and pro-
fessional organizations are looking for in their employees and
members—and, incidentally, to identify exactly what work I
might be suited for other than the underrationalized and basically preindustrial labor of freelance writing—I took thirty-one
official or practice tests. The tests ranged from tests for bar-

tenders, postal machine mechanics, radio announcers, and travel agents to tests for addiction specialists, geologists, foreign service officers, and FBI agents. (I did not take the exam for state troopers, however, having taken offense at some of the questions in a preparation guide for that test: "When driving a full-sized car, are you tall enough to see over the steering wheel?" "When standing next to a full-sized car, can you easily see over the top?" "Can you climb over a full-sized sedan either lengthwise or from side to side?" The writers of the test seemed to suspect me of being a dwarf.)

My results were not always encouraging; I passed only three tests.

There is not yet a test for freelance writers, of course. It occurs to me that perhaps this is just as well.

SO YOU WANT TO BE A COSMETOLOGIST

In addition to a written test that includes questions on bacteriology, trichology, dermatology, and histology, aspiring cosmetologists in New York State must pass a three-hour-long practical exam. At the busy, dark premises of the Wilfred Beauty Academy at Broadway and Fifty-fourth Street, I took the first four of seven parts of the mock version of the practical exam that Wilfred students must pass before taking the state board examination.

I entered the classroom area, its air redolent with the aroma of singed hair and perfumey fluorocarbons. I joined a group of about thirty white-lab-coat-wearing students who were under the tutelage of the obdurate Ms. Valentine. A short, middle-aged Hispanic woman with full, round cheeks, Ms. Valentine has a slightly regal bearing and luxuriant blonde hair—the empress dowager of Wella Balsam. But upon introducing herself to me she explained, "They call me the Drill Sergeant."

Pleasantries dispensed with, she reached into the three-foot-tall wooden cabinet in which wigs are dried and pulled out a male rubber mannequin head with slightly chiseled, epicene facial features. Its hair was done up in curlers and covered with a hairnet. Then, with a clamping device, Ms. Valentine used her impressive strength to briskly attach the head to the worktable closest to the wig dryer.

Ms. Valentine barked out the command to begin the first part of the exam—the "comb-out"—and then urged us to be assiduous about "relaxing the set." Upon seeing that other students were "effilating" (teasing) their heads' hair with combs, I followed suit; but upon snagging and almost breaking one of the comb's teeth in the resultant tangle, I decided that this was not the proper avenue to hair relaxation. I recommenced with a brush. When a bell sounded at the conclusion of the twenty-five minutes, I had fashioned a sort of churning mass of blondeness—Gunther Goebbel-Williams after having strayed too close to an air duct. Ms. Valentine strode around the room and, jabbing her finger into some coiffures, briefly combing others, took notes. Her look of unenthused calm suggested a high level of professionalism.

For the hair-shaping phase of the exam, I was given a water sprayer, plastic clips, shears, and a female mannequin head with long, straight brown hair. Handing me an illustration of a head of hair sectioned into four quadrants and one encircling fringe, Ms. Valentine explained that I would have thirty minutes to "section, remove excess bulk, and blend." This sounded like a tall order. Indeed, it was—I spent twenty-four minutes effecting a fringe and quadrants. During this time, Ms. Valentine slunk down the aisle four times, each time yelling a new command: "Razor!" "Blunt cutting!" "Effilating!" "Thinning shears!" This was not creating an environment in which I felt I could do my best work.

Upon looking at the clock I realized that I had only three minutes left; it was with a great sense of urgency that I launched into my excess-bulk removal and shaping.

In the twenty minutes given for the permanent waving segment of the exam, I resectioned the hair and then, using wee, slippery pieces of tissue paper, put about one third of it up in curlers. At the conclusion of the segment, Ms. Valentine announced that we would break for lunch. Some ten seconds later four girls had swarmed around the wig dryer out of which they stealthily pulled the Tupperware containers full of chop suey and rice and beans that would serve as their lunches.

After lunch we fingerwaved. According to Ms. Valentine, fingerwaving—the process by which one molds hair into even, 1930s-style ridges—is the most difficult part of the exam: "Sometimes students just break down crying during it." She gave me a plastic bottle of fingerwaving lotion—a sticky, viscous substance evocative of whipped spit. I labored diligently during this twenty-minute leg of the exam; although I was unable to create the plates and ridges of hair with which the other students were transforming their heads into what looked like well-lubricated armadillos, I *was* able to create a mottled, wavy look that had its own eerie beauty.

At the conclusion of testing, I asked to see my exam score-sheet. Ms. Valentine smiled bleakly and slightly maternally. Next to where she had written that I had garnered a thirty out of a possible fifty on the comb-out, was written "too fluffy" and "removed by brushing"; next to my thirty out of a possible fifty on the hair shaping, she had written "poor." She had not even bothered to score the permanent waving or fingerwaving sections.

"So I'm not ready for my own salon," I said.

"The comb-out was the only part that was close to passing."

"Yes, I felt good about that part," I said. "But will someone hire me if I can only do comb-outs?"

"Don't worry—you will not be hired soon."

"Maybe I could specialize. Maybe I could just do comb-ou—"

Ms. Valentine extolled the virtues of a proper Wilfred training; I thanked her for her guidance and left.

SO YOU WANT TO BE A SCENIC ARTIST

The painter of theatrical scenery who is interested in gaining admittance into Local 829, the United Scenic Artists, fits into one of two categories: Track A is for scenic artists with two or more years of professional experience; Track B is for people with "more traditional design and/or painting skills." Deciding that my own painting history is "more traditional," I applied for the latter. No résumé, letter of recommendation, interview, or portfolio is required for Track B admission into the union; one must simply pay $150, successfully complete a Home Project, and pass a studio painting test.

One month before the painting test, I was mailed two 8" × 10" color reproductions of paintings: the Home Project. I painted larger versions (3' 9" × 5' 2" and 4' 6" × 6' 0") of the two reproductions onto cotton duck. This year's paintings were "Drapery, Molding, Marble, Wood," a picture of a marble-arched wooden door on top of which someone has carelessly draped a lot of striped fabric, and "Still Life," a picture of a typical cliffside picnic.

On the Saturday morning of the eight-hour painting test I arrived at the basement of the ABC/Capital Cities studio at West End Avenue and Sixty-sixth Street at eight-thirty A.M. I stacked my rolled-up paintings on top of the other candidates' work at the entryway. Inside the studio the test's organizers had marked out some forty-five 5' ½" × 4' ⅞" painting areas on long rolls of muslin spread out and stapled to the floor. I picked a spot and unloaded my supplies. The other candidates, most of whom were in their twenties or thirties, were hunched over their areas of canvas, applying grids. Just before nine we gathered round, and one of the union members gave us a short speech in which she welcomed us to the Track B exam, told us to "relax and enjoy" ourselves, but explained that if we didn't stop painting at five P.M., one of the test's organizers would take the paintbrush from our hands. There were three palettes of paint for our use—Muralo, Iddings casein, and Rosco Super

Saturated acrylic; the paints were located in some fifty plastic buckets at the far end of the studio.

When we returned to the work area, we each had a sealed manila envelope lying on our canvas. Upon opening their envelopes to reveal lovely prints of a watercolor goldfish, most of the candidates started to frantically complete their gridding, some of them using plumb lines and one using a clear plastic sheet with gridding on it, which he taped on top of his watercolor. Others of us relied on rulers and yardsticks, calmly reasserting the "more traditional" upbringing.

After I had gridded my own muslin, I walked over to the paint area and filled nine small plastic containers with paint. As I was carrying four of these back to my work area, a male candidate in glasses and a gray workshirt came up beside me. His self-confidence was nervous-making.

"I see you're using the Muralo," he said.

"Yes," I said, slightly defensively.

"How come?"

I had chosen Muralo because there had been fewer people in line for it. But I did not want to reveal this to this man.

"I, unh . . . I like a paint with a little *spank factor* in it," I said.

This confused the man and he went away.

As I painted, I found it difficult to capture the gauzy effects of watercolor. The man to my left, a Russian, was getting wonderful results with many thin washes of color. I emulated his style with some success.

At one-ten, although no one else seemed to be eating, I squatted at the bottom of my workspace and ate the lunch that the union's guidelines had suggested I bring. I chose not to conclude my meal with any of the Oreos or Pecan Sandies that the local had provided, loath as I am to eat anything served by someone who has just opened and stirred several hundred gallons of paint.

At about four-ten I decided to chat up one of the organizers. He told me that the work of this year's group of candidates was *much* better than last year's.

"I'm crazy about *this* guy's work," I whispered, pointing to the Russian.

"Yes, it's nice," he offered.

"*Very* Track A," I said. "My work feels . . . *flat* to me. It, it doesn't quite come up off the canvas."

"Yes," he said, warily. "You lost some of the water effects you had going. If it'd been me, I would've avoided *everything* but the Super Saturates."

"How come?" I asked.

"The undercolor doesn't work up on you."

I nodded in agreement.

I resumed painting.

At the end of the exam, I spoke to a smiley organizer.

"Do you like mine?" I asked.

"Yes, you did a nice job," she said.

"Everyone else's is much better than mine."

"No, you did fine."

"I have problems with undercolors," I confided. "I have an undercolor problem."

"Well, if you fail the test you can always take it again," she said.

"You, unh, do you think I'll fail?"

"I can't tell you that," she said warmly.

Three days later I received a form letter telling me that I had failed and that I could schedule a review of my work for the fall. There was no mention made of an undercolor problem.

SO YOU WANT TO BE A MACY'S SALESPERSON

On a lovely, balmy spring day, I went to Macy's and applied for a sales job. After receiving a pass from a guard stationed at the entryway to the employees-only part of the store, I walked down several long corridors to personnel. Upon arriving at the personnel desk, I was handed an application attached to a clipboard and told to have a seat and fill the application out.

I jotted down my particulars, claiming to have done a lot of catering and to have been a salesperson for four years at someplace called the Brookfield Shop in West Brookfield, Massachusetts. Upon doing this, I noticed that the application asked, "What businesses, jobs, or professions do you know about from having a close friend or relative who worked in them?" Anticipating what kind of answer would endear me to the personnel people, I instantly thought of my sister, and wrote down "Nurse." Then, when asked to elaborate upon what the best features of that job were, I simply jotted down "Helping people get better"; when asked what the worst features were, I wrote, "Watching people die."

In response to "What are the most important things that make a company a good place to work?" and "What are some things you didn't like about jobs you've had?" I made obsequious comments about "effective communication between workers and management," "opportunity for advancement," "too much downtime" and the like.

The personable young woman who took my application from me gave it a cursory glance to make sure that I had filled everything out. Then, smiling, she asked if I had time to fill out another form. I readily obliged.

The second form was a booklet with some forty multiple-choice and true-false questions about my personality and behavior. Although I tried my best to divine what qualities are sought in a Macy's employee, it was not always easy to know how to respond to the questions. I answered in the affirmative to "Do you shop here often?" and responded "true" to "As a child I was always the one who tried to keep the class quiet when the teacher left the room." However, when posed "Do you always follow your orders quickly and cheerfully?" and "If there is no one else around to notice what you are doing, do you always pick up the paper and trash others leave around?" I answered no, fearful that I might seem irksome or fascistic. I tried to add a dash of moral probity to my personality profile by answering "true" to "It bothers me when a smart lawyer uses

the law to get a criminal off." Given that the successful completion of this questionnaire would, I assumed, lead to an interview with a member of the personnel staff, I was somewhat surprised by the question "When interviewing for a job, how much
difficulty do you experience in talking to the interviewer?"
Wouldn't the person interviewing me be able to answer this for
him or herself? I could only imagine that the personnel staff is
so busy picking up the paper and trash that others leave behind
that they are unable to focus on this issue.

The statement that proved the most difficult to respond to
was a statement of the "Have you stopped beating your wife
yet?" variety: "If I had had a fair chance in life, I would have
been more successful." Given that I feel that I *have* had a fair
chance in life, there is no way for me to answer this. I sat and
thought about how I would answer variants of the statement—if
I had had a less fair chance than I had, I might be less successful; if I had had a fairer chance than I had, I probably wouldn't
be applying for a job at Macy's—but I was stymied by the question in its present redaction. My inability to answer began to
gnaw at my self-confidence. I impulsively circled "false."

When I handed in my booklet and answer sheet, the
woman who took them from me thanked me and told me that
someone would call soon. But I did not receive a phone call.
Two months later I called the personnel department and was
told that applications are only good for thirty days and that I
should reapply. "We'll be needing more people for Mother's
Day," the woman whom I spoke to told me.

Upon returning, I filled out a second application in much
the way I had before. The chief difference was, when queried
again about jobs that I was familiar with, I thought of my *other*
sister, and wrote "Primate Center Manager." When asked what
the best features of the job were, I wrote, "Overseeing staff,
organizing events"; when asked what the worst features were, I
wrote, "Seeing chimps die."

I was not asked to take a personality test. I did not receive a
phone call.

SO YOU WANT TO BE A DOG GROOMER

How do you prepare a cocker spaniel for being taken to the Holiday Inn at the Newark airport in order to be groomed for the National Dog Groomers Association of America's certification test?

There is no way, I decided. The only thing for me to do was to try to acclimate the dog to the potential vagaries of the nonprofessional grooming experience by inviting the little fellow to pass a night in my home. I called Clifford's owner and arranged to pick him up the night before the testing.

Clifford is not inconvenienced by the limitations of tact; he is a paunchy five-year-old who has heartworms and who mistakes irritability for personality. Imagine Broderick Crawford on all fours, in an ill-fitting suit. I could not allow his reputation for having bitten several people in the past to dissuade me from deciding to work with him; suffice it to say that the response to my search for a dog had not been overwhelming. That his owner has no pretensions to Clifford's being a show dog made the prospect of using him all the more attractive. Clifford was the natural choice: he had the required eight weeks, if not more, of unimpeded hair growth.

Upon arriving at my building, however, he immediately established what kind of houseguest he would be. He would not climb my stairs until jerked. He bid an upturned snout to the kibble and other savory treats offered him. He would not allow me to effilate his groin area. I did not want to press my luck with him; the more I looked over the guidelines and Breed Profiles that the NDGAA had sent me—"It is advisable when testing," one read, "to try and use a dog not sensitive to burns, so you can clip clean and close"—the more anxious I became. Indeed, when it became clear after walking him that night that Clifford's paws required washing, I prevailed upon my boyfriend Jess to lower this unpleasant battleship into the harbor of my bathtub.

Clifford spent much of the evening barking at my refrigerator. We awoke bleary-eyed the next morning at five forty-five and drove to the Holiday Inn Jetport. Going inside and confirming with the two judges that I was the owner of a Greenwich Village dog salon called Ruff Trade, I registered myself while Jess encouraged an increasingly vexed Clifford to urinate in the parking lot. The testing was being conducted in the Frank Borman Room; chairs had been stacked on the side, and large sheets of plastic had been taped to the carpeting. Two female groomers dressed in smocky, pastel groomwear had set up their tables and were talking to their uncaged dogs; I set up my table next to a power-pak, into which one of the women encouraged me to "plug-in." When I saw that the other woman's dog was a cocker spaniel whose hair was far more fluffy and lustrous than Clifford's, I nervously helped Jess guide the addled Clifford into the adjacent Chuck Yeager Room for a last-minute comb-out.

Several minutes later we took Clifford into the testing room and eased him onto the grooming table just as the younger judge began circling the room with a clipboard to inspect each of the nine dogs. After putting her nose up to Clifford's side and inhaling, she palpated his ears. Clifford grumbled ominously. "Your dog has mats," she said. It was true; I had neglected to brush them out the evening before. "That's part of my grooming process," I explained to the woman. She wrote a note on her clipboard.

Seconds later she announced the commencement of grooming. The room whirred to life with the buzzing of electric clippers. I took my clippers and, running them along Clifford's side and back, discovered that this was not entirely pleasurable to him. He growled loudly, causing one of the other groomers to look over at us with concern. The Breed Profile for the cocker spaniel advises that one closely trim "the folds in the lower jaw area (flews), where the hair is apt to hold saliva"; I considered doing this, but decided that I was not anxious to see Clifford's reaction to my applying electricity to his saliva. Falling back on my cosmetological training, I took out my flame-tempered #10 shears and began to reduce some of the excess bulk on Clifford's legs. When I proceeded with this activity on and around his stomach, he began to make a low-pitched rumbling sound reminiscent of large aircraft. For reasons unclear to me even now, I then decided that this was the time to work on Clifford's mats. Picking up my comb, I lifted his left ear. But upon my touching said comb to the hair behind his ear, Clifford snarled and lifted his left lip, revealing a glistening incisor.

This behavior was distressing to me—as it would be, I'm sure, to any groomer. There seemed to be little that Clifford was going to allow me to do to him; surely I would fail the test if my dog exhibited no change in his appearance. Fortunately, I had had the presence of mind to bring along a few extra supplies; it was thus with a sense of professional ardor that, clamping Clifford's mouth shut with one hand, I pulled a lipstick from my bag with the other and proceeded to smear my snarly friend's snout with Clinique Citrus Pink. When I saw that the top third of the other cocker spaniel's ears were being clipped so unattractively "clean and close" that you could see the veins and skin underneath, I applied a generous daub of alcohol-free Dep styling gel to Clifford's left ear and then curled several of its long tufts of hair on his ear up into a curler. Waiting for this to set, I applied two liberal coats of Hai Karate cologne to his back and midsection.

My nontraditional grooming methods were at first almost wholly uninteresting to the judges and other groomers, four of whom were having a passionate discussion about bringing one's children along on the dog and cat show circuits.

"That's the only thing about cat cages," said one woman. "You can't fit a kid in there."

"*Bet* me," another countered. "*Bet* me. My friend Marie has a Siamese and she tours constantly and I've seen her put her kid in one. *Easy.*"

At the conclusion of the hour-and-a-half exam period, the younger of the two judges picked up her clipboard and made her way over to Clifford and me. Silently she ran my comb through Clifford's hair. She lifted his right ear. She lifted his left ear.

"You hardly cut any of his hair," she said.

"I know," I responded. "This is what I call a Lite Groom."

She looked at me suspiciously. Then she went back to the older judge and whispered in her ear. The older judge was a muscular, compact woman who seemed to be perpetually on the boil. She walked over to us looking like a woman with a mission. After raking my comb through Clifford's right hindquarter, she said in a forceful tone, "This is totally unacceptable."

"Oh," I said, somewhat forlornly. "What about the ears? I was trying to get some *volume* with his ears."

"Not with mats you don't!" she said. She continued to look him over, wincing as she fully beheld the lipstick.

"I unh . . . I was trying to capture a sense of the unexpected," I offered.

"No, I'm sorry, this dog is not acceptable. You should familiarize yourself with our Breed Profiles." She looked again at the Citrus Pink.

"It's lipstick," I said. "It's my grooming signature. I like a dog with a *face*."

She exhaled loudly and laid my comb down on my table next to one of the curlers. She explained that I had failed the practical part of the test but that I could take the written part.

I put Clifford and my supplies in the car and then returned to the testing room. The written test consisted of twenty-nine true or false questions and thirty-two outlines of dogs to be identified by breed. The older judge corrected my test while I waited, telling me I got a 56 percent on the written and 0 percent on the practical. The written critique of my practical work included the comment "Dog smells doggy." I declined to point out that this was unlikely since the dog was wearing a nationally distributed men's cologne. Both the critique and the older judge encouraged me to review the association's Breed Profiles and to attend more dog shows.

We drove home in silence.

SO YOU WANT TO BE A CEMENT MASON

Having mailed in an application in which I claimed to have the required "three years of full-time satisfactory experience as a cement mason, plus sufficient full-time satisfactory experience as a mason's helper," I walked to Seward Park High School on Grand Street one Saturday morning to take the written civil-service test for cement masons. About two hundred men were already waiting in line when I got there.

"It's all who you know," said the man standing in line behind me about the difficulty of getting work as a mason. "It's all Mob. Completely Mob-run."

I did not pursue this line of conversation, surrounded as we were by large Italian men.

The test consisted of eighty questions, almost all of them specific to the trade. I did not know what screeding is. I did not know what the proper tool for preventing honeycombing is. When asked "Which two of these tools have the most similar purposes: a) strike-off rod and bull flat b) edger and jitterbug c) bull float and darby d) groover and darby," the tools all sounded to me like dance steps of the thirties and forties; however, my subsequent search for mentions of the Trunky-Doo was completely in vain.

Ever since I took this test, I have spent more time thinking about sidewalks.

SO YOU WANT TO BE A PSYCHIC

When my friend B.W. returned from Miami one day and told me that he had read about an organization that certifies psychics, something about his calm and assured tone made me think that my vocational ship might finally have come in. I called the Florida phone number he gave me and spoke to an employee of the Universal Centre in Cassadaga. A New Age seminarium with an extensive metaphysical bookstore, the

Centre has three psychic readers who are available from ten
A.M. to five P.M. every day on the premises or from ten A.M. to
four-thirty P.M. over the phone (MasterCard, VISA, and
American Express accepted). But the woman whom I spoke to
knew nothing about certification; she said that the man who
was in charge of it was Dr. Sekunna, the founder of the Centre.
She gave me his phone number.

I told Dr. Sekunna that I was a psychic who had been giving
readings for seven years. He explained to me that people interested in becoming readers at the Centre must give an accurate
reading for either Dr. Sekunna or one of the other Centre members; upon successful completion, the candidates "work with"
and train under Dr. Sekunna. for a period of months or even
years.

I asked Dr. Sekunna if I could give him a reading over the
phone.

"Sure," he said.

I paused dramatically.

"Orange," I said. "It's a, it's a color that has become important to you. It was not until very recently."

"That's true. Orange is to me a very earth color. It's an earth
spiritual color. You'll find that a lot of Eastern mystics and yogis
use the color orange in their spiritual work. In the past few
years I've been very attracted to the color orange as a very spiritual color. If I was going to wear a robe, it would be orange."

"I'm seeing a little man with a beard who is living not in the
hollow of a tree, but very close. He's very in touch with the
woods. He is a sort of modern leprechaun. He has bells on his
shoes."

"I'll try to explain that one to you," Dr. Sekunna said, as he
began to tell me about a Centre member who had moved from
Miami to the more rural Cassadaga area. "You look at this guy
and you want to call him a leprechaun. He's got an impish type
of personality."

I was warming to this endeavor.

"I'm sensing . . . I'm sensing *cheese*," I intoned. "I'm not sure if it's a Roquefort or something from the Pyrenees—but it's some kind of *blue cheese*."

"Well, I enjoy all kinds of cheeses," he explained. "It's what I think I shouldn't eat so much of."

"That's no doubt where it's coming from," I explained matter-of-factly. "I'm also sensing that the underside of tables is perhaps something that fascinates you."

"The underside of tables?"

"Yes, the underside of things," I continued calmly. "From a *dog's* perspective."

This seemed to give him pause. But then, finally: "Yes, I'm an investigator in life. I like to see what's on the bottom as well as what's on the top."

When I had finished my reading, Dr. Sekunna said I was "very highly sensitive." He gave me the name of a numerology book that espouses a simpler, "more spiritual" approach to numerology than most; although I have "an affinity with numbers," he felt that I "get annoyed by numbers" and that when I was studying math as a child, I probably felt that what was being taught me was incorrect.

Twelve days later Dr. Sekunna unexpectedly called me back. Saying he had been looking over my chart, he tried to encourage me to go to Florida and take five hours of palmistry lessons with him for one hundred dollars. If those went well, I would then continue training for "a month or two."

"The more I've been thinking about you, the more I realize you're a touch person," he said. "If we worked on that sensitivity that you already have, and then add palmistry skills, we have the ability to have you make four or five hundred dollars a week."

"So you, you think I'm a touch person," I said.

"You *are* a touch person!"

"I've always wondered."

"Absolutely. You're a touch person."

Having asked me if I am "locked in to New York," he then explained that he hoped to open another Centre within a couple of months.

"This is exciting," I said. "And you think potentially you see me at this new Centre or do you think maybe there would be a spot opening at the current Centre?"

"I'll have a slot for you one way or the other."

Call me psychic.

Cafe Manhattan

HENRY ALFORD

ACTUAL SELECTIONS FROM MENUS AND SPECIALS BOARDS
FOUND IN MANHATTAN RESTAURANTS AND DELIS.

APPETIZERS

Anti pasta $3.49

Cream cheese and ox $3.50

Roast breast of Griggstown
pheasant wrapped in autumn
greens and crushed with smoke-
house bacon $28

Old turkey platter $4.95

Breast sandwich................$2.20

Tuna Nickwash $2.75

Smoke with fish
and cucumber $3.50

Mesculin salad

Lady's finger, sautéed and cooked
with tomato and onion......$4.75

Sautéed couch $10.95

Heart of palm with
golf sauce

Sour pig's fore shank

Hot open turkey
sandwich potato...............$6.95

Pasta from the sea $9.95

Colston Bassett Stilton Farmhouse Appleby Cheshire, Farmhouse English Somerset, Keen's
cheddar, banana chutney,
bread...............................$12.50

Loose vegetables................$4.95

Cream-cheese festival $1

"Fresh" fruit cup $1.75

"Asparagus"

ENTREES

Angel-hair pasta with wild
mushrooms, sun-dried tomatoes
and basil. After five years, as
great as ever....................$16.50

Fish curry: Fish marinated in
intricately blended spices
in the Stone Age $8.95

Beef goulash with spatial
and red cabbage...............$11.95

Grown beef $3.75

Grilled fresh tuna
served with soap................$7.95

Baked zit..........................$4.25

Omelette imp $8.95

Special big leg
with rice $3.25

Meatball's plane $3.25

Seafood containing
shrimp others....................$8.90

Dow Shew Sheemy: A different
type of sheemy made of bean
curd stuffed with ground pike.
The curd is light yellow with a
firm custardlike texture. It is
quite bland and may require getting used to.

Scallops: fried, sautéed,
broiled on organate $16.95

Live main lobster

Scallops, mushrooms,
smelt roe baked in our
special dynamite sauce
(148 cal.) $4.50

Fresh grilled lobster topped
with whipped buttery butter
sauce (seasonal price)

Peppered filet mignon
sautéed with interesting
mushrooms $19.95

Dumping meat pasta
in cream sauce

Everything dog $1

Peking duck (order in
advance): Waiter serving
on table, wrapped with
pancakes $28

SANDWICHES

Live wourst $2.59

Philadelphia "Swiss cheese"
steak hero $3.50

Buttler bagle ....60 cents

Olive leaf on roll $2.25

Reuban $4

Ruben...............................$3.99

Rubbin special..................$3.50

DRINKS

Sodas by Coke
and Pepsi...........................$1.25

Chardonnay, the Monterey
Vineyard: Big, forward and
mouth-filling wine $15

Fog Cutter: A nitemare
of gin, rum and brandy

Hot and ice flavor coffee

Toast-free coffee

Nicaraguan coffee
for peace $1.30

Caffe Americano: Our
premium espresso combined
with piping, hot water $1.35

DESSERTS

Chocolate mouse tort........$5.50

"Special" halo-halo is served
with ice cream, purple yam jam
and shredded young coconut
sport toppings $3.50

Fluffy balls of milksolids
in syrup $2

Yogurt: It is a good source
of protein and calcium. The culture that makes yogurt, "yogurt,"
is healthful for the ecology of the
intestines.

• • •

Everything is baked fresh right
here in our own.

Ask waiter for availability.

Corporate charges welcome. . . .
enjoy the comfort of reliable and
courteous service and expertly
arranged food that many apparel,
handbag and home-furnishing
firms have in the past.

The management reserves the
right to impose certain decency
regulations.

The manangement reserves the
right to assign and designate all
seating arrangements.

No potato on weekend.

• • •

The Young Man
and The Sea

HENRY ALFORD

It is the duty of the introspective, literary male writer, in the course of his career as an introspective literary male, to write a story in which he unbosoms universal truths while engaged in the act of fishing. Bobbing upon the watery depths, alert to the sudden presence of thorny verities, or of haddock, he must descend deep into the pit of his humanity and then mine that rich ore of his profession: awful splendor. So when, earlier this summer, I went to the Hamptons for three days of fishing, I knew that this was more than an opportunity to savor the blandishments of one of the Eastern seaboard's loveliest settings; this was an opportunity to practice eliciting stunned awe from the *Esquire* subscriber base and, perhaps, to make a dazzling literary metaphor of my dead father.

I started with sportfishing. At eight o'clock on a sun-shiny Wednesday morning in Montauk harbor, I boarded *Lazybones,* a fifty-five-foot "party boat" that can accommodate forty-five. I told the ruggedly handsome mate who collected my $25 half-day fare, "I'm hoping to encounter awful splendor today." His expression betrayed bafflement. I explained, "You know how in fishing stories, the fisherman looks deep into the beast's eye and has a harrowing moment of self-realization?" The mate matter-of-factly responded, "That's not going to happen today." What was going to happen was fluke, or summer flounder. Each fisherman was given a rod as well as bait resembling indelicately prepared sushi. As we chugged out to the fog-saddled sea, I fell into conversation with a courtly seventy-three-year-old, ponytailed gentleman. "My dear boy, you've never eaten fluke?" he said to me spiritedly, laying his hand on my shoulder. "The most delicious thing in the world." My brain flashed: possible father surrogate?

I would like to be able to tell you that I now understand the wisdom of this man's statement, and that fluke is at present my daily bread. But over the course of the next four hours, I caught only one fish, and it was wee, well under the fifteen-inch minimum length. This would have been less damaging to my confidence were fluke fishing not so easy (you simply let your hook drop to the bottom then wait) or were the woman fishing adjacent to me—a first-timer who had confessed to mild seasickness—not so spectacularly successful. "Attaboy, lady!" the mate who'd collected my fare yelled at this woman after she had reeled in five fluke and one striped bass in the first two hours: "She's throwin' 'em over the rails!" When I asked this woman, "What's your secret?," she told me, "It's called 'I-don't-know-what-the-hell-I'm-doing.'" I smiled bleakly. At one point her line got tangled with another person's on the other side of the boat; moments later, the mate who untangled the lines appeared with an eighteen-inch fluke and said to the woman, "Here, this was on your line."

Fluke—or, as I came to think of it, Bizarre Coincidence—was apparently not my fish, and my inability to apprehend any of regulation size was keeping me from having important literary thoughts. At the conclusion of our voyage, I skulked back to my rental car with not a little embarrassment, neatly dodging the man who had called me "my dear boy," only to find that I had left my headlights on and my battery was dead. Six phone calls produced an intense, burly mechanic from B&B Auto Service in Montauk, who jumped my car. I explained that I was on business, writing "my big fishing story," and needed a receipt. As I sheepishly closed the car's hood, I was filled with the strange delusion that my fellow *Lazybones* fishermen—now wandering around the parking lot lugging plastic baggies filled with the fluke they had caught and had had filleted by the mates—would ritually mock me by smearing their fillets on my face and genitals. This did not happen. However, as I pulled out of the parking lot two minutes later, the mechanic roared his tow truck perpendicularly in front of me, cutting me off: I had failed to close my hood all the way. He jumped out of his truck and slammed it shut, yelling, "This way, they won't have to buy you a new windshield, too!" From inside my car, I gave him a meek wave, as if to plead, *Release me from this festival of inadequacy.*

You will nod empathically, I think, when I tell you that on my next outing I gravitated to the soothing and picturesque. Indeed, I have seldom undertaken a more heart-stirring and visually glorious activity than that in which I found myself engaged the following morning: fly-fishing from a kayak, just offshore from the Shinnecock Indian Reservation in Shinnecock Bay, Southampton, at 7:30 A.M.—the earliest I have ever been awake east of Mastic-Shirley. I had engaged the services of North Sea Kayaking instructor Steve Lancia ($145 for three hours). Our first fifty-five minutes were spent standing onshore, practicing, without a fly on my line, the graceful art of casting; I slowly transformed my semaphore of intent into a surgical strike of aggression. Once we were out on the water, each in our own Old Town kayak, the combination of location and activity engendered in me a golden, International Coffees–type glow. Birds twittered, clammers clammed. I felt ready—ready to remark upon the noble proportions of a dying tuna, ready to behold a bluefish and then gravely announce, "We are all our fathers' sons."

But where were the fish? Finally, two hours into the outing, I had a strike. Steve, boyishly excitable, screamed, "Yes!" I reeled in hurriedly. Steve was genuinely enthusiastic: "I am so happy for you. I'm gonna get my camera. This is it, man. This is everything." I kept reeling in. Steve thought it might be "a blue." I was hoping for striped bass but would not sniff at a blue. When my quarry flashed in the water, Steve announced, "I think it's a skate"; we were sliding precipitately down the scale of fish desirability. The fish burst from the water. Steve exclaimed, "A sea robin! Very nice." He tried to put a spin on it, saying, "It's a beautiful fish—see the wings on it?" to which I murmured, "The showgirl of the fish community." Now, I don't mean to cast aspersions on showgirls, but for those of you who have never looked at a sea robin with the startling proximity that a kayak can afford you, here is the gist—think of a demented Genghis Khan. Add cancer-pocked flagella. Dip in polymer. In short, an entity to keep as far away as possible from the word *bisque*. An entity unlikely to elicit philosophical insight. We returned the fish to the water; I thanked Steve for his company and guidance, then headed on my way.

Bad luck runs in streaks. And so, although it should have surprised me when, upon returning to my lodgings at the Sea Breeze Inn in Amagansett, I discovered fourteen members of the Anglers Club, all on an Anglers Club fishing trip, it did not. I simply thought, "Of course. And then the innkeeper will turn out to be Mrs. Paul." Six minutes later, hearing the phrase *creel limit* being flung across the porch, I hustled into my car and sped off.

Heavy drinking commenced. Heavy drinking (so essential to manly contemplation) continued. As I remember it—it is almost dawn as I write this, and I am well into a bottle of Seagram's—it was at this juncture that I had my first epiphany. Namely, I was in the wrong Hampton. If you're looking for penetrating writerly aperçus, you don't go to Southampton, the tatty, spinsterish aunt of the Hamptons; nor to Montauk, the Hamptons' jovial, beer-gutted cousin. And you certainly don't go to East Hampton, that whorish geographical bauble. No, you must hie yourself to Beard-Tugging Central: Bridgehampton.

Down on Bridgehampton's Mecox Beach, notepad at my side, I watched a gorgeous sunset and found myself scribbling the notation *flutelike cry of the loon*. I thought: Yes. Yes. Perhaps I'm making my search for awful splendor too difficult, I thought. Maybe the equation Scenery + Boat + Pursuit of Fish was excessively ambitious, and should be divested of its third and most time-consuming component.

And so I headed off the next day to boat around Georgica Pond, the site of homes owned by Steven Spielberg, Martha Stewart, and Ron Perelman. Renting a kayak from Main Beach Surf & Sport in Wainscott for $65 for a half-day, I told a friendly employee named Lars that I was "a journalist in recovery" and that I was "hoping to reconnect with my troubled childhood." He applauded this pursuit. It took me two hours to trace the perimeter of the beautiful, sun-dappled pond, a period marked by two renditions of the *Hawaii Five-O* theme song, a flirtation with a truculent swan, and a vague desire to present myself at the Spielberg compound as a sea-weary Schindler Wasp. Near, but not at, Martha Stewart's house, I saw a blonde, forties-ish woman in a white sweatshirt. Thinking that maybe my journey would lead me to The Mother, not The Father, I yelled across the pond, "Martha! I've brought the swan's-head gondola lawn chairs with the matching jabot drapery!" The woman squinted and walked away.

Perhaps speed would provide the antidote, I thought. So I drove up to the northern coast of East Hampton, to the lovely Cedar Point Park, where, at a Main Beach outpost, I rented a trimaran ($50 a half-day). The wind, coming from the northwest, was fierce, whitecaps dotted the water like tainted meringue. Indeed, so awesome was the wind that, although I am a mature salt, if not an old salt, I prevailed upon Tom, the twenty-three-year-old Main Beach employee manning the outpost, to sail with me. I sat in the one-man cockpit and worked the foot rudders while Tom worked the sail. The pontoons slapped against the water, exploding in a miasma of salty spray: Neptune's facial. We rocketed forth with startling speed; lightning would be faster, except it zags. Mirth abounded. I started laughing, and was unable to stop. There are moments in life that require precise words, and so I will try, through the dampening fog of the Seagram's, to summon up the proper ones. *Cowabunga* is one. Also, *tubular hellcraft.*

But still no awful splendor. So galvanized was I by sailing, however, that I decided to try fishing again. But when I arrived at Montauk harbor without a boat reservation the next day at noon, I discovered that the only option available to me was the Viking line's casino cruise, at a mere $3 (off-season) for a four-hour ride. I joined the fifteen other passenger-gamblers. As we cruised out to international waters, I went to the upper deck and lay in the sun without my shirt on; a mustachioed senior in a denim cap remarked, "I guess you lost your shirt!," to which I responded, "Good one." The slot machines broke down with some regularity during the voyage, prompting the mates to fix them, and to encourage us to buy drinks. At one point I almost tripped over the guts of a slot machine that cluttered up an aisle: issuing from its viscera were what must have been 700 sweat-soaked slugs and quarters. Awful splendor.

I returned my car the following morning to the National Car Rental office at La Guardia. I explained to a soft-spoken National clerk that while I was writing "my big fishing story" out in the Hamptons, my car's battery had died and I had hired a mechanic. The woman apologized and offered me a $25 rebate. "But as it turned out," I told her, "it worked well for the story." To the limited extent that she was interested in this statement, her interest was marked by confusion. "That mechanic," I announced, "was the spitting image of my late father."

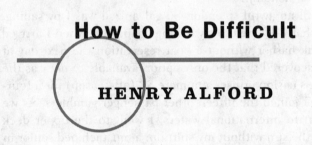

How to Be Difficult

HENRY ALFORD

We live in a time in which, increasingly, people are celebrated—nay, rewarded—for their ability to harass and vex. And you don't have to be Speaker of the House to join the fun, or even a bilge-spewing talk radio host. Almost anyone can play, provided they follow the successful models laid out below.

Teen-age girls:

Suggest that the theme of the prom be Human Rights Violations. Insist that Ritz crackers would make really good earrings. Make your own cosmetics; ask your father where you can get some placenta. Invest the lyrics of popular songs with an unrealistic amount of meaning. Ask if you can read a poem at the renewal of your parents' wedding vows; recite "Because I Could Not Stop for Death." Refuse to eat veal. Regale your family with the atrocities of the vealing process; quote the dimensions of your own room in attempt to elicit sympathy. Say that you aren't going to read any more books unless they are written by J. D. Salinger. Emblazon your mother's hardcover copy of "The Catcher in the Rye" with the note "Merry-Go-Round = Life." Accept responsibility for toilet-training your little brother; put him in the bathroom, slam the door and yell, "You're not coming out till I see some *results!*" Clog your father's fax machine with an article about the orgasm. Sign your library card "Mrs. Christian Slater." Practice screaming "I'm on the phone!" even when you are not.

Decorators:

Own a small dog. Ask to be referred to as an "interior dramatist." Whenever you are talking to a new client, allude to something called Teardown Month. Warn the client that you are in the process of deracinating your palette. After touring the site, tell the client that you think her taste is "brave." Report that many of the rooms are "problem areas." Tell the client that you have only one word for her, and the word is "ormolu." When the client asks where you found the wooden fruit crate you are charging her $700 for, say you are reluctant to reveal provenance. Speak primarily in bulletins, e.g., "An announcement: The voile has arrived." Threaten to revoke your assistant's swatching privileges. *Love* the swan's-head gondola chair with matching jabot drapery, but yank off the gold braid trim and wail, "Less, less, less!" Worry the tasseling. Faux-marble the toilet. When the client makes a suggestion, say that you are not in the indulgence business. Bill daily. When the client asks if your hourly travel fees are charged door to door, say: "No. Pajama to pajama." Call the client the night before she is scheduled to move in and tell her she can't because you are still sconcing. Sob. Use the small dog as a hankie.

Film critics:

Call your column "Death in the Cinema." Begin your review of "Presumed Innocent" with "The wife did it." Always sit in the front row. Smoke a lot. As soon as the lights have dimmed, start screaming "Focus! Focus!" Complain to a colleague that the editing of your work into capsule reviews has been spotty. Saddle your review of "Dumb and Dumber" with a discussion of hermeneutics. Invoke Barthes. Invoke Bazin. Write that the screenplay of the film in question is onanistic. Say that the film has no discernible Rosebud. Refer to the camera's "phallus-lens." Suggest that the star's performance is nothing but a series of cold symptoms. Dismiss Jack Nicholson as "just another Jack Nicholson impersonator." Say that the name Streep always makes you think of a French person asking you to undress. Refer to Ellen Barkin as She Who Does the Barking. Write a book called "The Grammar of Film." Begrudge Siskel and Ebert their success. Have complicated feelings about Gene Shalit's moustache.

Opera singers:

Storm dressing Room 1. Say that you're still trying to get used to not opening the season. Sing at half-voice. Alter the tempi. Observe that the second soprano's German is so bad that everyone can understand it. Say that the coloratura is "sharping" her notes; add that her perfume is clogging your resonating cavities. Tell the tenor that you saw the director's "Siegfried" in Bayreuth, and it was more "Rinse Cycle" than "Ring Cycle." Offer to pay to have the French horn's valves cleaned. Say that the castrato is looking at you funny. Have a snit with the donkey trainers; encourage the director to "lose the camel." Say that, although your part is small, audiences will *expect* you to take the last bow. Refuse to let your character die: when the executioner appears, turn his sword aside and present him with unsliced stollen. Feign surprise at applause. Tell the stage manager you've run out of places to put telegrams and roses; ask if it would be possible for you to take over his "little desk area."

Divine beings:

Thwart the exceptional. Concentrate the wealth. Answer prayer, but late, and without attention to detail. Intervene in a manner that suggests you haven't been following the story. Break up the Beatles. Let good things happen to bad people. Let bad behavior be mistaken for talent. Require compromise. Create gossip, infection, butter. Make toilets in Europe difficult to flush.

Encourage Andy Rooney. Give people hormones before they have completed their educations. Create the impression that hair color determines personality. Make people wait for long periods of time, often under fluorescent lighting. Let the shrinking of elderly people's bodies coincide with their sudden desire to own very large cars. Deny Maggie Smith and Dr. Mathilde Krim bodily immortality. Let there be berets. Let there be child performers. Let there be autobiography. Let there be Cher.

•• NEWS QUIZ ••

The News Quiz is topical comedy in convenient quiz form. Four days a week, in the on-line magazine *Slate,* I post a new question about the great events of the day, to which the readers reply with answers that are meant to be simultaneously funny and true. (Of course, I mean "true" in a large and abstract sense, and I intend something small and concrete when I say "funny" or when I say "lawn ornament"—which might be a tiny bunny or one of those gnomes that look so much like Senator Thurmond.)

In addition to the new question, each edition of the News Quiz features yesterday's question, five particularly amusing answers it received, my wrap-up, and the literally correct answer. I also run an extra, some additional piece of topical comedy. I've chosen ten samples of the quiz that have run since its debut in March of 1998. I hope they give you a chance to reflect on the recent past and to consider if perhaps your own lawn might look better if it were home to a small concrete fawn.

—Randy Cohen

1/14/99 "WOON RIVER"

When the Woonasquatucket River near Providence, Rhode Island, moved into the number two slot, behind New Jersey's Passaic River, signs went up along its banks: "Peligro! Los Peces De Este Rio No Se Deben Comer." Loosely translated, what would that be in idiomatic English?

"Ice Cube! Get back on the boat because a giant, man-eating snake lurks in these waters."
—Tim Rogers

"Danger! Vaguely racist jokes based on a limited knowledge of high school Spanish ahead."
—Dennis Cass

"Pellegrino! The Pescis and Esther Williams Won't Come Unless They Get Some!"—Tim Carvell

"Pelicans! The feces in this river are not safe to eat."—Steven Levy

"Welcome! The INS invites you to enjoy fishing and swimming here!"—Karen Bitterman

"Alas! The fish in this river are impotent."
—Steve Smith

"Drink this water, but we can't promise that John Travolta will represent you in court."
—Jon Garfunkel

"Warning! Use that stupid cell phone around me and I'll make you eat it."—Daniel Radosh

"Don't even THINK of parking here."—Deb Stavin

"Warning! The fish in this river are the exclusive property of Jack-in-the-Box Restaurants, Inc."
—Steven Miller

• RANDY'S WRAP UP •

When someone makes a movie about the Woonasquatucket (Adam Sandler, call my people), he'll have a rich riverine tradition to draw on. *Heart of Darkness, The African Queen, Deliverance*—each is a kind of flooded road movie. There are hundreds of them, if memory serves, and I can assure you that it doesn't. In *The River*, Mel Gibson and Sissy Spacek struggle to save their farm from flooding caused by Jewish bankers. In *Wild River*, Elia Kazan rats out his hillbilly coworkers to the TVA. *River of No Return* is the one where Robert Mitchum escapes savage cartoon Indians by floating down a river on Marilyn Monroe. There are Rivers of Death, Grass, Tears, Stone, and No Return. There are Rios Bravo, Conchos, Grande, Lobo, and Rita—this last featuring Abbott, Costello, and singing cowboy Nazis. That's a memory I'm sure of. What I'm less sure of is: When John Travolta turned down the $20 million that his clients clearly wanted, why would Meryl Streep risk her life to row him through the rapids?

AQUATIC ANSWER

"Danger! River Fish Are Not Safe to Eat!"

The Woonasquatucket trails only the Passaic for dioxin in its sediment. Informed of the problem, Robert Vanderslice, head of the Rhode Island Department of Health, swiftly ordered an interagency urban rivers team to post the bilingual signs, put on a slide show, and hand out brochures. The source of the dioxin is unclear. Legal action is pending. Swimming is discouraged.

EITHER/OR EXTRA

- "We believe that killing is not an acceptable management tool for us."—Either Bill Gates is announcing a policy change at Microsoft, or Richard Avanzino is promoting humane animal shelters for the SPCA.

- *Tara Road* by Maeve Binchy, *River's End* by Nora Roberts, and *A Sudden Change of Heart* by Barbara Taylor Bradford.—Either they're just not trying at the National Book Awards, or there's a new kind of giveaway in specially marked cases of Coca-Cola.

- "My monument has won!"—Either this is a line in a gay porn remake of *Spartacus,* or architect Peter Eisenman is delighted that some good has come out of the Holocaust; he got a commission.

- "After this past week, when people here say Yankee trash, they think it's redundant."—Either yet another person is offended by Mayor Giuliani's swaggering no-nothingism or . . . oh, wait, it is Mayor Giuliani's swaggering no-nothingism.

The Yanni Files

KURT ANDERSEN

Don't misunderstand: We're still very, very proud of the entire Yanni concept, as proud as we were the day twenty years ago when we dreamed it up.

Do we begrudge the fact that our notion has become the most popular entertainment product on the planet?

No—indeed, we're deeply moved.

Do we begrudge the fact that we don't share in the current Yanni revenue stream? No, because money was never the motivation. The process that turned into "Yanni" was a bar bet, a lark, a nutty what-if marketing experiment.

Friends often ask, "If you had it to do over again, is there anything about Yanni you'd redesign or retool?"

And we always say, "Yes—the hair." Back in 1978, when my friend Tibor and I first talked about inventing a character along these lines, Doug Henning and Tony Orlando were superstars; we knew that the dark shag haircut and the big, droopy mustache would work. In the event, the look became dated pretty quickly, but once it was integral to the Yanni brand—along with the billowy shirts and what we used to call "the waterbed smile"—a relaunch was out of the question. After the New Coke debacle, there was no way we were going to risk a New Yanni fiasco.

But those were seat-of-the-pants decisions, choices made casually over kirs at Maxwell's Plum. From there on, we introduced rigor into the creative process, starting with the name. We wanted unique; we wanted international, yet not particular-country-identifiable; and we wanted a word that didn't mean something unsavory in any major language.

From our original, computer-generated list of hundreds, we presented seven names to focus groups in Canada, Switzerland, and Singapore. "Smoofie" and "Zazu" had high negatives, and we encountered some significant pushback on "Yahweh"; "Rafi" and "Radu" scored well only among children and fashion models; the focus groups liked "Tin-Tin," but we were unable to clear the rights for North America. "Yanni" tested well in every country and among all age groups—and significantly better than either Yañi or Yänni.

One of our wisest choices, in retrospect, was to create a virtually complete oeuvre before we had even hired a performer. Did we invent "sampling" during the winter of 1978 in that recording studio in Westchester? All we know is, we and the White Plains Pops went in on January 3 with dozens of eight-track tapes (the *Planet of the Apes* and *2001* soundtrack albums, a bootleg of the *Wide World of Sports* theme song) and emerged two weeks later with forty-nine hours of brand-new Yanni music.

Despite everything, we also remain proud of our decision to hire and train three different men to tour simultaneously as Yanni. Although employing several Yannis at once ultimately led to our departure from the enterprise (interested readers may refer to the landmark National Labor Relations Board ruling, Yanni vs. Yanni vs. Yanni et al.), the multiple-Yanni concept was inarguably groundbreaking in non-animal, live-performance entertainment. (As most people know, there are six Yannis on the current two-hundred-concert "Tribute" tour, including the

Uzbeki Yanni, who performs exclusively in republics of the former Soviet Union.)

Sure, we made mistakes. That first season of performances in Esperanto was an idea whose time had not yet come. The "spiritual" component of the Yanni brand was part of the act we tried to phase out when the astrology craze faded; we just didn't see the whole New Age thing coming.

In planning our "Yanni: The Man of Peace Live at the 38th Parallel" concert special, we should have double-checked the North Korean promises of assistance, but once again the idea—Yanni plus international monument equals event programming—has been validated by the success of shows like "Yanni: Live at the Acropolis."

Pursuing our largely non-Yanni-related careers for the last decade, we have been content to watch, anonymous and silent, as our brainstorm succeeded beyond all imagining. But after the most recent PBS pledge drive, we decided we could remain in the shadows no longer. According to the December 26 issue of the *Public Broadcasting Report,* the program "Yanni: The Tribute Concert from the Taj Mahal and the Forbidden City" appears to have been more successful than any other PBS broadcast in generating pledges during 1997.

Yes, that makes us proud. But it also galls us: Back in the early eighties, during Yanni Phase One, when we proposed to PBS that they broadcast a Yanni program ("Yanni in Arizona: Live from London Bridge"), and we argued it would be great for fund-raising, a PBS executive actually laughed in our faces. "What do you think this is?" he said as he ushered us out of his office. "Some cheesy commercial network?"

**Human sacrifice was the old-fashioned way
of throwing money at a problem.—M.O'D.**

A Prayer for
Bill Clinton

DAVID M. BADER

The Jewish holiday of Yom Kippur—The Day of Atonement—is near, and with it, the perfect opportunity for President Clinton to express his contrition once and for all. Indeed, during the recent White House Prayer Breakfast, the president quoted from The Gates of Repentance, the prayer book for the Jewish High Holiday services. This solemn volume is a virtual catalog of apologies, including one prayer ("For the sin . . . ") in which worshippers atone for a long list of transgressions one by one, beating their breasts with each plea for forgiveness. While the traditional litany is more than adequate for the average sinner, it is perhaps not nuanced enough for Bill Clinton's needs. Herewith, a more presidential version:

> I atone for my sins, though I have not violated any of the Ten Commandments, as I read them.

> I atone for atoning by alluding to previous non-atonements.

> I atone once again, though I have already atoned, as stated earlier.

(biting lower lip) I atone for biting my lower lip.

I atone for not offering Monica Lewinsky a distant ambassadorship, perhaps to Kenya or Tanzania.

With regard to Footnote 274 of the Starr Report, I atone for not trying that with honey or syrup.

I atone for the deplorable tactic of having private detectives dig up dirt on members of Congress. In passing, however, let me call your attention to an interesting piece in *Salon* magazine about Dick Armey and a sheep.

I atone for not correcting my attorney Bob Bennett when, on my behalf, he gave a judge a sweeping denial of any kind of sexual relationship. At the time, I thought he had used the present pluperfect hortatory subjunctive future participle of a verb. So you can see how it happened.

I atone for the hubris of comparing my own sexual misconduct to that of John F. Kennedy. Yes, I know, I am no John F. Kennedy.

I atone for being more mature, grown-up and "European" about extramarital affairs than Congress or the media.

I atone for buying a stuffed animal, joke sunglasses and T-shirts for Ms. Lewinsky.

I atone for calling in Betty Currie, my devout, church-going secretary, on a Sunday, to try to get her to testify falsely, that backstabbing blabbermouth.

I atone for saying to Ms. Lewinsky that Kathleen Willey was "small-breasted." Not that I would personally have any direct knowledge, of course.

I atone for needlessly prolonging this scandal with seven months of specious legal arguments in the Federal courts.

Apparently there is no "presidential mistress" privilege. Whoops!

I atone for the damage I have caused thus far to the presidency, the legal system and the moral climate of the country. However, Paula Jones' lawyers left me no other possible course of action.

I atone for putting my vice president in such an awkward position and will tell him as soon as he is located.

I atone for subjecting the entire nation to "this journey I am on." Rest assured, you feel my pain.

I atone for all the new strategies and defenses we are about to roll out.

For all these sins, forgive me, as I have already forgiven myself.

Independence Day

DAVE BARRY

This Year, Why not hold an old-fashioned Fourth of July Picnic?

Food poisoning is one good reason. After a few hours in the Sun, ordinary potato salad can develop bacteria the size of raccoons. But don't let the threat of agonizingly painful death prevent you from celebrating the birth of our nation, just as Americans have been doing ever since that historic first July Fourth when our Founding Fathers—George Washington, Benjamin Franklin, Thomas Jefferson, Bob Dole and Tony Bennett—landed on Plymouth Rock.

Step one in planning your picnic is to decide on a menu. Martha Stewart has loads of innovative suggestions for unique, imaginative and tasty summer meals. So you can forget about her. "If Martha Stewart comes anywhere near my picnic, she's risking a barbecue fork to the eyeball" should be your patriotic motto. Because you're having a *traditional* Fourth of July picnic, and that means a menu of hot dogs charred into cylinders of industrial-grade carbon, and hamburgers so undercooked that when people try to eat them, they leap off the plate and frolic on the lawn like otters.

Dad should be in charge of the cooking, because only Dad, being a male of the masculine gender, has the mechanical "know-how" to operate a piece of technology as complex as a barbecue grill. To be truly traditional, the grill should be constructed of the following materials:

- 4 percent "rust-resistant" steel;
- 58 percent rust;
- 23 percent hardened black grill scunge from food cooked as far back as 1987 (the scunge should never be scraped off, because it is what is actually holding the grill together);
- 15 percent spiders.

If the grill uses charcoal as a fuel, Dad should remember to start lighting the fire early (no later than April 10) because charcoal, in accordance with federal safety regulations, is a mineral that does not burn. The spiders get a huge kick out of watching Dad attempt to ignite it; they emit hearty spider chuckles and slap themselves on all eight knees. This is why many dads prefer the modern gas grill, which ignites at the press of a button and burns with a steady, even flame until you put food on it, at which time it runs out of gas.

While Dad is saying traditional bad words to the barbecue grill, Mom can organize the kids for a fun activity: making old-fashioned ice cream by hand, the way our grandparents' generation did. You'll need a hand-cranked ice-cream maker, which you can pick up at any antique store for $1,875. All you do is put in the ingredients, and start cranking! It makes no difference what specific ingredients you put in, because—I speak from bitter experience here—no matter how long you crank them, they will never, ever turn into ice cream. Scientists laugh at the very concept. "Ice cream is not formed by cranking," they point out. "Ice cream is formed by freezers." Our grandparents' generation wasted millions of man-hours trying to produce ice cream by hand; this is what caused the Great Depression.

When the kids get tired of trying to make ice cream (allow about twenty-five seconds for this) it's time to play some traditional July Fourth games. One of the most popular is the "sack race." All you need is a bunch of old-fashioned burlap sacks, which you can obtain from the J. Peterman catalog for $227.50 apiece. Call the kids outside, have them line up on the lawn and give each one a sack to climb into; then shout "GO!" and watch the hilarious antics begin as, one by one, the kids sneak back indoors and resume trying to locate pornography on the Internet.

Come nightfall, though, everybody will be drawn back outside by the sound of loud, traditional Fourth of July explosions coming from all around the neighborhood. These are caused by the fact that various dads, after consuming a number of traditionally fermented beverages, have given up on conventional charcoal-lighting products and escalated to gasoline. As the spectacular pyrotechnic show lights up the night sky, you begin to truly appreciate the patriotic meaning of the words to *The Star-Spangled Banner*, written by Francis Scott Key to commemorate the fledgling nation's first barbecue:

> *And the grill parts' red glare;*
> *Flaming spiders in air;*
> *Someone call 911;*
> *There's burning scunge in Dad's hair*

After the traditional visit to the hospital emergency room, it's time to gather 'round and watch Uncle Bill set off the fireworks that he purchased from a roadside stand operated by people who spend way more on tattoos than dental hygiene. As Uncle Bill lights the firework fuse and scurries away, everybody is on pins and needles until, suddenly and dramatically, the fuse goes out. So Uncle Bill re-lights the fuse and scurries away again, and the fuse goes out again, and so on, with Uncle Bill scurrying back and forth with his Bic lighter like a deranged

Olympic torchbearer until, finally, the fuse burns all the way down, and the firework, emitting a smoke puff the size of a grapefruit, makes a noise—"phut"—like a squirrel passing gas. Wow! What a fitting climax for your traditional old-fashioned July Fourth picnic!

Next year you'll go out for Chinese food.

Parlez-Vous Francais?

DAVE BARRY

This summer, for my vacation, I went to Paris, France. I went there to follow in the footsteps of such great writers as Ernest Hemingway, Henry Miller and "F." Scott Fitzgerald, all of whom, for the record, are currently dead.

I blame the Parisian drivers. Paris has only one vacant parking space, which is currently under heavy police guard in the Louvre museum. This means that thousands of frustrated motorists have been driving around the city since the reign of King Maurice XVII looking for a space, and the way they relieve their frustrations is by aiming at pedestrians, whom they will follow onto the sidewalk if necessary. Often the only way to escape them is to duck into one of Paris's historic cathedrals, which fortunately are located about every twenty-five feet (or 83.13 liters).

Nevertheless it's very pleasant to walk around Paris and feel—as so many Americans feel when they're in that incredibly beautiful city—fat. Because the fact is that we Americans look like enormous sneaker-wearing beef cattle compared to the Parisians, who tend to be very slim, with an average body weight of thirty-eight pounds (7.83 meters). It's odd that the French appear to be in such good shape, because the major activity in Paris, aside from trying to run over pedestrians, is sitting around in cafés for days at a time looking French.

Sometimes we Americans try to blend in to the café scene, but the French immediately spot us as impostors, because we cannot pronounce the Secret French Code letter, which is "r." They have learned to say "r" in a certain secret way that sounds as though they are trying to dislodge a live eel from their esophagus. It is virtually impossible for a non-French person to make this sound; this is how the Parisian café waiters figure out that you are an American, even if you are attempting to pass as French:

WAITER: *Bonjour. Je suspect que vous etes American.* ("Good day. I suspect that you are American.")

YOU: *Mais je ne portes pas les Nikes!* ("But I am not wearing the sneakers!")

WAITER: *Au quais, monsieur pantalons intelligents, prononcez le mot "Rouen."* ("OK, Mr. Smarty Pants, pronounce the word 'Rouen.'")

YOU: *Woon.* ("Woon.")

WAITER: *Si vous etes Francais, je suis l'Homme de la Batte.* ("If you are French, I am Batman.")

The other sure-fire way to tell the difference between French people and Americans in a café is that the French are all smoking, whereas the Americans are all trying to figure out how much to tip. The tourist guidebooks are vague about tipping: They tell you that a service charge is USUALLY included in your bill, but it is not ALWAYS included, and even if it IS included, it is not necessarily TOTALLY included. On top of that, to convert from French money to American, you have to divide by six, and I have yet to meet anybody who can do this.

And so while the French are lounging and smoking and writing novels, we Americans spend our café time darting nervous glances at the bill, which is often just a piece of paper with a lone, mysterious, not-divisible-by-six number scrawled on it such as "83." We almost always end up overtipping, because we're afraid that otherwise the waiter will make us say another "R" word. I frankly don't know how the French handle tipping, because in my two weeks in Paris I never saw a French person actually leave a café.

Not that I am being critical. As a professional journalist, I like the idea of a society where it is considered an acceptable occupation to basically sit around and drink. In fact, I liked almost everything about Paris. The city is gorgeous, the food is wonderful, and they have these really swoopy high-tech public pay toilets on the streets that look as though, if you went into one, you might get beamed up to the Mother Ship. Also Paris has a terrific subway system, Le Metro (literally, "The Metro"). I always felt safe and comfortable in the Metro, although one time, when I was waiting for a train, the loudspeaker made an announcement in French, which was repeated in English, and I swear this was the whole thing: "Ladies and gentlemen, your attention please. Robbers are in the station. Thank you." None of the Parisians seemed the least bit alarmed, and nobody robbed me, which was a good thing, because I would have had no idea how much to tip.

I have run out of space here, but in next week's column I will tell you about some of the famous tourist attractions of Paris, such as the L'Arc D. Triomphe, Notre Dame, the Leaning Tower of Pisa, etc. So until next week, as the French say, *"Au revoir."* (Literally, "Woon.")

An Aesthetically Challenged American in Paris (Part II)

DAVE BARRY

Today I'll be concluding my two-part series on Paris, France. In writing this series, my goal, as a journalist, is to provide you with enough information about this beautiful and culturally important city so that I can claim my summer vacation trip there as a tax deduction.

My topic in Part Two is the historic tourist attractions of Paris. The Parisians have been building historic attractions for more than 1,500 years as part of a coordinated effort to kill whatever tourists manage to escape the drivers. The key is stairs. Most tourist attractions, such as L'Arc de Triomphe (literally, "The Lark of Triumph") and the Hunchback of Notre Dame Cathedral, have some kind of lookout point at the top that you, the tourist, are encouraged to climb to via a dark and scary medieval stone staircase containing at least 5,789 steps and the skeletons of previous tourists (you can tell which skeletons are American, because they're wearing sneakers). If you make it to the top, you are rewarded with a sweeping panoramic view of dark spots before your eyes caused by lack of oxygen. Meanwhile, down at street level, the Parisians are smoking cigarettes and remarking, in French, "Some of them are still alive! We must build more medieval steps!"

Of course the tallest monument in Paris is the Eiffel Tower, named for the visionary engineer who designed it, Fred Tower. The good news is, there are elevators to the top. The bad news is, pretty much the entire tourist population of Europe is up there taking flash pictures of itself. There are so many people crowded into the smallish observation area that you get the feeling, crazy as it seems, that the whole darned Eiffel Tower is going to topple over. Ha ha! In fact this has happened only twice since 1991.

Paris also has many excellent art museums, the most famous being the Louvre (pronounced "Woon"). If you plan to visit it, you should allow yourself plenty of time to see everything—say, four years—because the Louvre is the size of Connecticut, only with more stairs. The museum contains 30,000 pieces of painting and sculpture, and as you walk past these incredible works of art, depicting humanity through the centuries, you cannot help but be struck, as millions of people have been struck before you, by the fact that for a whole lot of those centuries, humanity was stark naked. To judge from the Louvre, until about 1900, everybody on Earth—men, women, children, gods, goddesses, horses—basically just stood around all the time without a stitch of clothing on. There's one gigantic painting of a bunch of warriors getting ready to go into battle, and all they're wearing is swords. You expect to see a comics-style speech balloon coming out of the lead warrior's mouth, saying, "Fight hard, men! If we win the war, we can afford pants!"

I think the reason why the *Mona Lisa* is so famous is that she's just about the only artistic subject in the Louvre who's wearing clothes. On any given day, every tourist in Europe who is not on top of the Eiffel Tower is gathered in front of the *Mona Lisa*, who gazes out at the crowd with the enigmatic expression of a person who is pondering the timeless question: "How come they keep taking flash photographs, even though the signs specifically prohibit this?"

I enjoyed the art museums, but for me the most moving cultural experience I had in Paris was—and you may call me a big fat stupid low-rent American pig if you wish—visiting a gourmet food store called Fauchon (pronounced "Woon"), which contains two-thirds of the world's calorie supply. In the great art museums, I eventually reached a saturation point and found myself walking right past brilliant masterpiece paintings by Van Gogh, Renoir, Matisse, LeRoy Neiman, etc., without even glancing at them; whereas after a lengthy period of browsing in Fauchon, I was still enthusiastically remarking, with genuine artistic appreciation: "Whoa! Check out THESE éclairs!"

In conclusion, I would say that Paris is the most beautiful city in the world, and its inhabitants have an amazing sense of "savoir-faire," which means, literally, "knowing how to extinguish a fire." I say this because one Sunday afternoon I was in a crowded café when smoke started billowing from a cabinet into which waiters had been stuffing trash. It was a semi-scary situation; I stood up and gestured toward the smoke in an alarmed American manner, but the French diners paid no attention. In a moment, a waiter appeared carrying some food; he noted the smoke, served the food, went away, then returned to douse the fire with, I swear, a bottle of mineral water. And you just know it was the correct *kind* of mineral water for that kind of fire. So the meal ended up being very pleasant. It was also—I state this for the benefit of the Internal Revenue Service—quite expensive.

Gardening Advice
from Mertensia Corydalis

*Q: A few warm days woke up my crocus. The leaves
are well out of the ground. What will happen if the
weather turns cold again? Will the flowers be ruined?
Is there anything I can do? What about the bulbs—
will they be damaged?*

—AGNES, LAMBDON

A: Dear Agnes: Looking now at the snow-crusted crocus in my own garden, I cannot forget the very day their
progenitors were planted. I crawled around on hands
and knees for hours one October day nearly thirty years
ago, making hundreds of holes with a dibble, while my
daughter Astrid toddled along after me, placing a crocus bulb in each hole ("Pointy end up, angel, hairy end
down, like Daddy"). Norton, my former husband, who
had taken to wearing Japanese farmer pants buttoned
at the ankles, clogs which never needed hosing off,
since he never stepped off the pea-gravel paths, and a
straw coolie hat with chin cord which could be pushed
back to hang behind his shoulders if he ever happened
to work up a sweat, walked up and down the edge of the
bed pointing with a bamboo switch, "There. And there.
And there." I wondered what it would feel like to
plunge a fat dibble into the flesh of a human foot.

Returning to your questions, Agnes, early spring-flowering bulbs are more often than not caught up in the cruel tantrums of late winter and sometimes the blooms are shredded by an ice storm or reduced to mush by a hard freeze, but the bulbs survive, leaving hope for the following year.

Fortunately, most years the blooms overcome adversity (it's in the breeding). Your questions tell me you are a new gardener, so I will give you a bit more advice. Always give yourself permission to rearrange or remove whatever displeases you in your own garden.

Q: *We are performance artists—perhaps you have heard about our presentation, in which we emerge, nude, from suspended black rubber chrysalides, wet with the vernix caseosa of newborns (actually fat-free lemon chiffon yogurt), interpret our life cycles through dance, and perish consuming each other in the act of love. We would like our garden to really make a statement. Can you suggest some out-of-the-ordinary plants?*
　—ANDRE AND AGATHE, BORGNE@CONFONDRE.ORG

A: Those of you for whom passing out bite-size Milky Way candy bars one night a year is not sufficient observance of Halloween might be interested in a special area of my own garden.

This small space, the Charles Baudelaire Memorial Garden, is anchored by a contorted hazelnut tree and a broken Doric column. I have made a little hobby of collecting the nearest-to-black plants that I can find. Some of the specimens include: *ophiopogon planisca pus "nigrescens"* (black mondo grass), *hemerocallis* Black Magic, a Black Jade miniature rose, Ink Spots and Taboo hybrid tea roses, Superstition bearded iris, black *alcea rosea* (hollyhocks), and pansies as deep and velvety as a party dress (and Jennelle's ears). Here is a tip: dark reds seem to be optically closer to black than dark blues and purples. In the future I hope to add a *pleurant*, an eternally mourning statue such as found in French graveyards.

Next time . . . a sedum for every season

You Could Look Me Up . . . Sometime

ROY BLOUNT JR.

A man wants to make a lasting mark. I don't mean just to be remembered fondly by colleagues, I don't mean just to have a moment of fame. I mean to leave something behind in the permanent record, so that, when posterity is sifting through the rubble of our civilization, someone will at least say, "Should we keep a file on this guy?" Several men with whom I have gotten loaded are now enshrined in sports halls of fame. My friend Dave Barry has been turned into a sitcom, so that, as long as there is a *Nick at Nite* . . . My friend Garrison Keillor is in *Bartlett's Quotations,* the son of a bitch. As for me, I have long dreamed of winding up in a dictionary.

A dictionary is a little like heaven. You turn to a page and there between *toggery* and *Tom, Dick, and Harry* are pictures of a *tomahawk,* a *tollhouse cookie,* and *Tolstoy,* all preserved together for the ages. Leaf back a ways and there you see same-size illustrations of *jellyfish, jellyroll, Jersey cow, Jerusalem artichoke, Jesus,* and *jet.* You have the glamour, the latent radiance, of various experts mixing together, all casually out of their elements, like a summit conference, an all-star game, or one of those comic books in which all the heroes join forces to stamp out some comprehensive new evil. Except in a dictionary the company ranges across centuries, scales, and genera. A *tank* and a *tankard* hang with *Tanzania,* a *tapeworm,* and a *tapir. Oil well, okapi,* and *Georgia O'Keeffe* rub shoulders with *okra.* And all of them sharp, crisp, essential. You could look them up.

Don't get me wrong, I don't expect to be defined (between *blotto* and *blouse*). I do figure, however, that I am due to be cited. After years and years of using thousands of words, at least half of them right, I feel entitled to go down as having provided a good example of at least one of them—ideally, a snappy one. Some years ago, while browsing in the third edition of *Webster's* unabridged, I saw a phrase by Roger Angell, who was then my editor at *The New Yorker,* cited as an example of the usage of *spang.* "Spang in the middle of the theatre district."

Hot damn, I thought. *Spang.* What a *good* one. As a matter of fact I was considering writing a baseball novel at the time (I'm still considering it), in which the centerfielder would be named Cesar Spang. If I keep typing away, I told myself, some day I'll be in a dictionary too, and then I can retire and set up a little stand by the side of the road with a big sign that says, "SEE THE CITED-IN-*WEBSTER'S* MAN! ONE DOLLAR! ALSO LIVE SNAKES MONKEYS ALLIGATORS VIDEO RENTALS SANDWICHES BAIT."

Then my friend Pauline Kael told me that she had once used *dum-dum* to mean not an exploding bullet but a dumb person, and when her editor at *The New Yorker* questioned this usage she said let's check it out, so they went to a dictionary and sure enough, that meaning of *dum-dum* was given. The writer cited as using it in that way was Pauline.

That is so cool, I thought.

Last year, the third edition of the *American Heritage Dictionary of the English Language* came out, and I figured my time had come. I am in fact—along with Bill Bradley, Barbara Jordan, Carl Sagan, Susan Sontag, Eudora Welty, and a lot of other people—a member of that dictionary's usage panel. Every so often I get a questionnaire on which I indicate whether it is acceptable to use *snuck* to mean *sneaked* (yes), or to refer to a woman as *suave* or a *lout* (yes), or to say "To *myself,* mountains are the beginning and end of nature" (no). I love this stuff.

My dictionary (whose shorter college edition just came out this fall, by the way) drew raves. Noel Perrin in the *New York Times Book Review* called it "surely the most pleasurable dictionary ever published in this country, and one of the most useful." And I was part of it. True, my sense of myself as a maven was diminished a bit by a review in the *Boston Globe* that said the dictionary "claims to be many things, but it does not claim to be authoritative. (Even the panel includes decidedly unauthoritative oddballs: actor Tony Randall and humorist Roy Blount Jr., to name two.)" You work all your life trying to get things right, and this is the recognition you get. But probably what the *Globe* reporter meant was *unauthoritarian.* I don't know about Tony Randall, but I can live with that.

Anyway, for my pains I did get a free copy of my dictionary in the mail, and I delved into it with relish. Lot of good stuff on Southern regionalisms. Did you know that "the verb *carry,* which to Southerners means 'to transport (someone) in a motor vehicle . . . ,' is etymologically more precise in the Southern usage than anyhere else"? Hmm, I thought, I wonder . . . In one of my books I used the word *tump,* and the copy editor asked me whether I meant *dump,* and I told her no, I meant *tump.* And that was that. Could it be . . .

And there it was:

The verb *tump,* used almost invariably with *over* in the intransitive sense "to fall over" and the transitive sense "to overturn," is in common use in the South. . . . But another citation, taken from Gregory Jaynes's parody of detective fiction . . . in . . . *Time,* indicates that *tump* may not be exclusively Southern: "*At the end he tumps over into his rice pudding, poisoned. Whodunit?*"

I sprang to the phone and left a message on my friend Greg's machine: "Go immediately to Madeline's bookstore [Greg's wife Madeline works in a bookstore in Savannah] and look on page 1,924 of the new *American Heritage Dictionary*. That's all I'm telling you. Read the whole page. Dammit."

So Greg had got *tump*. In my dictionary. In fact, he had received credit for *de-Southernizing* the word. Probably when the researchers noticed my usage of *tump* they said yes, well, but of course he's Southern. The truth is—where do you think Greg is from? Memphis. But I wasn't going to complain about that. *Time* isn't Southern, so, okay, the whole thing was good for my people. And I was happy for Greg, the son of a bitch.

Greg is younger than I am and has published ten fewer books. He is bound to have had articles in fewer periodicals than I have, because I hold the unofficial American record: 107 different magazines and newspapers, not counting reprints. And he is not a member of even the oddball quotient of the *American Heritage* usage panel. So surely the day would come when I would pick up my dictionary, to look up some *other* word, and there I would be.

I looked up *scrooch*. I have used *scrooch* several times in writing, and you don't see it that often in, you know, writing.

Scrooch. "To hunch down, crouch," said the *American Heritage*. Well, not exactly. To scrooch is to compress oneself *in a direction*. You can scrooch down or you can scrooch over, as in "Nanette, scrooch over on the couch, sugar, so Aunt Lotty can sit down too." Once I paid a call on Flannery O'Connor, and she told of a conversation she had with a man who referred to a "scrooch owl." "You mean a screech owl?" she asked him. "No, a scrooch owl," he said. "That's one of those little owls that land on the same limb as another bird and then scrooch over, and scrooch over, and scrooch him all the way off the end and grab him."

Not only had my dictionary defined *scrooch* without con-sulting me (I could have gone down there to the office and scrooched for them; they could have used a picture of me scrooching as an illustration)—not only that, but my dictionary had cited someone else's usage of the word: "'the hot kind of hot Indiana hot weather that sends the family dog scrooching under the pickup truck to enjoy the shade' (John Skow)." Perfectly good example—the dog is hunching his way *up under* something. The definition, though, was inadequate. I could live without being cited in connection with that one.

I looked up some other words. I browsed. Some very interesting stuff. (Did you know that Dr. Seuss probably coined *nerd*? Or that the first time an alligator appeared in English, spelled anything like the way we spell it now, it was in *Romeo and Juliet*? And it was stuffed?) I browsed a little harder. When Pauline Kael was in the hospital for a heart operation, I called her in hopes of making her feel somewhat better by informing her that she had been cited for *anomic, choirboy, funky, interiorize,* and *unstoppable.* Surely *funky* brought some color to her cheeks, but otherwise, she said, she would prefer to be remembered for livelier words. "So-and-so got *trashy,*" I said, mentioning another critic who once wrote an ill-informed (OK, semi-ill-informed) mixed review of my work so why should I give the son of a bitch any ink?

"I think I had *trashy* before him," she said.

By this time, I would have been happy with *interiorize.*

I was not turning up. What was I supposed to do, go through the entire goddamned dictionary page by page? That wouldn't be cool. Soon enough, no doubt, the phone would ring, and some friend would be telling me I had been cited for, I don't know, maybe for some really refined term that I couldn't even remember using. And I'd be able to chuckle and respond casually, "Oh, well, that's nice. It isn't *funky,* but it's . . . "

Could it be that I was cited for *nice?* That would be better than nothing. No, Shakespeare and Milton were cited for *nice.* Couldn't be expected to get in ahead of them. I didn't get down on myself.

The phone didn't ring.

So here's what I have done, over the last few weeks. I mean,

I didn't do it full-time, just a couple of hours a day or so. I have *gone through the entire goddamned dictionary page by page.*

I was glad to see that Flannery O'Connor got *scoot,* as with a hose. Tallulah Bankhead got *slick* (*as a sonnet,* interesting). Louis Armstrong's *dig,* Margaret Mitchell's *tomorrow,* and Richard Nixon's *stonewall* could hardly be faulted, and I was personally pleased that Jimmy Carter got *strength.* I envied Hunter Thompson for *booger,* Jimmy Breslin for *boozehound,* and William Safire for *hoohah,* but I was willing to concede *snob* to Tom Wolfe, *sumptuous* to Anaïs Nin, *something* to Virginia Woolf, *netherworld* to Malcolm X, and *affect* to John Paul II. You know who is cited for use of the very word *define?* Gloria Vanderbilt. Okay. But I don't know about John Glenn, who, in spite of being the dullest person ever to campaign for a presidential nomination, is pictured and defined on page 770 as the first man to orbit the earth, and then *on the very next page* is cited as the first person to use, in writing, the word *glitch.* The son of a bitch.

And how about these people, all of whom I have worked with or hung out with at some time or another (so where was I when they were using all these words?):

Linda Ellerbee, in fact, got *hang out.* Garrison got *snuck;* also *combine, couple, octet, reek, soul* (*soul!*), *unalienable,* and *unnameable.* Calvin Trillin got *collegial* and *factionalize.* Russell Baker got *clean* (*someone's*) *clock,* and *not half.* Bobbie Ann Mason got *hoot* and *frag.* Stephen King got *feel.* Dudley Clendinen, *johnnycake.* Lloyd Rose, *Philistine.* Gary Fisketjon, *rip off.* Pat Conroy, *rootedness.* Tom Boswell, *backstab.* Jeremiah Tax, *guileful.* Curtis Wilkie, *spring* and *distinctive.* Jerry Footlick, *fountainhead.* The late Pete Axthelm, *troll.* Jane Gross, *dervish.* Christopher Hitchens, *hooch* (although it does not derive from his name). I was somewhat consoled to see that Nicholas Lemann's name was misspelled in his citation for *ticket,* but for *fluid* he was spelled correctly. Frank Deford got *shaft* (the verb).

I got it, the noun.

By that I do not mean that I got cited for *shaft,* the noun. I mean I got the shaft. That's how demoralized I am. I am explaining my jokes.

I got nothing. Not the word *nothing,* Bosley Crowther got *nothing.* I got nothing as in not anything (Anne Tyler got *anything,* as well as *chomp*). Unless I just scanned right over my name, which I feel is unlikely, I am not cited in my dictionary for anything at all.

There are other bones I might pick with my dictionary. It doesn't seem to realize that *dickens,* as in *what in the dickens,* is a euphemism for *devil,* and it doesn't mention that a child can be called a *little dickens.* I disagree (as Louis Armstrong would have) that *all right* "is usually pronounced as if it were a single word" and therefore probably should have evolved into one, like *already* and *altogether.* (*Already* and *altogether* are different from *alright* in that they are adverbs—sometimes they are pronounced as two words, and when they are they are spelled that way: "Are you all ready? Okay, now, all together." All right? All *right.*) I never saw the University of Mississippi referred to as *Old Miss* (see the definition of *Oxford*): It's *Ole Miss.*

Furthermore, whoever wrote the "word history" note for *limerick* says "let us sum up by saying . . . " and then says one of the worst limericks I have ever read. It is a *rotten* limerick. I do not deign to quote it, for it is a *miserable* limerick. It is such a sloppy, misshapen limerick as to be no limerick at all. It doesn't scan worth shucks, it resorts to lame, old-fashioned inversion ("Or from poets it came," indeed!), it only *rhymes* once. I hereby challenge whoever wrote that so-called sorry-ass immetrical bit of scarcely even limerick-resembling twaddle to step forward and deny that I—just to take a random example— can write a better limerick than that in nine seconds, drunk. For instance:

> *A certain word-lover named B.—*
>
> *That is, incidentally, me—*

Turned phrases galore.
Where is he, therefore?
Not in the dic-tion-a-ry.

Don't try to pretend that you're not reading this, either, Mr. or Ms. "let us sum up." You have read a whole lot of words I've written, you are bound to have. You just don't want to admit it, you drivelly, unfunny, rhyme-poor, rhythm-impaired, anonymous, slack-lined, unauthoritative . . .

Hey. No one is cited for *son of a bitch*.

I Go to Golf School

ROY BLOUNT JR.

"Have you ever been close to death?" Paul Bertholy asks me, with a fierce glint in his eye. At first I think this is one of those questions of his that requires a ritual answer, like "What is the Golden Exercise?"

But no, this is one of those questions of his that requires me to say, "Well . . . ," and then he tells me that he fainted in the middle of the road yesterday and when he came to he saw that a big truck had stopped just inches short of running him over.

"The truck driver was shaking," he says. "I wasn't afraid."

I believe him. He tells me of the time when, thirty years ago, when he was about my present age, he was attacked by a two-hundred-pound college running back. Bertholy turned, as if to run, and then uncoiled a perfect left-hand-of-a-golf-swing that caught the football player in the throat. Bertholy then got the jock down in a choke hold.

"He was begging me to let him live. I said, 'No, I'm going to kill you.' Didn't I, Missi?" he asks his wife, Missi. Missi says he certainly did.

"He dumped in his pants," Bertholy says with grim satisfaction.

Bertholy is wearing, for reasons that will emerge later, a kind of bunny suit, only the ears don't stick up. The flaps of his hat turn down over his ears, so that the only part of him that isn't covered is his face.

This is my first golf master. The three people whom my second golf master, Mel Sole, wishes he could have a conversation with are Harvey Penick, Mahatma Gandhi, and David Niven.

As for me . . . Is there a snake-killing school I could go to? Because I think I would shine there. The first time I saw myself hitting a golf ball on video, I looked *exactly* like a man killing a snake. The action appeared to come to me just naturally. I've done very little snake-killing over the years, certainly never had any instruction in the art of it, but my feeling is, you don't really swing through a snake. You hunch over awkwardly so that you don't seem to present a real threat, and then, never mind the elaborate courtship of the swing, you just want to jump on his bones. You execute a kind of hurried hacking motion—and make sure you break that right wrist and get a little scooping action going so you flip the snake up in the air a ways, but not so far up ahead of you that he has time to recover before you run take another whack at him. And you don't need to get your hips involved. It wouldn't be sporting; snakes don't even have hips.

My only weakness as a snake-killer would be that I don't have anything against snakes, by and large. But then I don't have anything against golf balls either, except that they sure do play hell with a person's swing. Frankly, I believe I might have more potential as a blind golfer than as a sighted one. When I see that ball lying there, all dimpled and bland, everything I learned in six days of individual attention from Bertholy and Sole turns into one flash of primitive misrecognition: *Snake!*

I have often come up with ideas, over the years, of how various sports might be improved aesthetically. In basketball, lengthen the net by three inches, to prolong the swish. In shot-putting, make the shot bouncier: That thud is a downer. In golf, eliminate the ball.

Thanks to the Phil Ritson-Mel Sole Golf School, in Pawley's Island, South Carolina, I actually have myself on tape taking a fundamentally sound practice swing with a nine-iron. And I have Mel Sole's voice saying, "You don't know how *unusual* that is for a beginner. What it's telling me is that you *understand* the principles, you *understand* what you need to do." Mel is a large, laid-back South African with a kind heart. "You've just got to train your subconscious to do that when the ball is there."

Ah. Train my subconscious. Great. Did Freud have golf in mind when he came up with the whole idea of the subconscious? I don't think so. Snakes, maybe.

I am a scratch golfer, as in starting from scratch. At fifty-six. Taking up the game so late in life, and with no definite prospects of living past ninety-nine, I may never shoot my age. But maybe I can get my handicap down under my age. First I have to progress to the point of actually playing a hole.

If I were abiding by the principles of Paul Bertholy, I wouldn't be swinging a club yet, much less trying to hit a ball with one. Bertholy caddied for Walter Hagen. He has won considerable renown—though not as much as either he or Missi thinks he deserves—as a teacher. He has developed a method, the Bertholy-Method (his hyphen), which is more like tai chi than like snake-killing or weed-whacking or posthole-digging or anything else that I probably have some natural aptitude for. To give you some idea of the philosophical nature of the Bertholy-Method, here is a "Memo from the desk of Paul Bertholy, P.G.A.":

THE BERTHOLY-METHOD

METHOD IMPLIES A REGULAR, ORDERLY, LOGICAL PRO-CEDURE FOR PERFORMING A TASK.

THE BERTHOLY-METHOD NOT ONLY OFFERS A PRECISE AND PRODUCTIVE GOLF SWING BUILDING PROGRAM, BUT IT IS ACCURATELY AND TOTALLY DIAGNOSTIC, PINPOINT-

ING THE EXACT MOMENT OF A FAULT OR INADEQUACY
AND HOW TO OVERCOME IT.

BEING LOGICAL, THE BERTHOLY-METHOD OFFERS INDI-
VIDUAL FLEXIBILITY WHERE IT IS REQUIRED,

THUS
<u>BECOMING UNIVERSAL.</u>

I embarked upon the study of golf by wrestling with the
Bertholy-Method for three days, five hours a day—two and a
half before lunch, two and a half afterward, plus a lot of precept-
chanting, in the Bertholys' house in Jackson Springs, North
Carolina, near Pinehurst.

What you do is, you swing a two-foot-long weighted pipe.
Well, before you swing it, you assume a certain number of positions with it, which are the positions through which the
Platonic or Bertholic ideal of a golf swing ("Golf destroys your
swing," says Bertholy gravely) passes. You do it in a room of his
house—a converted garage, I believe.

Bertholy is a silver-haired banty rooster of a man, eighty-
five years of age. In 1979, when he was sixty-five, he shot a 67
on a 6,600-yard course and a 29 on a 3,200-yard course of nine
holes. Now he takes on students, one or two or three at a time,
at a hundred dollars an hour. He roaches his hair straight back
from his forehead; when it was red, he must have looked even
more intense than he does today. Intense, but in control. I sat
down in the Bertholys' breakfast nook, on the first day, and the
master began to talk. "All other sports are angry men's games.
Golf is not an angry man's game. The madder you get, the
worse you play. As emotion gets high, the kinesthetic gets low."
He sounded at least peeved, however, when he proclaimed that
"Golf instruction is the most backward single body of knowledge in human history. You're the sucker, the fool, the patsy of
all the so-called teachers in the world."

I couldn't take notes fast enough. So I have transcribed the
following rapid-fire reedy run-on Midwestern near-monotone

passage from the Bertholy instructional video, to give you some idea of the man's rap. He mentions Walter Hagen, and is off:

"I watched that man and mimicked him, and I have very high powers of mimicry—I have, oh, at least ten accents, and a fella said 'Gee with all the accents you have, how many languages do you speak,' and I said 'None, I'm still trying to speak English,' as you can well see here when I'm talking to you now. Say 'Catacolamine.' Would you say that, Mr. Kotay?"

Mr. Kotay, the cameraman, says, "Catacolamine."

"Catacolamine. That's a hormone developed by the human brain from laughter, from fun, so you must have some fun while you're learning the golf swing, if it's boring you're soon going to lose interest. We were so poor when I was a little boy my mother never vacuumed the living room floor, she weeded it. We were so poor when I was a little boy Santa Claus never flew over *our* house, he flew through it. So be able to poke fun at yourself. There's no such golf shot as a bad golf shot unless it has an adverse mental effect upon the ensuing shots. I'll repeat that. There's no such thing as a bad golf shot unless it has an adverse mental effect on the ensuing shots. A missed golf shot will never hurt my golf swing, it will only hurt my vanity. And vanity is a luxury of fools. Golf is a game of misses, it's not a game of hits. You must learn to accept your misses. So there are two distinct divisions, one is the building of the golf swing and once the golf swing is built the other, oh, almost mysterious division, is the playing of the game. Playing the game is done by a total control of one's mentality and emotions. So I have built a cocoon for that, to protect the mind so you can play. So first we'll teach you how to build a swing and then we'll teach you how to control your mind so you can play under pressure and win the world's championship. Okay, so position one, platform rod and claw. The toes are talonized. The buttocks are extended. . . ."

I believe that the Bertholy-Method is sound. I believe that if I pursued it diligently, I would develop a good swing. I *did* pursue it earnestly when we adjourned to the converted-garage room and began to assume the various positions. And I could see that holding the various positions was conducive to muscle-memorization of a good swing. But . . .

For one thing, Paul Bertholy has recently become, as his wife puts it, "allergic to everything." It happened to his daughter before him. Apparently it is happening to a number of people these days. You can air every possible residue of cleaning fluid or whatever out of a house, but *something* in the rugs or the atmosphere will affect Bertholy adversely and he will feel faint.

Hard as this must be on a man who has been so active all his life, Bertholy maintains a chipper attitude. He just has to go lie down a lot. So his assistant, Laverne Hess, an engaging woman in her sixties who looks much younger and has excellent form, takes over the hands-on instruction. And she is good at it. She gives you nice little nonauthoritarian tips like "Don't let your waggle give you a shank," and a comparison of the proper lateral hip movement to dancing the bump. But she would get to talking about how every time she is heading into the last few holes with an excellent chance of breaking par her husband will get mad and stop playing and make her stop, and I would get more interested in that than in my own progress, and then Bertholy would reappear, take one look at me, and snap, "What is the number one enemy of the golf swing?" And I wouldn't know.

And he would say, "The number one enemy of the golf swing is reflex action."

And I would say, "Oh, right," seeing his point in at least an abstract sort of way (my reflex action being to kill snakes), and he would say, "Repeat after me: the number one enemy of the golf swing is . . ."

And I would repeat after him, but sullenly. It ill befits a man of my age to pout, but if there is one thing I hate, it is being told to recite something.

Or else Bertholy would appear suddenly and snap, "Gimme a five."

Not "Gimme five." "Gimme *a* five." That would be the fifth position. But there were so many positions, and some of them had stages to them, that I could never remember which one was number five. And I would feel the disfavor of Bertholy, who still feels the favor of Walter Hagen.

And because of his allergy problem, when he would pop in like that, he would be wearing an outfit that looked remarkably like the kind of fleecy pajamas you zip a baby up in. White. With a fleecy hat that covered his ears.

And when we broke for lunch, Missi Bertholy, who is eighty, would serve soup and a sandwich and tell me her family's entire history, which was interesting, but I found that I could devote only so much energy to sympathizing with her over her father's having remarried. It must have been so long ago.

Let's face it. I am not the ideal Bertholy-Methodist. I get fidgety when I open a book—the book I have in mind is the Bertholy-Method instructional book—and the first thing I see is a photo of the author in a bathing suit and knee socks, flexing, with the caption, "Bertholy at 65. Note impressive deltoid development," and the next thing I see is a page that says:

STOP WISHING

The Universal Method of the Future

THE BERTHOLY-METHOD

The Magic Method of Fine Golf-swing Achievement,
the Only Golf Instruction That You Will Ever Need

And then on the next page:

At every crossroad on life's highway to
the future, there is a spirited individual who
is assailed by hordes of men blinded by
dedication to the traditions of the past.

The Bertholy-Method will safeguard your
golf-swing ascendancy and playing capability.

Here is another memo from the desk of Paul Bertholy:

THE MENTAL COCOON
LEARN TO CONCENTRATE. MEMORIZE
THIS PRE-SHOT ROUTINE THOROUGHLY.

THE BIO-FEEDBACK PRE-SHOT ROUTINE
FOR ALL FULL SHOTS AND PITCHES:

CHECK GRIP

TAIL OUT

PINCH KNEES

LEFT SHOULDER TO TARGET

CHIN BACK

KEYSTONE WAGGLE, <u>HOLD</u>

ONE THOUSAND, 2 THOUSAND, 3 THOUSAND
POINT LEFT KNEE B—E—H—I—N—D THE BALL

LEAD WITH LEFT KNEE (LEAD)

TUG WITH LEFT ARM (TUG)

TURN CHIN BACK (TURN)

I just now discovered this memo in the packet of instructions that arrived in the mail before I flew down for my lessons. Typed in clear capital-letter English above "Memo from the desk of " is this instruction: "MEMORIZE THOROUGHLY OR DON'T COME TO THIS SCHOOL, PB." I never even noticed this memo. It's a wonder I came away with as much in the way of proper muscle memory—kinesthesial recall of how unnatural the various stations of the golf swing feel—as I did.

The reason I looked so extremely unlike Walter Hagen in the first video Mel Sole took of me, when I went on to the Ritson-Sole school, is that I have tended all my life to drift in and out of muscle Alzheimer's. I can have a set of motions down pat one minute, and the next thing I know I look like a man falling downstairs in a lawn chair.

That is the kind of person I am. No, I withdraw that. My first day at Ritson-Sole, I took a psychological test. I don't like psychological tests. I keep thinking I will turn in my answers and an alarm will go off and several armed policemen will enter the room and arrest me for the murder of JonBenet Ramsey. But this test merely established that of the four basic types of person and/or golfer—Driver/Slasher, Persuader/Talker, Analyzer/ Methodical, and Craftsman/ Swinger—I am primarily a cross between Persuader/Talker and Craftsman/Swinger. My instruction was geared to me accordingly. Maybe if I were a cross between Driver/Slasher and Analyzer/Methodical, Mel would have had to hit me with a two-by-four to get my attention and then would have shown me diagrams; I don't know. As it was, he actually let me hit real balls with a real club, and taped me, showed me what I was doing right and wrong on a computer-ized split-screen video, with voice-over, that I got to take home with me, and offered encouragement for three hours or so for three mornings.

He also encouraged me to come up with a rhythmic key word or mantra to repeat as I bring back the club, pause at the top, come through, and finish. His key word is "Geronimo," coming down on the *ron*. I knew this wouldn't work for me, because I associate "Geronimo" with bailing out, which is the baseball term for letting your hips rotate out of play, which in golf I believe is calling spinning out. I used to bail out. Now I spin.

Word association is another one of my weaknesses on the links. For instance, *links* is German for *left,* so it makes me worry about whether golf will move me to the right politically. A friend of Mel's uses *ta-ra-ra-BOOM-de-ay* as his key word. I liked that, but I wanted a mantra of my own. I tried *Popocatapetyl,* but that reminded me of my late mother, because she used to say "Popocatapetyl" (the name of a Mexican volcano) occasionally as she did housework, for rea-sons I have never wanted to look into. I went with *Mo-ni-ca Le-*

WINSK-y for the time being, just because it came so readily to mind, but it's too topical, and it causes the expression "Presidential kneepads" to pop into my mind when I am trying to keep my front knee behind my hands or wherever I am supposed to keep it. Once late at night in the very pleasant condo accommodation that came with the three-day Sole-Ritson package, I got to drinking and swinging my Bertholy leaded pipe, and the Persuader/Talker in me somehow convinced the Craftsman/Swinger that I could turn my swing into a thing of beauty and a joy forever by keying it to the last two lines of Coleridge's "Kublai Khan":

> *For he on honey-dew hath fed,* [top of the swing]
> *And drunk* [moment of impact] *the milk of paradise.*

The next morning, however, it occurred to me why *drunk* had seemed, the night before, such an operative term.

So I haven't settled on a mantra yet. Then too I wonder—if I ever do manage to get a classic golf swing into my subconscious—what if a taste for saddle oxfords and certain plaids that I think of as Boca Raton tartans comes with it?

Then too I saw in the paper the other day where somebody on the seventh tee at a golf course in San Diego hit a drive that ricocheted off a tree to the green of the sixth hole and hit Billy Baldwin, the actor, right in the nose, requiring him to be rushed to Los Angeles for emergency plastic surgery. Do you realize how many Baldwins there are out there? The odds are pretty high that if I take up golf seriously I will hit at least one of them. And I don't have anything more against Baldwins, really, than I do against snakes.

And then my old baseball instincts kick in, and chip shots seem an awful lot like hitting pop-ups on purpose. And every time I see white shoes on a man engaged in sport, I recall, with a shudder, the sight of Joe DiMaggio, when he was a coach for the Oakland A's in the seventies when they wore those awful green-and-gold uniforms—the sight of Joe DiMaggio in *huge* white shoes.

On the other hand . . .

Several times I actually—*WINSK*—hit the ball right, thanks to some mysterious combination of Persuader, Craftsman, Bertholy, and Sole, and—*yyyyyy*—the damn thing flew some considerable distance straight.

And I was close to dying and going to heaven.

•• NEWS QUIZ ••

4/7/98 "RISKY BUSINESS"

The current Youth Risk Behaviour Survey of ninth-through-twelfth-graders reveals that three in ten boys and one in ten girls have done something in the past month. What?

"Fantasized about Tommy Tune . . . and his incredible gams."—Larry Amaros

"Been members of the Russian cabinet."
—Aaron Schatz

"Gone to eighth base."—Larry Doyle

"Been honest about their behavior while filling out the survey."—Bill Franzen

"Smoked a cigarette after sex with a teacher. (Is 'smoked a cigarette after shooting a classmate' too dark? Maybe I'm not getting out enough.)"
—Beth Sherman

• RANDY'S WRAP UP •

The sex, the drugs, the guns—who was it who said "Loathing and high auto insurance rates are the tribute age pays to youth"? Why, I believe that was me. And who was it who explained the 67 percent rise in military discharges since "Don't ask, don't tell" by saying: "We think the rise is almost exclusively explained by the increase in the numbers of people stating they are homosexuals. We think they are voluntary statements. We can only speculate as to why they are doing this"? Why, I believe that was Pentagon spokesman Kenneth Bacon. And who was it who in 1991 cut his wrists, mixed alcohol and pills, and tried to jump out a ninth-story window? Why, it was Milli Vanilli's Robert Pilatus, who died of a heart attack yesterday at age thirty-two. And who was it who said "Far more disgraceful than not to have sung on a Milli Vanilli album is actually to have sung on a Madonna album"? Me again. And why would I say such a thing? We can only speculate.

RECKLESS TEENAGE ANSWER

Smoked a cigar.

The survey, in Friday's "Morbidity and Mortality Weekly Report," found that between 1991 and 1997 smoking rates among high school students increased by one third, and among African-American high school students by 80 percent.

In a related story, plaintiffs in a Minnesota lawsuit took possession of 200,000 pages of tobacco company documents hours after the U.S. Supreme Court refused to block their surrender. "It sends a very chilling message to any trial lawyer that attorney-client privilege is not as sacred as it once was," said Greg Little, a lawyer for Philip Morris.

LEFTOVERS

"I'm not sitting here like some little woman standing by my man like Tammy Wynette."

—Hillary Clinton, 1992

A Graceland for Adolf

ZEV BOROW

The state of Bavaria said today that it had found an investor to turn the site of Hitler's 262-acre retreat at Berchtesgaden, his official summer residence near the Austrian border, into a tourist attraction.
—*New York Times*

Selections from the audiotape
accompanying the walking tour of
"Berchtesgaden: Hitler's Summer Retreat":

"Welcome to Berchtesgaden, Hitler's fabulous place in the country. Naturally, the führer had his own special nickname for his beloved retreat, an Austrian folk expression that translates roughly to: 'All the small birds are dead now.' Yes, Hitler loved folk expressions. And hated birds. [Pause] Stand straight! [Pause] The führer would arrive here at the start of summer weekends, exhausted from tyranny and evil. Close your eyes and imagine how it must have been then, without the adjacent petting zoo. Hitler would arrive, gaze at his surroundings, and likely feel the beginnings of a smile, perhaps the first to creep across his cherubic face all week. For here, all the small birds were dead, exterminated actually, in 1938. Open your eyes now, and, at your own pace, walk ahead . . .

"The front door. Now, we'll have to ask all Jews, Catholics, and Macedonians to wait out front while the tour continues inside . . . Just kidding—all are welcome! Step in and see the wonders of this palatial home. Move along . . .

"Growl if you like sauerbraten! Welcome to The Jungle . . . Room. And you thought only Elvis liked panther skin! This positively wild place is where Hitler would entertain some of the most fabulous Nazis in the world with lots of alcohol and late-night 'winner-take-all' Scrabble. Notice the custom-made swastika-shaped waterbed and accompanying shag rug. And dig that groovy mural! Walk ahead. Eyes forward.

"Hitler loved to surround himself with pretty things, and various kinds of poisons, especially here in his bedroom. The flower-print bedspread and matching snapdragon wallpaper are the perfect complement to Hitler's collection of hand-carved cat figurines. The shelves toward the back bay window—the führer made those curtains himself!—hold a dizzying collection of flavor-infused arsenics. Truly, a room where both Laura Ashley, and a trained assassin hired to kill Laura Ashley, would feel right at home. Now, march.

"Hitler's study, a refuge from his topsy-turvy world where he could jot down any little thought that popped into his head, say, a haiku to his dead mother, a nifty Polish joke, notes on an idea for a screenplay about cops, cops gone bad, or just a doodle of his imaginary friend, Sandy, who Hitler believed lived in the attic and came up with the strategy for invading Russia.

"When Hitler was stressed, more often than not this was where you could find him, in Berchtesgaden's gym. He'd spend hours here, practicing karate with his bodyguards, screaming into a full-length mirror, enduring marathon taebo workouts, whatever. Yes, Hitler was extremely flexible. Why not let one of our armed guards twist you into a pretzel? A German pretzel. Ha!

"The yard. Nothing relaxed the führer more than being astride a rideable lawnmower. An early proponent of organic fertilizers and home mulching, there were few things as important to Hitler as a green, healthy lawn. In fact, Hitler once said that if he had another life to live he would still try to conquer the world for the Aryan race, but first he'd conquer the menaces that are dandelions and nasty weeds. *Achtung!* Time to go . . .

"Sure, Hitler loved human suffering, but he also liked music—for marching, for dancing, for making one feel less sexually inferior. Music. And this was his music room. Look, behind the vintage Moog synthesizer is Hitler's old accordion. That's right, as a teenager the führer was in a rock band, albeit one that included an accordion player. The group, named Torchyr, after a joke Hitler's uncle used to tell, actually grew quite renowned in the clubs of Munich with songs girded by knowing pop structure and meticulously crafted harmonies.

"Hitler's garage. Here's where the führer would pore over ball bearings for his still-unfinished collection of kit '30s Fords, sniff turpentine, or just fiddle at his work bench. That old fashioned loom—Hitler loved to loom—in the corner has the teeth marks of a madman, and behind that are some really sharp knives. Indeed, here in the garage one can't help but get a sense of just how creative a man Hitler really was, and, while at Berchtesgaden at least, how happy and at ease. [Pause] This concludes our tour. Thanks once again for coming. Peace."

Upcoming House Votes

ZEV BOROW

Nearly 60 years behind the times, the House voted today to condemn the Nazi-Soviet nonaggression pact of 1939. The measure, a nonbinding resolution, was brought to the floor by Representative John M. Shimkus, Republican of Illinois. He is of Lithuanian descent, has a pocket of Lithuanians in his hometown of Collinsville and wants to try to highlight his support for the Baltic states' past efforts against Soviet repression . . . With time on their hands, many on the House floor are eliciting votes on topics they can boast about to the folks back home . . .
—*New York Times,* October 10, 1998

Representative Sarah Lichi, who represents Pennsylvania's 22nd Congressional District, wants the House to approve a resolution condemning the stock market crash of 1929. "Let's face it," she told reporters, "that crash wasn't good for anybody." The congresswoman says her district is "loaded" with people who invest in stocks, "and this 1929 deal, it makes them nervous. And that's not fair. Or right."

"C'mon, *nobody* wins that many games," says Congresswoman Beth Jintlow. Jintlow represents California's 11th Congressional District, which includes most of San Diego, and has proposed a resolution wherein this year's World Series champs, the New York Yankees, would be classified as "Lucky. Not great. Just real lucky."

Congressman Steve Monte, of New Mexico's 4th Congressional District, is drawing up a bill he says is "way, way overdue." It would formally approve a resolution in which the Vietnam war would be declared "won" by the United States. "It's not like we got blown out anyway," explains Monte. "It was a close war." Monte says his district is heavily populated by people who don't like to think of the United States as "a loser." "Besides," says Monte, "most of 'em are getting old, and between you and me, tend to be a little loose in the floorboards. This would be nice for them."

"In my district we're not ashamed to admit that we expect a lot of Robert Redford." This is what Representative Milt Tannenburg, who represents a large portion of western Maine, says is the impetus for his proposed resolution, the pertinent language of which reads: "The filmed adaptation of the *Horse Whisperer,* starring, and directed by, Robert Redford, was a piece of melodramatic offal." "Look," says Tannenburg, "everyone knows I love Redford. And people in my district even liked that *Up Close and Personal* thing. But 'a horse whisperer?' In a flick where there's not even any half-believable horse whispering!"

Victor Rodeo, a congressman representing parts of St. Louis and its suburbs, wants Congress to approve a resolution condemning the 923 A.D. pillaging and plundering of the Visigoths of what is now northern Austria by the Huns of what is now middle Austria. His district is composed almost entirely of second- and third-generation Americans of middle-Austrian Visigoth descent.

Differing slightly from many of his colleagues, Terence Roy Erickson, a representative from Kentucky's 11th Congressional

District, has proposed a resolution that would label the Spanish Inquisition—a nearly century-long period during the 1400s in which the Spanish monarchy and religious leadership brutally tortured anybody who wouldn't convert to Christianity—"not all bad." Apparently, the nickname of the high school football team in Pineland, Kentucky, the largest town in Erickson's district, is The Inquisitors. "I don't think the kids like to think of their team name as something with necessarily bad connotations. And I'm a congressman who cares about kids. Yes. Fine. The Inquisition was not a fun period of time for some people. But, well, these are *our children*."

"It has got to stop," says Congressman Richard Heinleman. Heinleman, a representative from Oregon, is trying to pass a resolution condemning Pontius Pilate, because, as he puts it, "I've got kids in my district wearing Pontius Pilate T-shirts, sunglasses, gold name plates. And, really, I can't blame them. Not with the way Congress has sat there, for decades now, and not come out—and I know this is debated in some circles—and condemned him for killing Jesus. Bennet talks about the death of outrage? C'mon, I'm talking about the guy who killed Jesus."

"Anyway you slice it, evil is wrong." Congressman James Goodman of Bergen County, New Jersey, wants his colleagues to approve a non-binding resolution declaring: "Evil Is Wrong." Goodman says that in his district "a lot of people have made it a point to come out against evil," though notes, "but, of course, this would be non-binding. If at some later date the country feels evil isn't so wrong, hey, it's nothing we can't fix."

Choose and hope, but the burger will be medium.—M.O'D.

Let's Hear It for the Cheerleaders

DAVID BOUCHIER

Strange things happen on college campuses in summer. I was nearly trampled to death the other day by a horde of very young women wearing very short red skirts and chanting something that sounded like "A fence! A fence!"

A fence might be a very good idea, perhaps with some razor wire and a warning sign saying "Danger: Cheerleaders Ahead." Long Island is host to more than a dozen cheerleader camps. For the educationally gifted, Hofstra and Adelphi Universities even offer cheerleading scholarships ("Give me an A! Give me an A!").

But I think there is some intellectual work to be done here. Cheerleading needs a history, a philosophy and, above all, a more sophisticated theory of communications.

The cheerleading phenomenon is almost unknown in the rest of the world. British soccer fans do their own cheerleading, with a medley of traditional songs, bricks and bottles. In less civilized parts of the world, fans express their enthusiasm by running onto the field and beating up the opposing team. Only in America do we have professional partisans to do the jumping and yelling for us.

Strange as it may seem to foreigners, the cheerleading industry has many ardent supporters. It is said to build self-confidence, positive attitudes and a mysterious quality called spirit, which seems to involve smiling a lot. Cheerleading also teaches the value of teamwork, something that women have often despised in the past as a male excuse for mindless violence and idiotic loyalties. "Be 100 percent behind your team 100 percent of the time" is a slogan that would be heartily endorsed by Slobodan Milosevic, the Orange Order and the Irish Republican Army.

Young cheerleaders also acquire valuable practical skills: impossible balancing tricks, back flips and the brass lungs they will need for child raising or being heard at the departmental meeting. Above all, they learn to compete, in hundreds of local and national events. Cheerleaders are clearly the corporate leaders and the political stars of the future.

Cheerleader culture is much broader and shallower than I had imagined. There are glossy magazines and webzines featuring the essential equipment: deodorants, contact lenses, Cheer Gear, makeup, party dresses and miracle diets. Novices can learn how to create a successful cheer routine with hot music, unique moves, fab formations, and multiple levels. They can also learn to make their own pom poms (called just "Poms"). There are international stars out there you've never heard of, and even a few anonymous muscular cheerleading males, whose job it is to support the base of the feminine pyramid.

Despite cheerleaders' obsession with pyramids, my research suggests that cheerleading began in ancient Greece, rather than in Egypt. The first cheerleaders were called Maenads, female attendants of the god Bacchus. Their task was to encourage the crowds to have a good time, with frenzied rites and extravagant gestures. The opposing squad, the Furies, were merciless goddesses of vengeance who would swing into violent action if their team was losing. The ancient Greeks must get the credit for being the first to give young women these important career opportunities.

So many teams were decimated by the Furies or led astray by the Maenads that cheerleading fell into disrepute for 2,000 years, until it was revived in a kinder, gentler form in the United States. But it's still a dangerous activity. In an average year, high school footballers lose 5.6 playing days to injuries, according to the January 1998 Harper's Index, a compilation of statistics. Cheerleaders lose 28.8 days. These accidents are blamed on excessive acrobatics and the passion for building taller and taller pyramids.

But all enthusiasm is dangerous, especially when it takes a physical form. If cheerleading is part of education, let's use it to educate by focusing on the message. Surely we can do better than waving our poms, doing somersaults and chanting:

> *Champs take it away*
> *Now Play by Play*
> *Move that ball*
> *Win win win.*

Let's face it, this is not exactly a stellar example of the sophisticated use of the English language. To reduce the risk of injury, and make the sport more educational and less distracting for the fans, I propose to substitute verbal skills for physical high jinks. Routines should become more static, and chants should become more grammatical, more literary and more conducive to the kinder, gentler society we all hope for in the next century.

> *Why don't you fellows*
> *Pick up that ball*
> *And move it carefully*
> *To the other end of the field?*

If we really want to teach good social values, let's chant this famous verse from Grantland Rice:

> *For when the one great Scorer comes*
> *To write against your name*

He writes not that you won or lost
But how you played the game.

Now there's a catchy message for the millennium!

And why not bring that youthful spirit and those brilliant visuals out of the stadium and into the workplace? Cheerleaders should be in every office, with a chant for every corporate game. In a lawyer's office, for example, a spirited cry of "Rule of Law! Rule of Law! Sue! Sue! Sue!" accompanied by some eyepopping dance steps, would give courage and purpose to desk-bound drones. On Wall Street, a simple chant of "Go Greenspan! Low Interest! Never Mind the Asians!" would create a positive environment for investment. And cheerleaders would share their boundless enthusiasm with the rest of us who, in the game of life, so often find ourselves on the losing team.

Lapses of
Photographic Memories

DAVID BOUCHIER

I may be the last person left in the world who takes snapshots on vacation and pastes them into a photo album. We have a treasure house of family history, a dozen formidable albums as big as medieval Bibles in which our holiday memories are lovingly preserved. The pictures have scarcely changed over the years. The main actors get a little older and grayer, but the prints are so small and fuzzy that it scarcely shows. Every vacation place looks exactly like every other. Photo albums give a reassuring sense of time standing still.

These albums are important family history. They certify that we've been there and done that. If the house went up in flames, we'd have no evidence that we ever left Long Island. Without these snapshots to jog our fading memories, we might accidentally go to the same places all over again.

Notice that I say snapshots and not photographs. A snapshot is quick, simple, and unpretentious. A photograph is supposed to be a work of art.

I spent a few years trying to take photographs. I set out on vacation weighed down with a huge load of camera equipment, including ten different lenses, electronic flash equipment, range finders, exposure meters and dozens of rolls of 35 mm film. I would have produced magnificent photographic art, worthy to hang in galleries alongside the pictures of Henri Cartier-Bresson or Ansel Adams. But it took too long to set up the equipment. By the time I found the right camera, the right lens, the right film, the right angle and the right exposure, the subject had usually moved on or had died, or the season had changed. Vacations were just too short for this kind of thing.

So I got rid of the fancy equipment and bought a simple point-and-shoot camera which, twenty years later, still produces almost-recognizable snapshots with 100 percent reliability.

Leafing nostalgically through the older albums, I notice that there are dozens and dozens of pictures taken on beaches, as if my family had lived perpetually by the sea, basking in the sunshine. I seem to remember that I spent almost all my childhood in gloomy classrooms in rotten schools, in the middle of horrible cities, and that it rained all the time. Yet the snapshots show this childhood paradise.

When adulthood allowed me to escape the classroom and the beach, my vacation pictures got more interesting. Female persons who were not aunts begin to appear, and I tried to live more dangerously. Later albums record numerous unwise activities, which, if they'd been captured on video, would certainly qualify for "America's Funniest." Here's me just about to fall off my motorcycle in Italy, just about to fall off my skis in Vermont, just about to fall off a horse in Arizona, and just about to expire of heatstroke during a ten-kilometer foot race in Mattituck. Those were happy days.

Technology has moved beyond the snapshot and the photo album. The modern vacationer carries a video camera, to capture all the happy activity and all the joyful sounds of holiday fun. The family will not thank him for this later. The video camera is an unforgiving gadget that shows us exactly as we are. The ordinary still camera can and does lie, if only you use it right. And now the camera has been further enhanced by the invention of digital photography that allows you to put your snapshots onto a CD-ROM disk and improve them later by brightening up the weather, or removing the images of young ladies you swore you never met. The President might like one of these for Christmas.

I'm going to stick with snapshots in albums. These memories are too precious to entrust to any computer. But it strikes me that they are also very selective. This nostalgic trip into the past set me thinking about all the vacation experiences I should have recorded on film, but didn't. Every vacation is a unique event, but you'd never know it from the snapshots. For example, what about the three days I spent locked in the tiny bathroom of my Athens hotel room after eating a second helping of moussaka? That bathroom was so familiar to me that I knew the cracks in every tile and learned the fire regulations in Greek, posted on the wall. But now it's just a fading memory. What about the spectacular body rash I got from eating English oysters, or the nasty incident with the camel in Morocco, or the tremendous flood that marooned us halfway up a mountain in France? Why did I never use the camera at these dramatic moments? Instead of all those picture postcard views full of sunshine and smiles, I'd have an authentic record of what our vacations were really like.

Personal snapshots should be a true history, and mine look more and more like a carefully constructed myth. I can't stop taking snapshots: it has become a habit, almost an addiction. But perhaps I'll succumb to the latest photographic gimmick, the disposable camera. This works more like the ordinary human memory. You take your snapshots, rewind the film and, just to keep the historical record straight, toss the whole thing away.

A Year-Round Tan
for the Asking

DAVID BOUCHIER

For the innocent Long Islander, one of the many hazards of midtown Manhattan is the cast of strange characters who lurk on every city block, distributing free literature. As a spectator sport, it's quite entertaining to watch the dance duets of the touts and the pedestrians who are trying to avoid them. But personally, being a polite suburban person and an avid reader, I find it hard to say no to anything in print. The result is that, within a few blocks, I become a walking scarecrow bulging with scraps of multicolored paper. This makes me a magnet for every other street person with a message.

It seems an awful waste of paper, and I feel that all this throwaway literature should be recycled. If I had the nerve, I'd stand on the corner of Seventh and Thirty-fourth, handing out my accumulated pamphlets to tourists and foreigners who are too courteous to refuse. But usually I dump the lot in a trash can at Penn Station, when nobody is looking.

One sunny day last week, moved by sheer curiosity, I decided to keep all my mystery messages and read them on the train going home. Perhaps I'd been missing something by being so self-conscious and puritanical. These squalid notes might lead me to the vibrant secret world of the big city, the places that no suburbanite can ever find, and that are not permitted to be advertised in *The New York Times*.

It was a big disappointment. I had collected a fistful of badly printed advertisements for one-hour photo developing services (why the hurry, I wonder?), sleazy-sounding nightclubs, burger bars, and one offer of guaranteed instant salvation available at an obscure storefront church in the Bronx (again, why the big hurry?).

But most of the advertisements were for tanning studios.

"Get a sexy tan without going to the beach," said one flyer. The photos showed machines like futuristic caskets, with the encouraging information that these are "8,000-watt 3-sided high-intensity upper body tanners." The lower body, presumably, just has to take care of itself, or perhaps they have separate tanning machines for that part. Certainly they offered special face tanners, and even hand tanners, in case you prefer to brown only the parts that show. People choosing this option obviously don't have much of a social life.

I wasn't tempted by the fast photo services: I can wait to see how bad my snapshots are. The nightclubs were in parts of the city where I wouldn't want to go without a Marine escort. The burger bars would send my cholesterol levels off the chart, and I don't think that I would qualify for instant salvation.

But the ads for tanning studios reminded me that yet another summer has passed, and I still had no tan.

In fact I can pinpoint exactly the last time I did have a good tan. It was in September of 1977, after I'd spent a long summer season working for a travel company in North Africa. I returned with the beautiful, dark bronzed color that is praised and envied by everybody. I have the photographs from 1977, and that tan really looked good. The dermatologist has been removing strange little blips from my face and body ever since.

Two decades seem a long time to go without a tan, especially if one's natural skin color is an unhealthy fishy white.

We're told every day that a tan will make us attractive and even sexy—and that by implication the lack of a tan will condemn us to a monastic existence with no chance of achieving self-esteem. This is a powerful incentive, and I would certainly need a very good reason to climb into one of their electronic coffins for a claustrophobic session with a bunch of ultraviolet tubes.

The French have a saying: "It is necessary to suffer in order to be beautiful," but this sentiment was coined in the old days, when the beach was our tanning studio. At least we suffered in the open air.

When my family went to the seaside years ago, everyone would lie on the beach until they turned brick red, and then peeled horribly. Really severe sunburn was virtually an annual duty. You certainly didn't want your friends to think you'd taken your vacation in Maine or Scotland.

People are more health-conscious now. And even if they don't care about health, they know that a youthful tan will quickly turn into a fine crop of middle-aged wrinkles. Like many other things, the fun has been taken out of it. Even if they do determine to get a tan in spite of everything, the pharmacy is full of tanning lotions containing sunblocks. In the distant days when I had a tan, suntan oil was just that—oil. You laid it on your skin as you might baste a chop on the grill, and for the same reason—so it would cook better. These new lotions advertise that they will prevent the sun from getting through to you, with chemical blocks more effective than a foot of concrete. In these circumstances, it seems scarcely worth investing in the boredom and discomfort of days on the beach, only to end up as white as before and saturated in chemical grease.

Thank goodness it's September. In ten days it will be October, then November, then December. Those horrible shorts can be stored away, our pallid limbs decently hidden. And when we see someone with a winter tan, we can respond with pity rather than envy. Some hustler on the streets of New York has sold them 8,000 watts of ultraviolet light, which we can get free, if we only wait a few months.

The Bane of Every Vacation: Souvenirs

DAVID BOUCHIER

Even the happiest summer trip has a dark cloud of anxiety hanging over it. What to get for Aunt Ethel, who looked after the cats? What about the cats themselves? We MUST take something back for mother. And dare we forget the lawn person, the chiropractor, and all the people we love to hate at the office?

The moment we think about souvenirs, all the pleasure goes out of the vacation. The last precious days and hours must be spent in a quest that is doomed to failure, because souvenir shops are always and everywhere the same. From Bridgehampton to Bombay, from Patchogue to Paris, they all sell the identical awful stuff.

This is because all the souvenir shops in the world get their stock from one central source, a giant warehouse in Outer Mongolia stuffed with billions of mugs and T-shirts with dumb messages and ancient jokes about age and sex. The rest of the global stock of souvenirs consists of stuffed animals, enough china fairies and shepherdesses to populate a baroque opera, a lot of peculiar "shell creations," cassettes of New Age music that sounds like whales with toothaches, twee little birdhouses that no self-respecting bird would ever inhabit, wind chimes, British bath products with names like "Sweet Almond" and "Gardenia," and so many candles that anyone would think Edison forgot to invent the light bulb.

When these objects get into the home, they sit around on the mantel for a while, gathering dust. Then, usually around Christmas, are consigned to the oblivion reserved for all holiday souvenirs. From there, they mysteriously make their way back to Outer Mongolia to be recycled. Next summer they reappear in the same souvenir shops, dusted and re-labelled and looking as repulsive as ever.

"Souvenir" is a French word, meaning "to remember." When we visit a new and beautiful place it's nice to bring home a keepsake. That's why most of the ancient monuments in the world are getting smaller every year.

History tells us that first souvenirs were brought back by the Crusaders of the 11th century, who upon returning from the Holy Land liked to bring back a piece of the true cross, or a Saracen's head, just for the memories.

By 1291, the modern souvenir industry had started up in Venice, making exquisite glass objects for tourists. Seven hundred years later, Venice is literally sinking into the sea under the accumulated weight of cute glass souvenirs. And glass is still the favorite souvenir material, even though it doesn't travel well in an overcrowded family car, or in the overhead luggage compartment of a plane, where the next passenger is just waiting to pulverize it with a carry-on bag the size of a Volkswagen.

But what do summer tourists take home to remind them of Long Island? I decided to check out souvenir stores in some popular local tourist spots.

The results were not encouraging. There were more plastic models of the Montauk Lighthouse than seemed reasonable, but almost nothing else with a specifically local flavor. What's wrong with some real Long Island stuff? For example, at the site of the ancient city of Troy, in Turkey, you can buy pieces of the original wooden horse of Troy for $5. Surely our local entrepeneurs can do better than that.

The defunct nuclear plant at Shoreham has become a place of magic and mystery. Like Stonehenge, nobody admits to having built it, and nobody knows what it's for or how to get rid of it. Why not sell it off in small brick-sized chunks, each with a certificate of authenticity?

Books are popular take-home gifts, and there just aren't enough attractive coffee table books about Long Island. Why not "Architectural Masterpieces of the State University of New York," or "My First Pop-Up Book of Strip Malls"? Drivers might appreciate a nice CD of soothing music for the ride home, titled "Long Delays Ahead, Exits 73–0." We have more sand than anything else on Long Island, but casual visitors seldom get to see it. Souvenir stores could do a brisk business in authentic pots of East End sand, labelled "Terminal Beach," or jars of genuine non-pasteurized water from Long Island Sound.

The profit potential here is enormous. But the whole souvenir business obviously needs to be rationalized and brought up to date. Instead of wasting good vacation time sweating in and out of tiny shops smelling of potpourri and hot candle wax, we should be able to order our souvenirs ahead of time, on the Internet, in the comfort of our own homes. Enter your vacation destination under "search," browse through the local offerings and choose exactly the right souvenirs, all localized and personalized. Just think, authentic gifts from Melville, Madagascar or Milan, delivered painlessly to your home address just in time for your return. The best part is, you wouldn't even have to go there.

Zone 5

Gardening Advice
from Mertensia Corydalis

Q: Ol' Betsy, as I call my lawnmower, is on her last piston. When I go shopping for a replacement, should I get a mulching mower or continue to bag the clippings?

— MEL, HILLCREST

A: I find it peculiar that a grown man, and a home owner at that, should be on a first-name level of intimacy with a piece of power equipment. Perhaps this carries over to your recreational activities as well. If you must mow, make it a mulching machine and keep your chemically treated clippings out of the public compost heap. Readers, I implore you. No more lawn-care questions. Please.

Q: My bearded iris had a lot of foliage but failed to bloom last summer. Could the problem be thrips?

— ALISTAIR, HAMFORD

A: "Alistair," don't even bother inspecting and dusting for thrips. I could see from my yard when you, the know-it-all, planted the rhizomes so deep that half the length of the leaves are covered by soil. If you lived to be a hundred, as will the iris, they will never bloom. Notice that when iris multiplies on its own, the rhizomes are right at the surface. Now what does that tell you? More's the pity as you will never enjoy the flowers' subtle fragrance of Grapette soda, the fleshy, erect curve of the standards, the saffron-hued brush at the base of each languidly draping fall. But then, I notice you never have any visitors besides your mother.

Q: *I am attracted to the idea of taking up home wine-making as a hobby. I would like to try something different, unique—like kiwi wine. How are kiwis grown?*

—MORRIS, SOUTH OLEANDER

A: Dear Morris: First, you must select a hardy variety of kiwi, which should be the only type available at your local nursery. Then you must have at least one male plant as a pollinator and up to three or four female plants in the harem. (So far we have spent about $35.) Since kiwi is a vining plant, you must build a trellis or arbor to support your kiwis (lumber $100, carpenter $300). Now you will need a few garden supplies: pruners ($25) and a bag of composted cow manure ($4). In September, when you harvest the kiwis, you will need a fruit press (minimum $100), a basic wine-making kit ($40 and up), bottles (let's say you opt for hand-blown Spanish bottles at $15 each), corks and a corking device ($45). After all this effort, you will want some handsome labels to show off a little (graphic designer: $750). Now you need racks to cellar and age your bottles of kiwi wine (lumber $100, carpenter $300). Finally, friendship-repairing gifts the Christmas following the one in which you give out your bottles of kiwi wine should be a minimum of $50 each.

Not to stifle your creative urges, but I recommend that you enjoy a good bottle of Nouveau Beaujolais (under $20), make a snack of a few kiwis from the supermarket ($1), and peruse a catalog from a nursery that specializes in wine grape root-stock (free).

Next time: Get tough on thug plants . . . siberians: the husky iris

Memo from Coach

CHRISTOPHER BUCKLEY

Welcome back! The fall Pixie League soccer season officially kicks off next week, and I'd like to take this opportunity to let you know the schedule and provide guidelines. I'm sure we all agree that, with the Grasshoppers' 1–12 record last season, there's plenty of room for improvement this fall!

With a view to maximizing our performance, this summer I attended the National Conference of Pixie League Coaches, held in King of Prussia, Pa. I did some valuable networking and came away truly "pumped."

Physical Training

Per my memo last June regarding the summer-training regimen, your nine-year-old daughter should now be able to: (a) run a mile in under five minutes with cinder blocks attached to each ankle (lower body); (b) bench-press the family minivan (upper body); (c) swim a hundred yards in fifty-degree water while holding her breath (wind); (d) remain standing while bowling balls are thrown at her (stamina).

Practice Schedule

Mondays, Wednesdays, Fridays: 5:30 A.M.
Tuesdays, Thursdays: 5:30 P.M.
Sundays: 7 A.M.
Columbus Day Weekend: 7:30 A.M.
Note: Live ammunition will be used at the Thursday
practice.

Video Critique of Games

Mondays, 8 P.M. Parents strongly urged to attend. See
"Camera Dads" sign-up list (Attachment E). Note: Professional-
quality video cameras preferred.

Game Schedule

Saturdays, 8 A.M. Important: Please be sure to have your
daughter there *at least two hours before game time* for the
pregame strategy briefing and pep rally. Note: As the girls will be
biting the heads off live animals, we will need lots of guinea pigs,
hamsters, parakeets, etc. See sign-up list (Attachment P). No
goldfish, please!

Halftime Snacks

Last year, there was some confusion about appropriate nourishment. According to guidelines established by the N.C.P.L.C.'s
Committee on Nutrition and Performance, "snacks high in carbohydrates, sucrose, and corn syrup have been demonstrated to
provide dramatic short-term metabolic gain." So save those low-
fat pretzels for your cocktail parties and bring on the Twinkies and
Ring Dings. Let's make sure that when the Grasshoppers hit the
field they're hoppin'!

Use of Steroids

One of the many things I took away from the panel discus-
sions at King of Prussia was that, contrary to medical guidelines, use of anabolic steroids by preteens is not necessarily a
hundred per cent harmful. (See Attachment Q: "New Thinking
on Performance Boosters and Mortality.") Grasshopper doctor

dad Bill Hughes will discuss the merits of stanozolol versus flu-oxymesterone and dispense prescriptions to all interested parents. (Participation encouraged!)

Note: If any Grasshopper parents are planning a vacation in Mexico, please see me about bringing back certain hard-to-get enhancers, like HGH (human-growth hormone) and EPO (erythropoeitin).

Parental Input on Player Substitutions

Much as I appreciate your enthusiasm, it is not helpful if in the middle of a tense game situation you abuse me verbally—or, as one overzealous dad did last season, assault me physically—because I have not sent in your daughter. For this reason, I will be carrying a Taser with me at all times. These anti-assault devices deliver up to fifty thousand volts of electricity, and leave the recipient drooling and twitching for weeks. Though I will make every effort to see that each Grasshopper gets her turn on the field, if you get "in my face" about it don't be "shocked, shocked!" to find yourself flat on your back in need of cardiopulmonary resuscitation.

Injuries

If your daughter has kept up with the summer-training program, there's no reason she shouldn't be able to finish out a game with minor injuries, such as hairline bone fractures or subdural hematomas. (Parental support needed!) Remember the Grasshopper motto: "That which does not kill me makes me a better midfielder!"

Cheerleading

If the coaches at K. of P. were unanimous about anything, it was the key importance of parental screaming from the sidelines. This not only lets our girls know that Grasshopper parents do not accept failure but also alerts the other team that if they win you will probably "go postal" (kid talk for temporary insanity) and try to run them over in the parking lot after the game.

See you Monday morning!

As I Was Saying
to Henry Kissinger . . .

CHRISTOPHER BUCKLEY

It is no secret that the late Stephen Potter (1900–69), author of the superb and wise *Upmanship* series, and I were very close. Many letters have been received here asking for advice with respect to the game—some would say art—of Name Dropping. In the spirit of the immortal Potter, now eternally "up" in the celestial firmament, we offer the following guidelines in the hopes the reader will find them useful.

The Surname Drop

The most frequently asked question concerns when to dispense with the last name when dropping the name. The surest sign of the amateur dropper is the Superfluous Surname Gambit. Classically: *I ran into Warren Beatty and Jack Nicholson.*

Many a gambit has come to grief this way. Contrast with the much cleaner *I ran into Warren and Jack.* (See the Counter Warren Gambit, below.) Note that the Surname Drop should only be employed when the given name is distinctive.

The Counter-Surname Drop

Our friend B. Conrad, of San Francisco, [...]
technique.

So you call him David? I've known [...]
We're close as can be, but I still call him [...]
I'm old-fashioned, but this first-name stuff these [...]
batty.

The Counter-Warren Gambit

J. Tierney, of New York, New York, introduced this one memorably at a dinner party. The guest, himself adept at the Surname Drop, had been going on at length about his great pal, Warren. Tierney let him exhaust himself, then suavely countered: *Oh, you mean the* actor.

"Actor" was pronounced disparagingly, as in "pig-farmer." This was swiftly followed with: *I assumed you meant Warren Buffett.*

While the guest was fumbling, Tierney finished him off with: *I wish I had more time for things like movies.*

Grandmaster Tierney will be familiar to our readers as the inventor of the famous Out-Box Ploy. The dinner guest is steered into Tierney's study on some pretext. Lying in the Out tray on his desk is an 8-by-11-inch glossy photo of himself, signed in large lettering: To Bill Gates, Glad I could help—JT.

Alternately: To Winona Ryder, With deepest affection—JT.

Formerly of Benefit (FOB)

The second most frequent error is dropping the wrong name. S. Blumenthal, of Washington, D.C., recently got himself into a big tub of hot water by announcing in a crowded restaurant that he is a close friend of President Clinton. This earned him multiple subpoenas and legal bills into the tens of thousands of dollars. He was last seen traveling in Europe incognito.

Consult your local newspapers for guidance.

Friend of Kennedys)

Currently under review. Once the *ne plus ultra* of Name
dropping, this category has become problematic. In general,
probably best to avoid, pending a final ruling by the committee.
But it is sometimes unavoidable. Some guidelines:

SAFE

—*Don't you just adore Arnold and Maria?* (See Surname
Drop, above.)

—*I don't know why John is going around bare-chested. He's
constantly borrowing T-shirts from me. What does he do
with them?*

UNSAFE

—*I used to hang out with the Skakel kids back in the '70s.
Boy, did we do some wild stuff.*

Royals

In America, caution must be exercised while royal name
dropping. The correct stance is that while one is delighted to be
on intimate terms with the royal families of Europe, one is fiercely
proud of the Revolution, Valley Forge, Bill of Rights, etc. This
republican imperative can be used to advantage. A variation of it,
the Confused Commoner Gambit, has been used with effect by
R. Atkinson, a British subject. He lets it slip that he has just spent
some quality time with the Prince of Wales. Then he adds:

*One minute you're calling him "Sir," and the next, you're
stuffing a crumpet down his trousers.*

This can be adapted to American usage. P. Cooke of
Lakeville, Connecticut, gets the ball rolling by serving his guests
Pimm's Cups, then shrugs:

*It's one thing not to bow. It is our American birthright. But
even though he's asked me to—repeatedly—I just can't bring
myself to call him Charles.*

A more modest approach is to steer the conversation
toward an apparently unrelated topic, such as tanning lotions,
and then to casually announce:

The Queen Mother has the most remarkable skin.

This can be followed with: *And just between us, is the jolliest of the lot.*

Immediately rebuke yourself for having said this, and intimate in the strongest terms that you do not want the remark quoted in the newspaper, especially since Ascot is fast approaching. Finish with:

It would make things in the Royal Enclosure damned awkward.

The Posthumous Drop

Safest of all, since chances of contradiction or being challenged are minimized. R. Clements, of East Blue Hill, Maine, uses this approach.

> RC: (*looking up from magazine, sighing heavily*):
>   *Thank god, is all I can say*
> LISTENER: *About what?*
> RC: *That it never got out about us. Miracle, really.*
> LISTENER: *About who?*
> RC: (*distracted*): *Oh, nothing.*

At this point, Clements excuses himself, leaving the magazine opened to an article about Princess Diana.

> RC: (*returning, wiping his eyes with tissue*): *Can I fix*
>   *you another?*
> LISTENER: *What did you mean by that?*
> RC: (*with a hint of defiance, fighting back tears*):
>   *Nothing. I shouldn't have brought it up in the first place.*

VARIATION OPENINGS:

I told her not to marry in the first place.

It's at times like this that I miss her the most.

I really wish that brother hadn't turned Althorp into a petting zoo. Charging the masses ten pounds just to view the grave. Honestly. . . .

FOLLOWED BY:

Of course, I'm no one to ask. I did practically live there for a while.

Listener's inquiries can be followed with an adamant refusal to discuss it further. A few minutes later, morosely interject: *Couldn't see a thing at the funeral. I was directly behind Luciano Pavarotti. Just my luck.*

Other Royals

Many novice droppers prefer to start off invoking intimacy with lesser royalty. There's no shame involved, but notoriety should be imputed to the LR[1] in order to compensate for his/her obscurity. T. Wilder, of Bethesda, Maryland, an advanced gamesman, began by using the following technique.

So, have you spent much time in Umvig-Glumstein?

The answer being reliably no, he proceeds:

Well, if you ever get there, let me know and I'll arrange for you to see Schloss Schlitz. For my money, it's far more dramatic than Mad Ludwig's desperate attempt at attention-getting, and yet it manages to be so—I don't know—gemütlich at the same time.[2]

Wilder has put several balls in play simultaneously: his own access to the notional castle, as well as the listener's unfamiliarity with European geography and conversational German.

Listener now on the defensive on several fronts, Wilder continues:

The current Graf is an old, old friend. Last of a line, direct descendant of Philip of Swabia, one of the less gaga Holy Roman Emperors, if you don't mind my saying. Isaiah Berlin and I used to get into such fisticuffs over it. . . .

Wilder has deftly implied that his views on the Holy Roman Emperors are controversial, even raffish.

[1]Lesser Royal.

[2]If he suspects that the listener knows a few words of rudimentary German, Wilder employs the Teutonic Escalator. In place of *gemütlich*, substituting: ". . . so—what is the German for it? *farble-flemmerchinzenecspritz?*" (chuckling to himself) "Yes, that's it. *Parsifal*, Act II, scene 3 . . . "

Anyway, the Graf is a dear old thing. Gives us the run of the place every August. Of course there are 236 bedrooms, so it's not as though we're constantly bumping into each other in the hallway.

He may now move in for the kill: *Anyway, if you're in the vicinity, I could try to fix it for you to stick your head in and have a poke around. I'd arrange for you to meet him, but he's a bit, you know, formal. . . .*

The DNA Insinuator

If no royal opening presents itself, steer the conversation around to how you faint at the doctor's office every time they take blood. Then:

I just got another letter from the Russian government. They're after me to give them a DNA sample so they can settle this damned authenticity question about the czar's bones. (Sighing.) I've been ignoring them for months. Well, they say they only need a drop or two. I suppose I owe it to the family. . . .

The Conversational Objective Correlative

Leave prominently displayed a misshapen lump inside a glass display case with a temperature gauge. Deflect the first inquiries, then somewhat wearily allow as how it is the pre-served heart of George III, King of England:

My great-great-great-great-grandfather was Nathan Hale. His brother, my great-great-etc uncle, never quite forgave the Brits for hanging him. He broke into the tomb and removed it. A bit grue-some, but I can't bring myself just to leave it in the safe deposit box. I must get around to giving it back one of these days, except I'm not really sure how to go about it. Don't let on, it would only create a huge stir.

The Star and Bar

Extreme care must be exercised here, as many Southerners tend to be meticulously versed in genealogy. Disaster befell P. Harding of Athens, Georgia, in the course of gambiting that he was a direct descendant of General Jubal Early, only to be icily informed by someone present that the General had died without issue. Harding counter-countered by saying that the General had had a liaison with a (beautiful) farm girl on the eve of the battle of Cedar Creek, and that the resulting love child was Harding's great-great grandfather.

Unfortunately, this only inflamed present company as it implied moral turpitude on the part of the Confederate god, and the evening ended in acrimony and remonstration.

One way to flush out any genealogically savvy Southerners is the Auto-Derogator Gambit. Declare, in a voice loud enough to carry the room, that it is now "universally conceded" that T. J. "Stonewall" Jackson was "overrated" as a strategist. If no one approaches you with a fire poker, then you may proceed to allow as how this new scholarship pains you, inasmuch as you are the general's great-great-nephew. The rest of the evening you may devote to refuting the new Jackson scholarship.[3]

The Geographical Preempt

Extremely adaptable. Can be easily inserted into any lull in the dinner conversation.

(With a trace of annoyance) *A week in Monaco is just too much. Three days would be more than enough. Rainiers, Hapsburgs, Hohenzollerns, Romanovs. After a while, one yearns to be among* ordinary *people.*

Or:

(With exasperation) *Five days at Balmoral! I have only so much conversation about grouse in me. On the other hand, I'm devoted to Princess Anne.* (Adding casually) *Are you going over this year?*

When a listener replies that he is not, nod sympathetically.

Just as well. She tells me the shooting's off this year.

---

[3]This is a variation on the Macedonian Sacrifice, perfected by D. Taylor of Brooklin, Maine, who uses it to affect aloofness, while claiming direct descent from Alexander the Great, "Or as we in the family call him, Alexander the *Occasionally* Great."

The Gnostic Parry

J. Turrentine of Los Angeles has written several monographs on Counter Strategies. His most popular is the Kissinger Refuse:

> GUEST: *I just spent the weekend with Henry Kissinger.*
> JT: *Isn't it exciting, his news?*
> GUEST: *News?*
> J.T: *He didn't mention? Henry does like to play this close to his chest. Still, if he had you out to the house, I'm surprised he didn't. . . . Well, it's probably for the best.*

In Case of Emergency

That's certainly not what Spielberg told me.

Cupping hand over the phone: *It's the White House. Do you have another phone I could use?*

I'm being stalked myself. And let me tell you, it's a damn nuisance.

•• NEWS QUIZ ••

10/15/98 "THE OLD SNIFF AND POKE"

A just released report praises the federal government's new HAACP program, and the **New York Times** *concurs, noting: "It is a definite step up from the old sniff-and-poke method." Method of doing what?*

"Census taking at old-folks' homes."—Brooke Saucier

"Having sex in the dark."—Evan Cornog

"Choosing a husband."—Deb Stavin

"Airport security. Just because I didn't want them to x-ray my laptop . . ."—Beth Sherman

"Selecting Supreme Court judges."—David Rakoff

• RANDY'S WRAP UP •

With a question bound to target the old, the infirm, and the morally dubious, it is not surprising that the most frequent target is ninety-five-year-old former segregationist Strom Thurmond, a man who is all three. So evil, so withered, has he become too easy a foil? Should his sobriquet "former segregationist" be stripped of its irony? Are there bygones that should indeed be bygones? No, there aren't.

Well, yes there are, but not Thurmond's bygones. His perfidy did not involve—what was Henry Hyde's felicitous bit of self-justification?—youthful indiscretions. It was not the uncharacteristic one-time act of a few hotheads, like when a New York City cop beats up a black man—OK, bad example. But the point is, we scorn Thurmond not for scattered actions, but for the persistent expression of profoundly held beliefs, i.e., for being on the wrong side of every issue throughout a record-setting career. (Born December fifth, 1902, and first elected to the Senate in 1954, he is both the longest serving and the oldest U.S. senator. He also holds the record for the longest filibuster, 24 hours and 18 minutes, against the civil rights bill of 1957.)

In an era that rushes to rehabilitate—at least to rehabilitate the rich and powerful—a time when Henry Kissinger is addressed on network television as "Dr." and not as "war criminal," it is nice to see that the News Quiz has a historical sense extending back more than five minutes. So let the scourging continue, but perhaps it needn't be restricted to his ass.

GOOD EATIN' ANSWER

It is a method for reducing contamination in meat and poultry.

In January, the Hazard Analysis and Critical Control Points system became mandatory at large processing plants; it will gradually regulate smaller plants. For the first time, HAACP sets specific microbial standards and prescribes testing, but leaves it to the processors to devise ways of meeting those standards. An Agriculture Department study shows that plants using the new system halved the number of broiler chickens contaminated with salmonella and cut down on tainted pork.

AUGMENTED QUOTATIONS EXTRA

(Each final sentence added by News Quiz.)

"Mink are particularly vicious creatures. They don't have any particular fear and will attack any sort of animal, whether or not they're hungry. But have you ever seen Barbra Streisand in the wild?"
— *Len Kelsall,* mink farmer

"There's no reason why polkas shouldn't be just as popular as rumbas. And dropping a cinder block on your foot; that could be as big as closing your hand in a car door."—*Frank Yankovic,* the Polka King, dead at 83

"They come back and they're not the same. They go off their feed. They won't settle down. They shouldn't have to go through what they went through. Goddamn your soul to hell, Barbra Streisand!"—*Len Kelsall*

Away from It All

FRANK CAMMUSO AND

HART SEELY

Bub and Satey thank you for renting on scenic Wrickey Lake. Please note these cabin rules and recommendations:

1: The locked basement is for storage only. Please stay out of this area.

2: The Vanderpools, who live on nearby Wrichard Bay, will remove your trash and recyclables, at no charge, nightly. Just leave unwanted items outside your cabin. (Note: Be sure to bring all wanted items inside.)

3: If, while hiking, you meet a group of stray dogs, remember that they generally are more afraid of you than you are of them. Simply toss aside whatever food you're carrying, then move slowly away. DO NOT RUN!

4: Please show respect for the flag that flies over the Vanderpool family compound. This signifies the Republic of Vanderpool, a sovereign nation separate from the United States since 1973. Trespassers could face inter- rogation or possible incarceration.

5: For day trips, we suggest nearby Potterfield (28 miles south on Route 182), home to the Exit 47 Truckstop, which offers a $5.95 All-U-Can-Eat Grand Seafood Buffet, Tuesday through Friday. (Best to go before Friday.) Further south is Mr. Wiggly's Sausage Barn, where families can tour "the magic of meat from hoof to bun." Free samples. Also, don't forget Happy Land Park, featuring Big Rickety, the world's oldest and fastest wooden roller coaster, and Ultimate Pee Wee Fighting every Friday, the winner receiving a $50 Savings Bond. (If planning to enter, don't forget child's birth certificate!)

6: At night, you may have dreams about the basement, or at times feel an overwhelming compulsion to see what's down there. Please, do not go in the basement.

7: Because of the high-intensity lines from Rainbow Valley Nuclear Units I and II, radios, flashlights and other electrical equipment may turn on and off sponta- neously. (No pacemakers, please.) Also, inside the cabin, you may occasionally experience minor electric shocks. MAKE SURE YOU ARE COMPLETELY DRY BEFORE USING ANY APPLIANCE!

8: You might hear shouts or explosions along Vanderpool Road between the hours of 11 P.M. and 4 A.M. These are routine field maneuvers conducted by General Vanderpool and his troops. If such noises occur, merely turn off all lights and remain inside your cabin.

9: Prolonged contact with lake water may irritate the skin. If problems occur, the Potterfield Burn Center (29 miles south on Route 182) is open 24 hours a day.

10: For religious services, you are invited to the Temple of Universal Truth, whose members are characterized by their shaven heads and black turtlenecks. Or visit their web page. Some of the acolytes may be a bit persistent about inviting you to join them on a journey. We recommend against it, unless you plan an extended stay.

11: Don't be surprised if your family hears "Girdie," the legendary monster that haunts Vanderpool Woods. The creature's fearsome roar could shake the cabin at about 5:18 each morning, as Girdie rumbles down the tracks in her daily migration.

12: Now and then, federal law enforcement officials may institute a blockade around the Vanderpool Republic. If such a policy is enacted, ask the highest-ranking U.S. officer for a pass allowing your family access to and from the cabin. Upon request, Kevlar vests will be provided.

13: During your stay, you may have the pleasure of meeting "the Professor," who lives in the woods not far from your cabin. He is harmless, though it's best not to offend him by flaunting electronic devices. If you're heading to town, the Professor may ask you to mail a package for him. You'll be amazed at the folks with whom our favorite hermit corresponds.

14: As the cabin continues to settle, the creaks and groans of aging woodwork at times may sound almost as if someone is in the basement, begging to be freed. For your own well being and your family's safety, please stay out of the basement.

Give One for the Team

Want the NFL?
It's a Question of Sacrifice

FRANK CAMMUSO AND

HART SEELY

Beginning in 2001, Hartford, CT—a city with 25,000 fewer residents than Syracuse—will have a National Football League franchise.

Hartford accomplished this by promising the New England Patriots a mere $400 million in financial incentives.

Well, what are we waiting for?

Let's make Syracuse the next NFL boomtown!

Of course, the naysayers will claim that Syracuse can't afford a $500 million giveaway, or for that matter, that we can't even afford our mayor.

We just say: HIKE THE BALL, AND GET OUT OF OUR WAY!

We're taking this city to the Super Bowl.

What's the plan? Bring an NFL franchise to Syracuse.

How can we do that? Get an owner to sell out his city. Don't worry. These guys sell out their moms, much less their cities.

Does this mean we'll have to raise taxes? No. In fact, we'll boost the economy and lower taxes . . . maybe end them altogether!

Where will we find the money? From Syracuse's greatest resource: The people!

PHASE I:
GIVING WHAT IT TAKES TO WIN!

The miracles of modern medicine have created an ever-expanding market for human body parts. Hospitals never have enough blood, bone marrow or vital internal organs. This is sad, especially when one recognizes that God gave each of us two ears, two lungs, two hands, etc.—one more than necessary.

We see a great fund-raising opportunity for kidneys.

Donating kidneys? Wait a minute. Are you sure this won't mean raising taxes? Absolutely!

To give of yourself will not affect the tax rate.

And no one *has* to donate their kidney.

We just say, give what you can. Stomach lining. A gland of some sort. Perhaps, an eye? But keep in mind that fans who donate kidneys will become Platinum Card Members of the Syracuse NFL Kidney Klub. They'll receive great discounts on franchise merchandise, preferred parking and one post-surgery hospital visit from their favorite player, or a team mascot.

Wow! All that, for a kidney? C'mon, what's the catch? No catch. In fact, our "Kidney Kollector" will come right to your front door. After subtracting costs of removal and storage, we estimate Syracuse will earn $100 per kidney. With 460,000 Onondaga County residents, that's a cool $46 million.

What if somebody doesn't want to donate? No problem. You can "buy back" your kidney—by contributing $100. This won't be as rewarding, and you'll feel less a part of the team. But Syracuse will still raise $46 million.

Then we get a franchise? No. We must find the most eligible NFL team owner and then apply the "Salt Lake City Formula" for luring sports.

How does that work? We give the owner a suitcase holding $1 million in cash. Then we invite him to Syracuse for one night and throw a party the likes of which this city has never seen! Here's where we must work together.

We make a secret pact:

For one night, everyone pretends we're somewhere else.

What do you mean? Think of it this way. For one night— just one night!—nobody whines about snow or mentions that stupid TV station's weather cat. People go downtown, wait for the subway and discuss Broadway shows. They pretend to swim in Onondaga Lake. And nobody moons the restaurants in Armory Square.

For one night, we can do this.

Next morning, we give the owner $40 million.

So then we get the franchise? No. But we have planted the seed.

PHASE II:
GO COLD TURKEY

Each year, Onondaga County government spends about $750 million. The Syracuse city and school district goes through $400 million. Add towns and villages, and local government spends far more than $1 billion per year. If all public operations closed for just six months—hey, give the kids an extended summer vacation—we'd save $500 million.

Wow! That much in just six months? Let's do it! Not so fast.

We don't want to be accused of sugar-coating anything here.

Fires will rage out of control, roads will crumble, garbage will pile up, and sadistic criminal gangs will rule the streets through sheer terror. Now and then, we'll yearn for "the good old days."

What will we do? Why not take a trip? Visit old friends.

It's a great big, wonderful world out there. Do you know that Utica is the "Handshake City?" Or that Cortland County has many fine campgrounds? And don't forget the North Country: If they survived last year's Ice Storm, they can certainly handle 460,000 tourists. And when we return, we'll have a cool $500 million.

Then we'll have a team? No. But we'll build a $500 million stadium and fill it with luxury boxes, advertising opportunities and tax-breaks for the owner. Then we'll get a team.

But you said this will boost the economy. How will that happen? Simple. We'll rename our team the Syracuse Microsofts. They'll play in "Bill Gates Stadium."

We think some computer work will soon come our way.

And if Gates doesn't produce, we'll try the Syracuse Foxes, playing in "Rupert Murdoch Field." Or the Broilers in "Frank Perdue Yards." Get the picture?

If you name it, he will come.

One last thing: By my count, there's still $5 million left. Think three words: 2008 Summer Olympics!

The body is a vehicle, and dreams are the in-flight movie.—M.O'D.

God, Help Me!

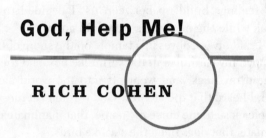

RICH COHEN

The recent surge in American spirituality has sent even the most secular adults into what has become a religion bazaar, where the boundaries are far more fluid and the rules less rigid than when they were children.   —*New York Times Magazine*

I was raised a Hebrew, and for a long time I was happy to have that religion. Being a Hebrew meant good ethnic food, doting grandmothers, stern fathers, sensible lectures, stories and more stories, and thousands of international bankers just waiting to bankroll any harebrained scheme I might come up with. And it wasn't just the bankers: in the beginning, the Hebrew God Himself was just as giving. I prayed to Him, and He smote mine enemies. When I was a boy, cut in the fashion of a young David, I was troubled by a bully who lived on a farm near my father's summer cottage. One day, after taking a beating, I appealed to the Hebrew God, and He responded, salting the fields of that farm. Later, someone told me, the sky above the farmhouse was filled with locusts, and that's when I knew the Hebrew God was the best God of all.

125

As I got older, though, I noticed signs of strain in my relationship with the Hebrew God. I did all the things I used to do—the lamb killing, the horn blowing—only now, to my adolescent self, these things seemed silly. The Hebrew God and I were growing apart. It was no one's fault. And rather than let bad feelings build up between us, I decided to make a clean break while the memories were still good.

I said my goodbyes in a temple on the shore of Lake Michigan, dropped my yarmulke in the yarmulke box, slid the gold star from around my neck, and went off into the world alone. Sometime later, I heard that the Hebrew God was mad at me—that He made people close to me curse my name, that inanimate objects became animate, that dogs filled the sky like birds.

But I was determined to move on and make the most of my freedom, so I turned to paganism. I became a keen observer of the seasons, enjoyed the occasional boar's head, celebrated the vernal equinox, and worshipped idols where idols could be found. Still searching, I stumbled into the arms of Islam. At first, Allah treated me well, spreading my seed like the stars in the sky: I couldn't turn around without getting lucky. Later, after I'd had my fill and the thrill began to wear off, the Muslim God turned demanding: read this, contemplate that, don't eat this, pray in that direction, wait till the sun goes down, wait till the sun comes up, yada-yada-yada. So, again, off I went.

I dabbled in the religions of the East. I saw the Buddha both clothed and naked. (May I suggest you see him clothed.) I tried my hand at various Christian sects. I traced the footsteps of the Apostles. I ate ham. I went to see a Pentecostal minister, who made me speak in tongues. Frustrated, and feeling tongue-tied, I called a shaman, who laid me down, fed me garlic, and said, "Be silent, and come out of him!" Dozens of unclean spirits rose from my body, like smoke from a house on fire. After the shaman left the room, one of the spirits stayed behind to thank me for his freedom. As a show of friendship, he then asked for the name of an enemy and promised to make that man's tongue cleave to the roof of his mouth. The last I saw of this enemy, he had assumed the shape of a goat, and his pathetic bleating was music to my ears.

And yet, despite all this good fortune, I am haunted by memories—things the Hebrew God and I had done together, warm, pleasant afternoons. I am no more satisfied than the day I discarded my Seder plate. A few days ago, as I was moping around my apartment after some past-life therapy, my neighbor Doug came over and said, "I am worshipping the Hebrew God. I just thought you should know." The next morning, I saw Doug at the mall, wearing a tallis and tefillin. What an ass kisser! I walk up to him, and the first thing he says to me is that he's won the Pick Four. Then I tell him I'm thirsty and want a drink, and he hands me a rock. "Oh, I forgot," he says, smirking. "He doesn't do that for you anymore, does He?"

Now I find myself wondering why I left the Hebrew God in the first place. How could I have been such a fool? But my therapist tells me I'm remembering only the good things. "What about the bad stuff?" she says. "What about His temper?" It's true. Who wants to be covered from head to toe with boils? Besides, I know that the Hebrew God is a stickler for etiquette, and Doug is bound to screw up. When he ends up blind and wandering through some desert, I'll be sitting at home, with a thirty-inch TV, a beer, and my healing crystals.

Autumn of the Matriarch

RICH COHEN

Esther Himmel, a willful stoop-shouldered woman in her mid-nineties, often feels betrayed by her own body. "My mind makes up to go somewhere my legs won't take me," she says. Several times each day, in fact, en route to Winn-Dixie or off to Eckerd Drugs for a bottle of Metamucil, she stops to rest, and it's in this way, sitting on a poolside chaise in the shadow of a eucalyptus tree, that she overheard Helen Greenwald tell the story of her husband's death.

Esther describes the tragedy in this way: "Helen asked Izzy to wash a dish. Helen was in the bathroom when she heard the crash. Helen thought Izzy had dropped the dish, but when she came out, she saw that what Izzy had really dropped was dead. . . ."

"Right away, I saw it marked as clear as in the *TV Guide*," Esther said of the impending days of political wrangling, filibusters and heated late-night meetings. After all, these were chaotic times. Izzy had been elected to chair the board of the Three Elements Condominium complex only a month before, and now there were the factions to deal with: the old and the young, the fearful and the confident, the ambulatory and the crippled. "Poor old Izzy," Esther thinks sadly. After all that, after the hard promises and coalition-building and schmoozing with enemies, and what's it all amount to? A broken dish. Within an hour of the death, the geriatrics who composed the constituency had gathered around the pool and by sundown had reached a rough consensus on the old man's political tenure. "Ach!" Elliot Freedman said with disgust. "Izzy come, Izzy go."

From the highway that makes its meandering way through South Florida, the Three Elements seems just another bleak retirement complex, a group of dreary buildings flung randomly down on North Miami Beach. Side by side, the buildings (Air, Water, Fire) form an isosceles triangle, in the center of which sits an Olympic-size swimming pool. The surrounding lounge chairs rise like bleachers, those along the water belonging by tradition to board members and other influence peddlers. Though she had never held office, Esther occupied a deep-cushioned chaise alongside the four-foot mark. This was largely due to her nature, which, at once meddlesome and disinterested, was admired by most residents. Dispensing advice, she routinely begins, "If I were you, and I'm glad I'm not . . . " One afternoon she spent an hour asking a large Russian-born woman why she was angry with her. "Tell me, fatso," she said. "Why do you hate me?"

About 1,800 people live at the Three Elements. All the apartments are identical: a small bedroom opening onto a living room, a kitchenette and a shelf-size balcony. In some bedrooms two single beds are pushed together to form a Hollywood double. Perhaps because she is a positive thinker or perhaps because she is ironic, Esther calls her own dwelling the Little Palace. "I've got to get back up to the Little Palace," she says, breaking away from lobby conversations. Standing on her balcony, she can see a murky canal that winds south toward the bay. Over the years, residents have spoiled the ducks that live on the water, and the birds have grown fat and dependent and aggressive. One day, while feeding the flock, Esther ran out of bread; the ducks chased her clear back to Fire, where she collapsed in hard-breathing relief. "They were just like crazy people," she said later. In the minds of residents, the ducks have become a symbol of aging and death. When a friend passes, they may say, "Well, the ducks finally got him."

The old men sit all day around the pool arguing condo history. "Ben Fox did not pass the law 'No playing in the pool,'" says Elliot Freedman, pointing at the list of Pool Rules. "Solomon Mizner passed that law. Ben Fox passed 'No running near the pool.'" Some Three Elements scholars have a particular field of study. They know the great pinochle champions or the instances of criminal activity.

Given time, all pool conversations eventually lead back to the origins of the Three Elements. In grave tones, the scholars discuss the original residents, northerners stepping from dank sleeping trains and out into the Florida light. Theories may vary, but most residents agree that the complex was, as much as the Berlin Wall or the Warsaw Ghetto, a product of history. "If there was no Adolf Hitler, there would be no Three Elements," says Mr. Freedman studiously. In the aftermath of the Holocaust, he explains, many Jewish people, who had spent the last 2,000 years on their feet, traipsing from country to country, decided it was time to find a homeland. Many, of course, turned their thoughts southward toward Israel. But there was another movement southward—to Miami Beach. Swamps were drained and settlements built. On Esther's bedroom wall, flanked by B'nai B'rith plaques and certificates from Hadassah, hangs a black-and-white photo of Esther and her husband, Moses, who died twenty-five years ago. Esther wears a wool sweater and Moses is in city clothes, and both sport beatific pilgrim grins. In those days, Collins Avenue, the main thoroughfare of North Miami Beach, was wide open. Standing on her balcony, Esther could see clear down the beach and out to sea. For the arrivals fresh from the North, the world opened like a fan. "The Jews have found their promised land," Moses liked to say. "And it's on north Collins Avenue, just across from the 32nd Street mall."

Who can say just when the bad times came? Most residents

link the changes in some vague way to the various economic booms that shook the economy, filling the city with fortune seekers, then leaving it with disillusioned poor. "The *shvartzers* and Italians and Hispanics, they all came," says Mr. Freedman. For most residents, though, the bad times came with the arrival of the Cubans, when Castro opened the jails in the early 1980s. Overnight, the city's flavor (language, music, food) changed from Brooklyn to Havana. "Be careful," Izzy would say, closing meetings. "Cubans are out there just waiting to knock down some old Jew." Collins Avenue—a boulevard of open vistas and quiet walks—became a strip, bristling with fast-food joints and seafood restaurants and cheap hotels with VACANCY signs. As a result, residents came to see the complex increasingly as an island, an enclave of old Miami awash in a sea of dark faces.

To some extent, this attitude emerged naturally with age and time. Most of these people had arrived in Florida while in their sixties. Now, thirty years later, their field of operations shrunk down to a TV, a sofa and a political maze, they have become old people. Over half are widows, whose husbands— decades after death—remain, ghosts in residence, engraved on buzzers ("Mr. and Mrs. Moses Himmel"). "A robber's less likely to attack a man's home," Esther explains.

And what about the children, grandchildren and great-grandchildren? No one comes to visit. Left to their own devices—like the schoolboys in *Lord of the Flies*—the residents have built a bizarre political system, a structure that outranks any in Miami or Washington. In the end, all law and reality is filtered down to residents through the actions of the board of directors.

For years, Elliot Freedman thought himself the De Gaulle of condo-complex politics. He awaited the clarion call, the triumphal elevator ride from his room down to the pool. He is a frail man with a pronounced stutter and an off-putting grin, who sees in himself all the elements of glory. Before mirrors, he stands in profile. He's a Polish-born Jew and a Holocaust survivor— Treblinka, then Auschwitz—with the blue number tattooed on his left arm. He doesn't talk about it. At seventy, with his wife dead and buried, he took a unit in Air. Within a month he realized this was a new world, a level place where the failures and accomplishments of a previous life, a life of haggling and hustling and snowy winters, were cleared away. No matter where you'd lived or what restaurants you'd frequented or what roads you'd traveled, everyone here was equal. The varied experience of all residents drained into this common basin: the kitchenette, the balcony, the living room. For Mr. Freedman, who had achieved nothing in life so great as his own survival, the change was invigorating. Here was a chance to lead, even be admired by, men who had outachieved him in the working world. But people soon recognized in him the hunger, the disappointments of his younger years. So even here he was pushed from the corridors of power. Like the old French general, he retired to his home, the barren apartment, to await the situation that would necessitate his intervention.

An opportunity almost arose in 1978. Esther's ten-year-old grandson was down in the pool swimming, and from her balcony Esther saw a bearded man holding the boy over the water by his ankles. She called the cops, saying her grandson was being attacked by a crazy bearded man. Arriving on the scene, police dragged the stranger from the pool (he was wearing a Speedo) and threw him against the fence and cuffed him. Old men and women watched from their balconies. By the time the bearded man explained it all—that he was the grandson of Heidi Baum, herself a resident of Fire, and was only teaching the child how to dive—the damage had been done. Sides had been chosen. The situation was close to a crisis, with Fire threatening to secede if Esther did not apologize publicly, when Elliot came down from his room to broker a back-room deal. Somehow, though, rather than becoming synonymous with harmony and good relations, Elliot's image got all tangled up with the incident. Just looking at him, people saw the half-naked, soaking-wet, handcuffed, bearded man. Mr. Freedman did not get a second chance until the day of Izzy's death.

★ ★ ★

The board of directors consists of fifteen members, each building being allowed to elect five representatives. The chairman is determined by a separate, complex-wide election. The constituency breaks down into factions, the big split coming over age. In the last decade, as people have begun to drop dead and new residents have moved in, the average age has fallen greatly. The new occupants are in their seventies, while the older ones, who still form the ruling majority, are well into their nineties. Most of the young crowd lives in Fire. There is also a minority bloc, which consists of one thirty-five-year-old black woman who moved into the condo complex sometime in the late 1980s. She keeps a low profile, though, and most residents are convinced she is really Mr. Himmelfarb's day maid. A few residents are not Jewish, but they usually pretend they are, which itself is an interesting role reversal. Even at the time of Izzy's election, it was clear that power was shifting away from the old residents and toward the young. "We still have some kick in us yet," Esther warned a seventy-three-year-old at the pool. In fact, most of the old are extremely wary of the young, whom they see as idealistic dreamers. While the old focus on security issues ("keeping out Cubans"), the young want to rid the pool of excess chlorine, cut spending and build a playroom for grandchildren.

Mr. Freedman's designs on the top spot became plain one morning when he pinned this note on a lobby peg-board: ELLIOT FREEDMAN GIVES OUT FREE HEFTY BAGS ON THE FOURTH FLOOR OF AIR. IF YOU SHOULD WANT A FREE HEFTY FROM ELLIOT FREEDMAN, COME AND SEE YOUR FRIEND, A TOUGH MAN ON CRIME, A MAN IN FINE HEALTH, ELLIOT FREEDMAN. Reading this, Esther was filled with disgust. Here, in two sentences, shrunk down like orange juice concentrate, were all the things she hated about the man. It was a bribe, and such a pathetic bribe. "He is a cheap shyster," she told everyone she saw that morning. "He tries to buy us with junk."

Still, his opponents were far from formidable. There was Yossi Franklin, an extremely old, wheelchair-bound man who first married at the age of seventy-five and has been married four times since. Yossi's current wife, Elaine, has no real idea what he did in the earlier parts of his life.

"Nor do I," Yossi says, shrugging.

"I think he was some kind of salesman," Elaine says.

"Yuh, yuh," Yossi agrees. "Maybe a salesman."

His candidacy was not trusted; people believed him to be his wife's creature, the pawn of her ambition. After all, it was she who entered him in the race and she who read his public statements. Some say that whenever he grows quarrelsome, which is quite often, Elaine switches his medication, leaving him to thrash about in a catatonic state. One day, as Elaine, standing poolside, read Yossi's statement on the importance of an alert government, the old man slumped and slid from his chair to lie motionless beside the pool. The next day, Elaine withdrew her husband from the race.

Izzy's son Gerald was also running. Soon after his father's death, the seventy-two-year-old son moved in with his mother. Gerald looked like Izzy: He had the same sunken eyes and downturned mouth, but the skin was a little tighter and the glasses not quite as thick. To many he seemed the logical choice, a member of the young generation who still appealed to the old. Here was a way to honor the dead man. Also, people are always drawn to the idea of political dynasty. That week the names Roosevelt and Kennedy were bandied about. Gerald told assembled residents, "I would be honored to serve." But despite his strong following and popular off-the-cuff remarks, he threw it all away—not unlike Gary Hart, allowing his quest for personal fulfillment to obstruct a higher calling. Within weeks of his father's death, he was misbehaving: breaking pool rules, coming in at all hours, entertaining women. A week of this sort of thing and he had ruined his own as well as his father's reputation: "What sort of man would have such a son?"

The field was left to Mr. Freedman. A lot of free Hefty bags were given away. Increasingly, it fell to Esther to present opposition. She dogged him, shouted him down, highlighted his faults. Esther responded to Mr. Freedman instinctively. "I react to Elliot as I would react to meat that's spoiled on my fork," she explained. Still, some wondered if she knew just what she was saying. Could she distinguish utterance from thought? One morning, as Elliot finished delivering a speech, Esther stood and said, "You, I wish Hitler had never let get away." Though many residents were offended by this and other like sentiments, an equal number were impressed. Here was an old woman, a woman for whom time was not plentiful, a woman who would say anything—and why not? Why should she waste her breath on lies? At the very least she was honest. All of a sudden Esther became very popular. Elliot's moment flowed from him like kidney stones. A woman on the third floor of Air painted a portrait of Esther, an idealized likeness, and hung it in the lobby of her building. Another fan told Esther, "You have a very beautiful bust line."

It's hard to say just when Esther decided to run for office. Maybe it was while she was standing in the shower with all the water running cold; or maybe it was when the dead squirrel got fished out of the pool; or when the dark-skinned man was caught skulking around the lobby. More likely it was the day that Elliot Freedman collapsed and came to, moments later, declaring his love for her. "Be my wife," he said and meant it. A few days afterward she took a landslide victory.

All that morning the rain came down in sheets. "God turned on his tap," Esther said. But in the early afternoon, a wind blew up from the Keys, moving through the trees, scattering clouds. By the time Esther made her way to the pool, shaking hands and waving all the way, the sun was on the water. Residents thronged the courtyard to hear her victory speech. It was all so strange. Years earlier, she had decided life was over; if she were needed here at all, it was as a prop for weddings and bar mitzvahs. Yet, twenty-five years after the death of her husband, fifty years after the Holocaust, eighty years after her arrival in New York and nearly a century after her own birth in the Polish woods, here she was, moving through the crowd, taking the place carved out by her own wit and skepticism. Elliot, back in his room, watched from the window as Esther promised more security, more peace, less tension, and all the while he was thinking only of Esther's eyes and puff of blue hair. "Magnificent," he said. "Ninety-four years old and still her own teeth."

Names of people and places and identifying characteristics have been changed.

Future Schlock:

Hip Products for Gray Boomers

CATHY CRIMMINS

Demographers predict that the last baby boomer will depart this earth in about 2075. We've always loved high-tech gadgets and products designed to fill our lifestyle needs. Will the last baby boomer and her friends, including us, still be ordering from those glossy catalogs?

You bet.

We won't think of ourselves as getting older, just as finding a new consumer niche. Our last decades on Earth will be just one happy string of 1-800 direct-mail opportunities.

Some gray boomer favorites around the year 2040, available on CD-ROM catalogs and the Home Shopping Network:

COOL STUFF FOR THE COCOON . . .

Airbag Bra/Necktie

For years you have enjoyed the protection of an airbag in your car. Now you can have the same protection wherever you go, with these airbag bras and neckties that promptly inflate if you stub your toe or if your vertical orientation changes at a freefall rate. Specify size (gals) or color (guys).

AM-FM Hearing Aid—A Yawn Turns It On

"Blah, blah, blah"—you've heard it all a thousand times before, and there's not enough quality time left in your life to listen to it again. So when the conversation gets excruciatingly dull, a single yawn automatically flips your hearing aid to your favorite preset AM or FM radio station. They'll think you're still paying attention to their tedious old tales, while you're grooving on your music, or listening to the news.

Applesauce®

The ultimate computer for the end user. Monitors your vital signs while you work and beeps when you need a nap. Large keys, easy-to-read screen, fleece-lined mouse.

Bone Dry

The first Chardonnay with added calcium. (Also available with extra estrogen and testosterone.)

Edible Book-Of-The-Month Club

These immortal classics and bestsellers, printed in large prune-juice type on 100 percent fiber paper bound with wheat gluten, *can be eaten,* page by page, as you read them. Why clutter your short life with more objects? Why make trips to two stores, when you can satisfy your hunger for learning and your yearning for food at the same time? Over two hundred titles to choose from in five mild flavors.

Karaoke Conversation Kit

Lip-synch along to favorite cocktail party chatter. You'll never feel alone again!

Memory Memoloop

Tend to forget what you were saying? This continuous-loop pocket tape recorder constantly records the last three minutes of your life. If you wander, don't worry; just play it back through the cordless earphone disguised as a hearing aid, and you'll pick up on your thoughts almost without missing a beat.

Remote-Control Spouse Identification

Remember the embarrassment when you didn't know which was your wife at the party? (No, you wouldn't, would you?) At the push of a button, her beautiful radio-activated acoustical necklace will identify and locate her anywhere within a 500-foot radius. Blinking tiara version is also available for the hearing-impaired. For forgetful wives, outfit hubby with an acoustical wristwatch or blinking toupee.

Smart Mirror

A breakthrough in self-imagery! Step in front of this conventional-looking mirror and great things happen: software works immediately to remove extra weight and wrinkles, projecting a 3-D hologram of how you really want to see yourself.

The Sony Walkerman

Stereo sound and firm support in one fine lightweight aluminum unit. Earphones attach directly to each miniature speaker on the walker's legs. Detachable storage unit for CDs and medications.

Steady-Cam Torso Stabilizer

The same technology that gave you the film shots you loved now keeps you from shaking and wobbling. Available without camera or with, so you can recap the day's events.

YesterDay-Timer

Forty years ago you were concerned about what you needed to do next week. Now it is hard enough keeping track of what you did do this morning. This miracle, pocket-sized computer-ized life log, with built-in video camera, audio transcriber, and physical monitoring probes, keeps track of your day's activities and displays them all, at the push of a button, in easy-to-read spreadsheet form. Did you eat breakfast? Take your medicine? Talk to Mabel (a black-bordered inset gently reminds you that Mabel has been dead for twenty years)? Or you can download the day onto CD-ROM to keep a permanent record for yourself and your friends.

MOVING DOWN LIFE'S HIGHWAY . . .

Bifocal Car Windshield

Why didn't someone think of it before? Now you can see the pedestrian walking in front of you, read the road signs, and take in the distant view, all with a single windshield. Just send us your bifocal prescription or a spare pair of glasses, and spec-ify the make, model, and year of your car. We will ship you your new windshield with easy-to-follow installation instructions.

High-Wheeler Weekend Collection

Now you can have a wheelchair for all your recreational needs. Choose from our sporty singleblade model, dune chair, all-terrain model, and, for that weekend in Aspen, the snomochair.

Hoovercraft

A riding vacuum cleaner for the homemaker who just won't be stopped. Available in facsimile BMW, Cadillac, Toyota, Ford Taurus, and nostalgic Country Squire station wagon models.

Lincoln Incontinental

Cushioned, doughnut-shaped bucket seats with optional hide-away chamber pot for the control-impaired.

Mustang Crank-O-Matic Bed

Still yearning for that Mustang Dad never bought you? Well, it may be too late for that, but here's the next best thing. A full-feature Crank-O-Matic hospital bed in the shape of that vintage car—convertible, of course. Facsimile dashboard houses controls to raise or lower head and feet, at three different speeds, while making true-to-life engine noises. Built-in AM radio plays genuine taped broadcasts from any year, 1962–1975 (specify), and the working horn will get anyone's attention, fast. If you can't pick up day nurses in this car, you're really lame!

HEALTH EMPOWERMENT

Build Your Own Pacemaker

No one cares about your heart as you do, so why should you trust it to someone else's hands? This new do-it-yourself pacemaker kit enables you to custom make and implant your very own pacemaker. Buy two, and assemble one for that special someone in your life—the perfect Valentine's gift. For an additional $5, we will engrave the message of your choice—two lines, with up to twenty-seven characters each line—on the pacemaker faceplate, so that your name or message will be engraved on your true love's heart forever. Presentation models come gift boxed and packaged with festive pink or blue 3-0 vicryl sutures.

Implosion Kit

Face it, as boomers get older, we get smaller. Our Implosion Kit includes everything you need to temporarily maintain the appearance of your original adult size until permanent arrangements can be made. Includes shoe lifts, phone books for chairs, invisible clips for temporary clothing hems, and assorted shims and extenders to bring you up, out, or otherwise closer to the things that recede from your reach.

Jet-Assisted Candle Blower

For that lung-impaired birthday boomer who still wants to get his or her wish. Developed at the Jet-Propulsion Laboratory in Pasadena. Two tubes invisibly concealed in handsome reading glasses frames are connected to a backpack or IV pole–mounted natural-fuel 8-horsepower jet engine. Just the push of a button sends a candle-extinguishing 140-mph gust of clean mountain air from the Rockies in a 5-foot sweep in front of that birthday boy or girl. Large-print microprocessor lets you set the jet speed to suit the body weight and bone strength of the user.

Make Your Own Medicines

This handy kit, complete with all necessary ingredients, an illustrated step-by-step guide, empty bottles, capsules, tableting machine, etc., contains all you need to make the top 100 prescription drugs taken by gray boomers, including antihypertensives, sedatives, antipsychotics, cholesterol reducers, antiarthritics, analgesics, and more! The deluxe model includes a mini-desktop computer already loaded with RxLabelPerfect, the prescription drug label-making program, and CANDA, a Computer-Assisted New Drug Application program, so that you can create your own clinical trials and file an original 650,000-page application with the U.S. Food and Drug Administration.

UltraBones

Osteoporosis: the scourge of old age since time began. Now nature and technology combine to banish brittle bones forever. UltraBones fools the body's normal metabolic system into incorporating a space-age graphite-titanium compound into bones and teeth instead of old-fashioned calcium. Graphite gives aging bones the flexible strength you know from high-performance tennis racquets, while the hardness and durability of titanium, used in supersonic military aircraft, enable you to shear childproof caps with a single snap of your mighty jaws.

YOUR HERITAGE

Franklin Mint Denture Collection

Each month for twenty-eight months you will receive one beautifully handcrafted enamel tooth, each completely different and produced in a limited, numbered edition. Order now and receive, free, a set of false gums to display them in.

Tanks Full of Memories

Forgotten your life, find it too boring, or just don't care, but still need to impress the grandchildren? Pick memories that make you the grandparent everyone wants. Kits come complete with scripted reminiscences, artfully blended joys and sorrows, together with supporting period artifacts. Send a photo, and your likeness will be seamlessly inserted into a lovely photograph album to document your newly minted history. So thorough, so real, that when you start getting senile you'll believe it yourself. Pick one life: *Men:* Soldier, Politician, Artist, etc. *Women:* Soldier, Politician, etc.

FINAL FUN

Am I Dead?

A reality home-test kit. Many gray boomers sometimes wonder whether they're really dead and just dreaming they're alive. The Am I Dead? reality check kit includes everything you need to check your continuing vitality—pocket mirror for breath detection, assorted pins to test pain response, brain-wave monitor, electrocardiogram, and on-line ObitSearch death list checking. Also includes the best-selling *100 Symptoms of Death,* compiled by a panel of the nation's leading thanatologists, medical examiners, and undertakers.

Condo Mausoleum

Ecologically and fiscally responsible boomers realize that we can't go on wasting precious irreplaceable real estate on cemeteries forever. New life-and-death Condo Mausoleums let you buy the place you want and stay forever. Live there until you die. Then your corpse or ashes are interred under the marble flooring in the foyer, behind the bathroom mirror, in the chandelier—use your imagination! For a 5 percent deduction on the purchase price, the next buyers agree to treat your resting place with dignity in perpetuity, and to admit friends and relatives to pay their respects on two prespecified days each year.

Natural Euthanasia Kit

When the time comes to leave gracefully, do it naturally, with traditional pure organic poisons such as hemlock and asp venom. No preservatives, toxic residues, or nonbiodegradable bullets to contaminate the environment. Comes with a booklet on tasteful scenarios that will make your departure a memorable event. Also available, the Rodale guide to natural embalming using only fruit juices and spices available in any kitchen cupboard!

OBITPERFECT

The latest software program from WordPerfect Corporation helps you compose your own professional obituary before you expire. An easy large-print, high-resolution tutorial takes you step-by-step through the process of writing a fascinating, dramatic, grammatically correct obituary in the standard form required by most newspapers. Order now and receive as a free bonus the fax component, which guarantees immediate delivery to national newsrooms upon your demise.

Plus, don't forget the extensive Gray Boomers Bookshelf, featuring important titles:

Pregnancy After 80
by Demi Moore

I'm OK, But Who Am I?
by Marianne Williamson

*Everything You Always Wanted
to Know About Your Bowels
But Were Afraid to Ask*
by Woody Allen

*The Oxford Book of Tirades
Against Declining Standards*
edited by Michael Medved

*Too Many Passages:
The Rite of Incontinence*
by Gail Sheehy

**The trash barrel near the leafleteer
is filled with leaflets.—M.O'D.**

What We Told the Kids

by Betty Markshuffle

PRUDENCE CROWTHER

There was so much talk in the papers of "teachable moments" that Russ and I began to feel we should prepare ourselves in case the kids started putting us on the spot about whatever they were picking up from their little friends or from the television. We weren't going to worry that much about Jasper, who's still breast-feeding—is that a euphemism?

There was one false alarm the day the report was released. We were having some leftover tamale pie that Friday night and out of nowhere Echinacea comes out with, "Mom, what are we here for?" I took a breath and threw Russ a help-me-out-here-hon stare, but he was suddenly deep into breaking up a clot of cornmeal, so I decided to buy myself some time by saying, "To help others"—that had been my mother's mantra. A full two seconds later she asks, "What are the others here for?" Fortunately Russ remembered a tip from one of the news weeklies and told her it was better if some things stayed private, and we had the impression that she was reassured to know that even in this tell-all age there are still some boundaries.

The next night we agreed we would take the bull by the hair

and ask them what they had heard. Jordy said his friend Max had told him the President had been fooling around with an "intern," which was what, exactly? I thought Russ was marvelous in using the occasion to talk about what it takes to get into medical school and how interns no longer have to work those long shifts, and that if, say, Jordy were doing a surgery residency he could end up operating on some pitcher's rotator cuff. It was perfect, since Chrys is doing an oral report on exactly that, so she got to show off. I was afraid we were in trouble later when it turned out Cosmo was still up when we caught the late-night news, but Russ said when he was putting him to bed he had only asked what "embracing a distinction" meant.

Monday Freesia was home with Cocksackie, and I don't work Mondays, so I thought, What the heck, let's watch. One of the announcers said that the report made no mention of the President actually having intercourse with the Lewinsky character, and naturally that did prompt a question. I asked if she had ever heard of the Amish people, which it turned out she was making an oral report on, so I got out the atlas and showed her that Intercourse is near Lancaster, Pennsylvania, where some of their farms are, and it didn't go any further, except she wanted to know if the word "impeachment" came from peaches, and I was able to say in all honesty that I didn't know.

I thought we were fine that evening because Newark was practicing giving us his oral report on graffiti, but then out of the blue Sharma asked where cigars come from. Oh Christ, I thought, now we're in for it, but Russ quickly told her that line about the difference between a woman and a cigar, that when a woman goes out she's out, but when a cigar goes out, it comes back. Is that it? Then Morris asked me if I'd ever heard of "Little Muddy Walters"—now *that* was a teachable moment, and soon we were playing records and dancing, more or less.

I assume we will continue to cope, as necessary.

Un Caballo in Maschera

PRUDENCE CROWTHER

HORSES IN MET'S *CARMEN* RECEIVED A TRANQUILIZER
—*New York Times,* October 24, 1998

Listen, I've done *Carmen* stoned, and I've done *Carmen* straight, OK? I know the ASPCA came out against this production: If the animal has to be high to get it to perform, that's an abuse of the animal, is that it? That isn't half of it.

My credentials for saying anything? Read this old *Playbill. Interrupted Melody, the Majorie Lawrence Story,* MGM, 1955. Remember, before she gets polio, where she defies the director of *Götterdämmerung* ("You vill *valk* za horse!") and rides Grane into the flames instead of leading him? That was my sire. A born Wagnerian, just like there are diving mules. He didn't even need a real bridle, it was cloth. Forget Eleanor Parker, he did it for Eileen Farrell, she was the voice. And *his* father worked with Flagstad at La Scala in 1938. That was back when they still used a live swan in *Lohengrin.* Do you think anyone knows how to gentle a swan today? Don't be silly.

Wagner was not for me. Eight women singing *"Hoyotoho! Hoyotoho! Brünnhilde! Hei!"* full throttle, I could never stay in

148

character. I made my debut in *Carmen,* Covent Garden, 1963. I was in the corrida in the last scene, wearing an old *peto,* the mattress that keeps the horse from being gored. A real Wardour Street number. We weren't tranquilized, but the bull was—a supposedly harmless three-year-old from Salamanca, not more than 1,200 pounds, with a pro doing the stunt for Escamillo. The torero was supposed to play the bull a little, then they would fake the killing with stagecraft. The house vet got the dose wrong and the bull passed out, so the next night they halved it. Talk about *whoa*—I was this close to tripe.

The next year I did it in concert for EMI, just some ambient neighing. I was anxious—well, Callas, though in the end she was darling—so they gave me a little something, but otherwise I only wore a pair of soft hobbles. It was interesting. It's much easier to fall for Carmen if she's not doing that gypsy vogueing they generally get into on the stage. *"Tra-la-la-la-la-la-la-la . . . "* It still makes my hooves tingle. No, it still makes my mane stand on end. Skip it. Incidentally, it's not as if drugs are the only issue. What about when the Cigarette Girls pour out of the tobacco factory and start smoking all over the place?

No, to rehearse a production humanely, you have to get one of these so-called horse whisperers to direct the animals. It's a misnomer, by the way, they don't whisper. The thing is, a horse is a flight animal. We need to join a herd to survive, even if that herd is the cast of *Carmen.* Stage right, hands on hips, that's not our language. But do you think a guy like Zeffirelli is going to learn how to play the role of the dominant horse matriarch? They even screwed that up in the film: Robert Redford forgot to keep his mouth slightly open when he was working with Pilgrim. And that part where the horse starts rearing hysterically because Kristin Scott Thomas's cell phone goes off? What were you supposed to think, that he'd been traumatized by an earlier phone call? Dreadful. But when they know how to work with our inherent willingness, it can be good. I saw a dressage habañera once in Bilbao that made Risë Stevens look like she was on crutches.

This sounds like sore apples, since I'm getting too blind to work anyway, but I think *equus* should be retired from the opera stage. Naturally *we* think drugs compromise our performance, but there's a more serious problem. Horses at the Met is really the middle-brow misperception of values in the face. Not just that the horses are more beautiful than the opera, but that the audience actually requires the thing in front of them in order to engage in a simulated imaginative experience. You know, they could use a puppet, or put some dowels together, and it would be better. In the end, my dear, it's an abuse of the audience.

Zone 5

Gardening Advice
from Mertensia Corydalis

Q: After the heavy rain last week a large circle of some fungus appeared in my lawn (snapshot enclosed). I kicked it all over and then stomped it flat, but then I wonder whether I should spray the area with a fungicide to prevent it from coming back.

— CHUCK, GLENGARRY

A: The toadstool colony that you marched over like a horticultural Wehrmacht is called a fairy ring. Judging from the photo you sent, it was definitely the most interesting thing that ever occurred in that patch of Astro Turf you call a lawn. You might have pried your children away from the TV set long enough to see the fairy ring, enchanting them with impromptu stories of pixies coming to visit. But I suppose their imaginations have been jack-booted by you, as well. This is absolutely the last lawn-care question I will entertain, and that's final.

Q: Last fall I planted rows of tulip bulbs in front of my house and lining the driveway. Now they are coming up this spring in random clumps in the beds. I'm just fit to be tied. I'll bet squirrels are the culprits. Can I do something to prevent this from happening again?

—BRENDA, PENNINGTON

A: Brenda, I never imagined that, in my lifetime, in the same sentence, I would ever hear the words "President" and "penis." But even more jarring is the juxtaposition of the words "tulip" and "row." Your neighbors, the squirrels, have the advantage over you in landscaping your property. They are outdoors all the time, they get both extreme close-up looks at your flower beds, as well as large overviews from the vantage point of trees. Thus, they are in a much better position than you to make aesthetic decisions about gardening. Plus, unlike you, the squirrels instinctively know that unstudied groupings of odd numbers of bulbs are far more pleasing to the eye than lines of goose-stepping Red Emperor tulips parading past the reviewing stand.

Q: Dear Mertensia: Some of my sunflowers turned out great—over seven feet tall. The problem is that for more than half the day the flowers themselves are facing my neighbor's yard, so I can't enjoy them. Are you supposed to orient the seeds a certain way to prevent this? I feel cheated out of all my hard work. My neighbor is getting something for nothing!

—HERRICK, HAMFORD

A: Dear "Herrick": We're really reaching into the Bin of Literary Obscurity for our pseudonyms now, aren't we? The reason your neighbor (as if I'm in such a fog I didn't recognize myself) is enjoying your surviving sunflowers (transplanted from a shaded location) is that they are heliotropic plants, focusing on the sun as we travel around it in the course of the day. Since my property is on your south side, the sunflowers are craning their necks in my direction during most of the day, casting their faces down in resignation as they prepare to spend the evening facing your side of the fence. I saw you out there trying to "adjust" them. Some people are so territorial, I'm surprised they aren't out lifting their legs to the surveyor's pins, marking their little parcel of turf.

*Next time . . . reflections on nematodes . . .
mucking out your pond for spring*

The Midwest:
Where Is It?

MICHAEL FELDMAN

Recent survey results suggest that most people don't know where the Midwest is, including many who live there (or would, if they only knew where they were). Asked which states comprised the American Midwest, respondents to a national poll could agree on only one: Iowa. But Iowa does not exist in a vacuum. "Are we not hog producers, too?" asks Wisconsin. "Do our whitefish cheeks not taste as sweet?" cries Minnesota. "Where do you think the corn palace is?" pipes up South Dakota.

Still, it's easy to be confused, even living here. In Wisconsin we regularly get tossed into the Great Lakes States, or tagged with the glamorous sobriquet The Upper Midwest. Occasionally we're just asked to check "glaciated" or "non-" (Milwaukee being the Queen City of glacier till, the place where even the Ice Age stopped). Territorial integrity has been hard to come by: Our doppelganger, Minnesota, is often mistakenly listed in atlases among "States, Scandinavian" (if that is a mistake; I mean what's really the difference between a finger lake and a fjord?), while Canadians think they can walk right on into North Dakota (where the border patrol has been less than vigilant) in spite of the insidious Canadian knack for blending in right up until they say "aboot," by which time it is often too late.

If, in fact, there is no Midwest (except Iowa) we have another potential Balkan situation on our hands to be resolved at an international conference in Dayton, even though Ohio is part of the problem—is it east? Is it west? What about Toledo? Then there is the always perplexing Indiana—hobnobbing with Easterners, lilting like Southerners—and yet accredited by *Midwest Living* magazine (that's right, published in Des Moines) as one of the twelve constituent states entitled to subscribe, along with Illinois (which, around Carbondale, most resembles West Virginia), Kansas (Great Plains, anyone?), Michigan (half of which sets its clocks to New York City time, thank you), Missouri (the Gateway to all four major directions), Nebraska (loaded with Heartland values, but excuse me, aren't those buffalo?), and the aforementioned North and South Dakotas, Ohio, Wisconsin, Minnesota, and the nucleus around which we all spin, Iowa.

Historically, much of the confusion regarding the exact location of the Midwest stems from the relative nature of terms like "mid" and "west," the legacy of the congressionally declaimed Northwest Territory, which, veneer stripped away, turns out to look a lot like Ohio or perhaps "Ohioland," as in "The Greater Ohioland Ford Dealers." Today many of us (with no particular ax to grind; I've had some good times in Ohio) would place Ohio in the East, at least as far as Columbus (and we'd concede that as well if it meant the Wisconsin Badgers never had to play at Ohio State again). To refresh your seventh-grade memory, the Northwest Territory was the region north of the Ohio River and east of the Mississippi comprising what today we think of as the heart of the Midwest (minus Iowa!); had the nation rested on its laurels in 1787, the Midwest would be the home of Starbucks coffee, and Bill Gates's high-tech hacienda would be carved out of a bluff in South Beloit. The Northwest Territory is not to be confused with the Northwest

Territories, encompassing Baffin Island and everything else that couldn't be conveniently stuffed into Canada, nor with the Northwest Frontier in Pakistan. The rule of thumb is, if Punjab is to the left and Pushwar is to the right, you are no longer in the Midwest and should call AAA immediately.

As America pushed willy-nilly westward toward its date with Manifest Destiny, it acquired another Northwest entirely, carelessly flinging aside the former and still perfectly good one, leaving it just a little hurt as well as up for grabs geopolitically. Congress never bothered to incorporate the Midwest Territories; if Lewis and Clark ever came through these parts, they didn't mention it. To this day the Midwest, which performs a great service to the nation by keeping New York and Los Angeles apart, is disparaged as the Fly Over States by jet-setting bi-coastals who would do well not to forget whose air space they're crossing (namely, the Midwestern home of the Strategic Air Command). In fact, the Midwest (and here I'm assuming we do exist) is the only region of the nation that came into being as a convenient place to store values; the Heartland, full of hardworking, religious but not overly zealous, family-oriented, parka-wearing (one for everyday, one for Sunday), tolerant, helpful folk who fall into two main categories: links or patties. Since the bulk of such people (no pun intended; many of us are large-boned) seems to fall in the middle of the country (once grits are served automatically at breakfast and seed caps yield to Texas T's, you've gone too far), the area they gravitated to came to be known as the Middle West, or, in racier modern parlance, the Midwest.

Which brings us back to the initial question: Where is it? Here's a little experiment you can try at home, using an ordinary atlas opened to the United States. You'll notice that the crease runs right through Fargo, Sioux Falls, Wichita, and Dallas—let this be the "Y" axis. Now, if you lean on the map, you'll see San Francisco, Denver, Kansas City, Cincinnati, and Norfolk running along the top of your forearm. Let this be the "X" axis. The point at which your forearm intersects with the crease would therefore be the center of the nation, or a spot about equidistant between Beatrice and Peru, Nebraska—let's call it Elk Creek because they'll probably enjoy the attention. Now, removing your glasses, place the tip of your nose directly on Elk Creek and, if your eyesight is anything like mine, everything you will be able to read on the map without moving your head will be the Midwest—Nebraska, South Dakota, enough of North Dakota to count them in, Kansas, Minnesota, Iowa, Missouri, Wisconsin, Illinois, Indiana up to about Kokomo, and, if you really furl your brow, Kalamazoo, Michigan. (I can't for the life of me make out Ohio, but no system is perfect. If they say they are, then they are.)

Since this coincides with the commonly accepted notion of the dominion of the Midwest without having to resort to cumbersome demographics, average household incomes, predominance of heavy equipment manufacturing, or number of acres in soybeans, and since it is consistent with a good deal of anecdotal evidence gathered from people who claim to be from around here, this then would appear to be the Midwest. Please commit it to memory; if there's still some doubt, please write for directions.

Come Stay with Us

Affordable Vacations with the Farm Families of the Beautiful Luling Peninsula

BILL FRANZEN

SPLINT'S HOLIDAY HOMESTEAD

We are an abstaining family willing to share our forefathers' century-old country home with travelers out our way. We strongly encourage you to partake in the day-to-day operation of our bountiful cattle farm. Activities include branding livestock, haying, and firewood production. Ambitious guests may want to join our sons (Noah, 38, and Joshua, 36) as they check their trap lines. Bring lots of old clothes and steel-toed boots—we have barbed-wire-resistant work mitts to loan you. Waterproof socks are a must. Be prepared to participate in the birthing of calves. Steak suppers, our specialty. No better apple-pie-doused-with-hot-fruit-sauce on the peninsula. Decaffeinated coffee is always on. Recently remodeled guestroom contains a large library of inspirational books. Fall visitors witness the most color this side of heaven. Our boys OK about meeting bus, if necessary. We ask that guests refrain from using perfumes and colognes in our home. No picture-taking. Minimum stay, two days. Prepare to enter the most fulfilling lifestyle Luling offers.

Who we are: Hort & Marliss Splint. *Where we are*: Planted by the Almighty at the geographic center of the peninsula. Eight miles due north on County Road 39. Turn at the Gaddis Sawmill sign. Go four miles west. After "one-at-a-time" suspension bridge, look for a Gulf station with a telephone outside. Call us for directions.

PRETTY PERFECT COUNTRY ACRES

Come! Flee the city and choose our historic cottage as your home away from home. (We thank you for your patience during renovations.) We operate a thriving egg business and maintain a large herb garden. Our children (Jack, 17; Terrence, 15; Ginny, 13; Neil, 12; Malc, 10; Marco, 10; Joannie, 8; Tyrone, 6; Ben, 5; Prink, 3; and Shung Chi, 1) are always eager to have company. Once the gang has initiated you on their "Tarzan swing" (Luling's only), they'll want you to get better acquainted with all our farm animals. Moonboots, our friendly Asian collie, loves strangers. You will meet, pet, and feed Kong and Mighty Joe, the big twin goats born last Thanksgiving; Sonny and Cherry, the pigmy goats; and Fran, the miniature black mule— all while Tuffy the Shetland pony looks on. A short llama ride away, peek in on our rabbitry, watch the bees make honey, and explore the caves where the turkey vultures nest. Also on hand to greet you are our clannish barn cats, two unpredictable peacocks, deer, a raccoon who's set up shop in the old Maytag, an ostrich, a people-loving buffalo, and a box of baby rattlers! Gruffy, our black Lab, has been with us for ages but it won't take him long to warm up to you, too. Meals will make you aware of the benefits of quality "whole" foods. Nobody else on Luling can make apple-pie-doused-with-hot-fruit-sauce quite like us. Grandpa has his workshop in the yard. He loves to tell stories. Some of our favorite nighttime activities include stargazing, collecting fireflies, and water fights. Of additional interest is our talent in taxidermy. Kyle just finished a tableau of comically posed small animals called, "The Pardon Came Too

Late." No other stay on Luling will compare with yours here! Mother Nature has endowed our acreage with beauty of the highest order. (Guided swamp walks available, if desired.)

Your hosts: Kyle & Brenda Fisk. *How to find us:* Easy, since we're at the exact geographic center of the peninsula. Drive north on Ten Curves Road till fruit stand. (Use low gears.) Bear right on winding gravel road. Twenty minutes later begin look-out for an orange school bus with a blue roof rack. That's our front yard. Remember, *we* are the prettiest way to experience Luling Peninsula.

DEITER AND VELMA'S LAZYBONE RETREAT

Come, please, liven our big home. Velma and myself immediately consider you family and serve out Luling's best home-cooking—as much of it as you can eat. We're a modest, many-treed hobby farm. On a lone cliff over the blue ocean. Scenery on the peninsula doesn't go getting better since our sunsets come straight off Hollywood. Children we love (ours grown and flown) and have done well especially with honeymooners. We sneak in to rouse you for a six o'clock hearty country breakfast. French toast, Luling bacon, Wiener schnitzel, hickory oatmeal, Johnson cakes with fresh maple syrup, bread, scones, muffins, jam, jelly, butter, cheese, and watermelon pickles. So have it good while sharing with Velma her interest in local history and genealogy. Afterward we'll be glad to give some tips for you to hike up nearby on the Dubenski Incline. But you may rather snooze the morning with us. Beneath the oldest maple on the peninsula. English lunches with roast beef, Yorkshire pudding, gravy, vegetables from our patch, baked potatoes, cabbage rolls with Velma's special sauce—you try it!—and fresh dairy milk, all you can pour. Big ravine down to the sea is the magnificent thing for walking off lunch. Or prefer to nod out with us in Hansel & Gretel porch swings left over from child days. Dinners served up from the blue ocean—Ahoya! Creamed scallops, scrod crepes, fried squid casserole. Dessert . . .

well, Velma's apple-pie-doused-with-hot-fruit-sauce is a local myth. Evenings spent back around our open fire pit. With stories and laughter over the day's adventures—know any good yarns of sailing? We love music, so if you play an instrument by every means, bring it!! It might just lead to family sing-alongs, then time for our hot cinnamony apple cider. Don't retire to your alpine suite before homemade fudge and ice cream. Other things are golf-carting to the hammocks or catching winks in the little red caboose built for my children. Take Velma's party-mix canister beneath the stairs and sleep before satellite TV in your room. If you're thinking around Luling, think of us first.

We are: Deiter and Velma VandeDor of Lazybone Retreat. *To get to us:* We'll be always from the commotion, get off the north shore highway, beyond once it goes west. Just before Country Road 39 falls south we are, but too far if you're seeing the landfill sign. Come on then! No finer breathtaking of the geographic center of Luling exists than you'll have from our dining table.

Desert Surprise:

Saddam Picks Bills

BILL FRANZEN

(The following is a transcript of an announcement by President Saddam Hussein, broadcast on Baghdad Radio and translated by the State Department.)

O Faithful Ones! Today your tireless Father-Leader was awakened by such divine revelations as to make the hairs on his arms stand up like so many vigilant Presidential guards circling one of his secretly located beds, O Lovers of My Safety! Your Shining Knight has been blessed with a glorious vision of the coming confrontation in the California city of Pasadena, between the stalwart Bills of Buffalo and the oil-crazed Livestock Men of Texas—now the den, I alertly note, of Devil's friend Bush.

O patient Bills! Trust that on Sunday your humiliating losses of the past will be as dust blown away by desert winds. Shout for your redemption and the victory of all honorable people, O Bills! Your Mesopotamian ally has seen for you in the Bowl of all Bowls many first downs, stubborn possessions of the ball, and a supreme defensive effort that responds decisively to provocations and territorial incursions by both aerial and ground forces of the Satanic petroleum state's arrogant young defilers.

O Bills! Nothing will thwart you as you gain more and more of the [word indistinct] of Dallas that is rightfully yours. Not the heathen alliance of the diminutive referees! Not the intimidations of the stadium's special-security apparatus "protecting" the "well-being" of the family of Steve the Canadian, your peerless field-goal kicker. And surely not, God willing, the threats and actions of roving bands of state police against your brave Buffalo loyalists waving banners denouncing Troy al-Aikman.

O you Bills! I have seen Super Bowl rings of victory fill the horizon for the great and steadfast warriors of the North. But this super-collision of men will require the sweat of every player. Sweat beading up on every righteous face and collecting in the chin strap until such time as God Almighty wishes it to drip down onto the turf of the Pasadenean battle site and puddles of sweat form and grow into salty ponds and then become treacherously muddy marshlands that will frustrate the aggressive territorial schemes of the petroleum state's Emmitt Smith.

O Men! Fight them, O Men of Buffalo! Struggle with these infidels, these colonializing oilmen disguised as innocent Boys-of-the-Herd! Shield your Jham-es Kelly—defend him from those who would sack—as if *he* were your Protector-King, but not quite, while he picks apart the cunning Dallas webs of defense. Pound the deviants until they can no longer carry out their insidious no-huddling schemes and they abandon their truly offensive coordinators and shed finally their armored body equipment and flee toward their dugout, tripping over spiky feet and falling headlong into their vats of impure Gatorade.

O Thurman Thomas, of sore hip and groin! Banish all worry! For the malicious herd can never avoid the long, lethal sword of their own sporting press, which will not cease shaming them until their decadent ranks are scattered as if by "free" American agency.

Then, back in the holy, cold Northland, the "God Is Great" banner will flutter and highlights of the duel will be broadcast again and again for all to see. Thus overnight, God willing, the epic battle will have achieved a valiant rating and a share to be recorded in numbers of light, and the humiliations of the vanquished oil monopolists, like Satan-loving Bush, will go on until the end of time or until there is installed for the Cattle Boys of Dallas a faithful new coach—or until the entire franchise, henceforth to be known as the Revolutionary Guards, is swiftly moved to Baghdad, where its safety will, of course, be guaranteed.

Return Saddam's Limo . . . Now!

BILL FRANZEN

Tariq Aziz was in town last week, meeting with United Nations officials to plead that sanctions against his country, Iraq, be eased—a plea that fell mostly on the deaf ears of those who'd rather see Saddam Hussein eased *out,* if you catch our drift. Well, we may have just the idea for Saddam—for speeding up his exit, we mean. See, recently, a publicity packet from the O'Gara-Hess & Eisenhardt Armoring Company, of Fairfield, Ohio, landed on our desk, with a lot of information about the company's new, forty-thousand-dollar "Personal Security Vehicle" system designed to help you in your Taurus or Camry "defeat random violence in North America," and right away we got down to work on what we imagined would be an exhaustive piece detailing how a New Yorker might personally secure his or her vehicle with the help of O'Gara-Hess & Eisenhardt—how, for example, O'Gara-Hess & Eisenhardt's chassis-mounted tear-gas-cannister launchers might get you your way with that Unification Church guy peddling roses at the entrance to the Holland Tunnel.

But then we got to talking on the phone with Bill O'Gara—

he's the company's president—and it came up that Saddam's personally secured limousine (or one of them, anyway) is sitting right out there at O'Gara-Hess & Eisenhardt's headquarters. Bill O'Gara explained it this way: "Back in the eighties, we built some cars for him. One happened to be back in maintenance in July of 1990. In August, he invaded Kuwait. So the car was impounded, as an Iraqi asset controlled by Iraq."

After getting off the phone with Bill O'Gara, we had this thought: Let's ease up on Saddam just the tiniest bit. Let's *send the car back*. Of course (and let's all do our level best to keep this part quiet), we ought to make a few minor adjustments to the car—just to lighten it up a bit for shipping, right? According to O'Gara-Hess & Eisenhardt, the following tinkerings shouldn't alter the vehicle's outward appearance much at all. Saddam— and this really shouldn't go beyond us—would probably not notice a thing.

1. Remove armor lining from doors and roof. Very carefully replace simulated-leather interior panels.

2. Remove explosion-resistant gas tank.

3. In the interest of allowing more light inside (you know, if he happens to notice, this sounds good, doesn't it?), replace bulletproof windshield with standard safety glass.

4. Remove the mine-resistant steel floorboards—well, you don't check under *your* mats, do you?

5. As for the "run-flat" tires that keep rolling even if riddled with bullets: Hey, there's only one way he'll learn that he's now hugging the road with basic radials.

•• NEWS QUIZ ••

Pleased with yesterday's result, who said this about what: "Thank God, once again the system works!"

"The Cleveland Indians on their pact with the devil."
—Beth Sherman

"A Nobel Prize–winning portfolio manager of Long-Term Capital, enjoying a rare lucky day at the dog track."—Jennifer Miller

"The manager of the Backstreet Boys, on payola."
—Brooke Saucier

"Claus von Bulow. Does it matter what the charges were?"—Adam Bonin

"Anonymous Russian toiler, standing in line to exchange stock certificates for bread."
—Norman Oder

• RANDY'S WRAP UP •

The system operates to the advantage of its owner-operators: That's the cynical assumption of most Quiz players with the maturity to demur from intestinal references. What's true at Caesar's Palace is true on Capitol Hill: The legal system operates in favor of those who own it, or at least those who rent a legislator. Still, the law offers a curious, if not entirely reliable, protection even to the poor and the weak; genuine progress in civil rights was achieved through the courts. The idea that the law must be applied to all, the equal protection clause, is the theoretical basis of the legal lives of children, which is pretty much just the constant lament, "That's not fair!" What they mean is: The rules are not being consistently applied. Even we adults who devised the system must be subject to its rules lest we undermine the whole sweet setup. The owners of Caesar's Palace realize that they too must bust if they take a hit at fifteen, draw a seven, and end up with twenty-two. But over the long run, the owners of Caesar's and Chase and Pepsico will win. As long as they get plenty of fiber.

WALK-IN-THE-SUN-ONCE-AGAIN ANSWER

Imelda Marcos applauded a Philippine Supreme Court ruling that overturned her corruption conviction, saving her from a possible twelve years in jail. Although she and her husband are believed to have stolen billions from the Philippines, this was the only case in which she'd been found guilty. "Justice prevailed," she said.

WHAT'S ON? SIMPLE SENTENCES EXTRA

(all drawn verbatim from Wednesday and Thursday *New York Times* TV listings)

Fran refuses.
Austin replaces.
Detectives discover.
Phil develops.
Mary decides.

Drew decides.
Dawson and Joey ponder.
Josh confronts.
Niles agrees.
The gang hunts.
Weaver vies.
Ross gets.
Lucy hides.
Benton keeps.
Sean makes.
A boy must.
Human bomb needs.
Birthmother voices.

Laws Concerning Food and Drink; Household Principles; Lamentations of the Father

IAN FRAZIER

SERMON ON THE TABLE

Of the beasts of the field, and of the fishes of the sea, and of all foods that are acceptable in my sight you may eat, but not in the living room. Of the hoofed animals, broiled or ground into burgers, you may eat, but not in the living room. Of the cloven-hoofed animal, plain or with cheese, you may eat, but not in the living room. Of the cereal, of the corn and of the wheat and of the oats, and of all the cereals that are of bright color and unknown provenance you may eat, but not in the living room. Of the quiescently frozen dessert and of all frozen after-meal treats you may eat, but absolutely not in the living room. Of the juices and other beverages, yes, even of those in sippy-cups, you may drink, but not in the living room, neither may you carry such therein. Indeed, when you reach the place where the living room carpet begins, of any food or beverage there you may not eat, neither may you drink. But if you are sick, and are lying down and watching something, then may you eat in the living room.

And if you are seated in your high chair, or in a chair such as a greater person might use, keep your legs and feet below you as they were. Neither raise up your knees, nor place your feet upon the table, for that is an abomination to me. Yes, even when you have an interesting bandage to show, your feet upon the table are an abomination, and worthy of rebuke. Drink your milk as it is given you, neither use on it any utensils, nor fork, nor knife, nor spoon, for that is not what they are for; if you will dip your blocks in the milk, and lick it off, you will be sent away. When you have drunk, let the empty cup then remain upon the table, and do not bite it upon its edge and by your teeth hold it to your face in order to make noises in it sounding like a duck; for you will be sent away. When you chew your food, keep your mouth closed until you have swallowed, and do not open it to show your brother or your sister what is within; I say to you, do not so, even if your brother or your sister has done the same to you. Eat your food only; do not eat that which is not food; neither seize the table between your jaws, nor use the raiment of the table to wipe your lips. I say again to you, do not touch it, but leave it as it is. And though your stick of carrot does indeed resemble a marker, draw not with it upon the table, even in pretend, for we do not do that, that is why. And though the pieces of broccoli are very like small trees, do not stand them upright to make a forest, because we do not do that, that is why. Sit just as I have told you, and do not lean to one side or the other, nor slide down until you are nearly slid away. Heed me; for if you sit like that, your hair will go into the syrup. And now behold, even as I have said, it has come to pass.

LAWS PERTAINING TO DESSERT

For we judge between the plate that is unclean and the plate that is clean, saying first, if the plate is clean, then you shall have dessert. But of the unclean plate, the laws are these: If you have eaten most of your meat, and two bites of your peas with each bite consisting of not less than three peas each, or in total six peas, eaten where I can see, and you have also eaten enough of your potatoes to fill two forks, both forkfuls eaten where I can see, then you shall have dessert. But if you eat a lesser number of peas, and yet you eat the potatoes, still you shall not have dessert; and if you eat the peas, yet leave the potatoes uneaten, you shall not have dessert, no, not even a small portion thereof. And if you try to deceive by moving the potatoes or peas around with a fork, that it may appear you have eaten what you have not, you will fall into iniquity. And I will know, and you shall have no dessert.

ON SCREAMING

Do not scream; for it is as if you scream all the time. If you are given a plate on which two foods you do not wish to touch each other are touching each other, your voice rises up even to the ceiling, while you point to the offense with the finger of your right hand; but I say to you, scream not, only remonstrate gently with the server, that the server may correct the fault. Likewise if you receive a portion of fish from which every piece of herbal seasoning has not been scraped off, and the herbal seasoning is loathsome to you, and steeped in vileness, again I say, refrain from screaming. Though the vileness overwhelm you, and cause you a faint unto death, make not that sound from within your throat, neither cover your face, nor press your fingers to your nose. For even now I have made the fish as it should be; behold, I eat of it myself, yet do not die.

CONCERNING FACE AND HANDS

Cast your countenance upward to the light, and lift your eyes to the hills, that I may more easily wash you off. For the stains are upon you; even to the very back of your head, there is rice thereon. And in the breast pocket of your garment, and upon the tie of your shoe, rice and other fragments are distributed in a manner wonderful to see. Only hold yourself still; hold still, I say. Give each finger in its turn for my examination thereof, and also each thumb. Lo, how iniquitous they appear. What I do is as it must be; and you shall not go hence until I have done.

VARIOUS OTHER LAWS, STATUTES, AND ORDINANCES

Bite not, lest you be cast into quiet time. Neither drink of your own bath water, nor of bath water of any kind; nor rub your feet on bread, even if it be in the package; nor rub yourself against cars, nor against any building; nor eat sand. Leave the cat alone, for what has the cat done, that you should so afflict it with tape? And hum not that humming in your nose as I read, nor stand between the light and the book. Indeed, you will drive me to madness. Nor forget what I said about the tape.

COMPLAINTS AND LAMENTATIONS

O my children, you are disobedient. For when I tell you what you must do, you argue and dispute hotly even to the littlest detail; and when I do not accede, you cry out, and hit and kick. Yes, and even sometimes do you spit, and shout "stupid-head" and other blasphemies, and hit and kick the wall and the molding thereof when you are sent to the corner. And though the law teaches that no one shall be sent to the corner for more minutes than he has years of age, yet I would leave you there all day, so mighty am I in anger. But upon being sent to the corner you ask straightaway, "Can I come out?" and I reply, "No, you may not come out." And again you ask, and again I give the same reply. But when you ask again a third time, then you may come out. Hear me, O my children, for the bills they kill me. I pay and pay again, even to the twelfth time in a year, and yet again they mount higher than before. For our health, that we may be covered, I give six hundred and twenty talents twelve times in a year; but even this covers not the fifteen hundred deductible for each member of the family within a calendar year. And yet for ordinary visits we still are not covered, nor for many medicines, nor for the teeth within our mouths. Guess not at what rage is in my mind, for surely you cannot know. For I will come to you at the first of the month and at the fifteenth of the month with the bills and a great whining and moan. And when the month of taxes comes, I will decry the wrong and unfairness of it, and mourn with wine and ashtrays, and rend my receipts. And you shall remember that I am that I am: before, after, and until you are twenty-one. Hear me then, and avoid me in my wrath, O children of me.

Only the empty restaurant forbids you to use its rest room.—M.O'D.

Flowers of Evil:
Ask Charles Baudelaire

FRANK GANNON

Q: What annuals are suitable for planting near the ocean?

If sufficient depth of topsoil (seven to nine inches) is provided and you give them sufficient water in dry periods (which drag on and on, furrowing into your soul, often), you should be in pretty good shape to grow almost any annual that strikes your fancy. A tip: don't get hopelessly drunk before you start, and don't approach the project through the miasma of despair. Also, remember the gloves and stay busy.

Q: The crowns of my veronicas are rising above the surface. Can I do anything about this?

Veronicas tend to raise their crowns if they're kept in the same spot too long. They've been stagnant and they're starting to fester; like madmen in the dark, with great wild eyes they are coming to get you, because your corrupted hand should never touch beauty.

If your heart is set on it, move the veronicas in a large soil bag. Then return to your life of error and sin, until you, too, die and fester in a very large soil bag.

Q: Is it all right to trim trees in the winter?

Yes, provided the temperature isn't too low. Also, check the trees. If black regments of larvae flow out of the trees like a dense, ghastly river, and the stench of death is overpowering, throw the trees away; it's way past trimming time. But bear in mind that you, too, will turn into a rotting mass, to be eaten by vermin. My love!

Q: Which trees and shrubs are suitable for sandy soil in a sunny location?

With proper care, arcadia and tamarisk should do well. Since half of horticulture is visual, you might think about putting one or two vile, rotting corpses, their legs in the air like lustful women's, out there somewhere. Use your own judgment, but I'd give the amount of shade more than a second thought for the corpses. Remember to mulch.

Q: How can I make a medium-size, manure-heated hotbed to get an early start on tomatoes?

Find some long two-by-fours and make a box. The size is up to you, but make sure that it's square. If you can make it voluptuous, that's a plus. Make it rich! Make it triumphant! Make it corrupt, rich, voluptuous, rich, and triumphant! Make it strange and untamed, and then wet it with your tears of anguish.

Grow your tomatoes earlier than others, and sing of their round red beauty. Sing of your depraved globes and know that they are your brothers! Brothers in pestilence! Oh, your mind and your early tomatoes spring from the very same vine! Use a 2-10-10 general fertilizer—unless you can live comfortably with the idea that you might need more potash.

Q: Should tulip bulbs be taken up each year and separated? Should they be covered with leaves in the fall?

It really depends on where you live. If you live in the Midwest, then I'd leave them where they are for two or three years, unless you're going to use the land for something else—like maybe a few naked black rocks over which flow a great deal of painful personal humiliation, until you lie palsied in your loins.

That's probably a long-term project. Forget the leaves, too. You probably have too much time on your hands, if you're asking questions like that.

Q: Which plants, besides geraniums, can be grown in a small home greenhouse for winter bloom?

When you set out your plants, you will find that a lot of flowers you wouldn't think of can produce winter blooms. But be careful. Studies at Cornell University indicate that if you're like other amateur gardeners, you'll probably wind up staring straight into the grim, still face of death. Go to your greenhouse without love or remorse, amateur gardener. Debud your chrysanthemums in sin!

Seriously, I'm always eager to help the amateur horticulturalist, because I know his ambitions and his many problems.

As always, yours for good gardening and hideous suffering.

—CHARLES BAUDELAIRE

Authors with the Most

FRANK GANNON

Mr. Blackwell, the fashion arbiter, rates the great American writers.

Herman Melville

We've seen the whale thing before and someone please tell this man that Biblical names are clever to post-office workers but not to anyone else. And you would have thought he might have heard that having someone named Bartleby who works in a law office and says "I prefer not to" is not exactly a fertile field for a tent and caterers on a Sunday. Herman grew up and wanted to become a major American writer but he seems to have forgotten that you don't go on a three-year voyage and invite only guys. Drab. Drab. Drab. A big white whale. Aren't we original? Reading Herman Melville reminds me of the time I tried to have a conversation with Donovan.

Emily Dickinson

Oh, Emily, are you in there? What has this tiresome woman been doing with herself? One would hope something more than writing more poems about old Mister Death. Hey, Miss Dickinson, there was a funeral in your brain, and guess who the flowers are for? I'll send you a note, Em—do read it. I don't want to hear any more from you about "drunken bees."

Nathaniel Hawthorne

Is there a better way to clear out a room than saying the word "Puritan"? had my fill of those dreadful black pointy hats at Thanksgiving. And that business about wearing a *letter* for punishment? No thanks, Hawthorne. I finished high school a long time ago, but when I *was* in high school I would never have been caught hanging around with losers like you.

Henry David Thoreau

Poor Thoreau. He spent so much time alone that he started to think he was the most interesting person in the room. Yes, Henry, do go on about your bean rows. Do you mind if I hang myself first? I once read Henry asking the pointed question "Shall I go to heaven or a-fishing?" All I can say to someone who uses the word "a-fishing" is "Gaak!" I don't care which one it is, but *do* go, Henry. Goodbye.

Edgar Allan Poe

He always seems to have just gotten off of a particularly nasty bus, and I picture him with an expression like one of those Mary Quant-manqués we had all over the place in the sixties. Always insisting that literature didn't have any *function*, it was just capital letters: ART. And the way the French carried him around on their shoulders! You know what people say, make one thing that appeals to reason and emotion simultaneously and you'll never be rid of the French. That's the way they are.

Henry Wadsworth Longfellow

Will someone shoot down this multicolored blimp from the sky? Please. If we promise to introduce you to some nice people, will you get it done? We will all live happily ever after if someone sends this man a telegram that says, "Hello, Wads, this is reality. You wrote 'The tide rises, the tide falls' three times in the same poem. We don't need that."

Amy Lowell

What's with the cigars, Amy *mia?* Could be you've entered the wrong contest here. Candidates for the Edward G. Robinson Memorial Bowl are meeting over at the Statler. Hurry.

Ralph Waldo Emerson

Should have "Rich and Bulgy" carved on his gravestone. The essay has just about vanished from the world of writing, and it's not surprising considering what Mr. Oversoul did to it. Overbearing is more like it. Waldo talked about self-reliance but what he should have said was "self-indulgence." It's frightening that in 1994, decades after we sent a man to the moon, somebody still needs to say, "I am sorry, Madam, no one here reads Ralph Waldo Emerson."

Long Day's Journey into Abs

FRANK GANNON

Infomercials disguised as actual programming are becoming more and more subtle.

—Associated Press

SCENE: *Night. An American-Victorian living room. Some lamps are on, but the atmosphere is one of subtle yet unrelenting gloom. It is a room that has seen a great deal of old-fashioned Irish-American emoting: silent suffering and suffering out loud. Enter JAMIE and EDMUND, drinks in hand. Their manner suggests an impending moment of clarity after years of alcohol abuse.*

JAMIE: I've been wise to Mama a lot longer than you. I'll never forget when I first found out. Caught her with a hypo. Jesus, I always thought that only whores took dope. And then you had to go and get consumption. We've been more than just brothers. (*He drinks.*) You're the only real pal I've ever had.

EDMUND: I know that. (*Drinks.*)

JAMIE: You know, Papa is old and he can't last much longer. If you were to die, Mama and I would get everything he's got, so you probably think I'm hoping—

EDMUND: Shut up, you damn fool!

JAMIE: Be realistic for once in your damn romantic life! (*Pause.*)

EDMUND: I'm sorry. We're all in bad shape. We're haunted.

JAMIE: Let me ask you something.

EDMUND: Wha? (*Drinks.*)

JAMIE: Can you spare twenty minutes a day?

EDMUND: What are you talking about?

JAMIE: I'm talking about twenty minutes a day. Twenty minutes a day in the comfort of your own home.

EDMUND: Well, I guess everybody has twenty minutes a day. (*Sighs.*)

JAMIE: Twenty minutes a day . . . to a new you.

EDMUND: That's a good one. A new me! (*Drinks.*)
(TYRONE *enters. He is sixty-five but carries himself like a much younger father.*)

TYRONE: Oh, both of you here. Tired of your filth and your whores?

JAMIE: They give me more than I ever got here!

TYRONE: Why don't you go back to them, the two of you. My heirs! My name—what a waste! Two drunks, and me a wreck! Done and finished!

EDMUND: You're the one to talk. Your money is more precious to you than your own flesh and blood.

TYRONE: I'll not hear this. It's just the drink talking and that blasted Swinburne. (*Mincingly.*) Oh, Algernon!

JAMIE: Speaking about money. I'm asking you, as your older son, do you have three easy payments of $59.95?

TYRONE: Did you say $59.95?

JAMIE: Yes, for God's sake. Three easy payments of $59.95.

EDMUND: Easy? Nothing is easy. (*Drinks.*)

JAMIE: This is. And consider what you get.

EDMUND: What *do* you get, besides a slow walk to the grave?

JAMIE: What do you get? A complete aerobic workout—a systemic workout of all the major muscle groups!

TYRONE: Where do you get that—from your godless, blasphemous dirty books? From your dirty two-bit whores?

JAMIE: No. It's available right now from one of the nation's oldest and most trusted names in personal fitness.

EDMUND: But what about someone like me? I'd like to get into shape, but I'm dying of consumption.

JAMIE: Look at me. I spend at least fifty hours a week drinking and having meaningless sex with whores. Yet with the Fitness Plus plan, I can get drunk, have oral and regular sex with prostitutes, and still have time to get a whole-body workout.

TYRONE: Wow, that is convenient!

JAMIE: And even if you're spending four or five hours coughing up blood, Edmund, the Fitness Plus plan can fit right into your life style.
(*They freeze as a Chopin waltz starts up on a player piano. The music stops as* MARY *appears in the doorway, wearing an old nightgown. Her hair is loose, and a strip of rubber tubing still encircles one arm. She stares straight ahead, oblivious.*)

JAMIE: (*in low horror*): Oh, my God! Enter Ophelia.

EDMUND: Enter Needle Nellie.

TYRONE: She's far gone.

JAMIE: Not too far. Mom? Can I talk to you?

(MARY *stops and turns.*)

MARY: I'm missing something—when will I find it?

JAMIE: Within two weeks, Mom! When you try the Fitness Plus plan—well, you'll get hooked on it! (*They all laugh hollowly.*)

CURTAIN

(The preceding was a paid program expressing the views of Eugene O'Neill and Fitness Plus Systems.)

Yankee, Come Home

FRANK GANNON

Early today, in keeping with his "everybody deserves another chance" policy, George Steinbrenner announced that in addition to signing Darryl Strawberry for the remainder of the '95 baseball season, he had also hired Robert Vesco as a third base coach. Vesco, the fugitive millionaire, had been under arrest in Havana. Fidel Castro was adamant about refusing to extradite Vesco, who is wanted in America for bank fraud, securities fraud and just regular fraud. However, when the Yankee chieftain gave him a call, the Communist dictator was more than ready to listen.

"I've always loved baseball," said the well-known Cuban kingpin, "so when Steinbrenner called my office, I thought he just wanted to talk ball. But then the conversation got around to Vesco. Steinbrenner told me about his 'everybody deserves another chance' policy, and I figured, why not?"

Steinbrenner, the widely despised tyrant of the American League, said: "Most people know Vesco as some sort of rene-gade financier, a guy who plays by his own rules, but maybe that's what we need around here. I mean, if there's a guy who can defraud people of tens of millions of dollars, a guy who is capable of international fraud on a massive scale, you want that guy in your dugout, not the other guy's dugout. Especially in tight games. And guess what? We were 20 games out of first the last time I looked."

For what it's worth, Vesco appears to be in excellent shape. His weight is almost exactly the same as it was when he was stealing millions of dollars from unwitting investors. Daily work-outs have kept the aging criminal in terrific physical condition.

Reaction in the Yankee clubhouse was mixed after the Vesco announcement. Don Mattingly, longtime Yankee first sacker, perhaps said it best: "Last year, for a couple of months anyway, all we had to concentrate on was baseball. Now it seems like we're returning to the old days when what happens outside the lines is more important than what happens inside the lines. I like Bob Vesco, and I have no problem with him. I never invested any money in anything that he was running, so I'm O.K. on that score. I think he'll look pretty good in that coaching box. I just hope the off-the-field stuff doesn't get to be a big distraction again."

Buck Showalter, the manager, says the Yankees helped Steve Howe, who was suspended seven times for violating base-ball's drug policy, and they can help Robert Vesco too.

"It's a challenge, one that you have to face a day at a time," said the Yankee skipper. "The way I look at it, maybe Steve Howe can help Darryl Strawberry, and Darryl Strawberry can help Robert Vesco."

Steve Howe says he's happy to have Vesco on the team, but he's getting tired of all the jokes "about Robert Vesco and me and Darryl Strawberry getting together and forming a quilting society. That's just not funny to me anymore."

Vesco's biggest challenge, outside of avoiding being arrested by Federal agents, will be, as for all Yankee players, dealing with the media. "I understand that news is news," says Vesco. "But when does it stop being news and just turn into sheer hostility? I'm here to help the Yankees win, period. I get a little tired of answering questions about Richard Nixon and where all the money I defrauded people out of is. That's all in the past. Nixon is dead, and I stole that money a long time ago. It's over. Period. Let's just play baseball."

Steinbrenner remains doggedly optimistic about salvaging the '95 season. "Baseball is about not quitting, and Bobby Vesco doesn't know what 'quit' means. The United States Government has been trying to arrest him for decades. He could have given himself up a long time ago, but Bobby Vesco doesn't give up. The Yankees don't give up, either. We were down in the standings a couple of weeks ago, and Bobby was under arrest in Cuba. Now we're in second place, and Bobby Vesco's in the third base coaching box."

What does the Steinbrenner-Strawberry-Vesco situation tell us about America?

I talked to Robert L. Permutation, Lancôme Professor of Game Theory at the Institute for Overly Formal Studies in Los Angeles.

"What the whole situation with the Yankees says to us is, for me, absolutely characteristic of the whole American love affair with sports and criminal activity," says Permutation. "You can pick your own take on the situation—Saussurian, Barthesian, Marxist, Foucaultian, Lacanian, Yogi Berrian—it still says something so essential, that sort of pre-Nietzschean frisson that is so close to the heart of the American labyrinth.

"We've seen this sort of thing before, of course," he says. "One thinks of Derrida in 'La Pharmacie de Platon,' of his reading of Hegel in 'Glas.' Or perhaps Leo Durocher in 'Nice Guys Finish Last.' But the one thing you can't challenge or refute is just this: As Freddy Nietzsche said so long ago, 'That which does not kill me makes me stronger.'

"The Yankees aren't dead yet, and let's not forget that—although I grant you it would be so American to do just that."

Zone 5

Gardening Advice from Mertensia Corydalis

Q: *Miss Corydalis, watering the garden takes so much time, and I'm never sure how much it really needs. I think we should install an irrigation system with drip emitters and a timer. My husband says we can't afford it and that it's adequate for him to go out every evening and water the garden by hand. What is your opinion?*

—PIA, MARMOT HOLLOW

A: Pia, it's been my experience that husbands, who normally leap at any opportunity to invest in gadgetry, love to spend the twilight of the day, hose in hand, lost in solitary reverie. So to keep the peace, pehaps you should defer. The only danger is that frequent, shallow watering encourages root growth near the soil surface, leaving the plant vulnerable during periods of intense heat. This summer is already unusually hot. Just today I had to insist that Tran, my garden assistant, remove his shirt to avoid overheating while dividing my veronica.

Q: *Finding myself with a lot of time on my hands, I'd like to take up indoor gardening as a hobby, specifically, medicinal herbs. My window only gets a few hours of sun a day and my resources are very limited. Any ideas?*

—JOHN, #895477, LUCASVILLE

A: John, very few people know this, but during the Falkland Islands fracas, I was a botanical rescue volunteer. Upon my arrival via commercial flight to Buenos Aires, the authorities prevented my boarding a commuter hop to the Falklands. I was detained a short time in an Argentine police station. (The guards were entirely civil, and I even had a good turn at tango with a guard named Rogelio.) To pass the time I started pots of gazania daisies in my window. I made do with a light reflector fashioned from the cardboard backing of notepads and bits of aluminum foil from Cadbury chocolate wrappers, using gravy as the adhesive. I hope this is helpful.

Q: *This is the third year for my lilac bush. Last year it bloomed but this year, nothing. I mulched and fertilized it, and last fall I shaped it up with pruners.*

—NIGEL, HAMFORD

A: Well, now you've done it, "Nigel"! The buds for next year's bloom begin to form immediately after this year's flush of flowers. The little styling you gave the bush last fall whacked off this year's buds. Also, save your energy. The mulching and fertilizing are unnecessary, although a few handfuls of lime would be appreciated.

Speaking of whacking, you have amputated my Nelly Moser clematis TWICE by insinuating your nylon string trimmer under my fence. If there is a repeat, I shall have to resort to retaliatory measures.

Next time . . . Wellington boots vs. French sabots, the footwear controversy . . . garden monument ideas for your pet's cremains

A Good Man Is Hard to Keep:
The Correspondence of Flannery
O'Connor and S. J. Perelman

VERONICA GENG AND
GARRISON KEILLOR

These imaginary letters were read at the Authors Guild Foundation's benefit dinner, "Literary Affairs," on February 27, 1995, at the Metropolitan Club in New York. Veronica Geng wrote and played the part of Flannery O'Connor and Garrison Keillor wrote and played S. J. Perelman.

Dear Sid,

Gone and got me a new dress. Black satin and it has what I hear tell they call a "plunging neckline." The lady in the fitting room at the Milledgeville store took a good hard look and then she said, "That idn't you." I said, "It is now."

Well, I reckon I sound most highly pleased with myself and for that I do thank you very kindly. "Plunging" is the word all right and I guess that is a fact.

Were they-all a bunch of geniuses in our panel discussion or was it near on to about the dopiest panel discussion ever? What I got out of it was a vision of yr starched white shirt front, blinding white like a nice new sheet of paper. What a lousy comparison, a sheet of paper hasn't got seven pearl buttons down the middle.

My mother is skeptical on this one point of your having ordered us up the room service at that Ritz. She says there is no Ritz in Iowa City. I have been telling her the juicy details so she won't want a television.

Anyhow, I was much taken with you and figure on putting you in a story. Have one going where this family on a car trip has an accident and goes into a ditch, and I need a man who comes along in a car and what all. He has blue eyes like yrs and a clean white shirt on and he has got him a picnic hamper with champagne in it and sandwiches and a portable Victrola and some jazz records.

> Yrs truly,
> F.

My little Peach Cobbler,

When I was a schoolboy in Providence, I spent my Saturdays sitting dazed and feverish in the balcony of the Pantages watching Mary Pickford in *Hearts Adrift* over and over until the manager pried my shoes from the floor and sent me home, and now I am in the same fever over you, but without the licorice whips. I do remember that it was the Hilton, not the Ritz, but passion is sweet no matter what the marquee, and I can't wait to make a fool of myself again as soon as possible. You are my ideal of Southern womanhood, and you have crept into my heart like kudzu. As for you putting me in a story, O.K., but be careful not to use the terms "rapier wit" or "dark flashing eyes" lest our secret be revealed and our names dragged into the gossip columns and our love cheapened. And please let me know when I can come to Milledgeville and see you. Do you have a refrigerator, by the way?

El Sid

Dear Sid,

Oh my.

Well, I thought I best ask my mama to see will it be all right putting up a New Yorker gent in the spare room. There is a nice rug in there and all. She says she don't mind but has yet to lay eyes on a man worth getting a new refrigerator for. Can you cope with an ice-box which it is pretty full up with peacock feed? Don't wear those nice shoes, we are awful muddy hereabouts.

As I recollect, the newspapers have a limited interest in my affairs and are blind dumb to boot, so if I was you I wouldn't get myself in a lather about publicity.

Now on this story. Yr character is seen from an omniscient pt of view. Not one living soul would reckanize you, human nature being suchlike that you don't even reckanize your own sef. Anyways, the details are all changed around now. The dark side of you has got to emerge and the sooner the better. He has got himsef a pearl-handled gun of some kind and is inclined to push these country people to the limit just on the pure meanness of it. I don't see fit to alter my method of working to your say-so.

Yrs truly,
F.

Mon amour,

I was stitching a plume on my chapeau, all in a flush over my upcoming trip to Georgia, when the mailman dropped your letter in my lap, and I must say it gave me a violent tic and I had to smell salts when I came to the part about the gun. Gallantry, my little chickabiddy, has its limits. First you say you are going to portray me in a story as a snappy dresser with a Victrola and blue eyes, and then I become a sullen thug who terrorizes innocent people at the point of a pistol. What do you say we segue back to the love scene, fade out on my dark side, fade in to a violent mist of perfume and ambrosia, you and me in closeup, our lips intertwined? Why not sell the mules, send your mother to a Bible camp, come north, and cohabit with me at the Plaza while we write a hit musical—you supply the colorful characters, the robust scenes of peasant life, etc., and I'll provide the verbs and prepositions—and we'll retire off the royalties to a Pre-Raphaelite snuggery in the Cotswolds and recline in a bower and adore each other? Meanwhile, could you reserve me a suite at a hotel near your farm where you and I could reconnoiter when you are done with chores?

Your Sid

Dear Sid,

Well, your plan is a real horror. To my mind the bidnis of living off of royalties is downright sinful, and I would as leave be strangled in my nightdress as do any such thing.

So I do thank you most profoundly as this is the exact feeling I was after and have been all day at the typewriter banging out the truth and getting the entire family gunned down in the woods excepting the old lady. Now she is face to face with the Misfit which is what I call him as you will surely agree is the word for him if you are able to take a good clean look into yourself. He has got the pearly-handle gun pointed right at her heart. MY HE IS AS BAD AS THEY COME. She looks into his pale blue eyes and then she says, "I'd like to kiss you but I just washed my hair."

Yrs truly,
F.

My little rosebud,

I must confess that surrealism is, to me, a powerful aphrodisiac and that I am thrilled by attractive women who say bizarre things. The dashing, sloe-eyed, silken-skinned Sid you know from the Sunday rotogravure was once a bohemian too, my sweet. Back when Edna St. Vincent Millay and I used to dip candles in her loft in the Village, I swapped symbolism with the best of them, wrote sonnets on mutability and decay, wore black silk shirts, read Rilke, drank espresso, the whole megillah, so believe me, kid, I can be as Gothic as the next guy. Kafka, let me remind you, was not a Southern Baptist, and if you enjoy spooky stories, I have a snootful—but why be obsessed with darkness when the bright lights beckon? My ticket to Georgia is purchased and sits atop the bureau, my shoes are polished, my hosiery is folded and wrapped in tissue, my white flannels are pressed, my heart is pounding like a triphammer, my palms are clammy with anticipation, but of course I won't come if I am only going to serve as the model for a psychopath. At the risk of sounding like Norman St. Vincent Peale, why not lighten up a little? If you want to wash your hair, come up to New York. We have hair dryers here.

Yours,
Sid

Dear Sid,

Well, we have us a disaster here with our icebox, which is of a mind to go crazy every oncet in a while. The only one who can fix it is a convict who comes down from the Atlanta pen, so I am waiting on him and can't travel. Besides my mother says there is not a man on the face of this earth who she would allow to visit without a good supply of ice on hand.

Please give my very kindest regards to Miss Edna whoever that may be.

Yrs truly,
F.

Testing, Testing . . .

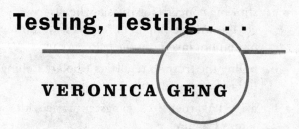

VERONICA GENG

> [A national-security official] suggested that I not publish my information on the link between organized crime and Russian nuclear-weapons security. . . . [A]nother well-informed national-security analyst told me . . . "Yes, our public posture is Pollyannaish, but there is some value in not panicking the whole world."
> —Seymour Hersh, *Atlantic Monthly,* June 1994

Caution: You are about to take the National Security Analyst Recertification Exam. Do not bring into the examination room any classified negativity or apocalyptic scenarios.

VOCABULARYOLOGY

public posture
pollyannaish
some value
panicking
the whole world

For each term, select the definition that will make Earth a nicer place and bring a ray of light to those whose lives would be a wee bit darker without it.

1. PUBLIC POSTURE is

    a. showing concern for Russia whenever we get too wrapped up in problems with our own plutonium inventory

    b. telling the truth to reporters who are itching to be threatened with censorship

    c. a 1931 Warner Bros. gangster movie with James Cagney

    d. the new French-designed toilet for urban spaces

2. POLLYANNAISH, the term used to reassure a layperson about the Russian mafia, describes the West's policy of

    a. Puzoisme

    b. Petrograderie

    c. Struwwelpetermania

    d. wondering if Boris Yeltsin's glass is half full or half empty

3. SOME VALUE is

    a. news value plus 20 percent discount coupon for a Happy Meal

    b. the mystique of the KGB as a force for order, now that Russia is trying something else

    c. vigorish on sales of Common Market products

    d. voodoo physics

4. PANICKING is

    a. a capitalist luxury

    b. a technical correction in the financial markets

    c. the God-given opportunity to invent Halcion

    d. a bipolar disorder caused by the similarity of
       the Russian words for "Heads will roll" and
       "Go to the mattresses"

5. THE WHOLE WORLD is

    a. the Beltway and Ann Arbor

    b. a Joan Baez song

    c. a fleeting nightmare during the human soul's
       brief transit from heaven to hell

Is this material churning up our apprehensions or grandiose control fantasies? If so, do not proceed until you have analyzed the feelings by visualizing and naming them in alphabetical order, as per the technique recommended in the official handbook by Maurice Sendak, *Alligators All Around*.

ESSAY QUESTION: Who Will Panic?

Construct a model panic-projection-and-resolution program, being sure to extrapolate from the "glad child" theory and principles laid down by Eleanor Hodgman Porter in *Pollyanna* and *Pollyanna Grows Up* (U.S. Government Printing Office, 1913, 1915).

Then show how your program becomes operational when, on a given tomorrow—gloomy or even rainy in parts of the international community—word leaks out that there might be something amiss in post-Soviet Russia. Impact your outcomes on lots of statistically representative lives, including these prototypes:

Mr. McGregor is a myopic old xenophobe whose idea of a weapon of mass destruction is an iron garden rake; should he scent worldwide panic, he might use it as an excuse to loot his retirement savings, thus incurring a disadvantageous tax bite.

The Red Queen is armored against her own emotional instability by the trappings of monarchy; her strategic capability notwithstanding, her secretary would keep any disturbing information from her, lest she flip out and make life miserable for everybody. Histories of trauma incline the Elephant's Child and Bambi to panic attacks, but the symptomatology suggests that these are triggered by loudspeaker announcements about the ozone layer and the rain forests. Stuart Little has ended up in a forced-labor camp, so he is pretty impervious to bad news.

The Cheese Stands Alone

VERONICA GENG

Will President Clinton bog down in political debts owed to party bosses, heavy-hitter campaign contributors, labor leaders, early supporters, and prominent Democrats who didn't hold grudges against him when they could have—i.e., Governor Mario Cuomo? Not if Clinton makes good use of Michael Dukakis's most creative legacy to political discourse: the cheese tray.

Back in July 1988, the *Daily News* reported, Dukakis met with Cuomo to

> *begin planning for the fall campaign in New York. Cuomo [was] asked whether he felt snubbed because he [had] not been invited to appear on the [convention] platform with Dukakis. . . .*
> *"I was sitting there with him. He offered me cheese. He offered me food. I said hello to his mother. I didn't feel snubbed," Cuomo said.*

Of course not! For no one feels snubbed when cheese is offered. In the Middle Ages, it was traditional for a man to indicate that a wheel of cheddar was en route to the family of a woman he couldn't afford to rebuff; and today there is no more certain sign of eternally dangled promise than a nice hunk of fragrant Bel Paese presented on a Ritz cracker or, even better, held out on the palm of the hand. In politics, as in love—as in all human endeavors where we try to say more than we can say in words or deliver in costly and irrevocable actions—it is to cheese that we turn for the tendering of complex emotions, subtle hints, and just plain reassurance.

Dukakis has never been given full credit for the eloquence with which he spoke the language of cheese. Clinton is said privately to admire him for this skill, and during the 1992 New York primary campaign, when a certain anti-Italian slur hung ominously in the air over the State Capitol, the timely offer of an herbed chèvre gift pack, from Little Rock Fancy Fromages, allegedly turned the situation around. But now Cuomo is just one of a great many allies to whom favor is due, and it remains to be seen how well Clinton will use assorted cheeses to work the ambiguous area that lies between snub and ambassadorship.

The following document was leaked to this magazine by a member of the Clinton transition team who has resigned his position on the board of directors of the National Council of Cheese Lobbyists:

THE HIDDEN LANGUAGE OF CHEESE

Swiss: This is a nightmare.

Stilton: There's a reporter right behind you. Don't make any kind of revealing gesture—just take the cheese.

Port du Salut: My wife will be doing that from now on.

Camembert on Wheat Thin: Any government contract you want, if you can persuade me my conscience is clear about Jesse Jackson.

Gouda: A ceremonial spot on Robert Reich's necktie.

Velveeta on Flatbrød: More figures needed from OMB on the worst-case scenario if we develop the courage to blow you off as a cynical parasite.

Feta on Pita: That was then, and this is now.

Cube of Laughing Cow on Toothpick: Sir (or Madame), does your hypocrisy know no bounds? The spectacle of you and your ilk turns even my stomach. Request denied.

Part-Skim Mozzarella on Saltine: See that man? He's a U.S. marshal, here to arrest you for trying to bribe a federal official.

Provolone: Get your snout out of the public trough!

Triple-Crème on Celery Stick: Boy, if things were only different, we could be somewhere, just the two of us, the banks of a trout stream in the Dordogne, trailing our fingers in the water and talking about books and ideas till the sun goes down, then back to the inn for oysters and white wine and a serious discussion about philosophy and life—but instead you're laboring under the misapprehension that kissing my ass at a fund-raiser bought you a free ride on the back of the American taxpayer, you toadying little weasel.

Schmierkase on Toast Wedge: Maybe by 1994 or 1995 something will shake loose, but I'd feel like a bum making promises I can't keep.

Herbed Chèvre Gift Pack: The Supreme Court.

American: Would you like to say hello to my mother?

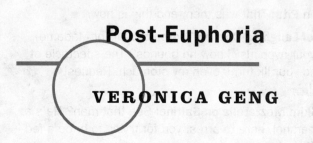

Post-Euphoria

VERONICA GENG

Frankfurt Stock Exchange
Frankfurt Germany

DEAR SIRS:

Specifically speaking, how does a stock exchange work? One would require approximately how many tables and chairs? And then what?

As fledglings, we are excited to be initiating such a body! Having in readiness for our members a fifty-litre samovar, we now await merely your input on final refinements of procedure.

> Gratefully,
> FREE MARKET
> PLANNING COMMISSARIAT

British Humane Society
London, England

LADIES AND GENTLEMEN:

Begging your advisory as per the ensuing hypothetical. Someone on my street, not me, keeps surrealist parasites in his basement as a hobby. Supposing he decided to release them from the holding pen—what would be the safest way? Should he just smash the pen open with a hammer and then run? I heard there is a danger that uninhibited specimens have a difficult transition phase and might form roving packs of killer strays. Is this true, or would they reenter the natural population?

Very truly yours,
CONCERNED SIBERIAN
CITIZEN (RET.)

Editor-in-Chief
Le Monde
Paris, France

ESTEEMED COLLEAGUE:

Our best regards to you and your enchanting wife.

By the way, how do you decide which are the news stories and which are the editorials? Is it by word count or, rather, a collective decision reached by secret ballot? Or perchance you leave this matter in the capable hands of your delightful spouse. In that case, might we consult with her now and then, purely on a professional basis?

With felicitations,
IZVESTIA EDITORIAL BOARD

P.S.: Please forgive the ironic idiocy of the above query if yours is one of the Western press organs which have been taking their instructions from us. Someone told us to forget about all that, so we had to.

Supervisor
Cook County Board of Elections
Cook County, Illinois, U.S.A.

DEAR SIR OR MADAM:

Knowing your reputation far and wide, we were just wondering. What if there occurred some voting machines of a highly democratic technology—for example, allowing multiple choice by means of extra slots and levers? Is there some method, in its sophistication a mystery to us, for insuring that a candidate with more votes does not obtain an unfair advantage over a candidate with not so many votes? There could be a situation where the latter is more deserving, due to family needs or health problems, etc., yet is passed aside by a hasty or whimsical electorate for a candidate they think they "want." Then idealism would cry out on its hands and knees to serve a higher justice. Is there a special device for this?

Also, do you happen to know how to get the ballots out of the machine—smash the whole thing open like a piggy bank, or what?

Sincerely,
SUPREME ELECTION REFORM
CENTRAL COMMITTEE

Mr. Akio Morita,
Chairman
Sony Corporation
Tokyo, Japan

Dear Mr. Morita:

This is not your problem, but in our admiration for your fantastic acumen we hope to presume upon your farseeing wisdom and topnotch business sense.

A woman named Yoko Ono has made us a firm offer of $30,000 in hard currency for eight hundred thousand hectares of state-owned pasture in the northeastern Urals. She asserts managerial skills such that over a five-year period she can transform the area into a profitmaking dairy farm equipped with automated milking system, carriage barn, historically restored rustic stone walls, manor house with large deck, hardwood floors, antique lighting, Tulikivi radiant fireplace, all-electric kitchen, aluminum siding, up-to-the-minute recording studio, and much more, and will then rent it back to us on terms to be mutually deferred.

Naturally we are tempted to gobble this while her enthusiasm is still at fever pitch. But the wife of our deputy agro-industrial minister suggests we ask if you know a hard-nosed tactic to sweeten our end of the deal.

Most respectfully,
Land Development
Inspectorate

Hughes Tool Company
U.S.A.

To the Board of Directors:

No doubt it is something out of the blue, receiving a letter from an unknown woman in Russia. I have selected your company because my husband is a fan of your unique oil-drilling equipment, which he appreciates only by remote lore and word of mouth but aspires someday to purchase for his business here. Having started from a single informal kerosene drum in a shed behind our dacha on the Black Sea, he has created over the years quite a formidable oil-and-gas-pumping endeavor, and now stands in position to operate on a mammoth regional scale.

However, I am concerned that he is the victim of a fairy tale about capitalist management principles. A small cohort of men visiting from your state Utah have attained influence over him. They are causing him to discharge fond employees of loyal longevity, and to sign many papers, and now they have him in a reclusion, lying in bed with long fingernails, watching a videotape of a film, *Ocean's Eleven*. Recently he sent out to me an elaborate pencil memorandum explaining how I should open herring jars in a certain way so germs from my hair cannot tumble in. He said that titans of capital have to protect themselves from poison elements, but I believe this to be a propaganda romance, indoctrinated by the Utah men. Finally, would it be a fact that executive decision-making power is enhanced by hourly injections of the substance "codeine"? This is what they proclaim, although they themselves are fanatically abstemious when it comes to even vodka or tea.

As I am too typical of our national unfamiliarity with these parts of the free enterprise system, I pray that you can inform my perspective before it is already too late and I smash open the attic with a hammer.

DESPERATE

TO WHOM IT MAY CONCERN:

I am free. What should I do?

•• NEWS QUIZ ••

06/2/98 "3D"

Proposed regulations in New York would limit its size to 78 feet long, 40 feet wide, and 70 feet tall. Size of what?

"New Jersey."—Patty Marx

"Miss Shelley Winters."—Susan Vance

"Any single stack of Lawrence Durrell novels at the Strand."—Chris Kelly

"The Sunday *New York Times*."—Andrew Staples

"The line for the ladies' room at Lincoln Center."
—Merrill Markoe

• RANDY'S WRAP UP •

Traditionally, when a world historic figure (or someone who thinks he is) wants to build a monument to his own greatness, he actually builds something: the Pyramids, the Panama Canal, the Chrysler Building, The Brooklyn Bridge, The Fifth Symphony. If the mayor of New York is an egotist, he is a new kind of egotist, leaving us with only less—crime (perhaps), hot dogs, street art, book-sellers, poor folks in college, affordable rental apart-ments, publicly financed parks, library hours, people walking the streets. Possible explanation: He is a mean-spirited little man with no vision. Alternative theory: He's very tidy.

ENORMOUS INFLATABLE ANSWER

Those dimensions limit the size of giant helium balloons in New York City parades. The guidelines were developed after last year's Macy's Thanksgiving Parade when a six-story Cat in the Hat plowed into a lamppost, raining debris onto the crowd below and seriously injuring a thirty-four-year-old woman.

Macy's has voluntarily withdrawn five large balloons, including the lovable yet deadly Dr. Seuss character.

CRIME & PUNISHMENT EXTRA: BASEBALL BRAWL VS. FIREMEN'S BRAWL

Last week offered two bench-clearing brawls in a single game between the Anaheim Angels and the Kansas City Royals, plus a drunken brawl between New York City firemen and other New York City firemen in the Bryant Park Cafe. A comparison.

The Spark
Ball Players: 4 beanballs
Firemen: long-standing station house rivalries

Number Involved
Ball Players: both teams
Firemen: 50–100

Duration
Ball Players: a few minutes
Firemen: six hours

Public Urination
Ball Players: no
Firemen: yes

Exposed Selves
Ball Players: no
Firemen: several

Teeth Knocked Out
Ball Players: none
Firemen: several

Old Lady Bullied and Humiliated
Ball Players: no
Firemen: yes

Staff and Patrons Terrorized
Ball Players: no
Firemen: yes

Initial Penalties
Ball Players: 12 ejections
Firemen: no arrests

Subsequent Penalties
Ball Players: most suspensions in 25 years
Firemen: no arrests

Statement by Authorities
American League Commissioner: stern warning that "Managers are expected to be strong leaders." Fire Commissioner: unconvincing pledge to conduct "aggressive comprehensive" investigation

Innocence: the mock-screams of school children. Cynicism: giving before the beggar starts his spiel. Existentialism: a walk without your wallet.—M.O'D.

Why Are Kids So Dumb?

A Defense

CHRIS HARRIS

Let us first extinguish any doubts: We're smarter than they are. Not only are we smarter now, but we were smarter as children too. Relative test scores? Don't bother; they can't even wear their baseball caps the right way. Teenagers have for years stood at the vanguard in the dumbing down of America, and this era's crop are no exception.

And now, yet another global survey has dumped our nation's progeny near the bottom of the educational trough. Children in countries we've never even heard of, like "Denmark" and "New Zealand," are beating us in geography. Undernourished waifs three countries from the nearest web connection are proving more adept in the sciences. And should any young. Americans ever acquire the math skills needed to *understand* the global survey, they would find their math skills sorely lacking.

Why? Theories proliferate, including one that suggests those aforementioned caps squeeze their brains until they literally pop and slip right out of the bottoms of their baggy pants. But perhaps—have a seat, please—perhaps things aren't nearly as bad as they seem. And perhaps, lest things *become* as bad as they seem, we must consider some radical changes in educational theory. After an illuminating reevaluation of our children's skills, a series of remedial actions are herein proffered, upon which, if we are to check any trend toward density, we must act immediately.

History

The reason today's children know less history than previous generations is painfully evident: There's *more* of it. As one youth explained, "[older Americans] didn't have to learn about things like that World War and colonies and the Emaciation [sic] Procla-thing and all that because they *lived* through it." To keep the workload fair, a cut-off mark should be chosen—perhaps 1698—which moves with the current year and before which no history is taught. After all, history repeats itself anyway—there's no point in being redundant.

Those who argue that students in other countries have encountered no such difficulty are guilty of gross simplification. Certainly, Swedes know their nation's history better than our students know theirs, but what history does Sweden *have*? It gets cold; it gets less cold. It gets cold; it gets less cold. It gets cold again; you commit suicide. Of course they have a better grasp.

Geography

Balkans, Baltics, Baltimore—youth today hardly know the difference. But the map will be redrawn many times over—remember, even the continents shift—before they're in charge. One can argue that students' ignorance in this area is in fact *more* insightful than our own "knowledge" of arbitrary details like what country we live in, for it accurately reflects the uncertainty with which international borders are placed in these ever-changing times.

English

The reputation of young people's vocabulary has been unfairly tarnished by an ageist, myopic definition of what constitutes *slang*. In years past, long, difficult words such as "extenuate" and "pugnacious" were the "hip lingo" of the times; these words now sound hopelessly dated, or "out." Today, really really short words (such as "cool" and "rad") are the speech pattern of choice. We can't reasonably expect them to use "lugubrious" or "obfuscate" any more than they do "groovy."

The size of youth's vocabulary has also been criticized, proving that any statistic can fall victim to a negative spin. The plain fact is that kids today do not have a *smaller* vocabulary, they have a *more efficient* vocabulary. Over 240 words, for example, ranging from "stylish" to "titillating," can now be expressed with the omni-word "phat."

Besides, English and its grammatical components will be rendered obsolete by the year 2010 anyway, at which point all communication will have been distilled into chat room abbreviations. A typical conversation:

webdemon: hi

netfudge:　wr　("wr" will stand for witty remark)

webdemon: LOL

netfudge:　?　("?" will stand for any question)

webdemon: xxx　("xxx" will stand for a series of sexual comments)

netfudge:　bye

webdemon: bye

Mathematics

The great irony of society is that the more and more powerful machines we create to do math for us, the more and more some people insist that math is essential for us to learn. Bull puckey! We have calculators, computers, ATMs, and CPAs: Math has never been *less* important to learn in the entire history of civilization. Kudos to the younger generation for recognizing this.

Moving Forward

And yet, one is still left with the nagging feeling that today's youth are a bunch of meandering dullwits. Again, we must act immediately to confront the greater problems of our current educational system; at least three additional improvements warrant our prompt consideration:

To illustrate one flaw, let us employ a simple analogy. Think of teenagers as a diverse infestation of roaches in a home, and education a highly toxic poison. Our current high schools, then, are a scattering of storebought traps: Occasionally a roach wanders in and picks up some chemical toxins, but many do not eat enough, and some stay away entirely. Much more effective would be the hiring of an exterminator, who cleverly takes the *poison* to the *roaches.* It follows that we should not simply wait for students to accidentally stumble into schools, but instead douse them with education wherever they already are. In newly designed *mall schools,* for example, learning will be subversively incorporated into the everyday activities of "hanging out"—math at the cash registers, social studies in the food court, and foreign languages at Au Bon Pain.

Second, we must emphasize the positive, somehow take better advantage of the areas in which this generation excels, for it does excel at many things:

- Skateboard tricks
- Gunning down classmates
- Singing whiny pop songs

. . . Or, as an alternative, we can decide to *not* take advantage of these areas.

Third, and with only the slightest air of defeat, we must remember that youth have always been—well—kind of dumb. Romeo and Juliet thought that love was the greatest emotion. Ha! A young Michael Jackson sang that "people make the world go 'round." Ha! Ha! And in the sixties, students actually believed that life would be better without the massive economic might of the military-industrial machine. Ha ha! Ha! Time, we may note with relief, corrects this type of blatant naiveté on its own, crushing and conforming these puerile ideas of youth into our known and established—and *right*—societal standards.

With this in mind, then, perhaps our best course of action in addressing the stupidity of the young is *not* to act immediately at all, but instead to *lean back and do nothing*. Don't help them, don't encourage them, and please don't give them any hints. Eventually the real world—as it did with us—will force smartness upon our children, just in time for them to grab hold the reins of the world and kick us screaming off the carriage.

Fourth, and failing all else, we can always just turn off the television.

Clarifications?

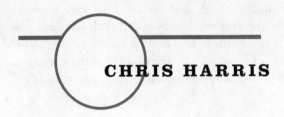

CHRIS HARRIS

Is It a Person, or a Pasta Dish?

	Person	Pasta Dish
Manicotti		✓
Righetti	✓	
Mussolini	✓	
Fettucine		✓
Al Fredo		✓
Al Pacino	✓	
Fonzarelli	✓	
Cannelloni		✓
Buttafuoco	✓	

Is It a Detergent, or a Major League Soccer Team?

	Detergent	MLS Team
Fab	✓	
Burn		✓
Wiz		✓
Tide	✓	
Dash	✓	

	Detergent	MLS Team
Clash		✓
All	✓	
Wisk	✓	
Galaxy		✓
Era	✓	

Is It a Third-World Country, or a Judd?

	Third-World Country	Judd
Tanzania	✓	
Wynonna		✓
Botswana	✓	
Rwanda	✓	
Naomi		✓
Argentina	✓	
Christina		✓
Malaysia	✓	
Ashley		✓

Did Jesus Say That, or Billy Joel?

	Jesus	Billy Joel
"Don't forget your second wind."		✓
"Only the good die young."		✓
"Drink it, all of you, for this is my blood."	✓	
"Blessed are the meek."	✓	
"Judge not, and you will not be judged."	✓	
"It's still rock 'n' roll to me."		✓
"I am the light of the world."	✓	
"I am the Entertainer."		✓
"I came to cast fire upon the earth."	✓	
"We didn't start the fire."		✓

	Jesus	Billy Joel
"Begone—Satan!"	✓	
"Even you cannot avoid—Pressure!"		✓
"Who touched me? Someone touched me."	✓	
"It's all about soul."	✓	✓

Is It a Death Row Rapper, or a Hostess Snack Treat?

	Death Row Rapper	Hostess Snack Treat
Nigga Daz	✓	
Thug Life	✓	
Suzy Q		✓
Tupac	✓	
Fruit Pie		✓
Tasty Cake		✓
Ice Cube	✓	
Sno Ball		✓
Doggy Dogg	✓	
Ho Ho		✓

Is It a Kevin Johnson Injury, or a Historical Midwest Destination?

	Kevin Johnson Injury	Historical Midwest Destination
Sprained Ankle	✓	
Pulled Groin	✓	
Broken Arrow		✓
Sore Hamstring	✓	
White Butte		✓
Abdominal Hernia	✓	
Upper Peninsula		✓

	Kevin Johnson Injury	Historical Midwest Destination
Lower Leg Contusion	✓	
Chicken Pox	✓	
Beaver Shoals		✓
Aggravated Calf	✓	
Fallen Timbers		✓
Woundod Knee	✓	✓

Is It an Earnest Female Singer-Songwriter, or a Repulsive Skin Disease?

	Earnest Female Singer-Songwriter	Repulsive Skin Disease
Alanis	✓	
Psoriasis		✓
Ani	✓	
Acne		✓
Tori	✓	
Eczema		✓
Erykah	✓	
Fiona	✓	
Melanoma		✓
Impetigo		✓
Joan	✓	

Is It a Supermodel, or a Mideast Nation?

	Supermodel	Mideast Nation
Jordan		✓
Naomi	✓	
Oman		✓
Iman	✓	
Yemen		✓
Yasmin	✓	

	Supermodel	Mideast Nation
Kate	✓	
Kuwait		✓
Claudia	✓	
Syria		✓
United Arab Emirates		✓

What We Talk About When We Talk About Little Green Men

CHRIS HARRIS

Now that their existence is—are we agreed?—no longer in question, we may redirect our efforts toward the finer details of their presence. Semantic issues must at some point be addressed ("We have positively identified that as a U.F.O" is not quite . . . right), but for the moment let us consider a more pressing concern: We know what they look like. We know what they drive. What, from these observations, can we deduce about our otherworldly visitors? As we piece the puzzle together, the developing image is not flattering.

First, God help them, they are unabashedly pro-American. Few countries seem as hospitable to spacecraft sightings and abductions as the good ol' U.S. of A. (Aliens also prefer the countryside and seem to love corn, facts that are already well documented.) And while they must be far advanced technologically, some narrow but deep pockets of ignorance apparently remain. For example, if their object is stealth, why must they employ colored, blinking lights on the outside of their spacecraft? Is it alien Christmastime? And why, for that matter, a saucer shape? Not only aerodynamically suspect, it also must give our aliens no shortage of grief trying to remember which is the front, back, or side of their craft. Worse yet, these saucers are often seen spinning rapidly, making our friends not only architecturally inferior but incredibly dizzy as well. We can only conclude that our alien visitors may in fact be much *less* technologically advanced than ourselves.

Physically, we can readily determine that the aliens are in relatively poor health. They possess inefficient optical nerves (hence the large, Ray-Ban eyes), underdeveloped remaining senses (note their small mouths and nearly invisible nose and ears), and, judging by their fragile bodies and spindly extremities, likely suffer from chronic calcium deficiency. One would not be surprised to hear of them invading drugstores in search of Centrum and similar multivitamins.

More disturbingly, they are incorrigible perverts. The typical abductee is without fail probed, prodded, and forced (forced!) to have sex with another abductee, who is often her teenage boyfriend with whom she had never before had sex but this explains her pregnancy so please don't get angry, Mom. *Real* scientists retain their subjects for a variety of experiments, including cancer treatments, genetic testing, and sociological insight. Not these alien "scientists." Sex, sex, sex. That's it. Even worse, whatever "knockout pill" they're using isn't doing nearly the trick it should in the memory-suppression department. As long as they're swinging by the pharmacy, perhaps they can pick up a little something stronger.

They like being naked, or at least no one has tracked any changing alien fashions, and they are remarkably humanoid in form considering they represent an entirely separate evolutionary tree; one might even say, all possible efforts at enslavement of the human race aside, that they look "cute."

Our mysterious visitors, then—sickly, perverted, overpatriotic nudists with a fifties-era grasp of technology—represent no immediate threat to our planet, little opportunity for enlightened exchange of ideas, and negligible value at cocktail parties. However, with some degree of effort and obedience school, they may eventually make excellent pets. The Roswell breed in particular shows great promise; we must ask the government to look into the matter.

Design Intervention
Solving the World's
Problems with Style

CHRIS HARRIS

Quit kidding yourself: Looks are everything. Super-models who can't act, sing or paint get paid fortunes for their acting, singing and painting. Companies blow thousands testing product names like "Olestra." We haven't had a bald President for thirty-five years. "And yet . . . " you murmur. Ah, no doubt you're thinking the same thing anyone would: "And yet . . . national borders pay no attention to image at all!"

So very true. Jagged boundaries, confusing shapes, and unfortunate names like "Greenland" pepper the globe. If nations were people—imagine Canada as your jolly drinking buddy, or Iran and Iraq as two bratty kids who should be kept away from sugar products—they'd be incorrigible slobs. Since image is so important to us, this blatant lack of regard for image—rather than poverty, war, oppression, etc.—must be the true source of much of the world's current malaise.

And why not? World maps are so common in this age, the sim-ple act of constantly viewing these monstrosities—for example, some intestine-shaped country like Panama, or the massive sper-matozoa we call Norway—has likely caused untold devastation worldwide. Consider the following scenario: *Little Johnny—or*

Johann, or Omar, or Chou—sits in geography class, trying to memorize the countries. He looks at South America. Does Chile resemble a chile? No, it resembles a string bean. Frustrated, the child drops out of school and joins a neo-fascist terrorist organization. A bit simplistic, perhaps but be certain that the extent of damage our current system has inflicted cannot be overdramatized.

This must change. It's time to retire our politicians and economists and militarists and diplomats from the international arena and, knowing that they could hardly be less successful, let *graphic designers* try their hand at world politics.

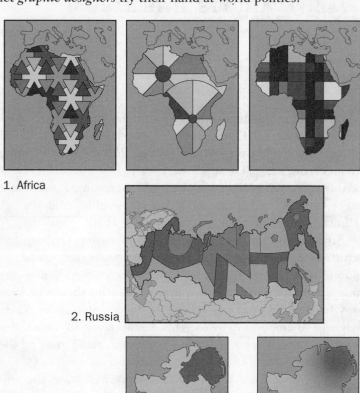

1. Africa

2. Russia

3. Ireland

Coincidentally, I happen to be a graphic designer. For the past six months I have labored over the international map, finding that even the most basic application of design theory to our nations' borders can markedly improve the global situation. Following I outline a three-phase plan to remodel the world.

PHASE I: CURRENT DISPUTES

First, a global makeover can provide immediate, effective and—yes!—pleasing-to-the-eye solutions to most of the world's current major conflicts. Consider the following examples:

Israel: The Homely Homeland

From an artist's perspective, the biggest problem in the Mideast is not the continued radicalism of extremists, or the status of Jerusalem, but the fact that Israel looks like a big, ugly fishhook. Hell, this was a *planned country,* and I've seen Rorschach tests with better layouts. However, if one "filled in" that ugly gap—with, oh, let's say, the West Bank—and likewise reattached that missing Gaza Strip, then Israel might look alluring, even sexy. On the contrary, this nation's shapely neck benefits not at all from the protruding "Goiter Heights," let it fall to Syria.

One need not have watched many late-night infomercials to understand the power of self-esteem. When residents—Jews and Palestinians alike—discover that their ugly duckling region has been transformed into Cinderella, the resulting *détente* will be nothing short of dramatic.

Introducing the New World Order

1. Africa looks just mah-velous with a slight reorganization of its countries into the stylish patterns of today and yesteryear. Note that on color maps, care should always be taken to make Cameroon an actual shade of maroon. 2. Mother Russia could solve its mounting budget deficit problems by redefining territory boundaries to spell out product names or corporate slogans, in this case "Junior Mints." 3. With the application of a few beauty tips, Ireland moves from terroristic to terrr-iffic!

Northern Ireland: Peace, Gradually

Now, let us turn our aesthetic eye to Ireland—a quaint island nation, charming and rustic and backwoodsy and—ack!—Great Britain drips into its northeast corner! This is blatant sloppiness, reminiscent of a preschooler's coloring outside the lines.

But we cannot simply cede the whole area to Ireland; distinct boundaries cause trouble in areas of mixed loyalty—not to mention being harsh on the eye. Fortunately, we have another option: the gradient fill. Starting with 100 percent United Kingdom territory in the northeast corner, gradually blend in Irish sovereignty as one moves out radially so that Belfast is two-thirds the former and a third the latter, and one reaches full Irish rule somewhere around Monaghan. The soft, gentle touch of fuzzy borders may also provide a solution to the ongoing Kashmir debate between India and Pakistan.

The Country Formerly Known as Yugoslavia

No doubt the greatest challenge to the power of the paintbrush lies in the former expanse of Yugoslavia. Death, discord and a general lack of manners persist across this region. Old-style politics and line-drawing have succeeded only in reaching a fragile compromise which is unsatisfactory for everyone. Equally horrifying, Croatia's borders stretch like a geriatric Pac-Man around a decomposed Bosnia-Herzegovina.

To most, the situation seems hopeless. But the fashion conscious eye recognizes just what this area needs: *polka dots*. Picture, against different background fills—Croatian in the Northwest, Bosnian Serb in the East, and so forth—lively circles of the other ethnicities' countries standing out cheerfully. Not only does each individual region (with some concession to a consistent pattern) get the nationality of its choice, but a fun, lighthearted feel is reinstilled across an area in desperate need of frivolity. Imagine how quickly tourism will pull these countries back to prosperity when families look at a world map and see the "happy clown countries" beckoning to them from afar.

PHASE II: OTHER COUNTRIES

Once these pressing crises are dealt with, the world can turn to correcting a number of geographic eyesores that undermine the entire globe's presentation.

For example, disconnected, countries give the world a hurried, slapdash feel, like a magazine that's poorly laid out. To solve this, eliminate that broken-off wedge of Russia near Poland. Likewise for the similar part of Oman. And while we're at it, attach that Upper Peninsula to Wisconsin.

Applying this guideline, one might fear the loss of Alaska to our northern neighbor. But those who would worry about a new, resurgent Canada, fear not: Our primary goal, remember, is a beautiful world map. Canada, for reasons unclear, is always *pink* on world maps. Pink is a horrendous color. Alaska can never become part of Canada simply because it will increase that country's territory, and hence the overall pinkness of the globe. Better instead to grant Alaska full independence.

And maybe Quebec, just to be safe.

Going . . . Going . . . Ghana

One hundred and seventy-eight countries? Busy, busy, busy! One major task will be to clean out all the "dust bunny countries": those redundant, cramped, and miniscule entities which serve no aesthetic purpose. To start, let's scrap Portugal entirely. And imagine how little Haiti will trouble us, once it's part of the new, improved Dominican Republic.

Malaysia, Swaziland, and Papua New Guinea will likewise no longer trouble geography students. You can say "later" to Liechtenstein, so long Singapore, and bye-bye Bangladesh. Does France stick too far into the Atlantic? Then perform a Brest reduction. Chop off the ends of Cuba so it looks more like a cigar. Give Kyrgyzstan some more shape, or at least some more vowels. Shake, shake, shake out Djibouti. Center Lesotho within South Africa. And—sorry, George—let Saddam have Kuwait.

PHASE III: MACRO-REENGINEERING

In the final phase I recommend totally renovating at least three of the world's larger areas. In Africa, we have a golden opportunity to once and for all throw out those antiquated, arbitrary colonial divisions with no respect for tribal boundaries, and replace them with a whole new set of arbitrary divisions with no respect for tribal boundaries. I believe a floral pattern of nations may suit this continent best, or perhaps a large paisley.

The other areas are Canada and Russia, two countries that could use some serious time on the StairMaster. I propose—contingent on their approval—their complete dismantlement, replacing them with a more dynamic montage. Imagine, in place of the former Soviet empire, a 50-nation depiction of Picasso's "Guernica," stretching from Moscow to the Bering Sea. What a moving testimony this would be to the power of art!

Afterwards, only an occasional tweak here and there, or minor changes to fit the latest styles, would be necessary.

This global reworking may initially cause some concern, particularly in those areas where such quaint ideas as patriotism and self-determination still prevail over a sense of style. But the entire process can be accomplished smoothly and quickly as long as a good attitude and a touch of humor are maintained throughout. For example, what if Turkey really *was* shaped like a turkey? Or, with minimal adjustments, we redrew Germany into a beer mug? One mustn't forget that when drawing international borders, the key word should be *fun*.

In conclusion, I truly believe that these ideas represent nothing less than the world's greatest hope for solving its most difficult problems. Through their application, we will solve most territorial disputes, end war, increase happiness, support the arts, and probably solve the healthcare crisis, although we're still working on those numbers.

Once its programs are in place, the United States of America Minus Alaska can then turn to solving some of its domestic problems in the same way. Our most glaring problem ("Hey, Rhode Island isn't an island at all!") can be quickly solved by switching it with Hawaii. Continuing on this glorious track, our descendants can then tackle the big questions, like: Is there any way to reattach that ungainly Baja strip? Or clean up Micronesia? Or does the ocean have to be blue—why not a deep burgundy? And why, for that matter, a sphere?

Short-term memory: six new names at dinner. Long-term memory: paying for the shared cab yourself. Amnesia: last year's guests gathered again.—M.O'D.

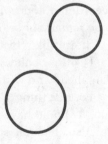

Too Late to Become
a Gondolier?

PAUL HELLMAN

I read that Coca-Cola CEO Doug Ivester set the goal of becoming head of Coke ten years before it happened. According to *Fortune,* he even set a target date that turned out to be remarkably close.

Stories like this always make me feel worse.

I will probably never become the CEO of Coke. Even if I plan ahead and write it on my ten-year goal list: COKE!!!

For one thing, I don't have a ten-year goal list. This is something I should have thought about ten years ago.

Also, I'm not sure I want to become CEO of Coke. Just because I respect Coke as a product and a company, where is it written that I have to be the CEO? Certainly not on my list. If I write this down at all, it's going to have to be sort of tentative: COKE???

Maybe, as a first step, I should forget about my ten-year goal list, and put it on my shopping list: Coke.

Let's face it: Some of us are drifting in our career. (And, I suspect, also in our boats. I'm not positive about this since I don't own a boat—possibly because of drifting in my career.)

Back to our career. Maybe we fell into something a while back, and now we're still doing it, despite our ambition.

This is scary. Not the drifting part. That's relaxing. It's the ambition part.

The ambition part and the drifting part don't always get along.

Don't assume you can just drift aimlessly forever. Eventually, you need a plan. For how to drift aimlessly forever. Otherwise, before you know it, ambition will assert itself, and you'll find your self doing something silly, such as updating your resumé, and shopping for boats.

It's good to have balance. There's nothing wrong with updating your resumé. Nor with ambition. There's also nothing wrong with drifting. (In a career. In a boat, it's nauseating.)

Here's a short list of balanced tactics:

Ambition Tactics	Drift Tactics
Network	Watch network TV
Try new things	Watch cable TV
Seek visibility	Wear scanty clothing
Take a risk	Wear no clothing
Publish articles in trade magazines	Trade magazines

But maybe it's time to *change* careers. The important thing here is to consider lots of alternatives, as opposed to actually doing any of them. For example:

President of Toyota! The last time Toyota selected a new president, I fantasized—that could have been me. We're all capable of doing more than we think.

The current president, according to *The Wall Street Journal*, is the first one not to be a member of the Toyoda family. Interesting. I too am not a member of the Toyoda family.

Also, he is extremely thrifty. He turns off the lights during lunch (so do I, unless I'm in a restaurant), and has memoed employees about using less toilet paper. (If that's what it takes to be president, I could do it!)

I'd like to ask Toyota why I wasn't considered. "Well, let's see," they'd say. "You're not Japanese, you have no automotive experience, and, frankly, you don't drive well."

It's always some flimsy excuse.

Cashier! This is one of the occupations with the largest growth, according to the Bureau of Labor Statistics.

These forecasts always seem whimsical. How do we know the Bureau of Labor Statistics isn't making the whole thing up?

Theory: Someone at the Bureau of Labor Statistics got *very* aggravated one day after spending an inordinate amount of time at the check-out line. "If only we had more cashiers," he thought.

If I worked at the Bureau of Labor Statistics, here are the growth jobs I'd be forecasting:

- Babysitters, especially ones who are available school nights.
- Car mechanics who don't overcharge or use words you don't understand.
- Handymen who actually show up at your house.

Gondolier! "Venice offers training courses for gondoliers, complete with exams and a three-year apprenticeship," reports *The Wall Street Journal*.

This sort of appeals to me. When I tell people I'm a consultant, they often look suspicious, as if it's a bogus job. Being a gondolier sounds more believable.

Also, there's a boat.

But mostly it's about options. I don't want to become a gondolier. I just want to fantasize that I could.

STRANGER: So, what do you do?
ME: I'm a management consultant, but I'm thinking of dropping everything, moving to Italy, and becoming a gondolier.

STRANGER: Is that your dream?
ME: Not really.

Anyway, it's probably too late. At some point you have to get realistic: You're never going to be a gondolier. It's just too much rowing.

Me and My Delusions

PAUL HELLMAN

I have this recurrent dream where I'm an important leader. Sometimes I'm a Fortune 500 CEO, sometimes a big-city mayor, sometimes a highly respected chimpanzee. In the dream, all the employees, citizens, monkeys adore me and happily give me their labor, votes and bananas.

I told this dream to a friend who is a therapist. He said he wasn't impressed. What do you mean you're not impressed? The whole point of the dream is that everything I do is impressive. No, he said, your fantasy is nothing out of the ordinary. Humans have a need to feel special. That's why your fantasy is so commonplace.

It's good to feel special. I remember when my daughter was in preschool. Each week her class selected a VIP who got a lot of extra attention, including wearing a paper crown (I think this was right around the time my CEO/monkey fantasy started). And all the other kids said what they appreciated about her, such as, in my daughter's case, that she played nice, shared toys and rarely bit anyone.

On the other hand, sometimes feeling special can cause

problems, such as when the universe doesn't agree with how important you think you are. Take last week . . .

I was on a business trip to a company in New Jersey. My client had arranged for a limo to meet me when I arrived at Newark Airport at 6 P.M. Although this was an ordinary limo, I still felt special. I love being met at the airport, even by a complete stranger. There they are, holding a sign with your name on it—it's like they're out there campaigning for you.

Also, the limo saved me from renting a car, which is always a bad experience. I usually waive most of the insurance and then worry that the rental-car agent will put a hex on my car. Not that they need to. I'm the kind of driver who needs maximum, industrial-strength coverage, the kind you'd sell to a legally blind cow.

The last time I rented a car I almost went out the wrong exit. THIS IS NOT AN EXIT, YOU MORON, the sign implied. It was the booby trap exit, with silver spikes protruding from the pavement, so that if you even thought about going out this exit, all four of your tires would immediately be punctured. This was the rental-car company's way of saying: "Ha, ha, we told you to buy that extra coverage."

So the limo thing was good. But the plane was an hour late, and when I arrived at the gate, no one was waiting for me, although there were a half-dozen drivers holding signs for other passengers. If this had been a campaign, the passenger Peter Hauser would have won hands down. His sign was large and bold. Peter Hauser was definitely going places. Peter Hauser was definitely leaving Newark Airport.

While I waited, I had the usual internal debate between the reasonable side of me ("I'm sure the driver will be here any minute now"), and the lunatic side ("WHERE IS HE ALREADY?").

Finally, my driver showed up with a small, pathetic sign. It didn't even have my name on it, just the client's name. I was grateful Peter Hauser wasn't there to see it.

It was now 7:30 P.M. I was tired, hungry and cranky. I

walked over to the driver and looked at my watch, the nonverbal way of saying, "You're late." Then he looked at his watch, the nonverbal way of responding, "Who cares?"

But then things got better. When I arrived at the hotel, it was having its weekly "customer-appreciation night." I started to feel special again. Lucky it was Wednesday! What happened on the other nights, the nights when there wasn't customer appreciation? Tuesday: "customer-loathing night." Get out of our sight, customers. You disgust us.

But this was Wednesday, and the hotel had put out free soda, chicken wings and meatballs—not the healthiest buffet. It wasn't clear whether the hotel was trying to appreciate us or kill us.

I started to feel underappreciated, mostly because they called it customer appreciation. If they had just put out some food, it would have been pleasant. But mixing customer appreciation with meatballs sent a weak message: "We appreciate you customers, but not that much."

I asked for a couple of bottles of spring water, and the hotel waiter said he'd be delighted to get them. He returned a few minutes later with two bottles, and a bill for $10.

"I thought this was complimentary," I said. He gave me a funny look, as if to say, "Complimentary? Don't flatter yourself."

So what I realized last week is that I'd be a terrible CEO. I already expect too much. As CEO, I'd be intoxicated by my own importance. The whole time I'd be thinking: I'm the CEO, somebody slap me.

Please don't mention this to the monkeys.

Eating the Desk

PAUL HELLMAN

The other day I was at a party where people talked about their hectic lives. One woman—let's call her Marilyn, because that's her name—complained that it took her all of Saturday morning to catch up on e-mail. "Everyone I know," she said, "routinely works at least part of the weekend." She looked at me. "You're busy, aren't you?"

It sounded like an accusation. I nodded my head quickly, as if to signal with this rapid movement that I was *incredibly* busy, so busy that I could barely keep my head still.

But actually, I hardly ever work on weekends. Occasionally, I take a three-day weekend. For example, I took this past Presidents' Day off, even though I am not, technically, a president.

Working hard has become a status symbol. It used to be that leisure time was a status symbol; now there's something wrong if you have too much leisure. You need to work yourself into the ground before you can really be at peace.

What exactly is "hard work"?

I imagine something *physical,* such as forging steel. Or forging anything. Forging art or coins can't be easy, and even something as straightforward as "forging ahead" is no picnic.

But most of us don't forge. I wish I forged, for the main reason that I'd enjoy saying I forged if someone asked about my job:

"It's not easy being a forger," I'd explain. "Heat it and beat it; that's our motto." Then I'd run out of things to say. "Excuse me, but I need to go and stand near a furnace for a while."

If you don't forge, or do manual work that's obviously "hard," then you end up talking about long hours. Hard work = long hours.

"I work seventy hours a week," someone boasted at the party. "That doesn't even count the time I spend at home."

Just once, I'd like to hear something different:

"I sleep seventy hours a week. That doesn't even count the time I spend at the office."

The day after the party, I had to fly from Boston to New York on business. I intended to catch the 8 P.M. shuttle, but arrived at the airport surprisingly early. It was only 6:45 when I parked the car, so I decided to make a run for the 7 P.M. flight. I sprinted to the gate. The agent had just locked the gateway door and was walking away. Then he saw me, checked his watch and reopened the door.

"Got a runner coming!" he yelled to a flight attendant at the other end of the passageway.

I ran down the passageway. The flight attendant gave me one of those looks. "If it weren't for people like you," he probably was thinking, "the transportation industry would be *a lot* more pleasant."

I didn't care. I had just gotten away with something extraordinary—stealing time. Maybe this was what it felt like to forge.

Then we sat on the runway for two hours.

My point, of course, is that the next time you're in a situation like this, you should definitely drive.

You can never really gain time. On the other hand, you can never really lose it either. The only time is present tense; only most of the time we're too tense to be present.

In a way, time is a lot like the jar of relish that's buried somewhere in my refrigerator. It seems like it's always been there, and always will be. Which, from a philosophical point of view, is really disgusting.

But it's good to have a sense of perspective. Who cares about a missing jar of relish? Why get upset about a thing like this? I feel better already.

WHERE'S THE RELISH!

To gain perspective, many time management gurus recommend the mental exercise in which you fast-forward to your funeral and think about what you want people to say.

(About me: "He was always searching for something. Often it was relish. Sometimes mustard or salsa. Why couldn't he organize his condiments?")

This reminds me of a friend's dream: *I'm buried under a pile of work and can't get away from my desk, even for lunch. But there's nothing to eat, so I start nibbling on one of the drawers. It's surprisingly tasty, with a crunchy, nutty flavor. But something's missing. If only I had some peanut butter to spread on this.*

The meaning of this dream is clear to anyone with a rudimentary understanding of Freudian symbolism. If you're eating your desk, *obviously* something's missing. And it's not peanut butter—any idiot knows that. It's relish.

Into the Giga Jungle

PAUL HELLMAN

Maybe you put off buying a computer until after the holidays, expecting a big price drop. That's smart. Not the price drop part—computer prices are always falling; it's some kind of law—but the procrastination part. When it comes to computers, you can never really procrastinate too long.

We, on the other hand, bought one before the holidays, which was not smart. Once we entered the computer store, we got confused. We found out that we're a lot like our old computer: reliable but slow-witted.

The old computer sits alone in the basement now. It's nearly five years old. That's human years. A computer year is less than a minute, so by the time you get one home and out of the box, it's more than 100 years old. That's why the store won't take it back, unless you also return the box and all the packing materials. Never underestimate the resale value of packing materials.

As you can see, we learned a lot. Now we can help you take what could be a confusing shopping experience and make it absolutely unintelligible.

I. RAM

Blah, blah, blah. The first principle—don't be overly impressed by superficial details like RAM (the computer's memory). JUST BECAUSE RAM IS CAPITALIZED IS NO REASON TO BE IMPRESSED.

"RAM is RAM." That's what one salesman told us when we asked about the difference between EDO RAM, which was in the old computers, on sale just a few minutes ago, and SDRAM, which is in the new ones. We took comfort knowing that RAM is RAM and looked forward to offering this explanation to others. There are lots of times when we have no idea what to say. Such as at funerals:

"Why did he have to die so young?"

"Well, RAM is RAM."

It sounded like a philosophy of life.

But it turned out to be wrong. Later, someone explained the main difference between the two types of RAM, using the kind of technical language we prefer: "SDRAM is better."

So that's what we bought. We'll believe anything. We're just grateful that no one said RAM is ham. Otherwise, we might have tried to buy a computer at the deli.

No matter how much RAM you get, it'll never be enough. Luckily, our new computer can expand to more than 300 MB of RAM, an enormous amount of power. That'll prove useful if we ever want to play a sophisticated computer game with our kids, like launching them into outer space.

II. Gigs

More numbers. Gigs tell you how much room you have in your hard drive.

Gigs are like bedrooms—a one-gig computer is like a one-bedroom house. Our old computer was like living in a high school locker.

This time, we bought a four-gig computer, and then discovered that it came pre-loaded with a gig of software. That's like buying a four-bedroom house and then finding other people living in one of the bedrooms. "They came pre-installed," the real estate agent might explain.

So we took back the four-gig computer and exchanged it, which was extremely gratifying—not so much the exchanging part as the taking it back part.

III. Level 2 Cache

We have no idea what Level 2 cache is. No one does. That's why you should ask a lot of questions about it—just to let them know they can't mess with you.

Whatever it is, it sounds good. We wish they would put it in more products. Why not low-fat milk, enriched with Level 2 cache? We'd buy it, and we'd gladly pay extra.

Most computers are reputed to have 512KB of Level 2 cache. We like the 12 part; it's a nice detail. Almost makes the whole thing believable.

Our old computer didn't have any. We can admit this now. The truth is, we never really noticed. But sometimes late at night, we felt a sense of lack.

We used to fantasize about being at the high school reunion. No one was talking about careers or relationships. They were talking computers. As we walked by, they ignored us. "No Level 2 cache," they whispered, "absolutely none."

IV. Help

Technical support is a must. Our new computer came with both presale and post-sale support. This is good. After we had purchased the first new computer, but before we had exchanged it, we wanted help comparing the two models. But whom to call? We were post-sale for one computer, pre-sale for the other. Obviously, we were a terrific candidate for help.

Post-sale sounded annoyed. "They're really two entirely different machines," they said, as if we were comparing a computer against a yogurt maker.

Pre-sale was more helpful. "The 4200 is really cute," they said.

We hadn't even considered cuteness. And pre-sale was right, the 4200 was extremely cute—it had an adorable look the fax machine could never pull off.

Then pre-sale mentioned that the 4200 had a loose CD-ROM cable. "Don't freak out, every computer has its quirks. If you buy it, we'll talk you through it."

That's what sold us. Knowing about the 4200's quirks made it seem more human. It was vulnerable, like us. Buying a computer taught us about vulnerability. We wouldn't have gone through this if we didn't have a loose CD-ROM cable somewhere.

•• NEWS QUIZ ••

5/4/98 "FUTURE NEWS: 'CORRECTIONS'"

"A picture caption on Sunday with an article about efforts to eradicate opium in Myanmar misidentified an armed man in a poppy field. He was a Burmese soldier sent to guard the field after it was discovered, not a militiaman from the Wa hill people."

Above, an actual item from the *New York Times* Corrections column. You are invited to submit a Correction likely to run over the next few weeks.

"An article in the Religion column Saturday stated that Episcopalians eat their young. It is the sea turtle who eats its young."—Patty Marx

"Because of an editing error, new wonder drug Viagra was not mentioned in any part of the Friday edition. The *Times* regrets the error."

—Beth Sherman

"In an October 1996 editorial, we endorsed the reelection of President Clinton. We should have said 'Vote for Bob Dole.' "—Dennis Levandoski

"In a recent Theater column, Jon-Robin Baitz's Off-Broadway play was misidentified. It is called 'Mizlansky/Zilinsky' or 'Shmucks,' not 'Lewinsky/Kaczinski' or 'Shmucks.' Our apologies to Mr. Baitz as well as to the former intern and to the former college professor."—Meg Wolitzer

"Due to late clarification from the producers of the Jerry Springer show, the Television section contained an inaccurate listing. In Wednesday's 'Younger Man, Older Woman,' Chip is indeed sixteen and Aida is eighty-five. However they are not lovers; they are grandson and grandmother."

—John Solomon

• RANDY'S WRAP UP •

So much *Times* and so little time. The Corrections column (into which some of you slipped the stiletto, and onto which others brought down the blunt object—and aren't they both fun to wield?) had it coming. But some crimes can't be effaced by amending a few facts. Consider, for instance, how the paper's proliferating sections—Circuits, Dining In, Dining Out, Dining Down, Dining, well you know—constitute an abandonment of public transportation.

When the paper was at its most urban and lead paragraphs gave you the essentials of a story, the News Summary ran below the fold on the front of the second section. You just flipped up the first section to read a concise account of the events of the day. This could be managed even on a rush-hour subway.

Then the *Times* became a fun magazine filled with color and zip and furniture photographs, and the News Summary scurried away to page two of the first section. To get at it now, you must juggle the eight or ten separate sections that currently comprise the daily paper (each with a big lovely, back page, ideal for a full-page ad), and fold it over, an act that cannot be done on any form of mass transit without elbowing your neighbors beyond the bounds of simple decency.

The New York Times is now designed to be carried in a car, by a commuter, driving in from the suburbs. It is no longer a subway reader's paper. It is no longer a city newspaper.

Correct that.

LEFTOVERS

"Their attitude was 'Keep a low profile and stay celibate.' "
—Reverend David Garrick,
former theater professor,
Notre Dame

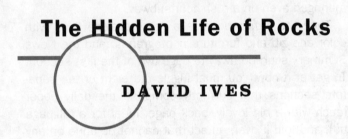

The Hidden Life of Rocks

DAVID IVES

Do dogs think we're God? Probably not.

—Elizabeth Marshall Thomas,
The Hidden Life of Dogs

Do rocks have consciousness? The question is absurd. *Of course they do.* The assumption that rocks lack an inner life, just because they're on the quiet side, is the kind of crude anthropocentrism that ranks Shakespeare as more "sensitive" than shale because he happened to write a few immortal plays. Lodestones have a better sense of direction than we— maybe because they're more frequently lost in the woods. Quartz is more beautiful. Why? Careful grooming. We're all aware that rocks eat sparingly. Lack of consciousness? No. Evolution has simply made them very picky.

Why should we think the lowliest limestone does not feel the same sorrow, exhilaration, and fear of hair loss many of us do? Why should we take granite for granted? Maybe gneiss *is* nice, and adamant adamant, but will the twain ever meet? True, rocks are extremely subtle in the way they express their emotions. Some might say coy. They're also loyal, attentive, and nonviolent. (Rocks don't break windows. People do.) Which of us humans really knows one another? Look at the hidden life of Rock Hudson. Who knows what lurked in the heart of I. F. Stone? Rocks certainly resist learning human ways. But given Mickey Rourke, why would they want to?

My interest in rocks began early. As a child, I had pet stones, in particular a pebble named Mr. Smithers that my father released into the wild after he decided I couldn't care for it properly. In college, my dorm mate was a twelve-pound lump of schist because nobody else would room with me. We've lost contact, but I couldn't name a more empathetic friend. (When I think of those intimate late-night talks when I poured out my heart!)

More recently, a neighbor in Cambridge was going away and asked if I'd watch her house. Touring her grounds I noticed two stones on a windowsill—obviously her pets and probably anxious at their owner's departure. Peaches was a golden-toned igneous gem, Tristan a hefty gray volcanic hunk. Clearly an alpha rock. Taking them home for better care, I realized that no one had ever investigated what rocks do when left by themselves. I decided to undertake the research myself.

Hiding at the kitchen door, I would observe them quietly. Luckily, the great slowness of rocks (an evolutionary adaptation) keeps their range relatively narrow. But they can be very territorial indeed. It's rare for one rock to enter another's territory with impunity. This is a function of demeanor: Over the millennia rocks have learned that the best way to face down a predator is to stand their ground impassively. They certainly wouldn't roll over and accept a pay cut the way I did.

After a week, I brought in a couple of strays: a vixenish red stone that I named Joan Crawford, and a savage, dirty, but robust specimen called Hercules. The atmosphere of anxiety at their entrance was palpable. After all, the new rocks were not domesticated. Ultimately, Peaches and Hercules became excellent companions. Joan Crawford and Tristan were less successful, and I often had to separate them.

In the wild, rocks tend to reside in packs (how else could they survive the Arctic winter?) with a hierarchy determined by size, the dominant rock being the biggest. Feral rocks have more solitary habits, living and feeding alone. City rocks prefer to sit in the park together or gather for bridge, though it can be hard finding partners.

No one knows what brings rocks into estrus. Seasonal changes? Temperature? The end of the television season? Stones can sometimes take the most obscene shapes—probably a form of sexual display. A worker at the Kinsey Institute for Sex Research, in a phone conversation, opined that the sex act between rocks is probably rather brief and businesslike but not untender, before she collapsed into either tears or hysterical laughter and hung up on me.

Interestingly, rocks flourish with classical music in their environment, and have a particular fondness for Schubert lieder. They shrink (ironically) from rock and cringe at jazz. Like us, they enjoy a warm bath (papaya bath oil is a favorite), and you might read them an Agatha Christie at bedtime.

Rocks certainly feel loss, as I discovered on my neighbor's return. I walked Peaches and Tristan over and told my neighbor I was returning her stones, placing them gently in her hand. She asked me what the hell I was talking about. Back home, I sensed the low spirits of Hercules and Joan Crawford, and put on some Mozart to cheer them up.

What do rocks ultimately want? Like all creatures, they want the security of an understanding group and a good video store in the neighborhood. They want their colleagues at work to stop thinking of them as weirdos. They want the paperboy to stop throwing the paper in the bushes. They want Mr. Smithers back.

I've come to admire these lonely, mysterious objects for their simple acceptance of things, for their almost Zen calm in the midst of a brash, hardhearted, and chaotic world. Millions of years after I'm dust, Joan Crawford and Hercules will still be here, patiently experiencing the universe. Walking around the woods with my rocks, jiggling them in my pocket, laying them out like tiny headstones marking the resting places of small unmemorable lives, I feel serene. Rocks, unlike my podiatrist, accept me without question for what I am: transient, anxious, and human.

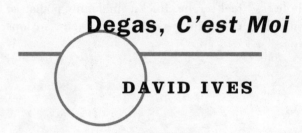

Degas, *C'est Moi*

DAVID IVES

I decided to be Degas for a day. Why Degas? *Pourquoi pas* Degas?

Maybe it was the creamy eggshell hue of my ceiling as I lay in bed that morning. Maybe it was all the cheap French table wine I'd been drinking. True, I didn't know much about Degas: dead French impressionist painter of jockeys and ballerinas. And true, I wasn't French, dead, or a painter of any kind. Yet weren't Degas and I united by our humanity? By our common need for love, coffee, deodorant?

I started immediately and brushed my teeth as Degas. Everything seemed different yet nothing had changed. In the shower, it felt strange, lathering an immortal. Equally strange, the immortal was lathering back. How had I become such a genius—I, who flunked wood shop at my Sheepshead Bay *lycée?* Had it been my traumatic childhood? My lost pencil box? Uncle Stosh's unfortunate party trick with the parakeet?

I tried to comprehend my greatness and immortality as I fried a couple of eggs, but the idea was too big. While considering the lustrous yellow of the yolks, I incinerated my muffin.

Being Degas would take some practice. I went out into the world with my dry cleaning.

Then I suffered a shock. First, the Pakistani on the corner sold me my paper just as before. Then my dry cleaner showed no change. Finally, as I headed down Broadway and people passed me by without a second glance, I realized: It *made no difference to be Degas.*

But maybe the other Degas had walked this invisibly through Paris—bumped into by bourgeois pedestrians and shouted at by men unloading cabbages at the Left Bank D'Agostino. Anonymous, I was free to appreciate the gray blur of pigeons, the impasto at Ray's Pizza, the chiaroscuro of the M7 bus. Anonymity continued at unemployment, where they seemed unfazed when I signed my claim "Edgar Degas"— maybe because the guy ahead of me had signed "Rembrandt" to his. Recalling my lifelong interest in jockeys, I stopped at OTB and put five francs on a chestnut filly whose jockey wore brilliant silks of crimson and green but who came in sixth. Who cared? I was Degas.

Famished by creativity, I stopped at Twin Donut. I was scribbling a priceless doodle on my napkin when I noticed someone staring, a young woman writing in a journal. Had she recognized me? She smiled slightly. Yes. She knew I was Degas. Not only that: She *loved* Degas.

Her admiring look redeemed all those years of effort. My work had given meaning to someone's life. Should I seduce her? It would have been traditional. But no. I'd only leave her, hurt her, go back to Doris. Not to mention what it would do to Doris. But wasn't it my duty as Degas to seduce this girl?

Too late. She had returned to her journal. I could imagine the entry: "Just saw Edgar Degas two tables over. So he likes vanilla crullers too! Suddenly this day is glorious and memorable. Wanted Degas to make love to me all afternoon. Should I tell Steve?"

Walking up Fifth Avenue, I forgot myself. The daily dreck intruded. Money. Job. Athlete's foot. (Had the itching fed my artistry?) It was blocks before I remembered I was Degas. The labor of hanging on to one's identity. *C'est trop!*

At the Metropolitan Museum I toured my work, amazed at how much I had accomplished, even without television. I stared into my fathomless eyes in a self-portrait (not a great likeness, really) and checked out my landscapes. "Bit smudgy, isn't it?" a man commented next to me. "So I had a bad day," I said and shrugged. He blinked, and moved off toward the communicants at van Gogh's *Sunflowers*. If those philistines only knew how Vincent cheated at *boules*.

In front of my *Woman with Chrysanthemums* I remembered facing that same canvas one morning a century ago, paralyzed by its blankness. I recalled how I had reached for my brush and the image crystallized: this pensive woman oblivious to the transcendent burst of color, the natural exuberance of the flowers versus her human sorrow, our blindness to the beautiful, the imminence of splendor . . . ! Would I ever have a day like that again? Would I get home in time to pick up my dry cleaning?

A guard told me to step back, I was too close to the painting. Inwardly, I laughed at the irony. He told me again, using a tawdry obscenity, and I stepped back.

When Doris met me for supper at the Acropolis, I was still exalted. She said she had typed twenty-eight letters at work that day, then ordered an Alka-Seltzer. I ordered a Reuben and told her I'd been Degas since morning. She nodded absently. I felt Degas start to slip. Her Alka-Seltzer fizzed in the glass. A man was staring at me from another table, something familiar about him. Doris said the toilets had backed up again. I looked back at the man and realized: It was Renoir. My old friend gazed at me with such pity that I had to look away. Now Degas was gone.

We walked to my place in silence. I sprawled on the couch with my hands over my eyes while Doris ran the bathwater. All my glory, all my achievements were utterly forgotten. Immortality? A cruel joke.

Then I looked through the doorway into the bathroom and

saw Doris standing naked with her foot up on the edge of the old lion-footed tub, drying herself. The overhead light was dim but Doris was fluorescent, luminous, with pinks and lavenders and vermillions playing over her skin. The frayed towel in her hands gleamed like a rose. She turned and smiled over her shoulder.

"Degas?" she said.

"Who needs him," I countered, and held out my hand.

You Say Tomato,
I Say Tomorrow

DAVID IVES

The public at large may not be aware that the human race is approaching a milestone in communication possibly as important as the invention of writing itself: the impending publication of the first complete dictionary of Unamunda, a language designed by its creators to unite all the peoples of the world in a single universally understandable tongue. To acquaint ourselves better with what was been called "the speech of the future" (or, in Unamunda, "da spinach della fuchsia"), we recently visited Donna Webmaster, editor-in-chief of what is technically known as "Webmaster's Drecktionary deli Unamunda," at the offices of Laxacon Press in Hindenburg, New Jersey.

On arrival, we noted that, for educational purposes, all the signage in the facility was worded both in English and Unamunda. The parking lot, for example, was divided into sections for "Employees" and "Visitors" ("Staph" and "Strep") and the offices, or "orifices," have a wing for "Editorial" ("Adda-Ting") and "Press" ("Pretz-Ling"). We also noticed that the mat outside Ms. Webmaster's office door did not say "WELCOME," as expected, but rather, "VELCRO." We stepped over it gingerly as Ms. Webmaster rose from behind her desk with outstretched hand.

"Belljar!" she said brightly. "Harvard U?"

It took us a moment to realize that this was Unamunda for "good day" and "how are you." We responded in kind with:

"Harvard *U?*"

"Wellesley, grappa," she said and indicated a couple of chairs: "Cha cha?"

We sat and she offered us beverages from a well-stocked sideboard. Like everyone else in the offices, Ms. Webmaster spoke only in Unamunda.

"Vassar? Tee?" she asked. And then, pointing to a Melitta: "Coffdrip?"

We declined, noting along the way an inspirational sign on Ms. Webmaster's desk, translated from Joseph Campbell's English into Unamundese. It said: "Follo yor blintz."

"Ms. Webmaster," we began, "you're the head editor of the drecktionary?"

"Iago arf da addatrix," she confirmed.

"And this is the first edition of the work?"

"Terd addition," she corrected, holding up three fingers.

"Sorry."

"Nor pablum."

"In Laxacon Press's literature on this project, you call Unamunda a triumph of American know-how, one of our greatest exports, and you claim that Unamunda will very soon be 'as popular as Coca Cola.'"

"Soda speek," she said with a show of modesty.

"Is the language very difficult?"

She shook her head in an emphatic no.

"Simplatico," she said. By way of demonstrating the ease, plastic beauty, and expressive range of the language, she regaled us with some translations of classic English texts into Unamunda. Longfellow's immortal lines from "Hiawatha," for example:

"Dinah shore di aldo gucci,
Biden simon mitzi gaynor . . . "

She had just launched into "Shall I compare thee to a summer's day" ("Shell-oil campari donnasummer day?") when a phone call interrupted her. She excused herself: "Squeegie. Tellaporn."

While the addatrix busied herself on the phone, we glanced over some nearby galley proofs for the Drecktionary. Of particular interest was an appendix containing a phrasebook for travelers. There, we learned that the Unamunda for "which way" is "quasimodo," "that way" is "a-la-modo," and "pseudo-Japanese detective fiction" is "mista-modo." These are not to be confused with the phrases for "auto breakdown" ("mess-da-moto") or "the hotel is far" ("remodo inn"). "Who" is "hugh," "what's" is "vutz," and "that's" is "putz." "How much" is "cuomo," while "about how much" is "pericuomo." Interestingly, the phrase for "Are you an undertaker?" is "Bury manilow?"

We had just learned the terms for "having to do with a parent's sister" ("auntological"), "brassiere" ("endtitty"), and "tell me what you're up to these days" ("lorna doin?") when Ms. Webmaster finished her call. We questioned her further.

"Ms. Webmaster, how many volumes are in the drecktionary?"

"Hesta williams."

"Sixty volumes!" we exclaimed. "How many entries does that add up to?"

"Pygmilion."

"Astonishing."

She shrugged, as if to say that the subtlety of Unamunda demanded so many millions of entries.

"The problem—or pablum," we said, "is that Unamunda seems to have a word for almost everything."

She smiled. "Nets-a-sarah-lee."

We chose an example at random from the proof pages: " 'A book in a bathysphere.' "

" 'Subtext,' " she provided.

" 'To die in the act of mating.' "

" 'Eggspire.' "

" 'Salmon in late spring.' "

" 'Maalox.' "

" 'Spoiled salmon.' "

" 'Dredlox.' "

" 'Salmon used as package stuffing.' "

" 'Padlox.' "

" 'An irrational fear of Christmas.' "

" 'Santaclaustrophobia.' "

"Ms. Webmaster, aren't all these reams of vocabulary a bit . . . "

"Redundulant?"

"*De trop?*"

"Detroitus? O contraire!" she protested. "Toledo, too late."

"But there can be too much of a good thing."

"Dots puzzible," Ms. Webmaster admitted. But she added: "Less is mormon."

We didn't quite get her point, but it didn't matter. The conversation was turning into a sort of crossword puddle anyway. We tried to encapsulate our feelings by confessing that the whole project seemed just a shade utopian.

"Da pravdaz enda pudding," she shrugged. "Yusay speech, eyecallit spinach."

"Unamunda," we ventured, "couldn't possibly be just another way to separate suckers from their money, could it?"

"Zucker vandabucks?"

"A scam," we said.

"E spam?! No no no," she protested. "Philanderopy."

An office assistant appeared in the doorway just then with some fresh pages on a tray. "Emily!" Ms. Webmaster greeted her. "Houseboy U?"

That was where we took our leave of Ms. Webmaster, wishing her all the best and thanking her for her time.

"Nafta-tall," she said. "My playshirt." She breezily waved us off with a final: "Achieu!"

The reader should note that the full sixty-volume set of the Drecktionary is only obtainable from a post office box in Guatemala and cannot be exchanged under any circumstances. What's more, payment must be in unmarked Swiss francs. So let the buyer beware. Caveat emptor, as the Romans used to say. Or, as Unamunda would have it: "Dik cavett emptier."

Chicken à la Descartes

DAVID IVES

[Gift-shopping for the contemplative cook? Need some food for thought? You might try "Favorite Chicken Recipes of the Great Philosophers," forthcoming from the Harvard Culinary Institute. Herewith an excerpt from the introduction.]

"I eat, therefore I expand. Edito ergo boom."

This statement, from René Descartes' great *Discourse on Flan* (1643), stands at the very heart of Western gastro-ontological thought. Is there "food"? What is "food"? And how long do you cook it? These are the perennial questions. Descartes was probably recalling the famous dictum from *Aristotle's Guide to Cheap Nicomachean Restaurants* (353 B.C.): "I eat therefore there must be food, or else I'd be pretty hungry by now."

Even before Aristotle, Socrates began the food fight in Plato's *Brunch* by claiming that the chicken before him was not true chicken, but merely the corporeal form of a higher, ideal chicken he'd had at a place in Thebes. His exchange with Aristarchon, an Athenian waiter, is worth quoting in full:

SOC.: I'll have the chicken sandwich and a pair of potatoes.

ARIS.: A pair of potatoes?

SOC.: I'm a peripatetic philosopher.

ARIS.: And yet our rulers call you a polis joke.

SOC.: O cute Athenian youth, in this life we are as in a cave, and see but the shadow of meals being eaten outside. If that's not bad enough, theirs is better, and they don't deliver.

Lao Tzu staked out the Eastern position in his *Tao Te Wings* (c. Thursday, 550 B.C.): "The sandwich is an illusion, only the Way is real. And even the Way is looking kinda doubtful." Unfortunately, the ancient Chinese character for "Way" can also be translated as "white meat." Stanton translates the same maxim as "What is chutney?" The gist, however, seems clear.

Then there is the fascinating chapter on snacks in St. Augustine's *Confessions:* "If someone inquires of me, what is a pork rind, I know. But if I am asked to explain pork rinds, they are a great mystery. Consider also shortcake—the longer one eats it, the shorter it gets. And yet the shorter one eats it, the shortcake does not lengthen. Uneaten shortcake should be of infinite length, or are my calculations off? Oh who can fathom the ways of the Almighty?" Unfortunately, the Latin word for "way" can also be translated as "flatulence caused by peanuts." The gist seems clear.

Spinoza was converted to the study of philosophy by being served a notorious and influential bowl of chicken soup in Leipzig in 1652. "There were spinach leaves floating in the bowl," he writes. "In a moment I realized that this chicken soup had a more meaningful existence than I, who had no spinach in me, and I set out to find the meaning of life. But first I had some herring."

The British empirical school cast doubt on the very existence of food, so it's not surprising they were a pretty scrawny lot. John Locke believed that we are born "without prior knowledge of chickens" but that we can be persuaded by advertising.

David Hume believed that there is no way for us to truly recognize "a chicken," but then he was shortsighted and known to stick his fork into his own hand. Berkeley believed that chickens only exist in the mind of God, though he conceded that the mind of God was somehow available in Covent Garden market for 60 pence a pound. ("If a tree falls on a chicken and nobody hears or sees it," he wrote, "can I legally take the chicken home?") It took the immortal Kant to resolve the matter in his *Critique of Purée*, where he wrote that the human mind is preconditioned by nature to perceive four essentials: time, space, time for lunch, and space for dessert. He also noted that the human mind instinctively perceives the right side of the menu first.

"Man is everywhere free," Rousseau wrote in 1771 in *Cooking with Wine*, "yet everywhere is part of a food chain." Unfortunately, the manuscript is unclear, and he may have written, "yet everywhere he buys his groceries from chains." The gist seems clear. Politico-polemical food literature dates back to Cicero's *De Gustibus*, usually translated as *Of Taste, or: Mind Your Own Business*. It culminates in Marx's *Kapital*, now largely dismissed as an economic analysis but very good on sauces.

The modern cuisino-philosophical tradition begins with Nietzsche and his controversial recipe for meat loaf in *Thus Baked Zarathustra*, intended as a slap at Wagner's bratwurst. Out of Nietzsche comes Sartre and the French existential school of cooking (7 Rue Jacob, Paris, write for details). Their works can be heavy, rich with distinctions between "eating-in-itself," "eating-for-itself," and "eating-with-somebody-else" until we reach the nouvelle existentialism of the 1970s, led by Derrida's decorative if unsatisfying plates of lo-cal nothing.

Ludwig Wittgenstein (who incidentally made great kreplach) influenced generations of philosopher-cooks with his *Tractatus Logico-Esophagus*. There, he investigated the relationship between language and food, deploying his arguments in numbered propositions:

3.1 "I call it spinach" is not a meaningful sentence unless one is referring to the cantos of Ezra Pound.

3.2 If one says, "You'll eat your words" to Joyce Carol Oates, she will be chewing a very long time.

3.3 If one shuffles those cantos and those novels, does one get "a pound of oats"?

3.4 Are the oats edible?

3.5 Why not?

3.6 Where did I leave the word for "spatula"?

Finally there is the great twentieth-century synthesis, Rombauer's two-volume *Joy of Cooking*. Traditionalist in flavor but with a modern rigor in the ingredient lists, this is one of the monuments of world philosophy. At this point one might quote the famous closing proposition of Wittgenstein's *Culinary Investigations:* "Shut up and eat."

Even More Memoirs by
Even More McCourts

JAY JENNINGS

Worse than the ordinary miserable childhood is the miserable Irish childhood, and worse yet is the miserable Irish Catholic childhood.

> —from *Angela's Ashes*

Any reader with an immigrant in his past cannot help but find his own forebears in *Angela's Ashes*.

> —blurb by Samuel Freedman on
> the jacket of *Angela's Ashes*

A weak, feeble collection of tired barroom tales told to capitalize on Frank McCourt's success.

> —an amazon.com reader's review of
> Malachy McCourt's *A Monk Swimming*

OY VEY, MARIA
By Shlomo McCourt

This memoir by a cousin of the McCourt brothers tells how the author's parents traveled from the slums of Limerick, Ireland, to America but got in the wrong line at Ellis Island and ended up in the Crown Heights section of Brooklyn among the Hasidim. "Worse than the miserable Irish Catholic childhood," he writes, "is the miserable Irish Catholic kosher childhood."

CREAM IN MY BLACK IRISH COFFEE
By M. C. Court

A distant relative of the McCourt brothers, the Brooklyn-based rapper who goes by the name of M. C. Court (his real name is Biggie Dog Flava-fu) explores his Irish heritage in this combination book and CD. A visit to his ancestors in Limerick is an eye-opening cultural experience ("Worse even than the miserable Irish Catholic childhood," he writes, "is 'Riverdance'"), but he credits the trip with changing his raps, which are now composed entirely of limericks, as in his song "Guinness Tastes Like (deleted)":

There once was a man who (deleted)
Whose (deleted) was so long, he (deleted)
(Deleted delete)
(Deleted delete)
And now he's (deleted) (deleted).

UNDER THE LIMERICK SUN
By Frances Mayle McCourt

The author, Brooklyn-raised like her nephews, trades her time-share on Hilton Head for one in Limerick, which, she is told, is in the heart of the Tuscan wine country. Imagine her surprise when finds that the "villa" she has rented for two weeks is a tumble-down rowhouse in the slums of Limerick. Nevertheless, with admirable fortitude, she sets about fixing up the place (which she cheerfully christens "Little Wopping Mistake") and engages in witty repartee with the eccentric locals, as in this exchange with a yeoman at the fresh-air market: "Do you have any fresh pomegranates? I'm making a delightful soup." "Shut your gob, you fecking Yank!" Recipes included.

SHOUTIN' AT THE LIAR'S CLUB
By Mary Bragg McCourt

This branch of the McCourt family settled in the South, but didn't fare any better than the other McCourts. "Worse than the miserable Irish Catholic childhood is the miserable Irish Catholic childhood with grits," the author writes. This tale is as much a memoir of the author's mother, Luann McCourt, as it is of the author herself. Luann is a hard-drinkin', hard-drivin', chain-smokin', husband-beatin' trucker in lime green stretch pants, whose life is a series of no-good men and worse luck. In the book's most poignant section, the author recounts her mother's struggle to overcome her lifelong battle with gerundism, a disorder that causes the sufferer to drop the final *g* from the ends of words.

MEMOIRS OF AN IRISH GEISHA
By Fiona "Kiko" McCourt

While other McCourts left for America to seek their fortunes as memoir writers, Fiona McCourt remained behind to become Limerick's most famous geisha. McCourt takes the reader inside the secretive world of her Irish geisha house, which is above a pub called The Shamrock and Samurai. She describes in detail the intricacies of the "cuppa" ceremony and recalls her encounters with Ireland's greatest literary figures, such as Joyce, Synge, and Mishima.

AM I ANYBODY?
By Nora O'Casey

O'Casey wrestles with the most troublesome question of Irish identity in our time: Can you be an Irish memoir writer and not be a McCourt?

Love Bug

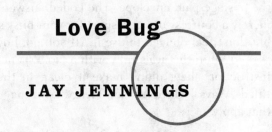

JAY JENNINGS

Dear Lorraine,

In that I have received no reply from you to mine of the 15th, 16th, 17th, 18th, 19th, 20th, 21st, 22nd, 23rd, 24th, 25th (A.M.), 25th (P.M.), 26th and 27th, I am now forced to cut off all communication with you and insist that you continue in your efforts to prevent yourself from responding to me. The self-restraint you have shown in this regard has been nothing less than herculean, and I am grateful for your forbearance.

Nevertheless, if we are to end our relationship cordially and respectfully, and if we are to move on with our lives, there remain a few loose ends to tie up. Though the recollection of some of these details may be painful, it is necessary for us to confront these issues head-on in a healthy and productive way.

First, the temporary restraining order. To me, the word "temporary" implies that you still hold out some hope of our reconciliation. I really don't wish to lead you on, and I'm afraid I can't promise anything at this time (because of the gag order and contempt-of-court citation).

I have not as of today received from you the answers to any of the 240 questions I asked you in mine of the 15th. (If your answers have crossed with this in the mail, thanks!) If you have not already done so, please send the answers to me at your earliest convenience in the postage-paid envelope. The coded answer card was merely a courtesy out of respect for your busy schedule, but don't feel obliged to use it. (If you do, however, be sure to fill in the ovals fully with a No. 2 pencil.) If the instruction sheet didn't make it clear, in the section titled "Ways I Have Abused Henry," you may fill in all that apply.

I have received a few calls for you here at the apartment, and, since you forgot to leave a forwarding number, I haven't been able to get in touch with you to pass them along. Agents from the Federal Bureau of Missing Persons would like you to contact them regarding your whereabouts. Someone (apparently) reported you as missing when it appeared that the loving, kind, and gentle Lorraine he (or she) once knew no longer existed. Evidently, he (or I or she) sent them the most unflattering photo of you we (or they) could find. It looks to be the one taken on that vacation in Cancún, when your face was all blotchy from sun poisoning and you were wearing that ridiculous sombrero just before you got sick after drinking too many margaritas in that cantina. At least that's my best guess about the picture's origin, after seeing it on those milk cartons ("Weight: 165"!) and on the special Web page (www.missing_persons.gov/hideous_lorraine.htm).

Regarding property that we purchased together: Since we both chipped in to buy that copy of Windows 98, I have filed a friend-of-the-court brief in the government's antitrust suit against Microsoft, in which I demand that you detatch the Internet Explorer browser from the Windows operating system and return it to me. Please comply as soon as possible.

In financial matters, I would like you to reimburse me the nonrefundable $250 fee for my gym membership, which was revoked (after only one day!) when I (coincidentally) showed up for the same aerobics class as you, and you screamed and became hysterical. I have enclosed a copy of the invoice, marked PAID, for my membership at the Only for Women Health Club. To show my goodwill, I will not charge you for the damage to the wig and thong that resulted from the ensuing scuffle with security. Make the check out to me, and on the memo line please write: "I have been grossly unfair to Henry."

That's all for now.

> Love (Platonic, of course. Didn't mean to get your hopes up!),
>
> Henry

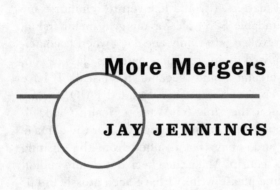

More Mergers

JAY JENNINGS

New York, NY, April 20 (AP)—In a move that rocked the Street today, Bert and Ernie announced that they had merged to form Bernie, a giant conglomeration of felt that will move them into the number two spot, past Big Bird and just behind Barney. In recent years they had lost sponsorship from the letter *P* and the number 5, and analysts say the move will help solidify their market share. "This is a logical move for us," said Bert. " 'Share' is our favorite word."

Concord, NH, May 14 (Reuters)—Continuing the wave of consolidation that saw Alabama, Mississippi, and Georgia join to form NationSouth, Vermont and New Hampshire signed a deal today that will combine the two into one state with the motto "Live Free or Whatever."

The deal involves a stock swap in which cows from Vermont and chickens from New Hampshire will be exchanged one-for-one.

Bangor, ME, Aug. 22 (Bloomberg)—Stephen King announced today that he had acquired Joyce Carol Oates in a deal that will allow him to increase production by as much as 125 percent, upping his output to at least one novel per month.

The new author, who will do business as the firm of Stephen, Joyce, King, Carol, and Oates, will be one of the most violent and critically acclaimed novelists working today. Though Mr. King sells more books than Ms. Oates, analysts say the acquisition of the respected writer will help him make inroads into new markets, like college literature classes.

"It's a win-win situation," Mr. King said in an exclusive interview with the *New York Daily Newsday Times*. "Joyce has the prestige I've been looking for and is one of the few writers who can keep up with my production schedule."

An earlier deal in which King had hoped to buy Upjohn Inc. fell through when King was informed that the company was not John Updike.

Washington, D.C., Oct. 3 (UPI)—In a deal that resonated in homes across the country, Cats announced yesterday that it had completed a hostile takeover of Dogs.

The new company, which Cats said would be called OnePet, will supplant the recently created Birdfishgroup as the world's largest supplier of domestic companion services.

Paris, France, Nov. 14 (Agence France-Presse)—In what is thought to be the biggest merger of all time, Men and Women have agreed to join forces into one sex, to be called Humanicorp.

The details of the arrangement are still being hammered out, but early negotiations have Men taking breasts. Women have agreed in principle to watch ESPN but have refused to give up self-respect. Sources close to both parties say that genitalia remain a sticking point. There are also serious antitrust issues that will need to be resolved.

A spokesman for Men, Bob, said that Men have been trying for years to merge with Women and that this was the culmination of a long-held dream for Men. Women were unavailable for comment.

Rome, Italy, May 30, 2305 (Religious News Service)—After several eons of discord and competition for the souls of Humanicorp, God and Satan have decided to merge in a deal that will join no less than Heaven and Hell.

"Some say I've made a deal with the devil," said God, who appeared simultaneously on CNN, Fox News, the major networks, all radios and personal computers, as well as in the sky. "But I prefer to think of this as two former adversaries setting aside differences for the good of consumers."

Those close to the delicate negotiations said that God would be chairman of the combined company and that Satan would hold the post of president.

Merger talks broke off several centuries ago in part because the executives could not decide who would run a combined company.

Reminded of his famous rebuff of God at that time, "Better to reign in Hell than serve in Heaven," Satan joked, "I take it back."

Satan's old organization, whose name is Legion, does not plan any layoffs.

The sudden success knows the caterer, but not his host.—M.O'D.

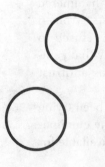

Rejected Polls

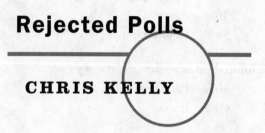

CHRIS KELLY

[These poll questions were prepared for a late-night network talk program. They were posted on the show's Web site and answered by thousands of Americans just like you. Inexplicably, these were not among the polls chosen to be used "on-air."]

I couldn't care less about the NHL.

    63%   Agree

    37%   Disagree

Least appetizing "honey-baked" foodstuff:

    17%   T-bone

    18%   Rainbow trout

    44%   Caesar salad

    21%   Banana

I'd rather watch a fire in a trash can than "Can't Hardly Wait."

    81%   Agree

    19%   Disagree

Bruce and Demi:

      36%   Didn't see it coming.

      64%   Saw it coming a mile away.

It doesn't, actually, get any worse than Mariah Carey.

      46%   Agree

      54%   Celine Dion

In a limited nuclear war, my money's on:

      40%   Pakistan

      60%   India

Favorite epoch:

      16%   Paleocene

      26%   Miocene

      58%   Pleistocene

Stevie Wonder has won Grammys in years when he didn't even record anything.

      95%   True

       5%   False

Worst *Horse Whisperer* sequel:

      37%   *The Goat Mumbler*

      20%   *The Mule Howler*

      43%   *The Camel Whiner*

Better schools:

      23%   Alphaville

      12%   Fat City

      65%   Funkytown

Someone should find the executives who decided to remake *Psycho,* and stab them in the shower.

    98%   Agree
     2%   Disagree

Hillary Clinton said she didn't stand by her man like Tammy Wynette. Now Tammy Wynette is dead. Coincidence?

    32%   True
    68%   False

If I were a stewardess, I'd rather:

    16%   Be groped by Bill Clinton
     0%   Be groped by Frank Gifford
    84%   Be sucked through the bulkhead
          by explosive decompression

Author of *A Pluralistic Universe:*

    38%   Henry James
    33%   William James
    29%   Rick James

An actual book by Jackie Collins:

    18%   *The Slut*
    50%   *The Bitch*
    10%   *The Cretin*
    22%   *The Sleaze Bag*

Gennifer Flowers was secretly taping people before secretly taping people was cool.

    88%   Agree
    12%   Disagree

Monica Lewinsky would do anything for:

    6%   Her country

  16%   Love

  78%   Skittles

Base 10 could kick any other counting system's ass.

  84%   Agree

  16%   Disagree

Best way to get Iraq to stop hating us:

  52%   Bombing them

  48%   Something else

Best describes a binary chemical compound containing one electropositive element and halogen:

 100%   Halide

Biggest chick magnet:

   5%   Carpenter

  15%   Fireman

  80%   Tubby, middle-aged, married, Arkansas bureaucrat

In about six months, those albinos from *Hanson* will be playing state fairs as:

  31%   "Hanson Goes to Hollywood"

  17%   "Right, Said Hanson"

   8%   "Hanson Politti"

  44%   "Hanson and the Beaver Brown Band"

"I don't wanna wait . . .

   5%   ". . . for our lives to be over."

  45%   ". . . more than thirty minutes for a pizza."

  50%   ". . . for them to stop playing that song."

Least appreciated Judd:

    14%   Ashley

    5%   Naomi

    2%   Wynona

    79%   Zeppo

Samuel Beckett said, "Nothing is funnier than":

    17%   Unhappiness

    23%   Folly

    60%   *Golden Girls*

If I was trapped in the shower, dying of thirst, I'd drink:

    17%   Shampoo

    21%   Conditioner

    62%   Cream rinse

In hell, bad kids have to eat macaroni and:

    22%   Tacks

    57%   Maggots

    21%   Yarnell

The best medicine:

    56%   Laughter

    44%   Tetracycline

They're never going to put this poll question on TV, because it doesn't mention any of the guests.

    52%   Agree

    48%   Luke Perry

Driving Mr. Crazy

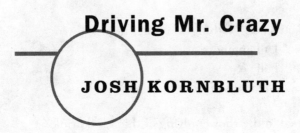

JOSH KORNBLUTH

This is a very short road story, about a very short trip, and the details of the trip were rather hazy to me even as I experienced them. Let me try to explain why.

I was visiting Los Angeles, so you can understand the hazy part right there. But besides the usual smog, there was a moral dilemma clouding my psyche. I had just been offered a part in a big Hollywood movie—one that, conveniently enough, was about to start shooting in and around San Francisco, my adopted hometown. The director, one of the world's greatest, had personally chosen me for this part. The problem, as I saw it, was this: In order to play that part, I'd have to kill people. At least four, including myself. Possibly more.

Not that they'd phrased it that way when offering me the part. No, all they'd said was, "You *do* drive a stick, right?" And I'd said, "Who doesn't?"—which, as I see it, wasn't technically a lie, because I'd put it in the form of a question. But shortly after hanging up the phone, I had to check my euphoria and soberly face one hard fact. Not only had I never driven a stick, I'd never driven a car. And now (in less than thirty-six hours!) I was sched-

280

uled to drive three fellow actors—one or more of them doubtless
the primary wage earner in a large, loving family—in the director's personally owned manual-transmission vintage car. At
night. On the highway. With the cameras rolling. And with more
than one key grip within killing range.

Balancing the moral alternatives in my mind—the advancement of my acting career versus the loss of human life—I
quickly reached the obvious conclusion. I picked up the phone
and called my little brother, thirteen years my junior, who was
(if you'll forgive the term) crashing in my Mission District
apartment after having just completed the ritual postgraduation
cross-country car trip. In a manual-transmission car!

"Look, I know you're exhausted and all, but I need your
help," I said. "Can you drive down to L.A. tomorrow morning
and teach me how to drive a stick on the way back?"

"Okay," he sighed blearily. Long ago, I used to change his
diapers, and ever since then, I've never let him forget that he
owes me.

That night, waiting for my brother to arrive and unable to
sleep, I went for a walk along Sunset Boulevard, wandering
moodily until I came to one of those twenty-four-hour liquor
stores. The cashier, a bored-looking man wearing the distinctive
turban of a Sikh, sat on a stool and regarded me with little interest as I brought a monster-sized diet Coke up to the counter. A
transistor radio was playing a song by Hootie and the Blowfish, a
band whose music makes me strangely nauseated and saps me of
all hope. As the man rang up the sale, I thought, Who am I fooling? I'll never learn to drive a stick by tomorrow night. It's all
over—my one shot at movie stardom will never come to pass. I
must call the famous director and tell him that for the safety of
the cast and crew, I can't take the part. I looked up at the Sikh
cashier. He caught my sad stare. After a long silence, he said
with feeling, "I *hate* Hootie!"

And in that moment, I realized that there was reason to live,
that there were strangers throughout the world who suffered as
well the slings and arrows of homogenized pop culture. And this

realization, I believe, is what gave me the strength to go forward with my adventure. The ultimate goal, ironically, was my participation in yet another product of homogenized pop culture. But how else are you going to get work in the movies these days?

At the smudgy crack of L.A.'s dawn, my agent stopped by. When I'd first met her, she was still driving a battered old Chevy that had carried her cross-country in the mid-eighties, part of a bold escape from her suffocating Long Island origins. At that time, the talent agency she worked for had just promoted her from assistant agent (read: secretary) to junior agent (read: secretary with a slightly larger office). But now, following her promotion to senior agent (read: dominatrix on commission), she'd upgraded to some shiny black Lexus or Nexus or Flexus . . . and the woman who stomped impatiently into my bungalow, clutching a DMV driver's ed booklet in one hand and a cellular phone in the other was a woman rapidly running out of patience with one of her more, er, marginal clients.

"Study this carefully," she commanded as if she were handing me the Talmud. "Pay special attention to the shapes of signs." Then her cell phone beeped, a slight crackling energy appeared around her, and—poof!—she was gone.

A couple of hours later, my dear, sleepy brother arrived in his beat-up Toyota hatchback. I eyed the gearshift with giddy anticipation.

I said, "Just one more time: Which one's the gas and which one's the brake again?"

My brother regarded me. Finally he said, "Uh, don't you need to get a learner's permit or something?"

What is it with the younger generation nowadays? Back in the seventies, when I was growing up, we lived to flout authority. As a result, we eradicated poverty, crime, and racism. By contrast, today's twentysomethings are squaresville.

But it was his car. So I got in the passenger seat and let him drive me downtown to take The Test.

Now I can't say I was exactly surprised to be the only non-immigrant adult applying for a learner's permit. But—surrounded as I was by a passel of pubescent surfer dudes and dudettes, along with the occasional Carmelite nun from the Balkans—I did feel twinges of the "otherness" said to typify the internal life of artists and Unabombers. Suddenly, sitting at my kindergarten-sized desk and clutching my half-pencil, I was seized with an unanticipated anxiety: *What if I fail?* If so, I'd be doomed not only to losing this acting job, but also to strolling eternally around the periphery of Hollywood rather than zooming jazzily into its evil heart.

I looked down at the test form. It was asking me about acceptable blood-alcohol levels. Just hours ago, I had read about acceptable blood-alcohol levels. I had read deeply in the matter. But at this moment, this awful moment (in the "now," as Buddhists like to call it—at least, those who drive), I was unable to summon from within myself any information, quantitative or qualitative, regarding acceptable blood-alcohol levels. Praying that my DMV examiner was a moralist, I drew an arrow to the question and scrawled, "*No* drinking is acceptable—ever!!" and moved on.

The shapes of signs. Nine times out of ten, if you were to show me a blank red octagon and say, "So, Josh, which traffic sign has this shape?" I would respond, "Jeez—the stop sign, of course." Sadly, this was the tenth time. As I stared at the blank red octagon on my test form, all I could visualize inside it was the face of my agent, saying, "Pay special attention to the shapes of signs." I rummaged madly through my brain for clues; all I could come up with was a vague sense that the word that belonged inside the octagon might also apply to my career's momentum. But none of the multiple choices was "Go Directly into Toilet," so I left that one blank.

It is sad to flunk a learner's permit exam. It is *humiliating* to do so when your little brother has accompanied you to the DMV. He was out in the lobby, reading a book by Baudelaire. When he saw me emerge from the examination room, he smiled expectantly and began to rise from his chair. Grimly, I gave him a thumbs-down. He quickly looked away.

I had two more chances. Slouching back into my tiny desk with Test Form #2, I thought about all those who had passed this exam before me: Don Rickles, Roger Clinton, Barney the Dinosaur . . . the list went on and on. Clearly, I reasoned, success should be within my reach.

Ultimately, it came down to the very last question on the third and final test. I can't even remember what it was: something about whether or not you should use your cigarette-lighter holder to breed deadly viruses, I think. In any case, I got it right and was able to stride proudly out to my brother and show him my hard-won learner's permit. He smiled faintly and walked with me back out to the car.

It's not that I didn't feel for him at that moment. Just a week or so earlier he'd been playing lead harmonica in a rhythm-and-blues band at his graduation, and female fans had been grabbing at his private parts (for real!) and passing him scraps of paper with their phone numbers. Now he was about to try teaching his aging and somewhat unbalanced sibling how to drive a stick. Does higher education really prepare one for life in the world? I think not.

There was an uncomfortable pause as he began to open the driver's-side door.

"Uh, look," he said. "Maybe you should wait to drive until we're out past the Grapevine." This sounded reasonable to me, though I had no idea what the Grapevine was. So again, as I had been doing all my life, I strapped myself into the passenger's seat.

We got on the Hollywood Freeway, then onto 405.

"Are we at the Grapevine yet?" I said.

"No."

Fine. I relaxed. It got a bit hilly. "Yeah," my brother said, "it's good for me to be handling this part, 'cause cars can overheat and stall around here."

I took a short nap. When I woke up, we were going along a flat stretch—mountains to the left, trees to the right.

"Well, we're on the five now," my brother said.

"Time for me to take over?" I said.

"Not quite."

"Are those orange trees?" I said.

"Orange trees or maybe almond trees," my brother said. We're both from New York and have no specific knowledge of trees.

"Huh," I said.

When I woke up again, my brother told me we were halfway through the San Joaquin Valley.

"So we're past the Grapevine?"

"It's kind of a tail-end-of-the-Grapevine sort of thing," he mumbled. "Pass me that diet C?"

The last time I awoke, we were crossing the Bay Bridge into San Francisco. The sun was starting its beautiful descent into the city's skyline.

I panicked. "We've got to be past the Grapevine now!" I said.

My brother looked reflective. "The Grapevine, perhaps, is an infinitely extending state of mind," he said. This is what happens when you let little brothers go to college.

That night, it rained in San Francisco. So the famous director decided to shoot our scene inside an enormous warehouse space—with me at the wheel of a car, *pretending* to drive, as highly paid technicians expertly simulated the look and feel of a highway at night. I pretend-shifted, pressed the pedals randomly, and paid special attention to the shapes of signs.

Nobody died.

The scene was later cut from the film.

Red Diaper Baby

JOSH KORNBLUTH

My father, Paul Kornbluth, was a Communist. He believed there was going to be a violent Communist revolution in this country—and that I was going to lead it. Just so you can get a sense of the pressure.

And anything my father told me I'd believe, because my father was such a physically magnificent man: He was big, and he had this great, big potbelly—not a wiggly-jiggly, Social Democrat potbelly; a firm, Communist potbelly. You bopped it, it would bop you back. It was strong.

And he had powerful legs, from running track at City College of New York. And he had these beefy arms. And he was naked—virtually all the time, naked in the apartment. And all over his body he had these patches of talcum powder—you know, Johnson's baby powder—I guess because he was a big man and he would chafe. Especially around his private parts.

And he had me on the weekends. I would have loved to have slept in late on the weekends, but I couldn't because my father wouldn't let me. He would wake me up.

This is how he'd wake me up: He'd come bursting into my room and then he'd stop in the doorway; and when he stopped, the talcum powder would come bouncing off of his balls—it was like the entrance of a great magician. And then he'd come running up to my bed, and looming over me he'd sing:

Arise, ye prisoner of starvation!
Arise, ye wretched of the earth!

I didn't know that was the "Internationale"; I didn't know that was the international Communist anthem. I thought it was my own personal wake-up song.

Check it out: "Arise, ye prisoner of starvation"—it's time for breakfast. "Arise, ye wretched of the earth"—it's five o'clock in the morning and I'm being woken up!

And if I didn't show the proper signs of life right away, my father would lean down over me—and his long, graying hair would straggle down, his beard would flutter down into my nose—and he'd yell, "Wake up, Little Fucker! Wake up, Little Fucker!"

That was his nickname for me: Little Fucker. Nothing at all pejorative about it, as far as my father was concerned. For my dad, calling me "Little Fucker" was like calling me "Junior" . . . "Beloved Little One" . . . "Little Fucker."

I knew from an early age that one day I must grow up and become . . . a Big Fucker. And I assumed that that would be around the time that I would lead the Revolution. Because my dad had told me over and over that all the great revolutionaries were also great fuckers.

But for now I was just lying there in my bed, my father looming over me with his—to me—enormous penis . . . swinging around, spewing smoke, powder, whatever . . . while I just had this little, six-year-old . . . training penis, if you will.

"Little Fucker." I didn't realize at the time that my father had his own language—not only his own English, but his own Yiddish. I used to think it was real Yiddish, but then my mom would say, "That's not Yiddish. What your father speaks is not

Yiddish. I went to Yiddish school in Bensonhurst—and what your father speaks is not Yiddish."

I'd say, "You mean, *ouska* is not—"

"No. There's an *oyska,* but there's no *ouska* . . . "

Well, in my father's Yiddish, there was a term *ouska. Ouska* was a prefix meaning "a lot of," "very"—as in, "I am ouska-cold, my son!"

I'd say, "Of course you're *ouska*-cold, Dad; you're *ouska*-naked. The window is *ouska*-open."

As it would be in the kitchen, where we'd go for breakfast. Dad and I would sit around the kitchen table having hard-boiled eggs (my father, not a soft-boiled kind of guy). And never little eggs: When Dad went shopping for eggs, he always got *ouska*-jumbo-large-size eggs, so we would not want for eggs. And we would smear on our eggs, in my father's language, "salad dressing"—meaning mayonnaise. And we'd drink juice—apple juice, orange juice . . .

And Dad would regale me with his stories of organizing in the South with the Henry Wallace campaign. (That's Henry Wallace. Henry. Okay?) And he'd drill me over and over in the catechisms of our faith—of Communism. Like how society has been driven from one stage to the next, driven inexorably by the forces of dialectical materialism, until . . .

I sense I'm covering old ground. But just to review:

According to Marx and Engels—and my dad—the first human society was Primitive Communalism: Everyone's just kind of dancing around, like at a Grateful Dead concert.

The next stage after Primitive Communalism was Slavery—which must have been a bummer of a transition.

Then from Slavery to Feudalism, and from Feudalism . . . Well, we've learned from history that it's very important after Feudalism to stop in Capitalism before moving on to Socialism. Very important to stop in Capitalism. Because that's where you get your appliances.

So you stop in Capitalism, you get your stuff, and then you move on to Socialism, and finally to Communism—and you're back at the concert.

After breakfast, me and my dad would move from the kitchen into the living room—although when I say "kitchen" and "living room," I'm being euphemistic. There was one basic room—except for my bedroom: Dad always insisted that I have my own bedroom for my privacy, he'd just come bursting in at any moment. But aside from my bedroom, there was just one basic room. That's because when my father moved into an apartment, the first thing he'd do is he'd knock down all the walls. I don't mean that metaphorically; he'd knock down all the walls.

The first time he did this we had to move—right away. Because we lived on the first floor, and the building came . . . ouska-down.

So we moved into the next building—same landlord, who insisted on giving my dad a lecture on the crucial architectural concept of the supporting wall. That's the wall you must not knock down.

So my dad went knocking around with his hammer to find the one wall that wasn't hollow, left that wall up, knocked down all the other walls. And all along the external walls of our kitchen-cum-bathroom-cum-living-room-cum-dining-room area were posters of our heroes, our gods: W.E.B. Du Bois, Malcolm X, Dr. King, Ho Chi Minh, Bertolt Brecht, Emma Goldman . . . And then, at the end of all these posters: my height chart. See how the Little Fucker measures up.

And then we'd go outside for our walks. When we went outside, my father—in his one true concession to society—would put on clothing. This is back in '65, when I was about six years old. Dad wore this one-piece, bright orange jumpsuit—a parachute outfit—with a broad collar and a big zipper with a peace-symbol pull-thing that would seal in the freshness of the powder.

Being Communists, we had songs associated with every activity. But me and Dad didn't just have generic walking songs; we had specific going-up-the-hill songs, specific going-down-the-hill songs.

We had learned our biggest going-up-the-hill song off an album by Paul Robeson, a great Jewish folksinger. It was a record my dad had borrowed from the public library, and then—as a revolutionary act—refused to return. (And my mom was a librarian . . .)

Going up the hill, me and my dad would sing:

Ey yuch nyem
Ey yuch nyem
O Volga, Volga
Ey yuch nyem.

Very hard to walk fast while singing "*Ey Yuch Nyem.*"

A lot easier on our going-down-the-hill song, which we had learned off an album by Doc Watson—a great Jewish folksinger from the Appalachians (another record that my dad had liberated from the library).

Going down the hill, me and my dad would sing:

As I go down in the valley to pray
Studying—

—as we went down in the valley to pray on East Seventh Street, between C and D—

As I go down in the valley to pray
Studying about that good old way
And who shall wear the robe and crown
Good Lord, show me the way.

My father couldn't hear me. He thought I wasn't singing. He didn't connect it with the fact that he was singing so *ouska*-loud he was drowning me out. So periodically he'd turn to me on the sidewalk and go, "Sing louder, my son—I can't hear you!"

Oh, fathers, let's go down
Let's go down, come on down.
Oh, fathers, let's go down
Down in the valley to pray.

"Try singing even louder, my son—and perhaps with more . . . melodic invention."

Come on, fathers, let's go down!
Down in the valley to pra-a-a-ay . . . to pray-yee!

"And a child shall lead them!" my dad would say, and then we'd hit the flatlands of Manhattan as we continued north on our walks toward Herald Square. And along the flatlands we'd sing what, for us, were "flat" songs—rounds—which were easier for me, more even between the two singers. And along the flatlands we would stop at the bodega to pick up supplies, and we'd stop at the pharmacy to get Dad's pills—and we'd continue north along the flatlands, singing rounds like:

Come follow, follow, follow, follow, follow, follow me.
Whither shall I follow, follow, follow
Whither shall I follow, follow thee?
To the greenwood, to the greenwood
To the greenwood, greenwood tree!

A nice, cheerful walking song—though confusing lyrically, to an urban child. "Follow thee to the greenwood tree—why? I'd much rather follow thee to, say, Chock Full O'Nuts."

Which was the kind of place we had to eat, me and Dad, because we had to live *ouska*-cheaply. Because my father . . .

Well, he was a schoolteacher—he was a very good schoolteacher. But my dad would get a job and be teaching his students with great passion, but at the same time he would be developing this anger towards his bosses: the principal, the assistant principals, the school board. And this anger at his bosses would build and build, until finally Dad couldn't take it anymore. This would take about two weeks. And at the end of those two weeks, Dad would go storming into the principal's office and yell, "Fuck you!"

Often the guy would never have seen my dad before. And he'd say, "You're fired! . . . If you work for me, you're fired!"

And then Dad would get another job, and he'd be teaching his new students with great passion but developing this anger toward his new bosses. And at the end of two weeks he would storm into his new principal's office and go, "Fuck you!"

And the new principal would go, "You're fired!"

So Dad would find another job—perhaps a little farther away from New York, as he lost his license to teach in this gradually growing radius. And at the end of two weeks at his new job:

"Fuck you!"

"You're fired!"

And another job:

"Fuck you!"

"You're fired!"

And another:

"Fuck you!"

"You're fired!"

This went on for years and years; my father never saw . . . the pattern. He never saw the cause-and-effect between "Fuck you!" and "You're fired!"

So we had to live *ouska*-cheaply. Which was fine with me: I loved eating at places like Chock Full. You could have a nice hot dog, maybe some coconut cake . . . then we'd continue north for further *ouska*-cheap adventures, like the Museum of Natural History—where, at the time, the admission was whatever you would care to donate. They've since changed that policy—I think because of my dad. ("Pay them a penny and not a penny more, Fucker!" "You're right, Dad! We're not gonna give in to those imperialistic paleontologists!")

We'd go running up to the dinosaur exhibit, where Dad would give me a tour. I don't think he was an expert in the field, but he did have his bright orange tour-guide outfit. "The Tyrannosaurus rex, my son—one of the largest . . . reptilian fuckers ever to walk the earth!" And other little kids would break away from their field trips and join us. The field was a lot more interesting the way my dad described it.

And then, after a weekend of this kind of *ouska*-fun, my dad—as the courts had mandated—had to return me to . . . my mom.

My mom, Bernice "Bunny" Selden: also Jewish, also a New Yorker, also a City College grad, also a Communist—but so different from my father in temperament. If my father was an out-there, *ouska*-Communist, my mom . . . *inska*.

And she had her own *inska*-wake-up song for me, too—and like I thought Dad had written the "Internationale" for me, I thought my mom had written her wake-up song for me; I only found out years later that Irving Berlin wrote it.

My mom would be getting ready to go to work at the library across the river. She'd go into the bathroom in her nightgown and come back out with her hair in a bun. Then she'd go back into the bathroom and come out . . . with another bun having been added, from some mysterious source. And she'd stand in my open doorway—which was easy for her to do, because for some reason she would not let me have a door. And she'd tiptoe up to my bed and she'd lean down and sing:

> *Oh, how I hate to get up in the morning*
> *Oh, how I'd love to stay in bed*
> *For the hardest blow of all*
> *Is to hear that bugler call:*
> *"You gotta get up, you gotta get up,*
> *You gotta get up in the morning."*
>
> *"You gotta get up, you gotta get up,*
> *You gotta get up in the morning."*

A pretty nice wake-up song. Unless you know the second verse, which to me gets to a surreal level of violence that I find almost Sam Peckinpah–esque:

> *Someday I'm gonna murder the bugler*
> *Someday you're gonna find him dead*
> *I'll amputate his reveille*
> *And stamp upon it heavily*
> *And spend the rest of my life in bed!*

I thought she could snap at any moment. So I'd get out of bed; I didn't want my reveille amputated!

But I still didn't have that get-up-and-go that the "Internationale" gives a kid. So she'd guide me gently up from my bed and lead me into the living room and sit me down on the couch, and then—this goes back to when I was at least four or five—she had this little motherly trick she'd play to get me going in the morning: She'd serve me a tall cup of double espresso—with whipped cream and a maraschino cherry on top, because I'm a little kid!

And I'd sit there sipping my double espresso on the couch, beneath the half dozen or so ceramic disks that she bought in Mexico, where she went to divorce my dad—which, by the way, was when I was six months old.

They were married for nine years, then I was born—then, when I was six months old, they divorced. From time to time I'd wonder why.

But then, a few months ago, I was reading this article in the *Village Voice* about a guy named Saul Newton, a crazed psychoanalyst who ran this psychoanalytical cult called the Sullivanians. They had a co-op on the Upper West Side. I was reading about this Saul Newton guy, and how he told his patients that the family is evil—parents are intrinsically evil, and they can only wreak havoc on their children; you must break up the family.

Reading about this guy—Saul Newton, Saul Newton, Saul Newton—and suddenly it hit me: "Wait a second! My dad's therapist was named Saul!" So I called up my mom and said, "Mom, I'm reading about this Saul Newton guy," and she said, "Yeah, that was your father's therapist."

Evidently Dad was an early patient of Saul's—sort of a test case. And after I was born, Saul convinced my dad that now that he had a family, and families were evil, his family must be broken up. So Dad left me and my mom up in Washington Heights and he got an apartment down on the Lower East Side.

And then, according to my mom, after a couple of weeks Dad started to miss us. He came running up the island to try to reconcile with us. But Mom saw him coming and escaped with me down to Mexico, where she got the divorce, bought big floppy hats, danced around in circles with strangers, and got the half dozen or so ceramic disks—each one of which depicts a woman escaping from slavery.

So I'd sit there under the disks on the couch, sipping my double espresso, as my mom went up to the old radio console and turned on WBAI—listener-sponsored, sometimes listener-taken-over WBAI. The morning disc jockey at the time was Julius Lester—he of the *ouska*-deep voice. And supposedly, Julius's program was a classical-music show. But what Julius would do is, he'd play about five minutes of a baroque oboe concerto . . . and then speak for hours about his various ex-wives and their sexual peccadilloes.

And I'd listen real carefully to Julius, and I'd sip my double espresso, and I'd listen to Julius, and I'd sip my double-espresso . . . and then I'd go running off to school—jazzed!

I was so excited my first day of kindergarten. After spending the first five years of my life exclusively in the company of my parents and their friends, that day—for the first time—I was going to get to mingle with the masses.

Boy, was I disappointed! That first day, I walked into my kindergarten classroom at P.S. 128—and I saw all these little kids running around screaming, pulling hair, bopping each other, crying. I thought, "How will I ever organize these people?"

Zone 5

Gardening Advice
from Mertensia Corydalis

Q: I found a charming iron terrace table and chair set that someone had tossed in the rubbish. It has a considerable amount of rust and chipped paint. I see in the home design magazines that this au naturel look is in vogue. What do you think?
— J. A. PRUFROCK, BRIGHTON

A: Alfred, what nonsense these interior decorators perpetrate upon the public! If you leave the set as is, and should you wear white flannel trousers, they will be ruined by rust stains. Sand the furniture down and paint it. Giverny blue-green would be a nice color choice. Do not be so slavish to the opinions of others. Take a walk on the beach. Eat a peach. You're not getting any younger.

Q: I have a bing cherry tree that looks like it's going to be loaded with fruit this year. How can I keep the birds away? The tree is too large to cover with netting. I have seen inflatable owls and snakes in the nursery stores. Do they work?
— DAVE, MT. VICTORY

A: Dave, here is how it works: The top third of the tree is for the birds; the bottom third is for your dogs and visiting raccoons. The middle third of the tree is yours, which you can conveniently reach without a ladder. Don't be greedy. At the end of the one week when the cherries will be ripe, you and everyone you know will be sick of eating them. And if the wildlife hadn't pollinated the cherry blossoms, you wouldn't have any fruit at all. Save your money for an inflatable girlfriend. It would offer you greater utility than the items you mentioned in your query.

Q: I have a shady area that is dark and boring. How about planting impatiens to add a little color? What is the lowest light intensity for impatiens to bloom?
                              —WILLARD, WESTBROOK

A: Willard, I see that you do not live in South Africa, so why would you imply to the viewer that these gaudy, waterlogged, pathetic little flowers just happened to land in some dismal corner of your yard, only to become compost at the first breath of light frost? Muster your powers of observation, if you have any, and notice that the understory of trees is dappled with light. Choose hardy native plants such as pulmonaria, whose white-spotted foliage will light up the darkest corner and bloom with lovely blue and pink flowers in May. By the way, what is throwing this shade in the first place? I suppose it is some hideous aluminum hut housing your riding lawn mower.

Next time . . . antiquing for vintage flamingos . . .
growing the right cucumber for your needs

Money

In Which the Famously Contrarian Humorist Explains Why the Rich Are Different from You and She

FRAN LEBOWITZ

[The following is a transcription of an interview between Fran Lebowitz and *Vanity Fair*.]

How do people get rich?

I started out in life asking this question. Whenever I saw a rich person I would ask where their money was from, and invariably, or should I say inevitably, the answer was a natural resource, or else an unnatural resource. Oil would be a common answer, or real estate, or steel—this was before computers. The answer was never the answer you wanted to hear. The answer was never "Poetry—their money's from poetry, Fran." Or "That's one of the great essay fortunes in this country." Or "You know, he's the biggest epigram magnate in Europe." And so I learned that I was not in the moneymaking end of the moneymaking business.

Have you ever thought of what you'd need to live comfortably, or even to live without having to worry about anything?

Yes. Hourly. First of all, I'm a buyer of lottery tickets. I mention this only so you understand what a recreational attitude I have toward money—how it is largely fictional and anticipatory. Although not as fictional as some people's. Once I was standing in a lottery line and the woman behind me, who was clearly a cleaning lady because she had all her stuff with her, said to the man in front of me, "It's a big lottery this week—$23 million." And the guy said, "No, it's not. It's $3 million." And she said, "No, it's $23 million." And they argued back and forth and finally he said, "Look up there." And he pointed to the sign where the amount was posted. And it was $3 million. And she picked up her cleaning stuff and said, "Well, forget it, I'm not waiting in line for *that*." And she left. I mean, after all, her time is worth something. It is impossible for me to extricate the thinking about money from the way I live now. Because the way I live now is primarily about thinking about money.

> *Do you think people should come by money*
> *through the sweat of their own brow, through*
> *the sweat of other people's brows, through lottery*
> *tickets, through dead people, or through some*
> *other means?*

It depends on what you mean by "should." Do you mean morally?

> *Yes, morally.*

Well, there are very few clean fortunes, I would say. Mostly people who earn their own money have done more damage to the society than people who inherit it. It's practically impossible to earn a fortune without getting a lot of people caught up in those gears. The kind of money that's being made now looks very clean compared with the money made in the nineteenth century. In the nineteenth century, fortunes were clearly filthy. People died building those railroads. They died in the mines. You could actually see the people dying so that the other people could make money. In these high-tech fortunes people don't actually die before your very eyes. But you do know logically that people are dying in some way for this amount of money to be made. I don't believe it's possible to earn a great fortune without hurting people in some way.

> *So would you agree with the adage that*
> *money is the root of all evil?*

No. I think it might be the leaf of all evil or the flower of all evil. I think human nature is the root of all evil. Money is just a manifestation of human nature. Any large undertaking, including the undertaking of making a great fortune, necessitates that other people die in the pursuit of it. But I do think that present-day money is a little cleaner. On the other hand, it doesn't really produce as much material benefit for society as the other. Maybe people died building the railroads, but then at least we had railroads. From the nineteenth-century fortunes we got the New York Public Library, we got the Frick. You just feel that the things left behind by these new people will be more annoying and less edifying.

> *You could make money writing for movies or*
> *television. Why don't you do that? Is it because*
> *you think it's selling out?*

It has nothing to do with selling out or believing that it's some lesser form of writing, both of which are perhaps outmoded concepts. It is simply because my main goal in life is to limit the number of irritating phone calls that come into my house.

> *You also seem to want to limit the number of dol-*
> *lars that come into your house. What's the basis of*
> *your apparent aversion to dealing with money?*

I was brought up with the notion that discussing money, thinking about money, or, in fact, exhibiting the slightest interest in money was unforgivably impolite. Bearing absolutely no relation to our circumstances, financial or otherwise, my parents raised me to be something along the lines of a nineteenth-century British aristocrat. I didn't write a check until I was in my early thirties.

You dealt strictly in cash?

Well, basically I dealt strictly in nothing. Before my first book came out I never had any money. I would get paid with a check which I would cash at the delicatessen. I never had a check so big that the delicatessen couldn't, say, take a roast-beef sandwich out of it and give me the change. After my first book came out I had a succession of business managers whose aggregate efforts resulted in me having no money again by the time I was about thirty-three, at which point I learned to write a check.

Do you agree with Calvin Coolidge that "the chief business of the American people is business"?

I think that in the current climate Calvin Coolidge might be regarded as almost a Beatnik, since it seems widely accepted that the *only* business of the American people is business—and that the appropriate model for all human endeavor is the business model. People constantly say things like "If I ran my business the way they run the public school system, I'd be out of business in three weeks." People seem to have the idea that these things are similar in some way. If they ran the public school system the way you run your business, people would be even less well educated than they are now, because the purpose of business is to earn a profit. This is not the purpose of education. Additionally, it is not hard to imagine downsizing in this context—grades four through nine being regarded as middle management and hence eliminated. It is equally easy to envision at some imminent point in time that during the State of the Union address, when the camera pans above the head of the president, instead of the great seal of the United States of America we will see the Nike symbol. Direct corporate sponsorship of the federal government.

People accept this sort of thing in every way now. People accept a level of commercialization of every single aspect of life that is shocking to someone of my age. You pay nine dollars to go to the movies and they show you commercials for twenty minutes. Not only commercials for other movies—which they get you to call trailers or previews, like, "How lucky for you. For your nine dollars we're throwing in seventy-five previews"— but also commercials for products like Coca-Cola. When they started showing these—which wasn't that long ago, although everyone now seems to be unable to remember a time when this did not occur—people in New York used to boo them, but now they don't. They expect to pay to see commercials. It takes two seconds, it seems, to get people used to this kind of thing. I, on the other hand, still can't get used to paying for television. A television bill. It's astonishing. And even more astonishing is that other people regard this as a technological advance, whereas to me it seems this is technology going back. I feel that if at first television had been cable TV—this enormous, clunky, cumbersome, labor-intensive, expensive system—and then some genius figured out broadcast television, people would have said, "Can you imagine? They don't have to dig up the streets anymore. They don't need the big wires. You can move your TV around. It doesn't have to be attached to your wall. And it's free. It goes through the air. It's a miracle of modern technology—of course, there'll have to be commercials."

What possession of the very rich would you most like to have?

A plane. The greatest use of money is to remove yourself from the company of others, to get you out of the general public. And there is no more general a public than the public that is sitting next to you on an airplane. A public which seems to believe that the thick blanket of orange gunk through which they descend as they land in L.A. is secondhand cigarette smoke.

What's your position on household help?

I'm in favor of it. I'd love to have a cook because I'm very interested in eating but not in cooking. And I don't like to eat in restaurants where the general public is so often to be found. I would really prefer to eat at home, except there's no food there. I have frequently been observed in other people's kitchens talking to their cooks, in the hope that they will like me so much they will come work for me for free. I would love to have a driver, a secretary, a maid, and a laundress. I don't really want to do anything for myself at all. Of course, the thing I would most like to have is a novelist. People always say, "Don't you feel embarrassed when people do things for you?" But I don't. Not in the slightest. I have only the deepest gratitude.

Do you think men and women see money differently?

Well, first of all, they see different amounts of it. Let's face it, as a friend of mine always says, men own the joint. It is often said that the advantage men have in business is that they don't take it personally. This is true. They hardly take anything personally, including, for example, their own children. Also, when you have a success, the first thing that happens is that you experience the reaction of your friends and relatives. And an enormous part of that reaction is envy. Most women respond to that envy by being upset, by feeling guilty, by feeling that they've hurt people's feelings. Men recognize envy for what it is—a sign of success. And it spurs them on. They're delighted: losing their best friend because they're successful—nothing better could happen. Having their brother never speak to them again—perfect. This incites them to further success. Hoping that these traits are environmental, people now try to train their little girls into them. I think it's fairly useless to try to train people into testosterone, which is the key element in money-making, and also money-keeping, which is just as important.

So I think it's basically a boys' game and they'll always win. Consequently, women will simply have to content themselves with not having to play football in high school—a more than fair trade.

So you're basically resigning yourself to never having the kind of money that men have.

No. Obviously, a person who's resigned herself to not having a lot of money does not buy lottery tickets. *Having,* I believe, is still a possibility. It's *earning* that seems out of the question.

Do you read interviews with people who have made a lot of money to try to pick up helpful hints?

I used to, but they were so riddled with lies that I gave it up. They always said that the way to make a lot of money is to not think about money. Just do something you love. Clearly what they love is making money. If what they said were true, then the richest people in the world would be good teachers and bad poets.

One assumes that you are not in the habit of carrying much cash.

First of all, I'm not in the position of carrying much cash. However, if I were, I doubt that I would. There is a credit card that enables you to get $50,000 cash anywhere in the world. I haven't the slightest idea as to what sort of emergency would require $50,000 in cash, other than a ransom demand. I used to know a guy, a musician, who carried a big wad of thousand-dollar bills. I once asked to see one out of sheer intellectual curiosity—I mean, considering the suspicion with which a twenty is scrutinized at Duane Reade, a thousand-dollar bill certainly seems like the very definition of what used to be called "focusing undue attention on oneself."

> *People believe that with the collapse of the Soviet*
> *Union worldwide Communism died a sorry death, and*
> *that capitalism is clearly triumphant. Do you agree?*

Not only triumphant but rampant. Not only rampant but annihilating. Annihilating in the sense that because of this victory
the distinction between capitalism and democracy has been
almost entirely eradicated. In the Soviet Union capitalism tri-
umphed over Communism. In this country capitalism has tri-
umphed over democracy. What we have here now is more and
more an almost totally unfettered capitalism which is inhu-
mane, tremendously disadvantageous to most people, and
essentially anti-democratic. The average person simply cannot
compete in such a brutal environment. That is what average
means.

> *Who do you feel is responsible for blurring*
> *the distinction between democracy and*
> *capitalism, the right or the left?*

The confusion between democracy and capitalism is fostered by
the right but vitalized by the left, whose insistence on eliminat-
ing the difference between public and private has resulted in
people identifying themselves by social grievance rather than
economic class. The right succeeds in getting people who are
struggling to pay their bills to worry about the capital-gains tax.
The left succeeds in forcing country clubs to operate as if they
were the source of some necessary municipal service. The left
should pay more attention to which Democratic president is
sending his daughter to private school than which private club
does not admit women or blacks or Jews. The point of being a
Democrat, not to mention a president, is inclusion: the public
schools are good enough for everyone's children. The point of a
private club is exclusion: not everyone's children are good
enough for them. Caring about the latter is not only not sensible—what is important is the public good, not the private bad—
but, in fact, violates the right to be idiotic in private. What do

they do in these clubs, anyway? Sit around saying things like "Thank God I'm here. No Jews! What fun! This is living, huh? Look! No Jews! I don't know when I've had a better time. And no women! Just men! And no blacks! Just whites! White men! White men who are not Jewish! It doesn't get any better than this." To some people, apparently, this is a perfect description of injustice. To me, this is a perfect description of a gay bar in Iceland. At any rate, in neither case is it a proper matter for public concern.

> *Can you imagine taking money from rich people to give to someone like you who doesn't have enough?*

No. We take money from the rich to give to the poor—not to the broke. Remember the poor from the 60s? Let us examine the welfare bill signed by our Democratic president that took away food stamps. *Food stamps.* In this rich, fat country. In this country, where one of the biggest health problems and certainly the biggest aesthetic problem is people being too fat, meaning too much food for most people. So, clearly, we can well afford to give away food stamps, which is to give away food. I have heard our governor, George Pataki, talking about a little problem he found in the welfare bill. The little problem was the impact the bill had on people he described as a group who found themselves in this situation "through no fault of their own." That's what he said: "through no fault of their own." I believe this group was legal immigrants, the only segment of the poor beloved by Republicans—i.e., the nanny class. Legal immigrants, "through no fault of their own," under the welfare bill, were losing health services or something. This presupposes the idea that everyone else who is poor is poor through "fault of their own." There is this idea now in this country that all people who succeed, succeed on their own, and all people who fail, fail on their own, whereas neither is true. The vast majority of people in this country stay where they're born. Very few people move too far from home. Rich people rarely become poor, and poor people rarely become rich. But we live in a society ruled by anecdote, so that we have no sense at all of what actually happens to most people.

Americans almost universally believe that poor people create their poor circumstances, i.e., their own misfortune. Whereas middle-class and rich people have misfortune befall them. The misfortune of the fortunate, it seems, always appears as an act of God. In other words, "no fault of their own." The misfortune of the unfortunate is, on the other hand, perceived to be a direct result of the slothful, irresponsible, ill-intended, but not unanticipated bad choice of the embryo that insists upon taking up residence in the body of a fourteen-year-old crack addict—not, apparently, an act of God.

I've always been kind of stunned that whenever there's a flood or an earthquake or a fire everybody in the affected area starts yelling for the federal government. "Where is our federal disaster relief?" And money is raced to Malibu as the movie stars' houses fall into the ocean, and money is raced to Newport Beach as the million-dollar houses go up in flames. And money is raced to the Midwest and West, to places actually called floodplains, where, funnily enough, they have these terrible floods. And right away the president gets on television and says, "We're sending money as soon as we can," because these unlucky people—how horrible for them—they lost their houses. Through a natural disaster—"no fault of their own." Am I the only person who thinks, Why do these people qualify for huge amounts of federal money? If you live in a place called a floodplain, I think you can pretty much count on there being a flood. This to me is an excellent example of "fault of your own." But at the same time no one in the country thinks that being born into poverty is a natural disaster. And whenever these acceptable weather disasters occur, I never hear one Republican say, "Government is too big here. We shouldn't be sending all this government money to these people whose houses were all washed away." And there's this prevalent political mantra about individual responsibility—people have to take responsibility for themselves. Well, I think you have to take responsibility not to build a house on a floodplain, not to build a house clinging to a cliff over an ocean, and not to move to a place where they routinely have earthquakes. If I said to you, "Oh, there was an earthquake today," you would instantly think, "California." So I think, Well, that's "fault of your own." I'm not saying these people shouldn't get federal money; I'm simply saying that Grand Forks, North Dakota, is no more an act of God than Newark, New Jersey.

It's been said that one of the boons of the future will be the disappearance of physical money. That we'll all walk around with Smart Cards, with money encoded on them. How do you feel about that prospect?

I probably wouldn't take to it, because I'm a reactionary and therefore constitutionally opposed to all innovation. This includes MetroCards and doctors who demand payment by check or credit card before you leave their offices. Doctors should either send bills or admit that they're retailers. New York Hospital is either a citadel of wisdom and healing, staffed by dedicated professionals, or just another store employing the usual assortment of surly salesgirls and bewildered managers. They can't have it both ways.

How do you respond, then, to escalating prices?

Well, it's hard for me to keep up with inflation because sulking, no matter how furiously, does not include cost-of-living increases. Also, I feel that among the things I learned in childhood were prices, by which I mean I see no reason for them to have changed. After all, five times five is still twenty-five and the capital of Delaware is still Dover, ergo: a pack of chewing gum should cost a nickel. It cost a nickel when I was a child—why should it cost sixty cents now? It's still chewing gum. It's not like they improved it in some way.

Is there anything that you would spend anything for—money no object?

Neurosurgery. I would not shop around. Who is the most ridiculously expensive neurosurgeon in the world? That's the guy I want.

If you acquired money tomorrow, would you stay in New York?

No. And not just me. The last big lottery was something like $45 million. Whenever the lottery gets that big the local news covers it. I saw on TV reporters going into the streets and asking people, "What would you do if you won the lottery?" And the first thing that every person said was "I'd leave New York." So now I realize that not only do I live in a city where all the residents want to leave but not a single one feels that he could get out for a penny under $45 million. That, as expensive as it is to live here, we imagine it would cost much more to get out. I myself would be gone like a shot.

Would you hide out in the proverbial house on the beach?

I know that's the dream, but I do not have this desire. I find the ocean very noisy. The surf pounding on the shore—sometimes when I'm at a house on the beach, I can't sleep because of the din, which to me, frankly, is just the nautical version of Con Edison drilling.

If you had a lot of money, would you give some of it away to an organization or goal or cause?

Yes, it would be very enjoyable to give a lot of money away. But people are always saying how awful it is that when people give money to an institution they tell them how to spend it. Well, what's the point otherwise? I would never give money to an institution without issuing instructions, if not edicts. There is no institution that I feel so accurately reflects my own judgment that I would let it just spend the money however it wanted. But I also would like to be like that guy on the old TV show *The Millionaire*, John Beresford Tipton. Remember him? He gave a million dollars tax-free to one person at a time. And he gave it anonymously. Exactly what I would do. But not because I'm a modest person like John Beresford Tipton, but because I believe this generosity would be likely to inspire the same number of irritating phone calls that writing a screenplay would entail.

Have you seen the ad with Sally Struthers asking for money for Third World children? Would you send her some of your money?

No. There seem to be a number of charities that show these children and they say that you get a specific child. They say, "You will have your own child and he will write you letters." Like the thing you want most in life is more mail. Clearly, the upside of being rich is you don't have to see your mail. And when they say that for the price of a cup of coffee—sixty-seven cents a day—you can support this child, my first thought, I am somewhat ashamed to say, is Where can you get a cup of coffee for sixty-seven cents? And my second thought is that I should move to this place where you can raise a child on sixty-seven cents a day because that must mean that for eighty-seven cents a day you can live like Peter the Great. But I would never send money to an organization like that, because I'm afraid that what they really do is send you the actual child and I, as you know, live in a place where the daily cost of raising a child is apparently something closer to $67,000.

If this current trend of your having no money continues, how will you fund your retirement?

I seem to be the only person around my age who has not been thinking about this for the past twenty years. The truth is, I don't actually work hard enough to envision a time when I would be working much less. Now, I realize that eventually—because I believe there will come a time when cigarette smoking will be illegal in this country—I will be compelled to become a smoking expatriate. And I'll live in a foreign country where I won't understand a word that is being said around me. Which in itself would be immensely relaxing. I'll move to one of those countries where you can raise a child on sixty-seven cents a day. Because if you can raise a child on sixty-seven cents a day—and children are, after all, still growing—you can probably retire on seventeen cents. I mean, *my* shoe size stays the same.

> **How many rich people are there in the world,
> do you think?**

Not nearly enough to go around.

•• NEWS QUIZ ••

4/16/98 "RAINY DAY FUN"

The list is: Drink antifreeze; eat a lot of loquat seeds; swallow an eighteen-inch stick; walk in front of a tour bus. List of what?

"What happens to Jerry, George, Elaine, and Kramer on the final *Seinfeld.*"—John Koski

"Options that Sylvia Plath considered and rejected because they didn't have that special 'this is all my husband's fault' quality."—Nancy Franklin

"What you must do if you wake up and find you've accidentally spent the night making wondrous, tender love with Senator Jesse Helms."—Meg Wolitzer

"The extras (over and above the standard Haftorah instruction and Chicken Kiev/Poached Salmon for fifty) in the new Busch Gardens 'Extreme Bar Mitzvah' package."   —David Rakoff

"The rarely played second stanza of a song by KC & the Sunshine Band:

> *Drink antifreeze;*
> *Eat a lot of loquat seeds;*
> *Swallow an eighteen-inch stick;*
> *Walk in front of a tour bus,*
> *Get down tonight,*
> *Get down tonight.*"
>   —Andy Aaron

• RANDY'S WRAP UP •

Ask a grotesque question, you get a grotesque answer. Or a Fox prime-time special. Which tonight means both "World's Wildest Police Videos" (Is that the one where the Rio PD executes homeless orphan boys? Wild!) and "World's Scariest Police Stings." (And is there anything more amusing than entrapment? Kids, hurry and finish your homework!) It's a perfect Rupert Murdoch product—police excesses as entertainment. Now if only there were a way to do it live, in Florida, and charge admission. Giulianiland? Get me Michael Eisner. And a cold compress.

ARTIFICIAL AFRICAN ANSWER

Causes of death among exotic animals at Disney's new Animal Kingdom theme park.

Among the dead—four four-month-old cheetah cubs (kidney failure from drinking ethylene glycol, an ingredient in antifreeze); two Asian small-clawed otters (the loquat seeds); a black rhino (the eighteen-inch stick); and two West African crowned cranes (hit by "safari-vehicle" tour buses in separate incidents). Disney officials say the rhino did not eat the stick while at the Animal Kingdom.

According to the *Orlando Sentinel,* on April seventh, the U.S. Department of Agriculture launched an investigation into a string of animal deaths at the park.

"At this point in time, we haven't found any intent or any violation of humane standards," said Captain Jerry Thompson, the commission's statewide inspection coordinator. "It's an unfortunate situation, but we don't find it highly unusual to have deaths in the captive wildlife industry."

Animal Kingdom, an $800-million venture eight years in the making, opens in Florida on April 22. Disney officials note that many of the one thousand animals in the park are not dead.

LEFTOVERS

"Out to get me? Oh, no, no, no. We enjoy good friendship with everybody around here."   —Giacomo Turano, after a five-hundred-pound chunk of steel and concrete fell onto his (unoccupied) seats at Yankee Stadium

"Who would put it past George [Steinbrenner] to do something like this?"   —Frank Albano, talk radio caller and Yankee fan

Trout

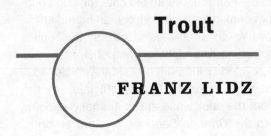

FRANZ LIDZ

I live on a wooded Chester County hillside overlooking the gurgling waters of White Clay Creek, about an hour's drive from Philadelphia. But on Opening Day, I can't get out of my driveway. It's not that raptorlike Philadelphia Phillies fans have swooped down on me. The pickups stacked up in my driveway—and for miles along the narrow road leading to civilization—are left by crazed fishermen. At six A.M. on the trout season's traditional Saturday opener, the White Clay banks are clumped with anglers eyeing clumps of stocked trout. At seven A.M., those anglers are as tightly packed as sardines, which are not stocked.

This year I figured, as long as I can't drive, I might as well cast. For verisimilitude, I ask my neighbor Lindsey Flexner to come along. He actually knows how to fish. "First, you'll need a fishing license," he advises. And so, the day before the home opener, I drive to DiFilippo's General Store on the edge of Kennett Square, a drowsy little hamlet that bills itself as the "Mushroom Capital of the World." That may be true, but it is also the world's apostrophe capital. One three-block stretch of State Street boasts Sam's Sub Shop, Kirk's Martial Arts,

Samantha's Cafe, Torelli's Men's Shop, My Sister's Shoes, Harrington's Coffee Company, Stephen's Menswear, Burton's Barber Shop, Rebecca Cooper's Consignment Boutique, Marston's Furniture, Clifford's Hair Fashions, Fran Keller's Eatery, B. B. Wolf's Restaurant, Kim's Nails, and Johnson's Catering. DiFilippo's, which is across the street from Fleming's Used Cars and catty-corner to Russ's Transmissions and Andy's Autotech, has a cryptic sign out front that reads:

HEY DADDY-O!
MONEY ORDERS—KEYS
STOP WE MAY HAV IT

Hey Daddy-O! I've always imagined that DiFilippo's interior was decked out like some Rat Pack bachelor pad, and that DiFilippo himself was a Vegas hipster who spoke in the finger-snapping lingo favored by Dino, Sammy, and Frankie: "Absopositively!" and "How's your clyde, Clyde?"

But the elderly fellow hunched over the register is more dinosaur than lounge lizard. I ask if he's DiFilippo. "Yep," says Leonard DiFilippo. I ask if the store is DiFilippo's or DiFilippos'. "Singular," he says. "Used to be plural, but my brother up and quit."

I tell him I want to buy a fishing license. "Trout?" he asks.

"Bingo, dingo!" I say enthusiastically.

The ancient hepcat coolly ignores the remark. As he completes the paperwork, I ask where to get gear. He points eastward and says: "Pete's."

At Pete's Outdoors (tucked between Rubinstein's Office Products and Granny Smith's Deli), I stock up on poles and nets and hooks and sinkers and hip boots. Then I drive home and await Opening Day.

Lindsey and his seven-year-old son, Dylan, show up the next morning at six. My ten-year-old daughter, Daisy, is already dressed and outside, clomping around in her hip boots. We bushwhack through the pickups to the Landenberg United Methodist Church; where the sign out front reads: TIME IS JUST

A STREAM I GO A-FISHIN' IN. A mechanic from Dave's Auto Service serves us a pancake and sausage "fisherman's breakfast." Daisy wraps her sausages in a paper napkin. "In case we run out of bait," she explains.

Bait we buy across the road at the Landenberg Store, which everybody calls Rosemary's. The sign by the door says: BAD DAY AT THE CREEK? WE HAVE FRESH TROUT FOR SALE. "You'll have no problem landing a trout," says the proprietor, Rosemary Bauer. "It's as easy as fishing in a toilet out there." An indelicate phrase, that.

In the last darkness before dawn, we join the swelling school of fly fishermen standing shoulder to shoulder in camouflage fatigues. They all seem to have festooned their hats with scores of dry flies as though at any moment they might dunk their heads into the current to land a three-pounder. "This has about as much to do with real trout fishing as putt-putt does with real golf," mutters Lindsey. "These aren't even real trout—they're hatchery dogs who've been raised on puppy chow."

Lugging a box of tackle and two plastic Baggies filled with worms, we immoderately compleat anglers climb through brambles of wild rose to the clear shallows. The camouflaged guy to our left yanks trout after trout out of the water. "It's all in the cast," he tells Daisy. She sails a nightcrawler along the edges of a granite outcropping, where most of the creek's trout population supposedly lurks. Then she slowly cranks the wiggler back in short, lively spurts. Daisy repeats this for forty minutes or so before asking: "When are we supposed to catch the fish?"

Dylan has already given up. He's in the middle of the creek, building a dam. "Look, I'm a beaver," he says, splashing a twig into the water. Lindsey, irritation mounting, tells him to be a quiet beaver. "Trout get scared off by a bunch of noise," he says. "They may be hatchery dogs, but they're still fish."

Lindsey casts earthworms for two hours before switching to Power Bait, a Play-Doh-like substance the color of ballpark mustard. The side of the container warns: "Not for Human or Pet Consumption."

"If it's not fit for humans or pets," I say, "then why feed it to the trout we're supposed to eat?"

"Just chew around the bait," Lindsey advises. He Play-Dohs a hook and says, "When fish are real finicky, you want something subtle." Around ten-thirty he subtly drops a hook into some weeds. A rainbow strikes, and Lindsey nets all seven inches of it. It flops on the bank, much to the dismay of Dylan. "I hate to see animals suffer," he says, and promptly grabs a log and bashes the fish's head in.

"Dylan," I say. "Remind me never to stub my toe around you."

Five minutes later my fiberglass rod bends as a fish struggles against my line. This one is only a chub, maybe two inches long. Three, fully extended. "It counts more," consoles Lindsey. "It's a native." I keep casting—mealworms, waxworms, church sausages. Yet my perseverance goes unrewarded: Over the next two hours I snag lots of fishermen's lines, but no fish.

Bad day at the creek, so we shuffle down to Rosemary's to buy a fresh trout. The third-grader at the door proudly displays his string of six big rainbows. Lindsey holds his tiny fish aloft. "Nice catch," says Rosemary. "Whose is it, Daisy's or Dylan's?"

Like I say, it's a very possessive place.

Jumpin' Jiminy

FRANZ LIDZ

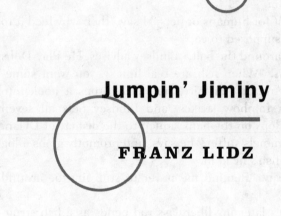

Cricket fighting along the Yangtze River begins silently in the last darkness before dawn. Cricket masters lug their chirping pugs in round clay cages. Sampans loaded with cricket enthusiasts pull toward the big new market that squats on a Shanghai bank like a concrete frog.

Even the Cultural Revolution couldn't suppress the ancient Chinese sport of cricket fighting. Mao was so fond of crickets that he took his favorite, How Peng Yiou, along on The Long March and cried when it ended an illustrious career in the belly of a cat. The Great Herdsman rallied his troops in the Manchurian hills with cricket fights and compared his men with the most durable and rugged insect combatants. Although it isn't recorded in The Little Red Book, we can imagine Mao exhorting his soldiers: "Comrades, you are as brave and as fierce as crickets."

The revolution considered gambling impolitic, but now, under Mao's more pragmatic successors, cricket handicapping is being rehabilitated. Matches draw as many as 20,000 spectators, though ringsiders have to watch the action through binoculars.

Shanghai matches feature a dozen bouts of five rounds each. Bookmakers wander the aisles between fights, quoting odds on a chalkboard. The bouts last from five seconds to five minutes. They end when one cricket is either flipped onto its back by its opponent, maimed, or killed. Champion crickets sell for as much as $150, the price of a good horse. While most compete about once a week, the legendary Moy Liao could do battle nightly—and did so for an entire autumn until he expired of natural causes. He was enshrined in a gold coffin.

Cricket fighting arose in the Tang dynasty (618 through 906) and reached its apogee in the last years of the Sung dynasty, when the royal court was so preoccupied with crickets that citizens could even pay taxes with them. One emperor, Nee How Ma, supposedly kept a cricket representing each of his courtesans and bestowed favors on the one whose love bug performed particularly well that day.

In the years of colonial hegemony leading up to the revolution, cricket fights became a source of nationalistic pride. Macao's notorious Cricket Riot of 1926 was set off by a match between a Chinese champ, Kual Tz, and Ko Ming, a Russian katydid (technically a grasshopper, as it makes chirping noises by rubbing its left forewing over the right rather than the other way around).

With an unruly crowd of sailors and vagabonds looking on, the Russian entrant answered the bell for round four, staggered to the center of the ring, and collapsed. So hopping mad was Ko Ming's trainer that he charged the opposite corner, mashing Kual. In the ensuing violence, thirty-five people were killed and the port of Macao was closed for four days.

In contemporary China, they still argue whether the captured-in-the-wild are superior to purebred domestics. City peasants, the honest rustic. The party line tends to support the populists. "A champion," says Bon Sui, "can spring up from anywhere."

Shanghai's most respected cricket referee is telling me this in a stall of the Yangtze market. He's hovering over a clear plastic box, about as big as a pound of butter. Inside this dinky arena skitter a black and a brown cricket, antennae quivering with prefight jitters.

"Time for the weigh-in," Bon Sui says, scooping up the combatants with a tiny net and placing each one separately on a postage scale. The brown bug tips the scales at five li; his black opponent, nine. A li is about a twentieth of a gram, Bon Sui explains, with a four-li cricket considered a middleweight. "The black cricket is a regular Mike Tyson," he says. "The brown cricket is more like Sylvester Stallone."

After the weigh-in, the brutes are spurred on by tickling with a single mouse whisker fitted into the shaved end of a chopstick. Modern trainers have experimented with chemicals and insect hormones, Bon Sui allows, though no cricket has ever been disqualified for taking steroids.

As a swarm of maybe fifty cricketeers presses in, Tyson makes a great leap forward and charges Stallone. Tyson rears back on his hind legs and unloads wild combinations with his short, white forelegs. Stallone folds his forelegs in front of him to ward off punches and lunges forward—straight into a barrage of overhand rights, crisp left hooks, and mottled brown teeth that snap his head back. Stallone clutches, leans, and absorbs an awful banging around his coxa and mandible. After two minutes of grueling but guileless fighting, Bon Sui declares Tyson the winner. An un-Rockylike ending, to be sure.

As Stallone's owner swats him out of the stadium, I ask Bon Sui: "Do you think the brown cricket might have been paid to dump the fight?"

"No way!" he says.

He's right, of course. It just wouldn't be cricket.

Space Travel Food

FRANZ LIDZ

There is no pie in the sky. The U.S. space shuttle stocks malted-milk balls, brownies, Teddy Grahams, granola bars, peanut M&Ms, and Butterscotch Krimpets, but there's not one pie in the pantry. Not even a Moon Pie. Which is probably for the best. The crust might flake off and float through the gravity-free cabin, gumming up the control panels.

It seems the big news, though, is that space food has reached new heights of sophistication. While not as yet out of this world, it's reportedly more palatable than in the days when astronauts sucked down Silly Putty meals from Brylcreem tubes. Nowadays, space crews choose from a menu of more than 100 nouvelle dishes ranging from shrimp cocktail to turkey tetrazzini. At launch, the orbiter even carries fresh pears, peaches, and pineapples, but because it lacks refrigeration, space shuttlers have to depend on packaged foods later in the mission. A lot of that chow originates in Houston area grocery stores before it's rendered inedible by government Space Chefs.

To be fair, however, I rise to the challenge and venture to the food laboratory of the Johnson Space Center in Houston for a little astronomy gastronomy. Dr. Charles Bourland, NASA's preeminent food scientist, has prepared a veritable extraterrestrial banquet. I hunker down at a lab table, surrounded by dozens of slate-gray bins, each containing dozens of slate-gray polyethylene pouches vacuum-packed full of Space Food. The list of sixteen space beverages that Dr. Bourland hands me includes tea, tropical punch, and that space pioneer, Tang. But not tequila: Spirits are barred from the heavens. Three brandy miniatures were smuggled aboard *Apollo* 8 in 1968, but Command Pilot Frank Borman vetoed the libation. "We're already high enough," he reportedly said.

Each food pouch Dr. Bourland offers in his seven-course meal is backed in Velcro. I fasten the pouches to my Velcro-dotted Space Tray and launch into my meal.

Course 1: Space Tortillas

Back in 1965, John Young smuggled a corned-beef sandwich aboard the *Gemini III* flight and littered the spacecraft with crumbs. It was another four years before astronauts were allowed to eat nitrogen-flushed bread. In 1985, payload specialist Rodolfo Neri-Vela asked for tortillas to wrap around his dehydrated and otherwise denatured grub. Tortillas have been a shuttle staple ever since. In a pinch, they also make swell space kleenexes.

Course 2: Space Beefsteak

Aficionados of the Three Stooges will remember the time Moe, Larry, and Curly inherited the deed to the Beefsteak Mines. I can still make out the pickax marks in my medium-rare nugget. By squeezing the laminated foil pouch from the bottom, the beefsteak emerges much like the monolith in Stanley Kubrick's *2001*. "This meat was developed by the army," says Dr. Bourland. "It should last five, six, maybe seven years." Mine carbon-dates to 1990 and comes with an itty-bitty packet of A-1 sauce, the liberal use of which is recommended.

"Beefsteak and turkey are the only items that come irradiated," Dr. Bourland assures me. The nuked flesh is dry and tough and answers the question, Whatever happened to Shemp?

Course 3: Space Rice Pilaf

Being high in space has little to do with haute cuisine, as Patrick Baudry discovered while riding in the *Discovery* in 1985. "What struck me up there," the French astronaut remarked, "is that you are in exceptional circumstances, with grandiose scenery, and the food you eat is ordinary."

Revolted by the American menu of chicken à la king and beef with noodles, Baudry brought jugged hare a l'Alsacien, lobster américain, baguettes, crab mousse, cantal cheese, and pâté. Unjugged, the hare induced nausea in the five human Américains aboard. "The shuttle can't vent odors," explains Dr. Bourland. "Believe me, you don't want to spend sixteen days in space with an open can of rabbit." I gape at the unidentifiable floating objects suspended in the pilaf.

Course 4: Space Italian Vegetables

Freeze-dried about the same time as Walt Disney, these veggies were rehydrated into a puree that looks suspiciously like Soylent Green. Even Dr. Bourland can't tell me exactly which Italian vegetables hide in this bubbling archipelago, though I spoon out what appears to be a chunk of Al D'Amato's cheek.

Course 5: Space Sweet 'n' Sour Beef

The alleged beef is soft and soggy, like a Tootsie Roll that's been soaked in a bathtub overnight. It floats in brown sludge that tastes like Klingon spit strained through Buzz Aldrin's socks. I try to wash away the taste with Space Orange-Pineapple Drink, which is a formidable color my thirteen-year-old daughter Gogo once called "hot yellow." I wonder for a moment what they do with the bathwater after they've soaked the beef.

Course 6: Space Lemonade

After sampling this elixir, I stop wondering about the bathwater. I'm reminded of a ball game I attended years ago at Wrigley Field. A pitcher named Tim Belcher was on the mound, and I sat next to a Chicago Cubs fan who was slugging back ballpark beer. He had already stacked up six jumbo cups and was flagging down a vendor for number seven. I asked: "How's it taste?"

"Taste!" he said incredulously. "Nobody tastes stadium beer. It tastes like nothing. It doesn't have a taste. Taste! I don't want taste. I want beer."

The same epicurean principle applies to the Space Lemonade I sip through a transparent space straw. Like ballpark beer, it seems specially designed just to flow through you. It may, in fact, have important medicinal qualities in that it so successfully flushes out Space Beefsteak.

Course 7: Space Banana Pudding

In lieu of such regional space desserts as Mars Bars or Milky Ways, or, say, Tribble soufflé, Dr. Bourland serves me a cup of banana pudding. I shovel in a mouthful and suddenly, like What's-His-Name gnawing on his madeleine, my mind floods with memories of grade school. This thermostabilized pudding is the color of pencil erasers and the consistency of mucilage. Or is it the other way around?

Before I depart, I scan the shuttle menu of Story Musgrave, a prickly astronaut who demands the same three meals every day. "I'm not here to dine," he snarls. "I'm here to work."

What's eating at Musgrave? I suspect the shrimp cocktail.

Piscopo Agonistes

FRANZ LIDZ AND STEVE RUSHIN

PART I

Last year's teen slasher smash *I Know What You Did Last Summer* proved that each generation of adolescents is new to the genre's creaky conventions. The formula calls for invincible, barely visible villains (*Friday the 13th*'s Jason, *Halloween*'s Michael Myers, *Nightmare on Elm Street*'s Freddy Krueger) shrouded in malevolent headgear (goalie mask, Halloween mask, felt-brim fedora) and wielding sharp, shiny implements (hunting knife, carving knife, razorlike Lee press-on nails). The most important convention is the sequel, the ceaseless serializing of serial killing.

Friday, Halloween, and *Nightmare* spawned twenty unholy offspring among them. And this week, the inevitable first sequel to *Summer* opens. In the original, an angst-riddled angler named Ben Willis (Muse Watson) wears a black sou'wester and brandishes an ice hook in a seaside North Carolina burg. Fisherman Ben terrorizes teen townies Julie James (Jennifer Love Hewitt), Ray Bronson (Freddie Prinze Jr.), and their innumerable soon-to-croak cronies. Julie and Ray live to see the sequel, and so does—surprise!—Fisherman Ben. This time the three are joined in the Bahamas (don't ask) by Karla Wilson (the mononymed pop star Brandy). The film concludes with the sine qua non of sequeldom, an ambiguous ending. With that in mind, we asked two of Hollywood's hottest young screenwriters to plot out endless "Summer" sequels. When they turned us down, we did it ourselves.

I Know What You Did in the Summer of '42

In this prequel to *I Know What You Did Last Summer,* the parents of Julie and Ray cope with the horrors of World War II by playing beach volleyball, catamaran sailing and lawn bowling in East Hampton with Hermie and Oscy, teenage heroes of the 1971 crypto-classic *The Summer of '42.* The older movie's Older Woman, Jennifer O'Neill, seduces a young beachcomber (Jonathan Taylor Thomas) who boasts of his conquest to multi-nymed classmates Jennifer Love Hewitt, Jennifer Jason-Leigh, Mary Elizabeth Mastrantonio, Mary Stuart Masterson, Mary Louise Parker, Sarah Jessica Parker and Sarah Michelle Gellar.

I Know What You'll Do Next Summer

Julie and Ray are transported to twenty-third-century Los Angeles, where the only living link to the city's past is Bob Hope, whose 392nd annual NBC Christmas Special is as fresh as ever. The great-great-great-great-great grandson of Fisherman Ben (Freddie Prinze Jr. Jr. Jr. Jr. Jr.) is not casting crankbait—he's casting movies! When he asks "Where's the hook?" he's in a pitch meeting! As president of 24th Century-Fox, Ben is still looking for fresh ideas. He tells his idea people to "stop living in the 2200s," and the studio releases the only non-sequel in the last 200 years. Alas, Romulo Ebert of the *Mars Daily Planet* gives the movie three thumbs down.

I Know What Hugh Did Last Summer

Fisherman Ben washes ashore on a private beachfront in Malibu, where Westec security guards frog-march him off the property, the summer rental of Hugh Grant and Liz Hurley. Grant tells Hurley he's "popping out for a Brandy." When Hurley finds him seventy-two hours later at the L.A. County Jail, Grant is performing *A Midsummer Night's Dream* with cellmates Willis, Robert Downey Jr., Sean Penn, and Christian Slater. A bootleg copy of the survellience video turns up at the Chichester offices of Merchant-Ivory, who turn it into . . .

I Dreamt What You Did Last Midsummer

In a well-intentioned homage to the 1935 Max Reinhardt masterwork (which featured Mickey Rooney as Puck and Jimmy Cagney as Bottom), director Kenneth Branagh brings nothing new to this familiar standard. Helena Bonham Carter quits in pre-production, cattily calling the film little more than "I Know What You Did Last Summer Stock." Preview audience response cards are hardly kinder, and Branagh hastily tacks on a new ending set in a Viennese sleep disorder clinic. Rex Reed writes: "Oscar's napping if he doesn't come calling on Kenneth!"

I Know You Took the Last Dim Sum

Fisherman Ben orders Chinese take-out in Manhattan. When the deliveryman (Jackie Chan) arrives with larceny in his heart and duck sauce in his beard, all hell breaks loose. John Woo directs.

Läst Sjommer Zum Zum Vlit Kjlåmmer

Death (Joe Piscopo) visits Stockholm, but is thwarted when Lufthansa loses his scythe. So Death takes a holiday. To the familiar Bergman themes—Godlessness, Life's emptiness, the thin line between sanity and madness—the Swedish auteur adds a new one: the utter hopelessness of finding a decent mochaccino around Stallmästaregården Norrtull.

I Know What You Did Last Summer, But Enough About You: Let's Talk About What I Did Last Summer

This $400-million epic from writer/director James Cameron goes wildly over budget when the egocentric "King of the World" summons to the set perceived rivals Larry King, Alan King, Don King, Billie Jean King, and cereal's King Vitamin. Insiders describe the increasingly paranoiac Cameron as "a royal pain." No animals were harmed in the making of the movie, set in an Azerbaijani abattoir, though Amnesty International decries the tortured soundtrack by Celine Dion.

I Know What You Did, Miss Sommer

Jonathan Winters summers on Cape Cod. Suzanne Somers, Pat Summerall, and Elke Sommer winter in Aspen. On the first day of spring, all four connect at O'Hare, where bomb-sniffing dogs determine this movie will be one. Undercover FAA officials—working in tandem with Transportation Secretary Federico Pena and Academy of Motion Picture Arts & Sciences poobah Jack Valenti—shut the production down, and order a cessation of any and all *Summer* sequels.

Based on a soon-to-be-true story.

PART II

Alexander Graham Bell's famous pronouncement—"Mr. Watson, come here, I want you"—was the first intelligible sentence spoken by telephone. And the last intelligible sentence spoken by a Scotsman, in any medium. Or so it would seem to unaccustomed ears. Ask Scottish director Bill Forsyth, whose 1981 film *Gregory's Girl* had to be redubbed for American and English audiences. Thick burrs were rendered thinner than cock-a-leekie soup.

Things have gotten worse. *My Name Is Joe*, a Glasgow-set feature from director Ken Loach, was recently released here with subtitles, as if it weren't even nominally in English. When we phoned him for comment, Loach was indignant. At least we think he was indignant. At least we think he was Loach. Frankly, we couldn't understand a word.

The same can be said for a whole rash of recent British movies: from the Newcastle horseracing saga *Eden Valley* (1994) to the Edinburgh junkie saga *Trainspotting* (1996) to the Nottingham boxing saga *24–7* (1998). To American audiences, these films might as well be in Northern Malawian CheCheewa. Moviegoers on these shores have long been baby-powdered by British actors who pamper every line as if the English language were a newborn's bottom. If we weren't savoring the plummy consonants in stuffy Merchant-Ivory productions, we were relishing the plumped vowels in stifling Elizabethan costume dramas. Lately, though, British movies have become both less mannered and less manored. And the grittier the fiction, the muddier the diction. The British cinema isn't dead, it's just not speaking as clearly.

"When I was growing up in Glasgow in the 1960s, to move ahead, to make money, to get a job anywhere that required opening your mouth, you had to speak BBC English," says Lex Braes, an abstract painter who now lives in Brooklyn (the borough that served as the setting for *Goodfellas*—a film whose dialogue was equally incomprehensible to British audiences). "These days it's not just OK to have a burr or a brogue over there, it's desirable. It's like New Labour—'Hey, we're all included.' That attitude carries over to the British cinema, where it's suddenly fashionable to have a regional accent."

If so, the height of British cinematic fashion may be *My Name Is Joe,* a film about a recovering alcoholic whose name we could never quite make out. Loach has been making pointed, poignant features about England's underclass since *Kes* (1969), a boy-meets-falcon tale that should have been closed-captioned for the Leeds-impaired. *Joe* is an even harder go. If you close your eyes (and you will), it is difficult to ascertain a single line of dialogue. The cast was voice-coached, evidently, by the guy who announces stops on New Jersey Transit trains. The title character has all the elocution of Mickey Rourke, which explains why the French loved him so. Peter Mullan, who plays Joe, won the best actor prize at Cannes.

Another British export in need of explication was last year's *Nil By Mouth*. Even the title could use a subtitle. Alas, the newly released video has none. Of Nil's cockamamie Cockney—which borders on Mockney—director Gary Oldman has said: "It's like watching Shakespeare. It all sounds like gobbledygook for the first ten minutes, you just have to work." *William* Shakespeare? Funny, we do not recall him writing, "A 'orse, a 'orse, me kingdom fer a 'orse." With the exception of a very few phrases in *Nil*—"Good mornin', Guv'nor"; "a coupla geezers"; "the ol' carrot-an'-onions"—what little we worked out could not be printed in a family newspaper. Volume 6 of the *Encyclopedia Britannica* contains fewer F-words.

Yet another picture lacking both subtitles and subtleties is *Among Giants*, which will be released stateside in March. *Giants* is a high-voltage electrical tower romance set in the vertical world of utility pylons along the Yorkshire Moors. This dizzying love story was written by Simon Beaufoy, whose growing Sheffield-based oeuvre began with *The Full Monty*, the 1997 crossover smash about redundant steelworkers baring the ol' carrot-an'-onions. *Monty* became the highest-grossing British film ever largely because non-British Midlanders didn't need a Berlitz course to get it.

Not so *Giants*. The most gripping—or rather, least gripping—scene in *Giants* sees a fearless Australian backpacker (Rachel Griffiths), imprudently mountaineering without her partner (Pete Postelthwaite), fall from a rock face and into oblivion (Joe Piscopo). What makes the fall doubly devastating for American audiences is that Griffiths is the film's only comprehensible actor.

The anti-social climber's calamity, which she survives, leads to the film's climactic exchange between Ray, played by Postelthwaite, and a coworker named Steve (James Thornton) who happens to be the hypotenuse of a bizarre love triangle.

THORNTON: "She gamma az inna, Ray! She fella sheeba fa fluv!"
POSTELTHEWAITE: "Whaa!"
THORNTON: "Jaga zina spittle, Ray!"
POSTELTHWAITE: (*despondent*): "Stu PaBasta!"
THORNTON: (*agitated*): "She fuga luvdja. *She fuga luvdja!*"

Stunned, as anyone would be by this revelation, Postelthwaite races to Griffith's hospital room and makes a moving bedside confession: "Beffa fubba hopang engla gland leega bunz maw."

GRIFFITHS: "Say good-bye to Steve for me."
POSTELTHWAITE: "Neela braygiz amuffa feffla!"
GRIFFITHS: (*tearfully*): "Ray, I'm sorry."
POSTELTHWAITE: (*tenderly*): "Mee tulip, goo timi zowap."

Stunned, as anyone would be by this revelation, Griffiths leaves town for good. The audience is left stranded on an electrical Tower of Babble.

Somewhere in this script, we are sure, has been encrypted the $600 Neiman-Marcus cookie recipe.

PART III

The days of the sequel are numbered. Or rather, Roman numeraled. *Lethal Weapon,* the Mel Gibson vehicle that went from zero to IV in eleven years, will have no '99 model. Rocky Balboa's five-bout film career ended in 1990, after a savage critical beating that left him, and moviegoers, with collateral brain damage. Arnold Schwarzenegger, whose most famous film line is "I'll be back," won't be: The Terminator's term limit was two.

Thank goodness, because the sequel and prequel have become cinematic Nyquil, putting audiences to sleep with their metronomic monotony. This film season, for the first time in memory, audiences will endure but a single sequel (*Austin*

Powers: The Spy Who Shagged Me) and a single prequel (*Star Wars: The Phantom Menace*). We may have seen the last of Kryptonite (*Superman*) and crypto-knights (*Batman & Robin*) and crypted nights (*Dracula*). This diehard genre—indeed, this *Die Hard* genre—is comatose. Have we finally felled this sequential Sequoia, silenced this sequential cicada?

If so, audiences will never have to see Denzel Washington in *Malcolm XX* or Brad Pitt in *Seven 11*. Then again, one lesson horror sequels teach is that the villain is never quite dead. The sequel may well rise from the grave and return in an altered state (a 1980 film curiously without sequel). It takes little imagination—and Hollywood executives have just that—to envision the grim future. Inevitably, as more studios consolidate and media mergers proliferate, companies will comb their back catalogue of successful sequels, gene-splicing different genres together to form lucrative new franchises. In fact, the following are already in development.

The Thin Man with the Golden Gun

If ever two franchise players needed filmic defibrillation, they are Dashiell Hammett's Thin Man and Ian Fleming's James Bond. By installment six of the Thin Man movies, the characters' sharp edges had been removed with a No. 17 sandpaper. The once manly 007 has been neutered, and worse, now has a license to shill. In this unholy matrimony, the new Thin Man (Alan Thicke) and his much thinner wife (Calista Flockhart) founder in a much, much thinner plot entailing a solid-gold Beretta (Robert Blake) and peppered with multiple product placements (Golden Honey Grahams, Rold Gold pretzels, Gulden's mustard . . .) The couple rubs elbows—or rather, elbow—with The Man with the Golden Arm (a woefully miscast Hideki Irabu), head of the reviled organization Jobless, Obscure Ex-Performers Inflicting Senseless Chaos on Public Order (J.O.E.P.I.S.C.O.P.O.). These franchises are revived; alas, the audience cannot be.

Father of the Bride of Frankenstein

You remember her: that twitching, lurching woman with a frightening muddle of hair and a scream like mating cheese graters. But enough about Diane Keaton, female lead in *Father of the Bride* I and II. This time, director John Frankenheimer stitches the 1991 lite comedy to the '35 horror classic—and meta-sequel—*Bride of Frankenstein*. Steve Martin once again plays the father. Martin, whose toy canon of *New Yorker* casuals is prescribed reading in Viennese sleep disorder clinics, finds his long-lost muse, which has been in a federal witness protection program since *Three Amigos!* (1986). Slated for 2002: *Godfather of the Bride of Frankenstein*.

Austin, Texas, Chain Saw Massacre

A (con)fusion of *Austin Powers* and *Texas Chainsaw Massacre* in which Mike Myers, as the dentally ill British superspy, has his part cut. Fortunately, doctors are able to sew it back on.

Bruce Wayne's World of Apu

A Bermuda triangulation of sequel machines: *Batman, Wayne's World,* and *The World of Apu,* Satyajit Ray's 1959 tandoori tour de force. A pirated copy of the soundtrack master tape has yielded an underground hit single in England: "My Pappadam Told Me." Already in the can is an arranged marriage between Ray's 1955 feature *Pather Panchali* and Peter Sellers's Inspector Clouseau. The result is due out next summer: *Pink Pather Panchali.*

Sherlock Holmes Alone

The Red-Headed League (lounge comics Red Buttons, Red Skelton, Redd Foxx, and Shecky Greene, working blue) opens a British branch of the Friars Club at 221-A Baker Street. Their relentless roasting, interminable toasting and Borscht Belt boasting exasperates the rabbit-eared resident of apartment 221-B, young Sherlock Holmes (MacCauley Culkin). So Mac enlists the aid of Emily Watson, Michael Moriarity, and Rupert

Holmes, whose "Pina Colada Song" is featured in the stunning opening sequence, set at the Hyde Park Hilton's rooftop tiki bar. Porn's Johnny (Wad) Holmes produces. As usual.

Rocky Road Warrior

Ice cream impresarios Ben and Jerry (Ben and Jerry Stiller) battle Baskin (*Mad Max*'s Mel Gibson) and Robbins (*Rocky*'s Sylvester Stallone) for control of a Nazi submarine in what *Daily Variety* is calling a "Häagen-Das Boot."

Hook Knows (What You Did Last Summer)

Wes Craven's sequel to Steven Spielberg's sequel to Walt Disney's animated film of John Barrie's children's book, *Peter Pan*. Starring Golden Globe winner Robin Williams (*Hook*) and Gold Glove winner Bernie Williams. The movie's *Hook Knows* title is unfortunate, as is the Yankee centerfielder's torpid performance. Indeed, the project has already been denounced by both the Anti-Defamation League and the American League.

2048 Hours

This puzzling film is a sort of Rubik's Kubrick in which Kubrick's rubric is Confuse the Viewer. HAL, the murderous computer from *2001* and *2010,* has been working malevolently at an airline reservation counter. He is *really* having computer problems: Ravaged by the Melissa virus, made anxious by Y2K hysteria, incompatible with the Apple of his eye, Hal (IBM's Big Blue) uplinks with Microsoft's mainframe and transfers $27 of Bill Gates's fortune to charity. Outraged, Gates enlists Eddie Murphy and Nick Nolte, the buddy team of *48 Hours* and *Another 48 Hours,* to help take a byte out of crime. Self-styled "King of All Sequels" Chevy Chase (*Caddyshack, National Lampoon's Vacation, Fletch*) cameos in multiple alien roles: a Vulcan, a Romulan, a Talaxian, a Comedian.

Gardening Advice from Mertensia Corydalis

Q: Miss Corydalis, you know how invasive wild violets can be. My lawn, which I had rolled and completely reseeded last year, is a sea of little purple flowers this spring. What can I use to kill them?
         —ARTHUR, UPPER LEXINGTON

A: Arthur, I believe you misdirected your question. You want to contact the wall-to-wall carpeting column. This is a gardening column. Here, we welcome a good ravaging by little purple flowers. Did Colette confide to her journals fond memories of Kentucky bluegrass nosegays? Did Proust bury his Gallic nose in a bunch of rye-grass blend? Enough of these tiresome lawn-care questions. No more!

Q: Dear Miss Corydalis: Three years ago I planted a one-gallon pot of zebra grass close to a tiny pond. Now it is about six times larger in circumference and looks out of proportion in its location. I want to transplant it, but can't seem to dig it up with a sharp spade. I tried chopping at the roots with a hatchet and, as a last resort, cut it back and sprayed it with an herbicide (it sent up new growth immediately!). Help!

         —WILEY, SAVAGE FLATS

A: Dear Wiley, Normally I would hit the roof seeing the word "herbicide" in my mailbag, but I understand your desperation. I know that bone-jarring feeling when you hit the stolons, as unyielding as steel cables, with your spade. Your teeth are probably still vibrating. You have about as much hope of budging this clump as you do of killing a vampire with a plastic fork.

Let this be a little Sunday School lesson for the rest of the readers—before you plant that innocent-looking gallon-size clump of ornamental grass, think long and hard about the location. And if the grass in question is a running type with fast-spreading underground stolons, such as many varieties of bamboo, the plant will go off on its merry way, if you are not careful, soon thumbing its nose at you from your neighbor's yard. The only advice I have to offer our friend Wiley is to hire a professional tree-removal company to dig out the clump, or if you're on a budget, detonate a do-it-yourself thermonuclear device.

Q: Dear Mertensia: I'm new to gardening and want to try my hand at roses. I recall a bright orange one my parents were particularly proud of called Tropicana. Should I buy one potted or bare root?
—LOIS, DUDLEY

A: Lois, Lois. Where is your brain? Why in the world would you crave a rose the color of a vinyl couch in the waiting room of your local muffler shop? Color aside, as a novice to rose growing, you have no business tossing your money away on temperamental hybrid teas. Instead, investigate sturdy shrub roses.

They only come in pastels and muted reds. They will serve you well until you develop some sense of color and knowledge of rose cultivation.

Next time . . . dwarf pomegranate—
the hot new conservatory plant

The Way of the Ear

SANDRA TSING LOH

Recently it was pointed out to me—in kind of a hurtful way, to be honest—that people in Los Angeles are aurally challenged. That is, at social events, we simply do not listen to Others. We do not ask them questions about themselves; we do not nod attentively when they speak; really, if we were to examine ourselves, we would realize that we simply have no interest in Others at all.

The criticism came from a denizen of San Francisco . . . which rankles a bit right there. In fact, let me be so bold as to say that after many visits, I've come to feel that San Francisco people listen to each other too much. What with the cappuccinos and the smugness and the flouncing and the book groups: In the end they have very little to say and should be punished for it. "Come to L.A.," I want to say, "where you will be good and ignored like you should be."

But I digress. The point is, yes we do listen here in our smoggy basin. Perhaps it is not all the caring giving loving listening that is offered on the front porches of tiny Midwestern towns. Perhaps much of it comes at a hefty price the unwitting

Mr. Spalding Gray monologist will pay later. But that is the way of modern "listening"—or at least controlling the flow of one's inattention. And there are at least ten ways we do this.

1: *"Pleasantly Playing Computer Solitaire While Trying Not to Make Too Much Noise Clicking the Mouse" Listening*

<u>Most Common Practitioners</u>: People with Retired Older Relatives

Nowadays, it is possible to perform various forms of Low-Impact Listening via the telephone. The advent of technological advances such as computer games and on-line services (like checking stocks) have enabled Low-Impact listeners to endure family phone calls much longer than in the past. Dangers include mouse clicks, heavy typing, or a sudden loud buzzer that goes off when you have finished Boggle.

2: *"I Married a Nut Case" Listening*

<u>Most Common Practitioners</u>: Every Human Couple

One of the duties of being married seems to be running from room to room while your spouse lumbers heavily behind, raving in a wildly disorganized fashion about someone who slighted them at work that day. Your job is to provide a buffer, so the loved one in question does not take this ridiculous monologue directly out into the world, where he or she will be humiliated. The upside is that you can often do laundry or watch CNN at the same time.

3: *"Defensive" Listening*

<u>Most Common Practitioners</u>: Every Human Couple, "Multicultural" Encounter Groups

Also known as "They're Mad at Me for Never Listening" Listening or "If I Don't Listen I'll Pay for It Later" Listening

4: *"Making a Deposit for My Monologue to Come Later" Listening*

<u>Most Common Practitioners</u>: People with Friends

What is a friend? A friend is a person who joins with you in the Universal Listening Contract, to wit: "You sit through my

Hour-Long Rambling Monologues About the Vague Problems of Life, I sit through yours." But so often people violate that contract, don't they? They do *their* hour, and then say: "What's going on with you? Oops! I'm late for a meeting!" That is why we kill.

But no. Sometimes when the Contract is violated, we merely reevaluate at the end of the year, like a board of stockholders. As we write Christmas cards, and we consider the bum portfolio that is the Satanically Self-Involved (SSI) friend. Sometimes we renew for one more year, in deference to past years of higher aural return, sometimes we do not.

5: *"Keeping One's Face Very Calm and Supportive While Secretly Waiting for Gristly Bits of Gossip to Drop from the Groaning Board of Personal Disarray" Listening*

<u>Most Common Practitioners</u>: Women with Friends

My SSI friend Lynn, on the other hand, had no saving grace at all except the graphic tirades she used to go into about her miserable sex life with her husband, Bruce, an aggressive tennis-playing lawyer. "We *are* having problems in bed," she'd sigh. *"Terrible* problems. He does a kind of weird *pinching* thing. And *giggles*. I told him it was a turn-off and he cried." Horrible story, yes, but somehow you cannot turn away.

6: *"Not In Tune with My Needs" Listening*

<u>Most Common Practitioners</u>: Graduates of 12-Step Programs

Here is the paradox. We all enjoy *delivering* Hour-Long Rambling Monologues About the Vague Problems of Life. At the same time, we do not want to think of ourselves as Pathetic. Because they always say the wrong thing, "Not in Tune with My Needs" listeners have a knack for making that happen. Example:

WHAT THEY SHOULD SAY: "And what do you think David's problem is, that he keeps picking on you? Maybe he's jealous—he seemed that way at the office party. Also, he's putting on weight."

WHAT THEY DO SAY: "You're so insecure all the time!

Maybe you need to *love* yourself a bit more, give yourself a big hug."

7: *"Watch How Well I Listen!" Listening*
<u>Most Common Practitioners</u>: Women's Groups, Touchy-Feely '90s Companies That Value "Human Process"
Now they smile and administer the hug to you directly, and you feel ridiculous and full of shame.

8: *"This Information Will Be Used Against You Later in Your Performance Evaluation" Listening*
Oops! What sometimes happens with 8.

9: *"Passive Aggressive" Listening*
<u>Most Common Practitioners</u>: Those of Us Who Still Insist on Suffering Through L.A. Cocktail Parties
Why do we still go? We all hate them. No one ever talks to us except for that one person. Sometimes it's the sharp-nosed blond in plastic earrings, sometimes the hairy pear-shaped guy in shiny NBC jacket. Either way, the story's always the same: He has been in L.A. just six months and has already landed a job scrubbing toilets on *Friends!* He can't stop talking about it!

Not that the career choice is pitiable. Indeed, such dogged, unattractive people seem to be the types who most often succeed in network television production. But if only they'd ask us about *us*! Questions like: "What is your name?" "Why are you here?" "What would *you* like to talk about?"

Unlike a normal person, the Passive Aggressive listener is somehow rooted to the spot, paralyzed by hostility. Her attention jumps off the hurtling train of the monologue—speeding alongside instead in her own pace car, counting conversational turn-off posts that whiz by ignored, marking each with the point of a tiny accusing finger and triumphal "Aha!" Not that I would know very much about this.

10: *"Active" Listening*
<u>Most Common Practitioners</u>: Leonard T. Reed
It turns out, there's only one person on the planet who does

Active Listening. He is Leonard T. Reed of Ventura, California. I have tested Len on many social occasions, sending over all the women who feel that *men never listen* to them. They all come back nodding, crushed, tears in their eyes: "He *does* listen . . . like a dream!" Currently we have Len Reed chained up in a basement in Van Nuys. Call us. Appointments are available.

Eleventh-Hour Bride

SANDRA TSING LOH

Enough months have passed; the wounds have healed; I can finally talk about my wedding. My wedding, since you ask, was like the great sinking of the *Titanic*. Then again, I knew it would be. That's why I was engaged for, oh, seven years.

Note how I keep referring to "my" wedding as opposed to "our" wedding—as if this were some auto-inflicted act. It is. Indeed, as the well-over-thirty (read "old") bride (for which there should be some special niche publication: *Old Bride Magazine*) plans her Special Day, the groom becomes but an extraneous character, a rubber mascot head, a blank screen upon which the ensuing drama of the bridal breakdown is to be shakily projected.

Sound ugly? Never mind. Postfeminist women still deserve that nuptial ballgown and tiara, even if it comes ten years late and we're feeling bloated. To this end, I offer these "11th-Hour Wedding Tips." That's right. While you should throw a big wedding, yes, I don't think you should spend more than two weeks planning it. Learn from my example. Two weeks is just long enough to complete the Hysteria Cycle without killing you both.

1: *Have the Wedding at Someone's House, Preferably Not Your Own.* For the years 1990–1994 inclusive, my dream was to get married on the cliffs of Big Sur—string quartet, sunset, strawberries, champagne. We'd put up our fifty closest friends at the picturesque Big Sur Inn for one magical, unforgettable weekend. I made one phone call, got a grasp on general price and feasibility, and fell into a depression for four years.

2: *Marry Lutheran.* Unless you're religious—in that case, of course, go with the home team. And I envy you: Jews, Hindus, Catholics—come weddin' time agnostics have far less leg to stand on. When my brother got married, his Christian service posited marriage as a three-fold braid: "Husband, Wife, and Jesus." Discussing this, my sister and I began to snicker—then sobered up upon pondering the alternatives. What would our three-fold braid be? "You, Me, and My Therapist?" "You, Me and VISA?"

I say, this is for life, so get all the help you can get. Anyway, bottom line: Make a big deal about going secular, and soon you'll find yourself lighting an aromatherapy candle, mumbling about some Great Spirit's circle of love, and being much more ashamed than if you had shut up and flown coach. Lutherans, which by coincidence Mike and I were raised as, give a short, decent service that soothes parents and stuns cynical, fortyish L.A. peers into a bemused and yet oddly respectful silence.

3: *Don't Sweat the Guest List: You'll Screw It Up Anyway.* a) Are they friends from college? b) Have they had you over for dinner in the last year? c) Would they invite you to their wedding? If the answer is no, said L.A. couple is sure to be the most pissed at your not inviting them. "But when do we ever hear from them?" you ask the air. And then at 3 A.M., two months too late, the lovely gift basket they recently sent will rise in the dark like a ghost. You scream. And so you are doomed to wander in rumpled wedding gown, botched guest list trailing, forever lost in the Palace of Guilt with its many alcoves and cupolas.

4: *Two Weeks Before, Let Slip to a Few Female Acquaintances That You Have Made No Calls Re: Caterer, Flowers, Decor, Etc.* Why? Because it's fun. "And what have you chosen for your wedding colors?" a distant (twice-married) female relative asked me mellifluously on Sunday night, thirteen days before Ground Zero. A howl of laughter, while a satisfying conversation stopper, was not enough to fully articulate my position. I pressed on:

"Wedding *colors*? I'm a person who can barely dress myself in the morning. Mike and I are getting married because we love each other. We've got the paperwork, our friends are coming, we'll have a big meal. That's it. It will be simple. This is a formal commitment between two adults, not a prom. We're too old to care about stuff like flowers and decorations and tuxedos."

To which she repeated, with a kind of eerie calm: "Sandra? What have you chosen for your wedding colors?"

5: *Immediately Take 60 percent of All Hysterical Female Advice Given.* And now, of course, the descent into madness begins. Wedding colors? Who gives a flying fig about wedding colors! Not you. But should you? Are you missing out if you bypass the wedding colors? Will that make you less than female? Less than bridal? Less than married? Just generally . . . less?

Suddenly a girlish pang of hurt wells up, a forgotten bolus of need from adolescence. You sense, vaguely, your Adult Head denying your Bride Head something princesslike, magical. What: There's a multimillion-dollar bridal industry in this country and you are not included? Who do they think you are? Gertrude Stein a-wielding gardening trowel? So what if you're in your mid-thirties! That's just five years older than twenty-nine! You're far from washed up. You want to live! It's your last chance!

6: *Bridal Salons: No.* Your huge plastic Bride Head, all circuits sparking like in the Disney Electrical Parade, will now pull you into a bridal salon, eleven days before D-Day. Suddenly the

Kate Hepburnesque white silk pantsuit that seemed so perfect is less than bridal, less than married, just generally . . . less.

You need the bridal white satin, tulle veil, rhinestone crust. Thousand-dollar dresses hang accusingly before you in plastic body bags, glinting bluish under the fluorescents. You shrug one on. You immediately see that these are duchess of Czechoslovakia dresses. And you're of sallow half-Asian descent: The vision you see swathed in beads before you suggests the cheery title "Communion Day in Little Tijuana!" You burst into tears.

7: *Rather Than Being Mere Food Service Workers, Caterers Are Sensitive, Misunderstood Artists Who Are Continually Being Oppressed by an Ugly, Boorish World. Fifty Dollars a Person for Papaya Brie Quesadillas Is a Fabulous Deal.* No. Put that phone down. You are hysterical. Have a smart, sensible friend discipline these people. Not the Wedding Colors one.

8: *No Matter What They Say, It Takes Stylists Eight and a Half Hours to Do Hair. "My Wedding Starts in Twenty-five Minutes and It's in the Valley," Has No Impact on the La Cienega Salon Person.* Trust me.

9: *Don't Kill Anyone at Your Wedding.* "Can Mike turn on the Nintendo?" one hapless eight-year-old asked after I'd spent twenty minutes, hair and gown increasingly bedraggled, marshalling the crowd—which, thanks to the Palace of Guilt, had swollen to two hundred—for toasts. I'm told my lips pulled back into a Hellraiser mask: The child in question let out a scream of terror. (Note that I did not follow tip number one: Do not get married at your own house.)

10: *It Will End.* The day after my wedding was the happiest of my whole life. "Oh my God," I thought, "I never have to get married again." Mike thought so too. And so on that first day as husband and wife, we were in bliss.

I Network with Angels

MERRILL MARKOE

If anyone has tended to be up for the existence of magical forces, it's me. I have loved the idea since my first encounters with fairy tales as a child. And not even the repulsive David Copperfield or Siegfried and Roy have succeeded in diminishing my ardor all these years later. I have continued to prove my willingness to play along by trying to believe in notions like E.S.P. and telekinesis, even while failing to understand the rationale for a magical power that would apply only to spoons and no other forms of flatware.

I do, however, draw the line at angels. And the fact that TV series, the hit movie *Michael*, and whole sections of bookstores are increasingly devoted to this topic has done nothing to convince me that I'm wrong. Nevertheless, one morning at the dentist's, as I was waiting to have my teeth cleaned, the available reading selection was so poor that I was paging through a local community center schedule. I was giving a couple of minutes' thought to the idea of attending a seminar entitled "ANGELIC ENCOUNTERS: How to Harness the Power of Angels in Your Life," just in the interest of fairness, when I looked down at the coffee table before me and saw the *People* cover story "Touched by Angels." At the time I felt I was motivated by the fact that there was nothing else worth reading on the coffee table. Now I wonder if it wasn't something bigger that presented me with those testimonials from people who felt that angels had interceded in their lives—showing up to provide a little last-minute change of luck in situations that could otherwise have been fatal.

For instance, a man named Don Spann fell off his own yacht, and after forty minutes of treading water, when he was "spent and barely conscious," heard someone calling his name. His first mate, "defying all odds," had found him and mysteriously somehow pulled him to safety. Now Spann is convinced he was helped by "a guardian angel."

Right next to *People* was a copy of the *Star*. And there it was again! Several more pages full of testimonials from people who had experiences with angels. In the case of one would-be suicide, the angel in question also mysteriously played her favorite classical music CD on her stereo! Said the suicide survivor, "Now my marriage is wonderful and my weight is coming down. Do I believe in angels? You bet I do."

And in yet another tabloid story, a woman reported that when a man with very kind eyes appeared unexpectedly to perform an act of kindness and then left, asking for nothing, she knew immediately that this had to be divine intervention. After all, what are the chances of something like that ever happening with a garden-variety human male?

Of course I now know that it was *more than coincidence* when the coupon from the Angel Life Guild presented itself to me in a mail-order catalog the very next day. Suddenly there was the opportunity to obtain free information about harnessing the forces of angels. So I checked the box marked "Yes, please send my secret angel information package." And then in the space for my name I wrote Zontar Mozincky. I don't know why I selected this particular name. Perhaps it was divine intervention. But I had a teensy-weensy suspicion they were going to sell whatever name I selected to mailing lists, and I wanted to track which ones.

A couple of weeks later, a letter appeared in my mailbox. Its words thrilled me to the core. "A secret angelic force is within you, Zontar Mozincky," it stated in bold letters at the top of the page.

"Congratulations, Zontar," it went on. "You've made the right decision! . . . Experts have determined that angels exist to aid each of us in achieving our full human potential." (This was bigger-league than I'd imagined!)

"Zontar . . . your angels are ready to help you release this Angel Awareness, your personal 'radar' of luck that keeps you constantly aware of Fortunate opportunities," the cheery letter explained. I read on to the bottom. "Zontar, please turn the page," it said.

And there, on the next page, was a coupon for Angel Prosperity cards, designed to show me, Zontar, what was holding me back from achieving what I want. I could hardly wait to harness this force! Twenty dollars seemed like a small price to pay, and I sent it off immediately. But as the weeks went by and I heard nothing, despair began building inside me. Of course, now I know it was *no coincidence* that I received another sign, in the form of a letter from the International Monetary Research Services (or I.M.R.S., as it said on the impressive letterhead).

"Dear Zontar Mozincky," it began, "I have been asked to send you this letter by the Director of the Investigation Section of I.M.R.S., a New York City firm. Ours is an organization totally dedicated to locating men and women who may have cash due to them by certain court rulings, settlements of class action suits, refunds of deposits, inheritances, escrow refunds, environmental actions, international war crimes, awards decisions, etc. Currently we are ready to launch an investigation on behalf of Zontar Mozincky to determine exactly what may be owed to you and from whom."

Wow! As I began to evaluate the consequences should I

decide to "send in the insignificant amount of $19.95 plus $3 shipping and handling to authorize the search for funds in the name of Zontar Mozincky," I received an even more compelling sign the next day, in the form of a letter from Anne Chamfort, "Golden Talisman Award Winner." "Elected World's Best Psychic!" is what it said under the photo on her letterhead. I was doubly stunned because I hadn't realized until that moment that World's Best Psychic was an elected position.

"Dear Zontar," it began. "As you undoubtedly know, your current environment is full of fairly strong negative waves. At least that's what I sense, and past events tend to prove I'm right!" A chill went down my spine. In recent months I had lived through fires, torrential rains, floods, road closings, power failures—how could I not read on? "I sincerely think that these terrible waves would have continued to harm you for many more years, if we hadn't made contact."

By the end of page six, there appeared a generous offer for a "genuine 'Pentacle of Luck' that will help you overcome your daily problems and protect your new positive waves (the ones that I am going to free in you)!" Plus a coupon for 185 days of "Intense Happiness!" I'd never have imagined that such a coupon could exist! Talk about being touched by an angel! The incredible good fortune would begin on December 24, 1996, and last through June 27, 1997—as long as we joined forces right away. And for the unbelievably low price of only $19.95 plus $3 shipping and handling I would get the "Free Gift of various occult work" to free me "from the terrible waves of frustration ruining my life" as well as *The Great Book of Secrets* (which would allow me to get the most from the lucky period awaiting me).

This made the offer from the I.M.R.S. seem almost puny. Excitedly I checked the box that said, "Yes, my dear Anne Chamfort, I would be delighted to have your help and I thank you very much for continuing to take care of me, even where many others have already lost interest." I didn't even want to *think* who those many others might possibly be.

Well, in the upcoming weeks, as I awaited my Angel Prosperity cards, the beginning of my 185 days of intense happiness, and *The Great Book of Secrets,* other phenomenal things began to happen. For instance, I received a letter that began "Zontar Mozincky, Nostradamus' Day of Destiny can change your life for the better—FOREVER!," from psychic astrologer Rochelle Gordon.

"Dear Zontar," it read, "For many the event which is prophesied to occur in the summer of 1999 will bring turmoil that will be severe and cataclysmic. But for others the changes can be like an answer to a prayer. In your case, a much deserved ZONTAR MOZINCKY prayer. Yes, the world will survive, and you, ZONTAR MOZINCKY, will be one of those who stand to benefit the most!"

I had never dreamed that this opportunity could be available, or that I would get a coupon for 365 days of happiness this time—and for only $19.95 plus $2 shipping and handling. All I had to do was check the box that said, "Yes, my dear Rochelle Gordon, I want to make the most of the next 365 days . . . that is why I am asking you to send me as quickly as possible in a sealed envelope with no distinguishing marks my secret guide to good fortune."

And the very same week, I learned that certain volumes of Dr. Wallace's Neo-Tech Discovery were being held in Zontar's name, including Neo-Tech III (controlling others) and Neo-Tech V (job power and sexual immortality). Okay, so this ran closer to $70. But what a small price to pay for sexual immortality! And who even knew such a thing existed, let alone that it was for sale!

I also learned that the name Zontar Mozincky was on an exclusive "list of names that have already won or may win cash over three million dollars." And that, "Beginning on February 12, an incredible 72 days of Good Fortune" were headed for Zontar Mozincky, the result of which could be *guaranteed* by Raylene Van Worth for $19.95 plus $2 shipping and handling. "It was destiny that brought us together," she wrote in her letter. "If I hadn't seen your name you might never have known about or used this chance to create happiness for yourself and your family!" Seventy-two *more* days of good fortune! If this wasn't the work of angels, what was it?

My big book of secrets magically arrived just before the start of my 185 days of happiness. It contained many valuable things, like the recipe for Prosperity Pasta Sauce "stuffed full of ingredients that bring prosperity and riches" such as "tomatoes, onions, basil, garlic, and marjoram!"

Then came the Angel Prosperity cards—forty thin pieces of paper, each with a single word printed on it, and a three-by-five-inch booklet to explain the meaning of each word. For instance: "FAITH: unquestioned belief not based on proof."

And the next thing I knew, it was December 24, 1996, and my 185 days of intense happiness began—with a bang. Someone broke into my car and stole my purse while I was out walking the dogs. But just as I was about to curse the whole angel thing as a big hoax and a rip-off, I remembered: The 185 days of happiness were not for *me*. They were for Zontar Mozincky. Zontar was the one with the power of Nostradamus, the psychic tech support, the power of angels.

That's what I get for wasting all my money using a pseudonym. Somewhere, perhaps in another dimension, Zontar Mozincky, wherever he is, has 622 days of happiness that really belong to me.

Phone Hex

MERRILL MARKOE

As we stare down the barrel of a brand-new year, what better time is there to look a few of our bad habits squarely in the eye and take the time to correct them? Which is why I am compelled to point out some violations of telephone etiquette that are really getting on my nerves.

Beginning with the hideous new GTE automated 411 torture that has actually caused me to scream out loud in the privacy of my own home for the first time in my adult life when, on multiple occasions, I answered the automated voice's question of "What city, please?" with the CLEARLY SPOKEN ANSWER "Los Angeles" and received the automated response "Our system did not understand." I have literally found myself yelling at the robot, "I SAID LOS ANGELES! Maybe you've heard of it? Los fucking Angeles! It's right around here! Get a map!" I never thought there'd be an occasion when I'd ever have to say this but, Please, dear God, bring back live operators!

And then there's the fact that I believe there should be a city ordinance against regular people using call waiting at home *after* business hours. It's allowing other friends to butt ahead in line.

But there's actually a bigger, much more delicate issue that I need to address. And first I would like to say that I *do not* hate children. I love children. Especially little toddlers. Who in their right mind doesn't enjoy watching them smear pudding in their hair and sit down in the dog-food bowl? Of course, let it be noted that most of the aforementioned charms are visual. The problem for me begins when the toddlers turn two because that seems to be the year that they begin to want to get on the phone. And I even understand why their loving parents don't want to deny them this simple pleasure. It looks so darling—a tiny child with grown-up equipment.

Why, it's as irresistible as one of those greeting cards with a puppy at a desk wearing glasses and a tie! Plus, they have no choice. Baby *cries* if you don't give her the phone! Well, you don't put them behind the wheel of the car just because they cry, do you?

I believe I am speaking for all right-thinking humans over the age of ten when I plead *Do not put your tiny children on the phone*. Or at least, don't put them on the phone with me! Because here's what little children do when you put them on the phone: NOTHING. They do NOTHING. NOTHING AT ALL! Not even audible breathing. So here's what the action is at my end. Silence. Maybe there's the added thrill of a little off-mike parental coaching, along the lines of, "Honey, can you say hi to Merrill?"

Meanwhile, I'm expected to entertain! Somehow it's now my job to amuse the silent child by making a wide variety of hilarious voices and imaginative mouth sounds. This is not as much fun for me as you might think. Which is why I feel I have no choice but to demand: the next time the impulse to put your tiny child on the phone with me overtakes you, just put your coffee table on the phone with me instead. This will also provide you with a visually amusing moment, not to mention that the coffee table won't get all bent out of shape if I hang up on it.

And if, despite my warnings, you do insist on putting the baby on the phone with me, be aware that there will be conse-

quences. I have selected a response that I feel is suitably puni-
tive yet not sadistic. I am going to read to your baby from the
newspaper. And I will spare them nothing. "Hello, baby," I will
say, for example, "I see where tens of thousands of North
Koreans will starve to death this year unless we increase our
foreign aid package." I'm going to tell them about Bosnia.
About Palestine and Israel. If there's another ValuJet crash, I'm
not going to leave out the part about the alligators down below.

And if that doesn't work, then the next time you call my
house, I'm going to make you say hello to my dogs. Although as
dumb as that might make you feel, you still come out ahead. At
least you get to hear a little audible breathing.

Happy New Year, everyone. You have now been warned.

Home is where the bills come.—M.O'D.

Birthdays:
So Now What?

MERRILL MARKOE

Despite the rollicking good time that is the aging process, I have never much liked having my birthday. But since they keep on turning up on an annual basis regardless of my feelings, I would like to share with you now the almost painless system I have invented for dealing with them.

1: DON'T IGNORE THEM.

I tried doing that for a while—the nadir came in 1992 when I went out to buy new tires and then sat alone at an empty sushi bar around the corner from a garage while they were being rotated and balanced. That experience made me realize that to ignore your birthday is to add to the punishment because of the additional pain points you accrue by feeling sorry for yourself.

2: ONCE YOU CONCEDE THAT YOU ARE GOING TO CELEBRATE, DON'T ALLOW ANYONE TO PUT YOU IN A SITUATION WHERE YOU HAVE TO LIVE THROUGH A SER-ENADE BY WAGE-DRIVEN RESTAURANT EMPLOYEES.

This recurring horror was visited upon me in childhood and

has resulted in a permanent state of agitation about eating near waiters gathered in groups of two or more.

3: DON'T GO SHOPPING FOR YOUR GIFT WITH YOUR MOTHER.

At least if she is anything like my mother, a woman who took the fact that my taste differed from hers as a personal insult. This resulted in a lifetime of gifts that I could never wear, display, or otherwise use. Which is why on my thirty-fifth birthday I tried to take the bull by the horns and go out shopping WITH her, an event that inspired many heated arguments culminating in a magnificent birthday crescendo in which my mother announced, as she angrily paid for the white sport coat I had selected, that "this is the last time I agree to doing this. I get no pleasure whatsoever buying you something I don't happen to like." It took me many years of therapy to unravel this confusing episode, so my advice to you is that whatever your mother buys you, just smile ebulliently and say nothing. Realize that the problem is not unlike the hole in the ozone layer . . . much too big to be solved by just one person in just one lifetime.

4: INSTEAD, DO FORCE A NUMBER OF YOUR FRIENDS TO GO OUT WITH YOU AND DO SOMETHING REALLY STUPID.

Your birthday is the one day of the year where you can successfully exert a bit of leverage. This year I managed to browbeat a group of my smart, sophisticated female friends into attending *The Hollywood Men: Legends of the Strip*.

I had never gone to a male strip show before because—well, they seemed dopey. But, as I mulled over my prospective birthday celebration, the idea of watching my poker-faced, irony-steeped feminist friends absorb this kind of display seemed to me well worth the price of admission.

Almost immediately, the evening began to shape up as something special. First, we went to a lovely restaurant, and while we were enjoying drinks out on a garden patio my friend Cynthia began to pontificate. "I believe you can look at life as either a soap opera or a sitcom," she said. And having spoken those words, she leaned back into an open candle and her hair caught on fire, thus instantly disproving her theory because she was able to combine the two options with great success.

I got up and smacked out the flames on her head before anything terrible happened. So I was able to be sort of a hero on my birthday. For the first time in my life I felt I actually *deserved* a few presents.

Then the party moved on into the depths of Hollywood to take a look at the first guys brave enough to leap into the void left by the late, lamented, now-extinct Chippendale's dancers. One might think that by the mid-1990s, men such as these might be more sophisticated, might have learned a thing or two about female sexuality. Ha! The name of the show alone should have been a leading indicator—in all my years as a resident of Los Angeles, I have yet to hear a man of even marginal sanity or appeal refer to himself as a "Hollywood Man."

The show was held in a former disco on Sunset Boulevard. We were shown into a dark, cavernous upstairs room full of tables, all occupied. The audience was 100 percent women; they were mostly, from the looks of it, attending bachelorette parties. And they were all bound and determined to be *full-out wild,* no matter *what.* This they accomplished, although the show itself did little to inspire them. It appeared to have been choreographed by someone whose answer to the question, "What does it take to turn a woman on?" would have been, "You must make her feel that every night of her life is just like Halloween." Instead of titillating nudity or seduction, we got silly costumes, agonizing grimaces, and smoke filling the room. If this was a sexy show, then so was *Casper.*

For some reason women's sexuality has never been success-fully represented in the world of showbiz. Female strippers know exactly what kind of moves and vibes and facial expres-sions it takes to turn men on. They are even professional and inventive enough within the boundaries of their job definition to have figured out how to work a damned aluminum pole into the proceedings. I believe that an in-depth exit poll of the women in attendance at the show on my birthday would have revealed that not a single woman present was turned on for even a minute.

Certainly not by the Greco-Roman vignette—or was it supposed to be ancient Egypt? Which was the period in history when it was very, very smoky and all the men would try to hump the floor?

Definitely not by the lame attempts at comedy. (I guess the person responsible for those must have read too many of those surveys where women list "a sense of humor" as one of their great turn-ons. How else to explain a guy in a G-string lip-synching to "Crocodile Rock" while wearing an alligator hand puppet and a pair of oversized "joke" glasses?)

And absolutely not even when various seminude guys ran out to fling themselves upon their audience in the hope of receiving tips. I was the recipient of a little of this action when a huge, sweaty, long-haired blond guy burst into my face for about thirty seconds. It wasn't arousing. It actually reminded me of the way my dog Lewis insists on greeting people when they come through the front door of my home.

The Hollywood Men would never have guessed how poorly their efforts were regarded, because all the women were simultaneously faking orgasm. That's the amazing thing about an all-female audience. Even though they have paid their hard-earned money to watch men parade as sex objects, they are still conditioned to appease that fragile male ego, wherever it might turn up. If a show full of female strippers had ever gone this far off the sexual mark, the male audience would have mercilessly booed and harassed them right off the stage.

But back to my birthday . . . I still had a great time because every time the show got a little too pathetic there was *still* some pleasure to be had laughing at the grim, deadpan expressions on my friends' faces as they dragged on their cigarettes, trying to decide what kind of facial expression to make when, say, a twenty-four-year-old guy in a jockstrap put two balloons into his

Superman top and wiggled around. It was at those moments that I realized how proud I should be for having solved my dilemma and achieved my goal. Now, if I could just figure out how to deal with Christmas, I would be a happy woman.

•• NEWS QUIZ ••

12/7/98 "NAME & SHAME"

British home secretary Jack Straw has proposed a "name and shame" initiative. So how would that work?

"It wouldn't."—Nell Scovell

"Certainly not as well as the old 'Maim and Flame' under Margaret Thatcher."—Kate Clinton

"Once your Furby learns how to say your name, it chastises you for spending $200 on a toy that will be passé by March when there are kids starving in Africa."—Daniel Radosh

"Leslie Howard! Evelyn Waugh! Ha ha, oh my, I do say that sounds like a girl's name! (U.S. version of name-shame humiliation: Val Kilmer, and her auntie Joyce Kilmer, ha ha ha!)"—Meg Wolitzer

"It shall become a capital crime to spell a British home secretary's name backward."

—Peter Lerangis

• RANDY'S WRAP UP •

It seems so quaint, so English, to propose shame as a social force. Shame relies on a sense of public life, not private entitlement, of waiting in line for a bus, not ramming someone with a Jeep Cherokee. It seems sentimental to suggest that freedom is about public life rather than an autonomous individual pursuing his own ends. (How did the Warren Commission put it? Ah—a lone gunman acting alone.) We Americans live with the ascendancy of the life, liberty, and property crowd over those poor saps favoring life, liberty, and the pursuit of happiness. Or, as Eric Foner says in *The Story of American Freedom*: Try telling the jerk in front of you at the movies to stop talking so loud into his cell phone and turn down his radio; see what he says about shared values. Hey—it's his radio. But of course this is no surprise in a nation whose president, knowing there was every likelihood he'd be found out, goes ahead and presents a Kennedy Center honor to Bill Cosby. ("The universal language of laughter"—I swear.) Shameless.

Of course, the awards ceremony is on CBS, so maybe he thought no one would see. Thank you; good night.

SHAME OR SHAM ANSWER

Straw wants public bodies to monitor private sector employment practices, "naming and shaming" firms with the lowest hiring and promotion rates of minority staff.

Overhauling the 1976 Race Relations Act, aimed at wiping out discrimination and opening up opportunity for black and Asian people in Britain, Straw has ruled out "positive discrimination"—i.e., affirmative action—but wants firms to have senior black staff act as mentors to junior recruits.

His proposals are, in part, a response to the Stephen Lawrence investigation. Ministers expect strong public criticism in the wake of the inquiry into the 1993 murder of this black eighteen-year-old, stabbed by a white gang near a bus stop in southeast London. Criminal proceedings against five white youths collapsed amid charges of police prejudice.

STOCKING STUFFER EXTRA

Holiday hints from the mail-order Oriental Trading Company in Omaha, Nebraska (*www.oriental.com*). This catalog of inexpensive novelties is arranged by theme— sports, luaus, dinosaurs, etc. Below, some products from the "RELIGIOUS," i.e., Christian, section. Why no other religions? Forget it, Jake, it's Omaha.

- "3-inch plastic CROSS MAGIC SPRINGS. Electric colors with cross shape. $13.50 Dozen."—The crucifixion as a plastic Slinky. I'm assuming it ascends the stairs.
- "2 ¼-inch 'SMILE, JESUS LOVES YOU' RELAXABLE BALLS. Assorted colors. $12.00 Dozen."—It's just fun to write "relaxable balls."
- "4 ¾-inch Vinyl RELIGIOUS EYE POPPERS. Flip the ball inside out, place it on a hard surface, and watch it pop! Assorted colors and designs. $4.80 Dozen."—Printed with these slogans: "JUMP 4 JOY!" and "LEAP FOR THE LORD." And yes, it's also fun to write "flip the ball."
- "3 ¾-inch Plastic GLOW-IN-THE-DARK PRAYING HANDS. $3.00 Dozen"—a classic. And I'm pretty

sure it's not made of that stuff that caused liver cancer in those lab rats.

- "16-inch SMILE! 'JESUS LOVES YOU' PUNCH BALLS. Assorted colors with rubber band handles. $6.00 Dozen.—I'm no theologian, but what happened to "turn the other punch ball?"

- "Stretchable CANDY CROSS JEWELRY. Each with a 1 ½-inch candy cross. Individually wrapped. 2 ½-inch Bracelets $1.95 Dozen, 4 ½-inch Necklaces $3.60 Dozen.—This is my blood, this is my body, and this is my candy necklace.

- "TESTAMINTS® Assorted peppermint-, spearmint- and wintergreen-flavored mints individually wrapped in Bible verse wrappers. (Approximately 140 pcs. per lb.) $4.80 Unit (1 lb.)."—Gives you the confidence that your breath doesn't offend and your soul isn't damned to hell for all eternity. Nice detail: the "T" in "Testamints" is a tiny cross.

Things That Are Confusing

PATRICIA MARX

After Iran and Iraq went to war against each other six years ago, you would have thought one of them would have had the courtesy to change its name so that people could keep track of which country was ahead. Needless to say, neither country did. Maybe Iran was hoping that confused mailmen would deliver arms intended for Iraq to Iran. Maybe Iraq liked having the name that was the preferred Scrabble choice. Maybe the forms were too hard to fill out. In any case, many smart, well-educated New Yorkers have trouble today knowing which is Iran and which is Iraq.

Both have oil; both hate the United States; both are predominantly Muslim; both prepare pita bread especially well; both are good places to go for an ornamental dagger or a tan. If they were people, their own mothers couldn't tell them apart.

There are differences, however. Most Iraqis are Arabs and speak Arabic. Most Iranis are Persian and speak Persian. Iraq was the cradle of civilization—Sumer, Akkad and Babylonia as well as part of the Fertile Crescent and the Garden of Eden were there. Iran is ostensibly where *Ali Baba and the Forty*

Thieves took place. Iraq is where, I think it is safe to say, Jeannie on *I Dream of Jeannie* came from. Finally, Iran took the hostages and Iraq did not.

I remember it this way: *I-racked* my brains trying to remember where I'd put *the cradle of civilization.* Then *I-ran* into *Jeannie,* who said someone (but not *a-rabbit*) had taken it *hostage.*

But your problems are not over. You may still humiliate yourself at a social gathering by confusing the following:

Contra/Contadora

A contra is a Nicaraguan antigovernment guerrilla, morally equivalent to our Founding Fathers. Contadora is the name of the alliance made up of Colombia, Mexico, Panama and Venezuela that has been trying to negotiate a peace settlement with Nicaragua. Many people mistakenly call the Contadora the Contradora. The Contradora is an organization against Dora, if it is anything at all. Furthermore, Contadora has nothing to do with Contadina, which is a company that makes tomato paste and other fine tomato products.

Sakharov/Shcharansky

The story of Soviet dissident Sakharov was dramatized on HBO in 1984. Soviet dissident Shcharansky's story has not yet appeared on television, although his biography was sold for a large sum to Random House.

First Cousin, Twice Removed/Second Cousin, Once Removed

Your first cousin's grandchild is your first cousin, twice removed. Your parent's first cousin's grandchild is your second cousin, once removed. You are not responsible for any relative more distantly related than that.

Bathos/Pathos

Bathos is pathos after too many drinks.

Howard Stein/Howard Stern/
Henry Stern/Harry Stein

Respectively, a politician who used to own the discotheque Xenon, a disc jockey, the New York City Parks and Recreation commissioner and a writer who used to write the Ethics column in *Esquire*.

Brooke Adams/Karen Allen

Karen Allen looks less like Margot Kidder than Brooke Adams does. Also, unlike Karen Allen, Brooke Adams starred in *Almost You,* a movie directed by Adam Brooks.

Muscular Dystrophy/Multiple Sclerosis

If you have to have one, choose multiple sclerosis, if only because it reduces your chances of ever posing for publicity photos with Jerry Lewis.

Euripides/Sophocles

Most important, Euripides wrote *Medea* and Sophocles wrote *Oedipus Rex*. If you're asked who's better, say, "Sophocles has the loftiness of Aeschylus plus the powerful psychological acuteness of Euripides." Whether Euripides and Sophocles are first names or last remains a mystery.

Puritan/Pilgrim

This is confusing because both have more than one meaning. Puritan is the name of a clothing company and a cooking oil. Pilgrim is the name of a glass manufacturer with a fancy showroom on Fifth Avenue and a French hand laundry on Second Avenue. Puritan and Pilgrim are distinct from Quaker, a breakfast cereal company, and Quaker State, a brand of motor oil.

M-14/MI5/MIT/M-19/MIG-21/M-1/M 104

Respectively, the U.S. combat rifle, the British intelligence service, the Massachusetts Institute of Technology, the leftist guerrilla group in Colombia, the Soviet jet fighter, the superhighway in England and the Broadway bus. It is possible, therefore, that one day on the M 104, a member of MI5 who holds a degree from MIT and usually drives to work on the M-1 might sell a secret about the MIG-21 to a member of M-19 who carries an M-14. But not probable.

Organic Chicken/Free-Range Chicken

An organic chicken is a chicken that has never eaten any thing sprayed with pesticides. A free-range chicken is a chicken that is not cooped up but is allowed to roam freely and eat whatever it wants, including organic chicken.

Sidney Lumet/Sydney Pollack

Sidney Lumet directed the movies you feel you ought to see but can never get around to seeing (*12 Angry Men, Fail Safe, The Pawnbroker, Long Day's Journey Into Night*). Sydney Pollack directed the movies you never wanted to see but then saw on cable (*The Electric Horseman, Jeremiah Johnson, Absence of Malice*). Also, Sidney Lumet has never made a movie with Robert Redford; Sydney Pollack has made six.

Iowa/Idaho

Sodomy is legal in Iowa but not in Idaho.

Penn/Penn State

People who go to Penn, short for the University of Pennsylvania, pay roughly $10,000 more a year so that you will not confuse their school with Penn State.

US/USSR

One has "The World's Best Cup of Coffee," but I forget which.

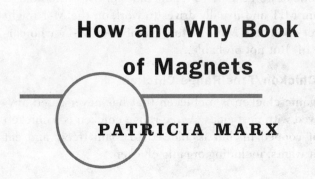

How and Why Book of Magnets

PATRICIA MARX

MIKE AND SUE DISCOVER MAGNETISM

One day Sue saw a little pineapple on the refrigerator door. Mike saw it too. "What's that?" they asked Dad.

"A refrigerator," answered Dad.

Mike and Sue giggled. Dad was such a dope. "No," said Mike. He pointed to the little pineapple. "What's *this* little thing?" Dad looked puzzled.

In came Mother to the rescue. "That's a magnet." she told the children. "Now go to sleep."

But Mike and Sue did not want to go to sleep so early. They were too curious about the magnet and too hungry for lunch. "How do magnets work?" asked Mike.

"A good question," said Mother, who believed in Creative Playthings and learning can be fun. "Watch carefully and I'll show you." First she got an old newspaper and cut out an article about Americans and how they eat too many sweets. Then she took the article and placed it on the refrigerator door and put a banana magnet on top of it. "Now go to sleep," said Mother, who was happy that her children were a little smarter than Dad.

"Gosh," said Mike. "It's like magic!"

"Not *like* magic," Dad corrected. "It is magic, Mike."

MIKE AND SUE LEARN ABOUT MAGNETISM

The next day in school. Mike and Sue learned more about the mysterious magnet. "How do magnets have babies?" Sue wanted to know. Mr. Smith was glad that his students were so curious and asked lots of questions.

"I'm glad you asked that question. Sue," said Mr. Smith, who had neglected to prepare class plans for that day. "A magnet is called 'man's true best friend,'" Mr. Smith explained to the class. "The dog who some people call 'man's best friend' is no friend at all because he bites."

"Do magnets have teeth?" asked Dot, the ugly fat girl who had no friends.

"That's a stupid question, Dot," said Mr. Smith.

"Then how do magnets eat if they don't have teeth?" another student wanted to know.

"Well," replied Mr. Smith. "Magnets have very sharp tongues that act like teeth."

Mike thought about the little pear magnet at home that could pick up paper clips. "Maybe it isn't magic," he thought out loud as other children stared at him. "Maybe," he thought, "the magnet's little tongue is picking up the paper clips."

Mr. Smith chuckled. "No, Mike, not quite. A magnet can pick up paper clips because it is 'magnetic.' You see, there are very little men that live on the magnet and run very, very fast and pick up magnetic objects like the paper clip. The men are so tiny that not even the tiniest human eye can see them. The men learn to run fast by practicing on a place that is called a 'magnetic field.'"

"Really?" asked Mike, who wondered where this magnetic field was.

"No, Mike, that is not what really happens but children are not smart enough to understand the truth," answered Mr. Smith.

Before the children went home for lunch, Mr. Smith promised that he would show them how to make a magnet. "But first," he told them, "we'll need some things." When the children went home, they got all the silverware from their mothers' drawers for the science experiment. Mr. Smith collected the silver and locked it in the cabinet. "All right. I have everything else we need to begin." Mr. Smith took a compass and put it on his desk. Then he got a big hammer and crushed the glass on the compass into millions of little pieces. As Dot swept up the glass from the floor, Mr. Smith showed the class how the little needle inside the compass could pick up paper clips.

"Wow!" said Mike. "A home-made magnet."

"Not so quick," said Mr. Smith. "It still has to be painted like a pineapple or a pear or a banana."

WHY ARE ALL THE MAGNETS ON REFRIGERATOR DOORS?

There are magnets everywhere—in the air we breathe, in the food we eat, even in our bathtubs. Everybody *else* can see them. What's the matter with you? Maybe something is wrong with your eyes.

HOW DID MAGNETS GET ON REFRIGERATORS?

At one time, eons ago (before even your great-great-great grandfather was born!), the earth was covered with out-of-door freezers called "glaciers" (glay-shores). Then, one day there was a nice day and the sun came out and the glaciers melted. This made mankind worried because he didn't want all of his meat to defrost and ruin so mankind invented refrigerators inside of his house. It was during this era that the first magnets began to creep out of the seas and grow on refrigerator doors.

HOW DO MAGNETS WORK?

Magnets do not *really* work. Trick photography only makes most of them seem to work. The others are on welfare.

HOW DID MAGNETS GET THEIR NAME?

There is a legend that in ancient Greece a shepherd boy named Bob, while tending his sheep near Asia Minor discovered that a magnet is "magnetic." From the word "magnetic," we get the name "magnet."

HOW DO MAGNETS HELP US?

Magnets help man by eating up all of the bugs in the refrigerator that feed on butter and eggs. In ancient times, doctors used magnets to suck the blood from their patients' arms and lower intestinal tracts. But today, modern science teaches us to use leeches.

HOW CAN I TELL THE DIFFERENCE BETWEEN A CROCODILE AND A MAGNET?

One sure way of telling the difference is to count the legs. On a crocodile there are four (1-2-3-4). A magnet has less than that. Another way to tell the difference is to look at the snout. A crocodile's snout is long and broad. A magnet has no snout at all. One last scientific test is to put the unknown in water. Most crocodiles will float to the top but magnets will sink to the bottom (unless they are pretending to be crocodiles). Use a river, not a basin of water, because most crocodiles will not fit in a basin of water.

HOW CAN I TELL THE DIFFERENCE BETWEEN AN ALLIGATOR AND A MAGNET?

You can't.

HOW MANY KINDS OF MAGNETS ARE THERE?

Nobody knows how many kinds of magnets there are but there are at least three—the pineapple magnet, the pear magnet, and the banana magnet. Some scientists think there may be ten or twelve million—or even more. Some scientists don't even care.

MAGNETS AS PETS

Keeping magnets can be an interesting and entertaining hobby. The beautiful coloring and conformation of these little creatures make them a constant pleasure to watch as they lie there among the other things you put in their cage. Since they need little light, water, or food, they are easy to keep alive.

A wide selection of tropical magnets can be purchased for little cost. Of course, certain rare specimens imported from far-away lands are very expensive.

Magnets like to live in cages. A good rule of thumb for choosing the proper sized cage is: the bigger the magnet, the bigger the cage. Don't worry about closing the magnet cage because most magnets are well-trained and will not escape.

Magnets also get along very well with fish and many children like to dump their magnets in their parents' aquariums.

A MAGNET EXPERIMENT: GRAVITY AND MAGNETS

You will need:

>   1 tea kettle
>   1 wax candle
>   1 banana magnet

Do this:

1. Set aside the tea kettle and wax candle. They are not necessary.

2. Throw the magnet into the air and watch it come down.

Why it works:

> The magnets obey the law of gravity.

OTHER THINGS TO DO

- Try to think up a way to "de-magnetize" the slug rejector on a vending machine. Then, set up your own little business with the free candy that you get.

- Put on a magnet skit with your friends. Each person can dress up like a member of the magnet family—Mr. Magnet, Mrs. Magnet, and the children magnets Mark and Minnie. Sell tickets to your parents and make money.

THE FIVE NEVER RULES

If you really want to have fun with magnets, you must first learn to play the Never Game:

1. Never eat magnets between meals.
2. Never put magnets on train tracks.
3. Never cross a street between magnets.
4. Never get into a strange car even if the driver promises to give you a magnet.
5. Never say, "Can I have a magnet?"
   Say "May I have a magnet, please?"

Joyce Maynard Looking Back:
A Chronicle of Growing Up
Vicariously in the Sixties

PATRICIA MARX

1962

1962 was the year Jimmy Wolf sat in The Front Row. It was also the year of the Pez Dispenser. It's a cliché but looking back I guess it's true—life is a lot like one big Donald Duck Pez Dispenser.

1963

March came in like a lion and went out like a lamb that year. Still, I will always remember 1963 because my mother had bought me a magenta dress with baby doll embroidery across the top (we called it the top then because we were much too embarrassed about the Real Life clinical term). Although I liked the dress very much (the baby doll was "in" that year), I hardly wanted to actually wear a magenta dress though magenta was still my favorite color and the proof of that is that it was the first crayon to be used up in the Giant Crayola Crayon Set that Rachel Franklin got me for my birthday just the other year ago. It may sound trite but it's true, too, life is full of irony. Of course, my mother, who is really not of the same generation, could not understand why I preferred to wear my last year's blue dotted swiss even though it was so tight I could not zipper it without starving to death and going to the bathroom a lot. Why can't we fit into clothes that are outgrown? Why does the rib roast have to burn when we leave it in the oven too long? Why does everything illegal have to be against the law?

1964

Somehow nature seemed more natural then. This was the year of the yo-yo and for some reason, none of us questioned the value or social consciousness of the instrument. We did not care if it was bio-degradable or full of calories. For us, in Miss Bolden's sixth grade class, the yo-yo was just a toy.

In this psychologically enlightened age, we often do not have the time to think about these real things. (Try asking a telephone operator for something *other* than a phone number, try asking a waitress at Howard Johnson's for human understanding when she asks if she can help you.) Caught up in a world of dog eat dog, we can not pause. Once I called up CBS to ask if they could postpone "Dr. Kildare" just one hour because I had a special student council meeting (concerning orange drink in the cafeteria) that would conflict with my watching. Like the taste of soggy banana walnut bread on a rainy May day, my request was ignored. The show must go on . . . but does anyone really know what time it is??? Is it a coincidence that love has no more letters than hate?

1965

Maybe it's not true for every American teenage girl growing up in the '60's, but in 1965 we got our first color TV. Of course, there's more to life than just TV, but it's also true that money isn't everything. Spoon-fed by the TV, my generation quickly learned that there were really not little men and women inside the boxes. With a TV "in every pot," we became Media Children, accustomed to having our thrills and excitement provided for us. I can't say none of us ever read books but it was a rare seventh grader who could actually read by the time he entered junior high. (In sixth grade, Kathy Smith, "The Class Brain," was sent to a special school for Brains because she could read silently without using her lips.) Now a junior at Yale, I am still surprised by all those intellectuals who go around with their heads buried in *The Teachings of Don Juan*.

Of course, written communication, like push-button telephones and the postal service ("Did you get my letter?" . . . "Oh, I forgot to stamp it," was a favorite joke of ours but it really isn't so funny because you can really hurt somebody like the time Jonathan Crichton fractured his ankle and had to be rushed to the hospital and the doctor said, "Jonathan, a joke is a joke," which is actually quite true if you stop to think about it) really does serve its purpose. It really is a wonder the things you can do with words!

1966

When I think of seventh grade, I think of Pascal's triangle and *Gilligan's Island* and points off for punctuation errors on Social Studies compositions. (What do you want, good grammar or good taste?)

That same year, Mitchell Merin gave Donna my best friend his ID with his initials (M.M.) but since Donna's mother said that Donna could absolutely NOT go to the Freshman Frolic and the word was final since Donna's father was on a business trip, that Indian giver Mitchell Merin took back his ID leaving only six couples in the seventh grade that were going steady if you count Shelly Bush three times since she was going with three boys which in my opinion only proved she was insecure . . . like everyone else.

Like opening a box of Cocoa Krispies and finding them half full, this made me realize that life is one big half a box of cereal. Newly philosophical, I pondered the universe. If a tree falls in the forest and there is no one to hear it, is there a noise? If Henry Ford had not lived would there have been an automobile? If there are as many grains of sand on Westport Beach (where I first learned how to play Frisbee in ninth grade until I stepped on a clam shell that went so deep the nurse nearly fainted and the doctor said, "Really, Nurse, it's only a little clam shell" which was actually quite true if you come to think of it) as grains of sand then isn't Westport Beach larger than we think it is and isn't man a mere speck of sand? Where have all the flowers gone?

1967

Like a cool glass of water at dusk, I discovered Kahlil Gibran in 1967. To say the least, I became aware of the true human condition and I also became a totally new human being—more aware, more enlightened, less blind. Why couldn't pi be a terminal number? Why was Joe's Dew Drop Superette always out of coffee ice-cream when you wanted it most? Why did there have to be learning disabilities? I searched for the answers.

Then I forgot Kahlil soon after Thanksgiving Vacation when we only got two days off instead of three because of the Teacher's Strike at Clambake High which was illegal only we didn't have the guts to protest because we were too chicken.

In this era of lies and deception, is it then a surprise that my generation probably tells about 35 percent more white lies than our predecessors? Raised in a world where one cannot judge a book by its cover, we come to expect the weather reports that are intentionally wrong, the speed limits on the turnpikes that never accurately tell us how fast the average vehicle travels and the various scientific hypotheses that always contradict each other. It is indeed a sad commentary on our age that most of the books now written are classified "Fiction." Like a lemon-lime fizzy that has been let loose in an electric waterbed, we cannot see the forest through the trees.

1968

"Blowin' In The Wind"—Peter, Paul, and Mary

> *How many roads, etc., etc., etc. . . .*
> *How many years, blah blah blah, blah blah blah . . .*
> *How many times, ad nauseum . . .*
> *The answer is blowin' in the wind.*

1969

In tenth grade, my generation was the Student Strike Generation. For the first time in sixteen years, we turned off our TV sets and marched in The Real Street. Peace was our cry. We hated war. (It may sound dumb now but things like war and peace really meant a lot to us then.) In a world where black is not white and white is not black, we wore armbands to show our anger . . . at L.B.J., at Hubert Humphrey, at Richard Nixon. (Where are they *now,* I wonder.)

Of course, protest is a verb, not a noun. Every age has its Battle of Hastings—ours was Washington, 1970. I went with Christopher Jacobs and a peace patch.

1973

Today as I sit here, watching TV, I know I am no longer a child. *Star Trek* is a rerun and Lassie seems to run a little slower. As I have matured, my dreams have mellowed. No longer do I want all the gold in the world. Today I will settle for a cup of Ovaltine and a blood transfusion.

Bad Numbers

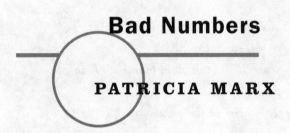

PATRICIA MARX

It took me a while to notice that the 2 on my telephone was broken. But finally, I figured out that pushing a 2 meant getting a 4. I tried pushing the 2 firmly. I tried pushing two 1's instead of one 2. I even tried pushing the 1 and the 3 down together and then taking my finger off the 1 to subtract.

Had I caused the problem? Lately I had received a lot of urgent literature from AT&T. I assumed, as I threw away the letters unopened, that AT&T wanted me to return to their phone family. But maybe, without knowing, I threw away the response card that asked if I wanted to keep my 2.

Life without 2's was not so terrible. I could order Chinese food and I could call most of my friends. Probably I could join a special-interest group and meet people who did not have 2's in their phone numbers. In New York you become friendly with people for all sorts of reasons.

I changed my phone message: "If your phone number has a 2 in it, I cannot call you back."

My friend Larry called and said, "I have three two's in my

number, so I guess I'll never talk to you again." A true friend, I thought, would change his number. "Is this a moral stance or a mathematical handicap?" another friend asked. Someone else suggested my 2 phobia was really a fear of intimacy.

The next day, my 2 problem spread to the 3's. I thought wistfully of the days when I could play "You Are My Sunshine" on my touch tone. Now I could not even play "Do Re Mi."

Oh, well. Hooked On Phonics (1-800-222-3333) was out of the question, but I could still call Dial-A-Dentist, Dial-A-Form letter, and Dial-A-Wagon. I could call Dial-An-Aetheist but I could not call Dial-A-Prayer. I could call Dial-A-Date but not Dial-A-Hunk. According to my calculations, I could not call 80 percent of my friends but, naturally, I could call the one person I was avoiding.

I changed my phone message: "If your number has a 2 or a 3 in it, I cannot call you back." I remembered the person I was avoiding and considered adding, ". . . Also, if your number has the numbers 876-8916, in that order, I cannot call you back."

I called the phone company. "It sure sounds like you're having trouble on the instrument itself," the operator said. "If you cannot do anything with the instrument"—she didn't have to rub it in—"I would recommend you call Telephone Repairs."

I called repairs and got a computerized message. "If you are calling about trouble on the line, press one. If you are calling about trouble with your instrument, press two—"

If my telephone number were a poker hand, it would be a full house—2 pairs, one set of three. Visually, it is pleasing, for the digits fall along a column on the telephone keyboard. This is not entirely accidental. When I moved to my current address, I did not wait to be assigned a random number. Instead, I informed AT&T that my brother was learning-disabled (he certainly is not) and, therefore, I required a numerical series that would be easy for him to remember. By the way, my present local phone company, Bell Atlantic, no longer allows you to select a phone number free of charge—probably because of dissemblers like me. (A "gold telephone number" costs $20.76 initially and $3.11 monthly thereafter.)

My phone number has cadence, but there is a downside. Callers seem frequently to misdial it, and always in the same way, making a pair of the second and third number, rather than the first and second. And so, for fifteen years, ever since I have had my phone number, Sarah and Herman have been regularly receiving calls meant for me. At least once a month, it seems, a friend reports to me that he has either hung up on Sarah and Herman's machine, talked to Sarah or Herman, or unwittingly dialed their number many times in a row. While trying to retreive my messages, even I have occasionally phoned Sarah and Herman, though never when they've been home. Oddly, I have never gotten a call for Sarah or Herman, which makes me think that they are either not as popular as I am or that my friends are more dyslexic than theirs.

A couple of weeks ago, when a friend told me he had inadvertently reached Sarah and Herman's machine at two A.M., I decided I must apologize—for him and everyone else in my wide telephone circle who has intruded upon them all these years. Also, I wanted to find out what Sarah and Herman thought of my friends. I felt sympathetic to this long-suffering couple and, in a weird way, cosmically connected to them. We were identical but for one digit. Perhaps they, too, felt a bond. After all, they could have changed their number to get rid of me, but chose not to.

I imagined Sarah and Herman to be retired and short. They received few phone calls, I supposed, and most of those they did get were probably from their children and grandchildren. Considering how disappointed they must be when yet another caller asked for me, it was especially considerate of them to be as patient and kind as my friends described them. I wondered how long it would be before Sarah and Herman moved in with one of their children, perhaps to Long Island. Their number would be turned over to a churlish Wall Street type. Unlike Sarah and Herman, the new guy would hang up immediately on my friends— and, with a vengeance, *69 anyone who hung up on him.

As it turned out, I got it wrong. Sarah is fifty-six, an artist, and beautiful, with shoulder-length gray hair and a face like the actress Vivica Lindfors. When I called to suggest we meet, she was agreeable—"It's like something out of, oh, a magazine article!" she said. Herman is seventy-nine, a retired lawyer, and very large—think Ernest Hemingway. He had come from the gym the day we met.

We had lunch downtown at Jerry's restaurant, not far from where they lived, and it felt kind of like a promising first date. As we walked to our table, Sarah mentioned that a man had phoned for me that morning. I felt a pang for all the calls I might have missed. We talked easily about a variety of topics, including how Sarah and Herman met (Herman had bought a painting of Sarah's fifteen years ago before and moved in with her five years later), their neighbor (she had asked Sarah to let me know that she always gets phone calls for Jacoby Hospital), bathtubs (Herman can't stand up in a tub whose bottom is curved), London (Herman's daughter lives there), their house in the country (they go every weekend), papayas (Sarah had just had a dream about one), and Freudian analysis (a natural segue from the papaya dream).

And, of course, we talked about the integers we had in common. To my relief, neither Sarah nor Herman were disturbed by the call from my friend at two A.M., nor any other late-night calls because, after ten, they turn off the phone in their bedroom and let a machine pick up. "I hope I haven't been rude to your friends," Herman said, concerned that his phone manner had been soured by the prevalence these days of "courtesy calls" (has there ever been such a misnomer?). Sarah assured Herman that he is never rude. Turning to me, he commented, "Sarah's more gracious that I am." At the end of the meal, Herman stood up. "Well," he said, "do you want to go back to the loft and see . . . The Phone?"

I did see The Phone. In fact, it rang not long after we walked in. Herman wondered aloud if he should pick it up or let the machine handle the call. "Pick it up," I urged. "It might be for me."

Sunken Treasure

DANIEL MENAKER

> The producers and actors are not alone in making money out of *Titanic*. The Scottish carpet manufacturer Stoddard Sekers International has also made a pile. The company was among the many that kitted out the original boat, laying two-inch-thick carpet throughout the first-class compartments.
>
> —*The London Times*

> Something will eventually make more money than *Titanic*. I just don't see anything out there right now, or on the verge, that could.
>
> —Hollywood producer Laurence Mark,
> in *Entertainment Weekly*.

At 4 P.M. on February 16, 1912, James Powell, the riveter who drove in *Titanic's* second-to-last rivet, saw several pied seagulls perched on his mansard roof when he got home from his final day of work on the ship. According to his wife, he suffered a fit in the tub that night, shouted out a few nautical expressions, and then, before she could help him, slipped down into the bathwater and practically drowned! She later sold that bathtub to a junk dealer for a mere three shillings!!

A set of early blueprints for *Titanic* included a reinforced, inflatable rubber gasket to go around the entire vessel at the waterline, providing true unsinkability but also limiting the ship's maximum speed to 3.5 knots. These blueprints were discarded but were later recovered by a Southampton chandler who had nothing whatever to do with *Titanic*. Not stopping to think that someday they might be worth something, he used them to start a fire for boiling water to make his tea!

Many of the workmen who built the ship found the upholstery on the settees in *Titanic*'s parlor suites garish. As it turned out, the draper who provided that fabric was none other than a man called Robert Sinker! Well, all right, his name was Robert Griffiths. But his mother's maiden name was Hull!! And there are no records to indicate that Griffiths wasn't in fact the Southampton chandler's second cousin. What's more, as passengers were boarding the ill-fated vessel, Griffiths was safely ashore in his storeroom, pressing his attentions on his assistant. Mysteriously, nine months later, the same assistant gave birth to a child with a birthmark on her right shoulder that two or three people said looked a little like a smokestack! Eighty years later, an elderly woman bearing just such a mark—only now it had moved to her left shoulder—opened a stall in Brighton where she now sells photographs of the dermatological phenomenon!!

A ginger cat belonging to one Mrs. Choade began losing its fur ferociously the minute it was set down on the great vessel's deck. The cat—whose name is unrecorded but could well have been Titanicat!—continued to shed until it was entirely bald. When the ship sank, Titanicat miraculously survived for half an hour in the icy water and was plucked from the sea in a stiffened condition by a ship's laundress who could easily have had another coincidental name of some kind—Lizzie Stern, maybe! She sold the cat for not much more than a song to the Seamen's Bethel on Staten Island, where it became a mascot and was renamed Lucky. It died in its sleep thirteen years to the day after *Titanic*'s second mate would have become eligible for his pension!

It's a well-known fact that the iceberg struck by *Titanic* broke into two parts a week after the collision. Many observers are pretty sure they saw a TV documentary that said the smaller part of the berg was spotted by a fishing boat off Greenland with six hundred and sixty-six puffins—never before seen at such a northerly latitude!—nesting on it. (Last week, a small-time mail-order company out of Bruges issued a new catalogue featuring one-ounce bags of shavings from what it claimed was a forty-pound remnant of the puffin section of the berg, inexplicably found afloat in the English Channel!) The larger part drifted south, and, according to the same source, it melted, evaporated, and then fell as rain into the reservoir for Bremen, Germany. Eventually, it reappeared as ice cubes aboard the *Lusitania*!

Taking into account box-office receipts, authors' fees for books and articles, salvagers' revenues, payments for expert testimony, and tchotchke retail purchases, each life lost from *Titanic*'s disaster has generated an average of $22,658,117—or three times what the White Star Line paid to have her built! And there's no end in sight: I've heard about projections for the year 2012 which indicate that revenues realized from the tragedy will surpass the cumulative budget for the earth from the dawn of man until two days before that Night to Remember!!

Copies of this article, each signed by the author, can be purchased for just $19.95. Or pick any three paragraphs for $12.95. Cash, checks, and money orders accepted. No C.O.D.s, please.

One Guy's TV

HOWARD MOHR

I've never been able to watch a whole football game on TV—or off—not even the Vikings, the home team named after the career pillagers in hats with horns who in boats discovered America. If any of you Columbus supporters are about to bristle and snort, I want you to know that thirty miles from my house on the Minnesota prairie, there's a normal American citizen living on a bluff over the Minnesota River Valley whose wooded backyard contains a big rock with a large iron ring attached to it. That ring, according to him, was used by the Vikings to tie up their ships back when the river was 180 feet deep and three miles wide. This was before the Mall of America but after the glaciers.

But if I don't watch football, you may ask, how do I keep the attorney general from appointing an independent counsel to investigate my manhood? Let's say I'm thinking about doing a little walleye fishing and I'm in line to buy a dozen leeches at a crowded bait shop, a familiar scenario during the summer. Let's say the guy behind me utters the eternal question: "How 'bout them Vikes?" No problem. I just say what any macho Minnesota dude with a thousand games and untold nachos under his belt would say: "You got that right." And he will say, "You can say that again." I avoid detail because the only football player I can think of is Joe Namath and that's because he wore panty hose in a magazine ad.

My father was a mechanic and truck driver, but not much of a sports fan. He took me to exactly one sporting event when I was growing up: women's donkey softball, where all the players rode donkeys bareback, slipping and sliding, dismounting periodically to push the dang thing around the bases. I liked it.

If ABC would run "Monday Night Donkey Softball," I'd watch it. If there was a NDFL, I'd support it. I would get excited about the Super Donkey Bowl. Heck, I'd watch donkey golf, donkey bowling, the "Donkey Nightly News," donkey talk shows, donkey infomercials. I would watch Barbara Walters interviewing Michael Jackson on donkeys. There's hardly anything on TV these days that would not be improved by having it happen on donkeys. I'd even watch a Danielle Steele miniseries if they'd do it on donkeys.

What I like on TV hasn't changed much since a June evening in 1948 when I was nine and saw my first pictures through the snow on a TV set in Snortley Hardware. Earlier that same year my parents had seen a UFO near White Sands, New Mexico, while cruising through the night on our way to California on the southern route, in a '42 Plymouth coupe powered by that hardy ninety-horse flat-head six.

Those two sightings are located in the Formative neighborhood of my brain, north of Puberty and east of Sleeping Bag Full of Tarantulas on Boy Scout Trip, southwest of Getting Sick and Throwing Up During a Church Hayride While Sitting Next to the Most Beautiful Girl in the Junior High Sunday School Class.

CLOSE ENCOUNTER OF THE TV KIND

In 1948 the only station in my neck of the urban Midwest was experimentally broadcasting a couple of hours a night, give or take a few time-outs for technical difficulties, toppled cameras, or the occasional studio fire. There was no daytime TV. Nobody I knew had a TV set until Mr. Snortley, of Snortley's Hardware, bought one for display. In a bold marketing move, he decided to open his store at night so people could see a picture on it.

I rode my bike over after supper, milling around with other kids. No adults showed up. Mr. Snortley, wearing house slippers and smelling of fried potatoes and onions, unlocked the door shortly after six, relocked it, and without talking, led us back to fasteners.

And there it was: Two hundred pounds of the future, silent and mysterious.

Mr. Snortley said, "I'm gonna turn it on. Stand back and shield your eyes. These picture tubes can explode and they're filled with poison gas."

It was music to our ears. Cool in the valley of death, Mr. Snortley fiddled with the controls as the station struggled to the air with its test pattern.

We didn't eat licorice or Milk Duds, we didn't go to the bathroom. We watched. "DDT in Paradise," "Happy Herefords," "The Corn Borer and You," "Detroit on Parade," "The Miracle of Dirt," "Silage," "Nematodes on Parade," and the pièce de résistance, "The Four-cycle Internal Combustion Engine."

Practical information presented on a miraculous invention in a hardware store full of useful objects. It was a hard act to follow. I suppose that was the day I started becoming my father, who mainly worked on cars and trucks but could fix any machine. Machines were his life. His philosophy of repair was simple: If somebody made a machine, then a guy ought to be able to take it apart, find out what's wrong, fix it, and put it back together. And he was that guy. That was his work. It was also his recreation.

He fixed things and I watched him, and often accompanied him to the sacred sites: the parts store, the auto graveyards, the shops of other mechanics. To this day, nothing pleases me more than a few hours in an auto junkyard. There's one up on a hill in the country about twenty miles south of me that has picnic tables, graveled lanes between the cars, and a map showing locations of make and model. Pretty darned relaxing on a summer day. But I like the old-fashioned junkyards best, where you bring your own tools and wander through acres of weeds and the Detroit dead. And when you find the part you need, you have to take it off the wreck yourself.

I'm a guy who likes to know how things work. I come by it honestly, there's nothing I can do about it, and I don't want to anyway. A fairly recent long PBS series on the design, manufacture, and testing of the Boeing 777 was perfect for me. Do the same thing with any complex machine, from nuclear power plant to heart pump to lunar module to copy machine, and I'll watch it.

With five-hundred-channel cable around the corner, I'd like to suggest, from my master list, a few programs that would make me erect a dish in my yard and buy a monster high-screen.

"The Joy of Car Repairs":

Twenty-four hours a day, mechanics working on cars, explaining things in detail. I see separate channels for Ford, GMC, Chrysler, and so on, with future expansion to other motorized machines such as bulldozers.

"Infrastructure, USA":

Twenty-four-hour examination and explanation of the hidden machinery that keeps cities alive: subways, furnaces, underground pipes and wires, traffic lights, telephones.

"Plumbing Verité":

The drama of replacing a toilet, sweating pipes, hooking up the water heater, and much, much more. Eventually channels for all the trades.

The following suggestions for guy programs are meant to be less technical, more relaxing.

"Sewers and More Sewers":

Continuous broadcasting of unedited videos made with remote rooter cameras used to inspect city sewer lines, with voice-over by technicians. "Yeah, Bob, I see there's a little roughness and clogging at the feeder junction on Maple Street."

"Going for a Ride":

Driving around in town and country with a camera and no particular plan, just looking out the window, stopping to eat, whatever. A changing cast of riders from many walks of life would do off-the-cuff commentary.

"Garage Sale of the Air":

Camera crews go from garage sale to garage sale, looking at stuff on card tables, with the off-camera personality holding something up or maybe asking what's wrong with the air compressor that says "Don't work, $2" on the tag.

I guess I'll tell you the whole UFO story next time, but suffice it to say that if the rotating saucer with porthole lights my folks saw in 1948 had developed engine trouble and landed in front of my dad's Plymouth, he would have picked up his tool box—he never left home without it—and said to the pilots, "Let's take a look at that thing." They'd understand him perfectly, because the body language of a mechanic offering help is understood throughout the universe.

Could my dad have fixed the antigravity hyperdrive? Piece of cake.

After This Word
from Motel 3

HOWARD MOHR

We're still under five bucks at Motel 3, but we change the sheets every week if they're slick. We don't give you free soap, though, and we don't put windows in the rooms because then we'd have to hang up some curtains and the next thing you know we'd be putting locks on the doors and charging six bucks. My uncle Don always stays at Motel 3 because it reminds him of home, where the walls are thin and the ceilings are low and people are yelling at each other all the time and throwing things. The smell from the restaurant next door is enough to make you gag, he says, but it keeps him from being homesick, anyway, and it's darn handy if your appetite comes back and you can keep anything down. At Motel 3 you can expect a fairly clean bathroom on almost every floor but remember to shake the handle and bring your own towels and toilet paper when you visit, and a can of bug spray. We'll leave the bulb burning for you and the door propped open with a brick so the air can circulate a little and dry up some of that mold on the foam pillow.

At High School 4 we still don't have foreign languages, and we don't have counseling, and we don't have urine tests either, and you can smoke in the lavatory and throw your butts on the floor. We're not all that particular. But if you're looking for up-to-date textbooks and teachers who play with a full deck and don't wear sidearms, then you can put your nose in the air and head for those other high schools and pay the price. At High School 4 you get a desk with dirty words carved in it and you get police protection. We just figure the main idea of education is to keep from being mugged. My uncle Teddy says it was good enough for him and it keeps taxes low and besides that, he says, you don't turn out so many smarty-pants students who go around inventing things and rocking the boat. Well, we'll try to keep some of those fluorescent lights flickering for you and remember to go through the metal detector before you head for homeroom.

At PETRO 6 we don't have double-hulled tankers or sober captains like some of those other oil companies. What we got is a carefree attitude and once in a while a few million gallons of crude ends up in some water someplace, but it's no big deal. My uncle Fred says if you're gonna rape and plunder the land, you might as well do it right and besides he thinks getting some high-test gasoline for that 480 V-8 Mustang he races is more important than a few sea otters somewhere he never heard of before. PETRO 6 will keep the lights on for you and those spark plugs sparking, and if you see an oily bird land in your yard, well, give it a bath for us, will you? And send us the bill. Your check is already in the mail.

We try to hold down costs at Nuclear Power Plant 6, so don't expect all the fancy safety features like the containment vessels they have in those high-priced reactors. We took the low bid, but we got power coming out of her most of the time and besides, a little radiation never hurt nobody, that's what my aunt Phebe says. She's been X-rayed so many times she glows in the dark, they think it's her gallbladder. Anyway, we'll keep the lights on for you unless those darned fuel rods stick again and we lose the coolant. And if you hear the alarm go off, don't worry, we got plenty of duct tape at the plant and pills to keep us awake. And if Nuke 6 takes a notion to head for China, like those pesky things will sometimes, we'll try to give you a little warning so you can pack up a few things and move away.

Divine Being One wanted me to tell you that the thing is, if a world that makes sense is all that important to you then just go ahead and travel to one of those high-priced planets out there, but Earth is good enough for my uncle Bill. He says you got your basic birth, and you got your death and what else could you need? Myself, I'd throw in a color television set and a LaZ-Boy. Well, remember to pray once in a while for something, but don't expect a reply or any amazing results because it just wouldn't be fair to the other people. We'll keep the sun on for you as long as we can and you try to stay out of trouble and don't clean your ears with a nut pick.

O.J.: The Trial
of the Next Century

HOWARD MOHR

1995

After a six-month period when white Bronco purchases reach an all-time high, the jury is finally selected in the O. J. Simpson trial.

The defendant publishes a book while he waits to go to trial. Judge Ito releases O.J. on his own recognizance for the book tour.

A briefcase-swinging fight erupts when the O.J. defense team is assaulted by the prosecution team for introducing new evidence that a busload of convicted felons with identical DNA was seen outside the Nicole Simpson home the night of the murder. Judge Ito clears the courtroom, warning that if this outrageous behavior continues he will prescribe Prozac for both sides and take away the TV cameras. The jury is visibly shaken by an aftershock of Northridge quake.

In her book, *Why I Think O.J. Is Innocent,* defense attorney Shapiro's mother refers to prosecutor Clark with the B word.

Phillip Morris tries to acquire the O.J. trial in a hostile takeover. Judge Ito calls it an insult to justice, the bid much too low for such a hot property.

First conception during conjugal visit announced by juror in graphic press conference, movie rights sold.

Defense team buys condo complex near courtroom, pays cash. Tired of commuting, need tax shelter.

Juror's touching audio, "A Sequestered Christmas," becomes instant hit worldwide, TV movie, Nintendo.

1996

Jurors form union, want health benefits, retirement package, dental, maternity, better housing, bigger per diem. Judge Ito approves purchase of house for each juror and family. Jurors collaborate on *We Don't Have a Clue*, published in June, bought by Redford, will star Streep, Cruise.

Congress, giddy with success on the balanced budget amendment, passes Constitutional amendment requiring the O.J. trial to be over by Christmas 1997.

O.J.'s second book published, critical examination of the early Shakespearean comedies. Given honorary doctorate at Harvard.

Son born to sequestered juror is named Ojito.

1997

Jurors form a rock group; Judge Ito agrees to provide musical instruments and costumes in renegotiated union contract.

MTV acquires video rights for undisclosed sum. First CD goes platinum. Two jurors buy the O. J. Simpson home in Los Angeles. Trial recessed for three months during the thirty-city national tour by "Bloody Glove."

National Enquirer launches *The O.J. Enquirer*, devoted entirely to the O.J. trial.

Bailout for the O.J. trial passed by Republican majority after it is learned that the defense team has not been paid for a year and the bill is in excess of $10 million. Republican president Joe Petersen says deficit spending trials are an outrage, agrees to one-time payment to the strapped defense team.

Knighthood, jeweled sword, granted to Newt Gingrich by Republican president Joe Petersen.

Thirty-five new O.J. books published, including five by authors claiming to be the murderer.

Trial does not end by Christmas 1997, thus violating the constitutional amendment requiring it to end. President Joe Petersen says it was a very naughty thing to do. Amendment repealed.

1998

One pound of marijuana found in jury snack room, smoke thick. Judge Ito rules that it is no more than any sane person would do in the circumstances, orders a better ventilation system.

The twenty-four-hour O.J. Channel premiers on cable. Reruns of football games, reruns of trial days, dramatic adaptations of books, game shows, first TV talk show hosted by murder defendant from cell during trial.

In a deal worked out by agents representing the defense and the prosecution teams, the O.J. trial is moved to Disneyland, where visitors ride through the new "courtroom" in open-top white Broncos. Features water slide and scary tunnel trip past the animated "murder scene."

Twenty-seven O.J. books published, down eight from 1997. The stock market reacts in flurry of December selling.

1999

"Bloody Glove" on world tour, trial recessed four months. Defense and prosecution teams go to Hawaii for R & R in same plane, President Joe Petersen picks up tab.

Two jurors marry each other. Defense team gives Tupperware, prosecution gives toaster oven. O.J. best man.

Congress makes the O.J. trial a national monument, "a powerful example to the world of what made America what it is today," says President Joe Petersen.

2000

Hardly anything happens anyplace in the world during the first year of the millennium, much to the disappointment of thousands of religious groups and their leaders. The O.J. trial has a slow growth year, no new TV movies, no books. "Bloody Glove" cancels national tour after lukewarm reviews of new release. Network news drops O.J. to number three for first time since 1994.

2002

Federal budget not balanced this year as prescribed by the constitutional amendment, so amendment is repealed by Congress. "The alternative was to arrest the government and impeach all the elected representatives and that would be silly," says Sir Newt Gingrich.

The total cost of the O.J. trial for the first time exceeds the federal deficit.

First defense-team attorney appears on *Forbes* 400 billionaire list.

2019

Ojito, the first child conceived and born in sequestration, graduates from law school, passes bar, and is appointed to the O.J. defense team. Prosecution cries foul.

The paper used so far for written documents related to the O.J. trial is calculated to have consumed all the trees in Oregon.

The Walt Disney Company buys the city of Los Angeles for expansion.

2020

Judge Ito rules that the sons and daughters of jurors may substitute for the parents in the event of death or disability. *Adult Children of Sequestered Parents* leaps to top of best-seller list.

Judge Ito rules that the children of the trial lawyers may replace their parents in the event of death or disability.

2021

Judge Ito retires and is replaced by defense-team attorney Ojito. The prosecution cries foul.

2042

Seven children and five grandchildren of the original jurors remain sequestered, as closing arguments are begun by the lawyer sons and daughters of the original defense and prosecution teams.

2044

The jury enters the courtroom for the last time in June with the verdict. Fifty years after being arrested, O.J. Simpson, nearly blind, arrives in a wheelchair, IV bottles hanging from the rack. The attendant turns up O.J.'s hearing aid. O.J. tries once to rise, tries again, succeeds.

The foreman of the jury says, "Not guilty."

Judge Ojito says to all gathered: "Business at this pop stand is done. Go home."

The Walt Disney Company, as part of a friendly takeover bid for outright ownership of America, agrees to pay off the national debt.

O.J. is given a lifetime contract with the Buffalo Bills.

Scrambling for Dollars

HOWARD MOHR

I don't believe in TV antennas mounted on housetops because of the inherent dangers, which I won't go into here and create panic. My antenna is in the attic, lying across ceiling joists and R-16 pink fiberglass insulation, pointed roughly toward the town of Granite Falls, twenty miles away, where a tall UHF tower emits signals for several channels.

On VHF I receive my neighborhood public broadcast station, Channel 10, directly from Appleton. No other VHF channel comes in on a regular basis with a picture that can be distinguished from an X ray of my gallbladder.

A satellite dish is definitely out of the question. My extensive research in the newspapers on the rack at the checkout counter at HyVee has convinced me that satellite dishes can give you 120 channels, sure, but they also collect bad karma that pools up in the dish and eventually runs over and into your basement and reacts with bed mite methane. You can imagine the medical implications of this.

Besides, a satellite dish doesn't go with our basic granola and compost-heap lifestyle.

Back in the old days, which was last year, if my memory serves me correctly, the UHF tower at Granite Falls was sending me a signal that included Channels 9, 11, and 4 from the Twin Cities. This kept me from being isolated from the center of culture there near the freeways and the Mall of America, and enabled me to watch several accounts of the latest mayhem, and the weather, too. Then—without warning—the Granite Falls tower began broadcasting FOX and ESPN and CNN and TNN. What a goldmine. Give a guy eight channels and what else does he need?

But pretty soon ESPN, CNN, TNN were scrambled. And then 9, 11, and 4 were scrambled. My mediocre picture was not only mediocre but looked like a paint spill. I understood that one could purchase a descrambler from the Scramble Company for a couple of C-Notes, but, goodness, a guy could buy two fifty-five gallon drums of granola with that kind of money.

So that left me with PBS and Channel 5, a Hubbard system, which to this day comes in loud and crisp because there are two separate relay towers very close by that send out UHF signals so powerful you don't need an antenna. You can't get away from it. It ghosts up everywhere.

You can pick it up on the end of your nose.

In fact, my friend Harold Mire—who doesn't even own a TV set these days—began hearing voices one day and went to the clinic about it.

The GP listened with his stethoscope to the side of Harold's head, just below his feed cap, and said, "It sounds like Angela talking to Mark."

"Angela who?" Harold said. He was completely news-anchor illiterate.

The doc told him there was no cure for it. But there was. The voices disappeared after Harold stopped wearing his gold-framed granny glasses during heavy sunspot activity when the grass was wet.

Apart from Channel 10, Channel 5 is my main source of televised information about the current state of the universe. I had invited Randy, Angela, Mark, Dave, and the whole gang into my home so many times that I was a little peeved that they hadn't ever invited me into their homes. They did sometimes show family pictures of weddings and new babies, though.

So let's say I was as happy as any guy has a right to be in the age of intrusive media. Did I need to look at some cretin on speed sell cheap jewelry in the middle of the night on 11? But I did like the occasional *M*A*S*H* rerun and *Night Court*.

So I did what any red-blooded tinkerer would do. I tried defeating the system, using native ingenuity and my elementary electronic expertise.

Here are the results of my descrambling activity. Patent is not pending, so feel free. More power to you. Not responsible for accidents.

1. Wear two copper bracelets of the kind used to cure arthritis. Grip the incoming antenna wire with one hand while slowly moving your head from side to side and rubbing your belly in a circular motion with the other. A steady rhythm is best, in sync with the wave patterns of the scrambler.

2. Build a large turntable powered by a one-horse electric motor. Use a gear reduction system (old Ford Escort transmission in low is perfect). Put the TV set in the middle of the turntable and position your couch and chairs on the perimeter. Vertigo is a serious problem with this descrambler and can create severe nausea and disorientation if you try to watch tennis matches or Joan Rivers.

3. Run back and forth in front of the TV set while fluttering your eyes. (Don't do this if the mailman is outside looking in through the window.)

4. Load an old Sears food blender with Silly Putty and turn it on to CHOP. The interference pattern completely cancels out the scrambling until the blender heats up and fails, slinging Silly Putty and metal fragments into the walls.

So what did the Scramble Company do? They stopped scrambling, and started reversing the images instead. Everything looked like the negative for a photo. Everybody had bad teeth. Even the beautiful anchor lady on 9 looked menacing.

This negative imaging was entertaining, I'll have to say, but dangerous. I grew to like it, it made all the shows somewhat interesting. But the Scramble Company probably found out that some families were watching more free TV with the reversed images than ever before. So they scrambled the negative image. Only people who really did inhale in the seventies and kept it up into the nineties would have found entertainment value in it.

The benefit of all this scrambling for money? Some people with limited budgets and big families decided to watch less TV and go to the free lending library more. I consider that a major plus for us out here, but certainly not for the advertisers who buy space on the commercial channels. I would think advertisers might seek cheaper rates for their Greater Minnesota scrambled messages. I don't know anything about business, but I don't think too many people would buy a made-in-Disneyland Chevy from a salesman who looks like an extra from *Dawn of the Dead*. However, I have been wrong before about consumerism.

I grew up listening to the radio. I like radio. It's free, and always has been. You can scan the dial at night and pick up cities all over. It's great. If somebody wants to start another American revolution, just let them try scrambling radio and then making us pay for it.

The most positive effect of scrambling?

Some people in Greater Minnesota (read "rural") are beginning to believe that the most useful thing a guy can do with a TV set is shut it off.

Gambling in the Schools

HOWARD MOHR

[When Minnesota jumped into legalized gambling, it was off the deep end without a lifeguard. First it was Canterbury Downs, a clean, well-lighted horse track that seemed more like a Lutheran church with betting windows. Then came Powerball, Daily Three, Gopher Five (named after the official state rodent), and Scratch-Offs. At the same time Native American casinos were springing up in the land of sky-blue waters, raking it in with blackjack and slot machines and high-stakes bingo. What could possibly be next?]

Parents and teachers who have been worried sick about finding enough money just to maintain public schools at a minimal level, worry no more. The Minnesota Legislature last week approved the Education Gambling Bill. The bill allows Video Gaming Devices (VGDS) in K–12 classrooms. Only two machines per classroom will be permitted, unless the class size exceeds thirty, in which case one additional VGD machine will be permitted for each additional ten students. Class size, however, will not be a problem once the gambling revenue begins pouring in.

Students in math classes will be instructed in probability, statistics, and hot streaks. The VGDs in kindergarten classrooms will operate with nickels only. All students will be expected to do their assignments and homework before gambling, unless they're on a roll.

Powerball and Gopher Five tickets will be sold only in the lunchroom during the noon hour. But the attractive neon Minnesota lottery signs will be permitted at the main entrance of the school and near the scoreboard at games.

Pulltabs and Scratch-Offs are specifically outlawed in the bill because they make a big mess, according to the powerful Janitor's Lobby.

Off-track horse betting will be handled in the Principal's office, with a $2 and $5 window initially, but with the option of a $100 window after the first year. Race results from the major American tracks will be broadcast to the students on the classroom Channel One. National scratch sheets will be available in convenient locations. The first half hour of the school day will be a "handicapping homeroom," but students will be encouraged to arrive early if they are psyched up and have the feeling that this is the day.

Each school system may publish and sell its own Tip Sheet or it can hire a professional tipster, such as "Gimp" Gordon or "Fast-Forward" Freddy, to be a counselor and role model.

Betting on high school sports will be forbidden, but the morning line for collegiate and professional sports will be broadcast on Channel One and posted in the principal's office near the sports betting window. As a safeguard, students will not be allowed to bet on sporting contests unless they have successfully passed Math II, "Point Spreads and Injuries."

Poker games will be operated as an extracurricular activity from the final bell until four A.M. The school will be the "house" and provide the dealers. There will be a 10 percent rakeoff for each pot up to a maximum of $10 per hand. Only Five-Card

Draw, Stud, and Hold-Em will be permitted. Midnight Baseball, Spit in the Ocean, or Mission Impossible will not be permitted because they are silly games of chance and would send the wrong message to students.

Gambling will obviously bring new life and big money to the schools, but there are other advantages:

1: Students will be prepared for jobs in the gambling industry after graduating.

2: Part-time jobs will be created in the schools for change walkers, dealers, security officers, and so on.

3: A wider variety of people will be attracted to the teaching profession.

4: Discipline will be better because the hope of getting something for nothing is one of the oldest drives for excellence.

A bigger gambling issue faces the Legislature soon: Should gaming be permitted in hospitals and medical centers? And if so, how much and what kind? Would patients be able to bet the ponies from their beds? Could nurses deal blackjack in the sunroom? Could you go double or nothing with your physician?

Gardening Advice
from Mertensia Corydalis

Q: Last fall I lifted my canna bulbs and stored them in the unheated pool house. It did not get too cold this winter. Do you think the bulbs will be OK to plant again this year?

—CHAD, NEW LEICESTER

A: What a pity! All that money and no taste. Do you live in the Yucatan Peninsula? I thought not. Then why are you growing tropical plants with big hot-colored blooms in the middle of what was formerly prime Ohio farmland? Refer to question number one in today's column. Throw the damn things out and collect rare dwarf conifers. You can afford it.

Q: Dear Mertensia: How do you get a pond ready for spring?

—FELICIA, CLAYTON

A: Inspect the pump and filtration system, replacing any cracked tubing and cleaning out any debris. Next you must remove the autumn leaves that have blown in. If the pond is small, lift out the leaves with a rake or even a doggie pooper scooper. Here, my garden assistant Tran and I first remove the pots of iris kaempferi and water lilies so they will not be disturbed by the thrashing about. Then, because my pond is virtually bottomless,

Tran strips to the waist, and, wearing no waders, plunges right in and goes at it, taking care not to puncture the butyl liner. There will be a bit of musky odor, but consider it part of getting the job done. Add the leaves and muck to your compost heap or apply them directly to the base of your plants, the rich, decomposing material like truffles fed to a lover; the rewards will be generous.

Q: Miss Corydalis, a friend tells me I need to have my lawn aerated. The lawn care companies want to charge several hundred dollars for this. I saw these aerating do-it-yourself devices you can mail order [The reader enclosed the catalog illustration]. Do you think they will work?

—Buck, Greater Maumee

A: Buck, since your lawn is out of doors most of the time, it's getting plenty of air. I suppose we're talking about thatch buildup, which would not be a problem if you were not having the turf bombarded with nitrogen four times a year. The illustration—from the sort of catalog that sells ice-cube molds in the form of breasts and Denver Broncos toilet brush concealers—is of a pair of spiked platforms that one buckles onto the soles of one's shoes. If you don't mind spending the afternoon doing a frenzied flamenco in full view of all your neighbors, you might manage to loosen up the thatch a bit. Otherwise, fire the chemical warfare service and let nature take its course. Finally, you have a lot of cheek sending me another damned lawn-care question.

Next time . . . on gazing balls
and composting pet waste

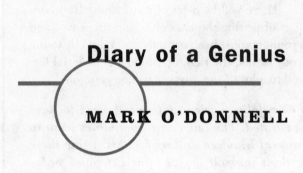

Diary of a Genius

MARK O'DONNELL

No responses to my job search again today. They do not understand my vision. Those bourgeois enthusiastic catch phrases are through—it's time for a New Advertising. I'm writing some copy that *criticizes* Hershey kisses: *"They're probably nothing but junk."* It will provoke people into defending them, or entice them to see for themselves. The insolence is bound to impress the teen market. It worked with me and Sandra Heller. When her parents hated me and told her I was a loser, she got serious with me. I wonder where she is now.

Father writes and begs me to turn my talents to literature, but he doesn't understand that Mmm Mmm Good controls mankind, not How Do I Love Thee. By the way—NOTE: Sex isn't working in ads anymore. Too dangerous. Besides, Margarine does not equal Matrimony, jaded buyers know that. The New Advertising must tap into the well of aging singles' loneliness *honestly:*

- THIS CHRISTMAS, TRY HEINZ GRAVY, COLD, RIGHT OUT OF THE CAN, ALL BY YOURSELF, STANDING UP, IN THE DEAD OF NIGHT.
- GIVE YOURSELF DIAMONDS—NO ONE ELSE IS GOING TO.
- FRISKIES' TREATS: PRETEND YOUR CAT CARES, IF IT HELPS KEEP YOU ALIVE.

I tried calling Sandra. Her so-called "husband" says she doesn't want to speak to me. He was intimidated by the British accent I adopted. I must remember: *Sexual desire is only a displacement of the urge to purchase.*

I watch the electric billboards in Times Square and all I can think is, They're "fun"—but they *don't work.* Too busy. Besides—they aren't "green," they blight the environment. We need Abstract Ad Placement for the New Age—We should offer premiums to average citizens to pepper their conversation with references to our products (we'd monitor them with implants), or, better yet, name their kids after them: *"Those are my youngest, Kleenex and Benadryl."* Must call that nimrod at BBD&O. Remember, act arrogant so he'll want to "socially raise himself" to what I'm offering.

Celebrity endorsements are fine, but not from dead or imaginary celebrities who can't defend themselves, not to mention get paid. Leprechauns and Santa should *not* be allowed to endorse products. Ditto Mother Nature, Washington, and Lincoln. I'd include Jefferson, but why bother, he has no holiday and no TV recognition factor. Columbus and Sir Isaac Newton—*only as figures of ridicule.* Candice Bergen, fine—if there's certified proof she actually exists.

★ ★ ★

Three words: *Homeless Poppin' Fresh.*
   (Can't find an oven? Expires uncooked? Explore . . .)

That martinet at BBD&O suggested I try pharmacological advertising, that I might find an "opening" there. He was intimidated by my *"Stave Off the Abyss"* pitch for Rolling Rock. He doesn't grasp that *Advertising is a lie that exploits the truth.* The landlord saw me sneaking in and tried a negative campaign on me. I used my English accent on him but I was nervous and it came out more high-pitched "baby talk"—but he did back off then. Must I turn to Father again? He wants me to concentrate on my poetry, but I reject poetry. Products are the only truly palpable things. There is no soul, despite what those twee herbal tea ads pretend. There are only marketing niches.

I see professional athletes plugging MTV—jocks and rockers, seemingly antithetical— Theory: *Everything that makes money must converge.*

Billions and billions served. Why don't they dare to be specific? Could the public not handle it? Would their fragile sense of reality shatter? *Vagary must end.*

Question: Advertising, or Advertizing? If only I knew.

That Pumblechook at the pharmacological agency has returned my "All-Blank" pages for Prozac. He didn't get it. I suppose he wants the product name somewhere. He didn't like my all-silent thirty-second radio spots, either. True art Shows, it doesn't Tell. He suggests public service spots. I don't believe in service, only in products. And even if public service is my fate, this I pledge: *I will never resort to rainbows.*

★ ★ ★

The Head Yahoo at Grey shot down my proposal of subtly inserting promotions into folklore: *"And when the miller's daughter* finally *presented the king with the lightest and tastiest snack cake in the world, he marveled, 'Little Debbie's are indeed the lightest and tastiest!'"* The goofus claims nobody reads folklore anymore. Well, the movies are already full of plugs—why not literature? *All's Well That Ends with Pepsi. The Old Man and the Coppertone Sunscreen and the Sea. Nausea, and Periodic Discomfort Relief.* . . . No one reads literature either, but the rates would be cheaper.

★ ★ ★

I screamed my ecologically pure commercials for Eagle Brand Potato Chips out my window all night but all I got was arrested. The Eagle people didn't even offer to post bail, much less pay me for the free promotion. What kind of world forces me to fight to be heard while the Snuggles Fabric Softener Bear Masters rule?

★ ★ ★

Home again. Father's check arrived. He complains that my sestina on Sani-Flush does not qualify as poetry. He's locked into nineteenth-century notions. *It rhymed, didn't it?*

I asked the stewardess downstairs on a date and she asked if I was the guy who'd been shouting all night. I said I was and she just shook her head and walked away, disappointedly, I thought. I guess she realized I'm married to my work.

Recited my Eagle Brand promos to myself, quietly, all night long. I'm thinking them to myself right now, over and over, secretly. I have discovered a whole new genre: *Advertising no one will ever even know exists.*

TV Guide, Soon

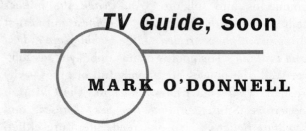

MARK O'DONNELL

SATURDAY

4 A.M.–4:30 A.M.

1 NY1—NEWS GRAPHICS WITHOUT NEWS

2 CBS

PUERILE AND JEJEUNE (CC) :30
Puerile (Fanny Post) gets Jejeune (Pooty Nelson) in hot water, literally. Burn Specialist: Edward Mulhare. (Repeat)

3 CORRECT TIME CHANNEL (Repeat)

4 NBC

WHO'S THAT GIRL?: THE SERIES (CC) :30
Madonna (Debbie Gibson) invites a homeless orphan to spend Thanksgiving (Burl Ives) with her. Dondi: Marky Mark. (Repeat)

5 FOX

METER MAIDS (CC) :30
Real-life minicam action from Denver. (Viewer discretion unnecessary.)

6 HOME BROWSING CHANNEL

Merchandise displayed with no phone number to call.

7 INTERACTIVE SEX NETWORK

THE BIG BREAK-UP—Discussion 1:00 (possibly more)
Hot babes you've never met tell you it's all over between
you.

8 WEATHER NOSTALGIA CHANNEL

Yesterday's weather today. (Repeat)

9 SCI-FI CHANNEL

STAR TRUCULENCE (CC) 1:00
Nadir (Shank Coltish) and Monitor Nod (Reef Brine) shoot
up tin cans on a peaceful uninhabited planet. The Galactic
Gatekeeper: Vic Tayback. (Repeat) (Closed-captioned to
overexplain significance of pretentious dialogue.)

10 NEWS FOR THE FAINTHEARTED NETWORK

Nice and upbeat headlines only. (Repeat)

11 ALL GAME SHOW CHANNEL

FAMILIAR FEUD :30
Not the right answer, the average answer. (Repeat)

12 CHILDHOOD SEXUAL ABUSE MOVIE CHANNEL

"Father Touched Me" (1995). Seattle family undergoes
years of histrionic litigation. Booty: Mason Gamble. Father:
Richard Crenna. Meredith Baxter: Herself.

13 RESTAURANT FOOD CHANNEL

No recipes, just platters of food and a check.

14 BISEXUAL SELF-HELP CHANNEL

"Lamp Unto My Dresser." Hosts: Leslie Less and Merle
Pesto.

15 INTERACTIVE GAY SELF-HELP CHANNEL

"C'mon, Get Happy." Guest: Cosmetician/faith healer Wage
Dandy does makeovers on viewers without even seeing
them.

16 STRAIGHT SELF-HELP CHANNEL

"Spit and Polish." Host: Frank Shard. Guests: The Millers
from next door.

17 A SEXUAL SELF-HELP CHANNEL
"The Hobby Hut." Delbert builds a birdhouse again.

18 LOCAL YOKEL CHANNEL
"Murky Inarticulate Drivel." Guests: His Self-Imagined Holiness Fatuoso Gha, street performer Oopsy Doodle, Sylvia Miles.

19 BUDGET TRAVEL CHANNEL
"Local Public Swimming Pool Round-up." (Repeat)

20 INCORRECT TIME CHANNEL

21 HBO
MOVIE 1:15—Erotic Thriller
"Slippery When Dead" (1995). Unexceptional potboiler made infamous when star Sharon Stone was killed by inadvertently overheated Vaseline. Kevin Dillon, Roy Scheider, Andrea Marcovicci.

22 THE DISNEY CHANNEL
LORD OF THE FLIES—sitcom—:30
Piggy has a tea party and everyone apologizes for being thoughtless. The Wildlife: The Care Bears.

23 THE DENIAL CHANNEL
Joy Brotherly says everything's fine, over and over. (Repeat)

24 DENIAL WEATHER CHANNEL
Sunshine predicted only.

25 TRADE SCHOOL CHANNEL
"Arc-Welding for Beginners"—1,390 min.

26 TBS
GULLIBLE'S ISLE
Gullible (Arnold Stang) kills everyone (Herman's Hermits) accidentally, but they come back to life as a testimony to the show's basic falseness and vapidity. (Repeat)

27 BIG BAND CHANNEL
Music, but no picture. Featured sounds: Tommy Dorsey.

28 EGGHEAD CHANNEL
MURDER MOST ELEEMOSYNARY (1994). 2:00
Joan Plowright portrays intellectual sleuth Camille Polio, tracking down a killer at a deconstructionists' convention at

Oxford (Peter Ustinov). Jacques Derrida: Carl Ballantine. (Repeat)

29 THE STATIC CHANNEL
(Temporarily out of service.)

30 MTV

31 TNT
MOVIE 1:30—Comedy
"Hoboes in the Haunted Hospital" (1942). Slapstick on the excruciating side, with hemophiliac Slappee Golden and the Bray Brothers.

32 THE PIFFLE CHANNEL
"The Making of the Best of Entertainment Tonight: Reprise Edition" (Repeat)

33 SPANISH NETWORK
MOVIE—2:10—Childish Drama
"EL HOMBRE DE LA LUNA" (1981). El classico de Steven Spielberg concerne del extraterrestrialle adorablo e su amigo suburbanito. (Parlando muy forte, e.g., "penis breath.")

34 AMERICA'S MOST AMATEURISH
HOME VIDEO CHANNEL
KINDERGARTEN BALLET ROUND-UP—320 min.

35 THE TRAFFIC CHANNEL

36 THE PEDESTRIAN CHANNEL

37 THE EVEN MORE PEDESTRIAN CHANNEL

38 C-SPAN
LATE NIGHT
Cleaning ladies mop the floors of Congress.

39 C-SPAN 2
LATE NIGHT TOO
Night watchmen patrol halls of Congress.

40 MAKE BELIEVE WEATHER CHANNEL
Snakes, manna, and oobleck reported mischievously.

41 COURT TV
Ongoing coverage of Abe Rosenthal Prolixity Trial.

42 BAD MUSICALS NETWORK
MOVIE—Bad Musical

"Honk for Happy" (1954). 95 min. Seems longer.
Typical superhighway musical involves plans to stage auto ballet with hundreds of cars to save kindly gas station owner somehow. Speedy: Gene Kelly. Pitstop: Vera-Ellen. Pops: Dean Jagger. Otto: Itself.

43 VIOLENCE NETWORK
"Eat Lead" (1987).—90 min.
Jean Paul Von Damnable kills and kills and kills and kills in Hong Kong. (Parental discretion unlikely.)

44 E!
PUBLICISTS ON PARADE :30

45 COMEDY CHANNEL
STAND-UPS NOT AS FUNNY AS YOU 1:00

46 ABSTRACT PRETTY PATTERNS CHANNEL
"SPIRALS FOR DAYS."—6,840 min.

47 HOME SHOPPING CHANNEL
(*Temporarily closed due to suspicious fire.*)

48 LE TELEVISEUR FRANCAIS
POUAH! 1:00
Chic, insufferable people mock America as they drive to Graceland. (Repeat)

49 EXTREMISTS CHANNEL
IRA TODAY :25
Gun-running and terrorist plotting announcements. (May be delayed due to excessive diatribes on the Muslim Fundamentalist Spotlight.)

50 THE WOMEN'S CHANNEL
WOMEN WHO HATE EVERYONE BUT THEMSELVES, AND EVEN THEN (1:00)
Host Yolko Ovum talks to Patty Reagan about getting a life. (Repeat)

51 THE MAN'S NETWORK
IRON JOHN—Robert Bly makes veal piccata with a grizzly bear, pantses George Will. (Repeat)

52 RELIGION NETWORK
THE LORD IS MY DETECTIVE. Rev. Travis explains that Jesus is tailing you, and He has photos.

53 PLAYBOY CHANNEL
"Chicks with Dorks Like You." (Fantasy)

54 THE WESTERN CHANNEL
MOVIE
"The Spurs Are Hers" (1958).—2:00
Barbara Stanwyck whips a man to prove her loyalty to a lawless town, and to sadism in general. Grant: Richard Jaeckel. Clutch: Edgar Buchanan.

55 THE INTERACTIVE HEALTH NETWORK
RASH ROUND-UP :30

56 THE LUCY CHANNEL

57 VIDEO MUSIC BOX
Pop stars singing about love but actually caring about no one but themselves.

58 HIGH SCHOOL EQUIVALENCY CHANNEL
STUDY HALL—120 min.

59 BULLETIN BOARD CHANNEL
Local announcements.

60 GRAFFITI CHANNEL
Obscene phrases from local youth.

61 TV GUIDE CHANNEL
Lists programming. (Repeat)

62 ESPN SPORTS CHANNEL
DEAD-OF-NIGHT BOULDER ROLLING 1:30
Dial Soap Invitational from Sisyphus, Saskatchewan, hosted live by the ghost of Steve Reeves.

63 ALIEN COMMUNICATIONS FREQUENCY
Nothing programmed yet, unless it's undetectable to earthly eyes and ears.

64 OLD NEWSREEL NETWORK

65 OLD DRIVER'S ED TRAINING FILM NETWORK
"The Last Prom" (1954). :30 (graphic violence)

66 OLD TV COMMERCIALS NETWORK

67 CARTOON NETWORK
SALLY STRUTHERS SHOW (non-animated)

68 ALL-NITE DELI SECURITY CAMERA NETWORK

69 BURNING YULE LOG NETWORK

70 PBS
"The Search for the Nile" (1 min.). David Attenborough goes to Egypt and readily finds the Nile. (Repeat)

71 PARANOIAC NETWORK
Eerie faces tell you they're going to get you.

72 THE OTHER GAME SHOW NETWORK
WHEEL OF FORTUNE :30
Nonentities struggle to reveal the hidden, and it turns out to be a cliché.

73 SENIOR CITIZENS CHANNEL
REMEMBERING WOODSTOCK 1:00

74 THE NAZI NETWORK
"BLITZKRIEG!" 1:00
High school students make strafing sounds with their mouths and heil each other for laughs. Hitler: Wally Joss. (Repeat)

75 MISSING PERSONS NETWORK
Faces of the missing on a rotating basis.

76 NOSTALGIC TEST PATTERN NETWORK

77 THE AQUARIUM CHANNEL

78 ALL ELVIS CHANNEL
MOVIE
"The Wild One" (1954).—80 min. Marlon Brando reminds some people of Elvis in this leatherclad motorcycle epic, but in any case, try it just as a break from all that Elvis.

79 MOSTLY VIOLENCE CHANNEL
MOVIE—Action 1:30.
"Run Roughshod" (1990). A barefoot Jean Bob Van Dim kills and kills and kills but then stops and rests in Bangkok. Nominal love interest: Jazmin Tayle. (Nudity, violence, but no actual genitals or guts hanging out of people, just blood and teeth and mashed-up faces.)

80 EMERGENCY BROADCAST SIGNAL NOSTALGIA NETWORK

81 BOOKS ON VIDEOTAPE CHANNEL
"Truman" (565 pp.). Page after slowly turned page of David

McCullough's biography of the late president, for readers without shelf space for actual books.

82 THE MARILYN CHANNEL
"The Misfits" (1961). 100 min. Marilyn looks neurotic and windblown in this peculiar drama without any cross-dressing to speak of. Clark Gable, Montgomery Clift.

83 THE THELMA RITTER CHANNEL
"The Misfits" (1961). 100 min. Thelma's funny enough here, but wait for "All About Eve." Marilyn Monroe, Clark Gable.

84 LIFESTYLE NETWORK
"THIS OLD BOMB SHELTER" :30
Beau retools his shelter into an underground disco, which is also passé, but not quite as much so.

85 CUTE KIDS NETWORK
"FULL HOUSE" :30—Comedy, Supposedly
While Jesse and Joey smirk and mug, Michelle (Mary Kate and Ashley Olsen) does the same, only more amateurishly. The Overweaning Local Bureaucrat: Olympia Dukakis. (Repeat)

86 THE FOREIGN MOVIE CHANNEL
"Breadfruit and Frederica" (Moldavian, c. 1962, 150 min.). A disturbed old grocer and a nonexistent teenager seem to spend an uneventful winter day in a parking lot, but it may all be an illusion in a young seminarian's mind. Vespa Venal, Molto Piccolo.

87 THE NICE SHADE OF SOLID BLUE CHANNEL

88 THE OLD JUNIOR HIGH SCHOOL HYGIENE FILM CHANNEL
"Give Me Puberty or Give Me Death" (1954).—:45

89 THE COCA-COLA CHANNEL

90 THE ROSS PEROT CHANNEL

91 GOSPEL COOKING CHANNEL
BAKIN' WITH MY MAKER :30
Cassioepea Brunell finds the strength to make Sunday go-to-meetin' brownies with a little help from the Man Upstairs, and none whatsoever from that no account Dexter. (Repeat)

92 MTV FOR THE DEAF (CC)

93 YOUR SUBSTITUTE FAMILY NETWORK

Your baby wakes up and cries, and you pretend to calm him down; your dog stirs fitfully; your wife dreams of someone, but you don't know it's not of you. (Repeat, you think.)

94 THE TIGER BEAT CHANNEL

"THE JASON PRIESTLEY SHOW"—1:00

Girl journalists talk about Jason dreamily, but he never shows up. (Repeat)

95 GUNS 'N' AMMO CHANNEL

Order guns by phone.

96 INTERACTIVE VIDEO DATING CHANNEL

97 THE MIRROR CHANNEL

High technology provides reflective screen.

98 SEXUAL TECHNIQUE CHANNEL

LOVE ALONG WITH MIDGE—Guest Robin Byrd shows Midge how to massage spouses as if they were total strangers.

99 THE RELENTLESS BIG COOL EXPLOSIONS NETWORK

100 NICK AT NIGHT

HATE THAT HOWARD :30—Vintage sitcom

Howard (Will Hutchins) simply tries to buy some flowers for Gina (Millie Perkins) but the florist kills him. Florist: Vincent Price. (Repeat)

101 THE MYSTERY CHANNEL

MYSTERY BIOGRAPHY 1:00

Host Peter Graves explores the fact that Bob Saget has a career.

102 PUBLIC AFFAIRS CHANNEL

WHITHER?—Jesuitical Discussion :30

Panelists former Senator Daniel Patrick Moynihan, former Governor Mario Cuomo, and defrocked Cardinal John O'Connor debate the use, and indeed the existence of, asbestos.

103 DOG BARKING TO DETER BURGLARS CHANNEL

104 ADULT FILM CHANNEL

MOVIE 2:00—Erotic Drama
"Will Wanda Never Cease?" (1993). Julienne Hover plays an insatiable social worker in what is supposed to be Beverly Hills. Cliff Burns, Drusilla Hellish. (Nudity, unconvincing language.)

105 GLADIATOR PETS CHANNEL
THE CRITTER PIT. 1:00
Cockfighting; two junkyard dogs in a washing machine; a python and a gerbil on an escalator. (Repeat)

106 INTERACTIVE HOME SHOPLIFTING CHANNEL

107 INTERFAITH NETWORK
GO THOU AND FIGURE 1:00—Discussion
Rabbi Saul Christopher O'Rourke discusses whiskey versus Mogen David with himself. (Repeat)

108 ALL-BLOOPER CABLE NETWORK
Outtakes considered too inane for network blooper shows.

109 THE INTERACTIVE PSYCHIC NETWORK
GUESS WHO'S PSYCHIC 1:00
Arthur C. Cabal takes phone calls, which shouldn't be necessary if he's so psychic. Foreseen: calls from lonely drabs.

110 OBITUARY CHANNEL
DEAD OF NIGHT :30
Scheduled: Obits for Bob Hope, former president Ronald Reagan, and victims of unexpected plane crash in Tampa.

111 ALL TRIVIA CHANNEL
GRAMMYS HISTORY IN REVIEW with Teresa Brewer.

112 VIRTUAL REALITY
THE CARLSBAD CAVERNS HOUR :60 (Footwear recommended.)

113 AMERICAN SECURITY SECRETS NETWORK
STEALTH TECHNOLOGY SHOW.
Informants TBA.

114 INTERACTIVE VIOLENCE NETWORK
WHAT ARE YOU LOOKING AT? 1:00
Mooky Finnegan doesn't like the way you're watching his show. (FCC requests adults trained in self-defense only.)

115 SECOND STRING SPORTS CABLE NETWORK
THE LESS THAN SPECIAL OLYMPICS (CC) 2:00
Rick Shroeder hosts squat thrusts, tag, and jumping jack finals from Fort Wayne, Indiana. (Pre-taped)

116 SPORTS AND PUBLIC AFFAIRS CHANNEL
WRESTLING WITH ISSUES :30
Congressmen Lex Luger and The Undertaker take on the trade imbalance; Vice President Colin "The Widowmaker" Powell literally takes potshots at the revised federal budget. (Repeat)

117 ARTS AND CRAFTS NETWORK
DOODLING WITH THE GIPPER :30
Late ex-president Reagan shares some of the thousands of doodles he drew during his White House years, and recommends felt tips. (Repeat)

118 LIMITED VIOLENCE CHANNEL
MOVIE 1:45—Action
"Dead to the World" (1994). Jean Marie Von Dumme knocks people unconscious all over Asia in his quest for a good night's rest. Late night revelers: T. K. Chang, Brad Woo.

119 THE ALL SATAN CHANNEL
HEAVY METAL ROCK VIDEOS PLAYED BACKWARD SHOWCASE 6:66

120 THE SOOTHING SURF CHANNEL

121 THE BIRDS SINGING IN RUSTLING BRANCHES CHANNEL

122 THE LULLABY CHANNEL

123 INTERACTIVE EMERGENCY ROOM NETWORK

124 INTERACTIVE DESPERATE BANKING NETWORK
Deposits, withdrawals, transfers, bankruptcy a specialty. The Teller: Andrew Tobias. Subject to cancellation.

125 THE ENVY CHANNEL
LIVING ROOMS OF THE LOADED 1:00

Host Ravening Leech leads a tour of unaccountably wealthy civil servants' homes in Colombia. (Repetitious)

126 INTERACTIVE JOB INTERVIEW CHANNEL
Sorry, no scheduled programming. We'll call you.

127 THE CHAOS CHANNEL
The ongoing faceless dark abyss. (Repeat)

My Genetic Memories

MARK O'DONNELL

You know what I miss? How bathtubs and stoves used to have those little feet on them, and you'd lose things underneath them. One of Vera's flapjacks got under the old Heat Queen and was there for most of the Truman administration. Finally gave it to the paper boy at Christmas, told him it was a flying saucer toy (flying saucers were new then) and he was glad to get it. None of those flippant remarks the delivery people are full of today. Everybody's a snideheimer now. I blame the television there.

And remember how the little ones used to cut themselves on the metal pieces of Erector sets? Sure, nowadays they wiggle their little plastic men and say, "I'm exploding everybody!"—but does anyone actually get hurt? No. Today it's all video games. Explosions but no consequences. I even hear how they're going to fight the real wars on video screens now. Never mind getting out in the fresh air. Not like it used to be. Not like the Thirty Years War. Even the kids got in on that one. There was none of this paperwork rigamarole to join up, if you ran away from home you were eligible. And those big blunderbusses, like trombones.

I guess today they'd say they were funny looking, but back then they got a lot of respect. Whatever happened to those Prussians, anyway? Or Hessians, whoever they were we shot at, or alongside, whichever. They worked hard. A year and a day for a schnitzel and a copper. Not like these mercenaries today. Today, they want the movie rights on the raid and free cable in the bunker.

That Tamburlaine could cut a rug through human flesh, too, without a lot of press conferences. One hand on the reins and the other swinging his, what would you call it, a scimitar? The way Vera used to go on about him, I was almost jealous, but then, I had made ritual sacrifices to Diana at her temple at Aricia; Vera never would let that go. It was for the hunt, but try explaining that to a woman. And the temple architecture was worth seeing. Solid, not like these prefab Halls of Fame they have now. It had caryatids. You don't see those on these new pinkie glass boxes with the silly hats. Unless they add them as a joke. It's all Disneyland now, no sincerity or terror like the Valley of the Kings. There weren't any flippant remarks around Rameses.

Of course, they couldn't do something like the hanging gardens again if they tried. Too expensive. Not enough old devil's-own Babylonian cleverness (boy, some of those strange musical instruments they dreamed up!). Plus a lot of those fancier plants were killed off by the ozone, or the flood. It's all hydroponic hothouse flavorless plasticky stuff now. Haven't had a decent apple since about Day One. That last Ice Age made the food taste funny. Those enormous Carboniferous era ferns, they were lovely to hide from predators under. I suppose they'd wilt in this namby-pamby temperate modern climate.

Oh, that reminds me, the woolly mammoth. There was a classic. I like my elephants with some hair on 'em. Jumbo was OK, but he had nothing on those Mesozoic babies. And the sloths of today—cannot compare. Mammals were fresh then. Oh, when we were all little tree shrews, remember that? Those little fingers! No thumbs, and we didn't want 'em. Life was simpler. Conceptual thought was something we didn't even think of. Makes me want to go suck an egg right now. I miss the night vision, too, especially when I have to take out the trash.

People are always going "Dinosaurs Dinosaurs" but they forget those gigantic dragonflies. Used to prey on us when we were grubs, and you know they could scare your tour group today. And that first fish that crawled out of the water. That took moxie. Fish nowadays, no moxie. Spineless. Well, they're not spineless, just no ambition. Want everything handed to them. No hands back then, so no handouts.

What I really miss is spineless deep-sea life. Wouldn't have that lower back trouble like I have now! That nice primordial soupy solution all around, none of this wind and rainfall we have to deal with up here. To tell you the truth, things were simpler when all life was unicellular, not just a lucky few. Nothing but tiny little wriggling amoebas and the big, big ocean. No appointments. No internal organs. We didn't even need land masses back then. Time just rolled along. Eons felt like epochs. It was so peaceful. None of those noisy radios like the youngsters carry around now!

Of course, for quiet you can't beat that long stretch before the Big Bang. That was nice, all that nothingness. So it was chaos, so what? We were young, we didn't care. Not a lot of rigamarole, and no flippant remarks. Vera says she's come to like the existence of things, but you know Vera—loves a houseful of knickknacks. Me, I'll take the void.

The Last Publicist on Earth

MARK O'DONNELL

The devastating meteor storms of 2016 ravaged the Earth terribly, sending what little was left of mankind underground, and then, when the alien saucer fleet arrived and enslaved the earth, well, the bop pretty much went out of the beach party. We never saw anything but their spaceships, so we never even figured out if they were organisms or robots, that's how cold and uncommunicative they were, so uninterested in publicity.

Humans themselves were out of contact with each other, scrounging in scorched fields for half-buried canned goods, or skulking in caves to avoid the aliens' light-speed police hovercrafts. There were no newspapers. There was no longer any television. There were no new movies to hype. There weren't even any publishing parties. Everyone was cowering in dank caverns. I faced my greatest crisis. How was public relations supposed to survive?

I was determined to not give up to the despair that had destroyed stand-up comedy and traveling ice-skating spectacles. And I was determined to not just endure, but to prevail. I vowed to generate publicity, not merely a whisper but a media, such as they were, blitz. Hype springs eternal. I found some fixable old ham radio equipment, which I took to my newfound enormous, burned-out tenement hideaway on once-fabulous Park Avenue. There I broadcast upbeat gossip tidbits about myself daily—I was my only source, after all—but I could get nothing but static out of the radio, static and that piercing, shrill tone the aliens make when they pass overhead taking potshots at anything that moves. I tried to figure out how a world without safety, food, or water might also hunger for puffery.

Finally, I discovered a dazed and dingy but still determined aspiring model in the ruins of what had been lower Manhattan. She had found a broken stretch of abandoned highway that she pretended was her own personal practice runway. She sneaked out and displayed her imaginary clothes between sweeps of the aliens' Oblito-ray. She needed that fantasy in order to survive.

I saw in her quivering muteness something I could mold into an icon. Pinups had vanished from the scene, along with walls, I guess. It was a society where all known celebrities had been destroyed or sent to swink in the titanium mines, there to get dirty faces and be whipped, so there would be no more glamour shots from them. This addled girl, graded on a curve, could take up the glitz slack.

My homeless superstar-to-be had no grasp of reality, and along with that stunned look in her eyes, she was basically like the models I had known before the apocalypse. I decided I would give my all to promote her. She would be my blank canvas, my Sistine Chapel, my Planet Hollywood. I called her Nova—meaning New, not, please, like the Disastrous Exploding Star—since she herself had forgotten her own name, and newness seemed like a good strategy, since the only time I heard human voices wafting from nearby buildings, they were wailing from vicious giant cockroach attacks and damning all that had gone before. *"Why?"* was the cry I heard most frequently. Now, there's a good question. Personally, I don't believe the widespread rumor that the aliens had destroyed mankind as vengeance for our broadcasting daytime talk shows into outer space.

Her big debut, which I planned carefully—hurling invitations into the wind and shouting the details loud and clear into several alleyways where I knew humans were cowering—was, inexplicably, a no-show. Oh, a few raggedly mutant types tried to get in—it was held in the open air, after all—but they didn't have invitations. The fashions I had designed myself, using a pseudonym, of course, to give the public the impression this was pure professionalism, not some little-guy operation. Well, not designed, exactly—I assembled them from leftover gauze I'd found in the ruins of a hospital. No one had seen anything that white in years, not since that perpetual sooty haze had settled in after the meteor storms. I called the look "neo-Mummy"—it seemed a whimsical-but-still-death-acknowledging slant in a fun-starved but fatalistic environment—and I whistled cool jazz (in lieu of a band) as she stumbled through her costume changes. The few people who did secretly watch her poison-fog-enshrouded fashion parade from their charred hiding places made anguished catcalls and threw bricks or stray bones. Then the alien police craft beam caught her glittering finale (actually, she was decorated with bits of tinfoil I'd found in the plastic rubble of a fast-food hull) and instantly vaporized her. Well, that's the glorious risk of high fashion—you have to do it in public.

Still, there was no coverage I knew of, so I had to file it under fiasco. I'm nothing if not fact-facing, so I realized that after that misstep, I should stay out of the public eye for a while. Somewhere I could plan my new personality positioning, and the passage of time would heighten public sympathy for my comeback. I fled by night in a rowboat to unknown New Jersey.

The leaf-clad natives here are very nice to me. The aliens seem less determined to destroy them than New Yorkers, for some reason, and the humans here covertly plant tiny gardens in their woodland hiding places. There are no press releases, but for now, strangely, that's all right. I do the covert watering. It never occurred to me that there might be life outside New

York City. Well, Los Angeles, but that was destroyed by the aliens' board of censorship.

I don't know when I'll get back to publicity. I like the relative ease of hiding from the aliens in a nice soft forest. Still, I can sense the Next Big Thing is out there, and I hope I'm smart enough to recognize it when I see it.

•• NEWS QUIZ ••

11/24/98 "AUSTRALIA, CONVICTS, GEORGE III?"

"This seems like the perfect place to release them."
Where? What? Says who?

"Monticello; my last remaining slaves; says Strom Thurmond."—Alex Balk

"New Mexico; D. H. Lawrence's oversexed girl-friends; says Freida."—Chris Kelly

"The *New York Times* op-ed page; tedious narcissistic ramblings; says Maureen Dowd."
—Jennifer Miller

"Netscape NetCenter; our constant busy signals; says Steve Case."—Steven Levy

"A chartered DC-9 at 35,000 feet; dozens of turkeys rescued from a poultry farm; says PETA activist Christie Brinkley. ('Fly! Go free!' she said as fellow activists looked on in horror.)"
—Tim Carvell

• RANDY'S WRAP UP •

Comedy attacks. It is difficult to be amusing in praise of something. But risking holiday sentimentality (with the ready-made excuse that it's just the chestnut stuffing talking), I'd like to mention some things I'm thankful for, like Tim Carvell's knack for transforming poultry pushed out of airplanes into a delicate bit of whimsy; the special way Jennifer Miller's eyes light up when she puts the boot into Maureen Dowd; Alex Balk's plucky determination to hound Strom Thurmond to the grave, along with his touching belief that Senator Thurmond will ever die, what with the satanic bargain and all. It's this kind of commitment, the sort of thing irresponsible doctors might call pathological, that makes American industry the envy of the more materialistic parts of the world, and the News Quiz such a pleasure to work on. Thank you all very much. (Especially the people whose feelings I've hurt by not mentioning your names here. I'm sorry. If this were a TV show, I could run a long list of thank-yous that you'd ignore on your way to the kitchen for another beer. And I'd be getting some fat residual payments, that great writers guild health insurance, and, geeze, just the weekly paychecks would be terrific. I never should have taken that swing at Brooke Shields.) Happy Halloween, everybody.

THE FEMINIZATION OF CULTURE ANSWER

Oxygen Media, a new cable network for women; hundreds of reruns of the *Oprah Winfrey Show*; says Oprah Winfrey.

The channel being created by former Nickelodeon president Geraldine Laybourne, Marcy Carsey of Carsey-

Werner-Mandabach, and Oprah Winfrey, will "super-serve women," says Laybourne. While most of the pro-gramming will be original, there will be plenty of room for reruns of Carsey-Werner shows, including *Cybil* and *Grace Under Fire,* said Ms. Carsey. That's superservice.

PARADE OF FUN EXTRA

Which of these is a Macy's Thanksgiving parade float from a proud corporate sponsor kids love, and which is one of the New York Public Interest Research Group's Twenty Most Dangerous Toys?

TOY OR FLOAT?

1. Mr. Peanut's Circus
2. Hasbro's Teletubby Po
3. Folgers Coffee's Rip Van Winkle Wakin' Up
4. Mattel's Baby Dil's World
5. Bell Atlantic's Maurice Sendak's Wild Thing
6. Playskool's Talking Pay Phone
7. Ocean Spray Cranberries Inc.'s Peter Pan's Pirate Ship
8. Hanes Hosiery's Party Time!
9. Unique's Flying Propellers
10. Betacarotine

Answers

1. float: and you know what kids love with those salted nuts? Mr. Beer.
2. dangerous toy: vinyl face made with phthalates, cause of liver cancer in laboratory mice

3. float: celebrating kids' willingness to settle for instant coffee?

4. dangerous toy: pieces could cause choking

5. float: kids are thankful for reliable local phone service

6. dangerous toy: plastic coins can lodge in child's throat

7. float: kids wave bye-bye to urinary tract infections

8. float: we gather together to count the lord's panty hose

9. dangerous toy: but not nearly as dangerous as rusty flying propellers coated with broken glass

10. actual part of parade, listed as "celebrity character for kids"

Memoir Essay

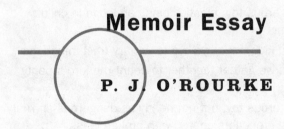

P. J. O'ROURKE

After years of effort in the author trade, I've discovered an ideal topic, an inexhaustible subject of discourse, a literary inspiration—me. I'm writing a memoir. I don't know why I didn't do this ages ago. It's so liberating to sit down at the keyboard and just be myself, as opposed to, say, being you, which I don't have the clothes for.

Actually, my memoir is still in the idea stage. But I'm full of enthusiasm. I'll give the secret of my success—the success I plan to have as a memoir writer. As far as I can tell, the secret is thinking about myself all the time. No doubt my memoir will be inspirational, inspiring others to think about themselves all the time. They'll see the meaning in their lives: They've been meaning to write a memoir, too.

So what if it's a crowded field? My memoir will stand out. It will show readers a side of life they little guessed at, the side with the writer sitting in his boxer shorts surrounded by six empty coffee cups and three full ashtrays playing Go Fish on his laptop.

Maybe they *had* guessed at that. But I'm going to recount my personal struggles, such as having to come up with things to write about all the time. I've spent decades looking for stories that would interest other people. I've surmounted enormous obstacles—thinking about other people, just for instance.

But enough about them. This isn't going to be a mere self-help book. This is the story of how one young man grew up to be . . . a lot older. That is probably the most serious issue I need to work through in my memoir. The issue being that I haven't really done much. But I don't feel this should stand in my way. O. J. Simpson wrote a memoir, and the jury said he didn't do anything at all.

There's also a lot of anger I need to deal with. I'm angry at my parents. For memoir purposes, they weren't nearly poor enough. They weren't rich either. And they failed miserably at leading colorful lives. My mother did belong to Kappa Kappa Gamma, which is a secret society, I believe. And my father was a veteran of the Pacific war, but the only casualty in his battalion was one fellow crushed by a palm tree. Furthermore, we lived in Toledo, Ohio. I suppose I could write a comic memoir. But, in today's society, there are some things you just don't make fun of and chief among these is yourself.

My parents also neglected to abuse me. They're gone now, alas. (Downside: no publicity-building estrangement when memoir is published, to be followed by tearful reconciliation on the *Oprah* show. Upside: I'm an Adult Child of the Deceased.) I've thought about asking my wife's parents to abuse me, but it seems too little, too late. I did have a stepfather who bowled.

Perhaps I'll keep the section on my childhood brief, just emphasize that I'm a survivor. That's what's unique about me, and there are 5.7 billion people in the world who know how unique I feel. This should guarantee excellent sales. And—here comes that literary inspiration again—memoirs do sell. Readers want to know what real people really did and really felt. What a shame that the writing geniuses of the nineteenth century wasted their time making things up. We could have had Jane Austen Reality Prose: "Got up. Wrote. Went out. Came back. Wrote some more. Vicarage still drafty."

Modern book buyers have become too sophisticated for imaginary romance and drama. They want facts—Roswell, New Mexico; the missile that shot down TWA flight 800; the Congress/Clinton balanced budget deal. Unfortunately, I don't have many facts like that, but I do have some terrific celebrity gossip. I've read all their memoirs.

I also know about some awful things my friends have done. I've noticed, while memoir-reading, that one of the main points of the genre is ratting on your pals. So I was gathering that material together and was about to commit it to paper when I realized that other memoir writers, as a class, seem to have very few friends who weigh two hundred pounds and own shotguns.

Probably confession is a safer route. I've done all kinds of loathsome deeds myself and am perfectly willing to admit them, if it sells books. But, thumbing through my memoir collection, I noticed another thing. Good memoir writers only confess to certain of the more glamorous sins—drastic sexual escapades, head-to-toe drug abuse, bold felonies after the statutes of limitation have run out. Nobody confesses to things that just make him look like a jerk-o. Nobody admits that he got up at four A.M. with a throbbing head after five hours of listening to the kid's pets squeaking in the exercise wheel and drowned the gerbils in the toilet. Most of my transgressions fall into this category and will need to be excised. I don't want to get caught writing one of those "unauthorized autobiographies."

This brings me to the other little problem I'm having with the story of my life, which is remembering it. There were the 1960s. I recall they started out well. Then there were the 1970s. I recall they ended badly. In between, frankly, I am missing a few candles on the cake. Also there were the 1950s, when nothing memorable happened, and the 1980s, when everything memorable was happening to somebody else. And the 1990s have gone by in a blur. But, no worries, I've been keeping a diary: "Got up. Wrote. Went out. Came back. Wrote some more. Drowned the gerbils."

Maybe I can make up for my lack of reminiscences by

inserting various vivid fantasies I've had. But this is cheating on the memoir form since I'm admitting that those things—the *New York Review of Books* swimsuit issue, for example—never happened.

Or, perhaps I should go back to all those challenges I've faced. I've had to endure enormous prejudice. True, since I'm a middle-aged white male Republican, the enormous prejudice came from me. But I still had to endure it. This is one reason that learning to love myself was another huge challenge. But I've overcome that, too. Although, now that I'm completely self-infatuated, I keep waiting for me to give myself a promotion. It's been a bitter disappointment.

Thank goodness. Bitter disappointments are crucial to memoirs. Thinking of something to write in this memoir has been a bitter disappointment so far. That means I can write about not being able to write. Should be good for a chapter, if I can make it sound bitter enough.

Wait. I'm forgetting spiritual transformation. I've been touched by an angel—and a big one, too, all covered in glitter. It got me right in the forehead last month when the dog knocked over the Christmas tree.

And I have a good title: "My Excuse for Living." That should count for something.

Anyway, I'm not daunted. The memoir is the great literature of the current era. All that we ask of art, the memoir provides. Beauty is truth, truth beauty, and if we can get a beauty to tell the truth then Kathryn Harrison's *The Kiss* is all ye need to know. Art justifies God's ways to man like *The Art of the Comeback* does. God is going to fry Donald Trump in hell, and He is perfectly justified. As with all art, the memoir holds a mirror up to life and if there are some lines of cocaine on that mirror, so much the better. Out of chaos the memoir brings order—a huge order from a major bookstore chain, it is to be hoped. The memoir is nature's handmaiden and also nature's butt boy, bagman, and patsy if *Behind the Oval Office* by Dick Morris is anything to go by. The memoir exists on its own terms, art for art's sake, if you happen to be named Arthur—vide *Risk and Redemption: Surviving the Network News Wars* by Arthur Kent. The memoir speaks to us, indeed it won't shut up. *Vita brevis est, memoir longa.*

And mine is going to be really long. I've got a major book happening here. After a whole morning spent wrestling with my muse, I've made a vital creative breakthrough. I now know how to give my memoir the moral, intellectual and aesthetic impact that the works of Shakespeare, Goethe, Dostoyevsky had on previous generations. As with all insights of true originality, it's very simple. It's called lying.

Art is eternal, but lunch is what's happening.—M.O'D.

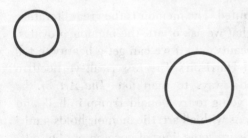

March

SAMUEL PICKERING JR.

Spring came late to Connecticut, and March was wintry. As soon as February ended, though, I began to dream about greenery. Moods blustered, and I forced change upon the month, imagining my restlessness reflected in bud and on wing. Around the feeders birds seemed more aggressive. One morning a nuthatch and a titmouse landed on opposite sides of the suet. Instead of ignoring the titmouse, the nuthatch shrugged his wings high over his back and then leaning forward thrust his head over the suet, so disturbing his dining companion that the titmouse lost his appetite. On the large groaning board outside the kitchen window, Vicki served a banquet of cracked corn and sunflower seeds. Early in March grackles appeared. When a pair landed on the board, they paid less attention to the food than to each other. Both birds hunkered down, pushing themselves into their chests. Then they expanded, necks and breasts swelling, their bills tilting upward, almost lifting them off the feeder. For a moment they swayed toward each other, but then the smaller bird jumped off the board and joined a companionable group of gray squirrels and mourning doves on the ground.

Songs of cardinals rang flowering through early morning. Wanting to see change, I roamed Storrs. People don't so much find what they look for as convince themselves that what they find is what they were looking for. On walks I imagined discovering signs of spring. One morning below the sheep barns a flock of bluebirds foraged through alder and black locust. A familiar sight, the birds spent winter in Storrs, but in March, they now appeared harbingers of another season. Throwing themselves off limbs, the birds seemed to melt like ice along the shore of a pond, sinking blue then rising orange, creating currents that stirred the air into a rich broth of "spring over turn."

As overturn sweeps nutrients up from the bottom of ponds, so spring mixes the high and the low. In spring the goldfinch gets another breast, and the adolescent's fancy turns to lust. Scattered among dry stems of Joe-pye weed near the wolf den were leaves from an issue of *Nugget Extra!* Instead of creating freshness, the new year revived old fleshly delusions. I raked through the table of contents and from the "Fiction" section snagged a tale supposedly written by Daltrey St. James, "Assuming The Throne! Toilet Tart Obsessed With Potty Play!" While the lead article in the "Pictorial" section was "Slave Buys Chinese Mistress The Right Spikes!" the "Fight" department featured "Tit-Tearing Female Fights!" I glanced at a picture. A naked man lay bound to a rack, nineteen clothespins pinching his privates, the ends of the pins sticking up thick as porcupine quills. "Not in these woods," I murmured. "Porcupines don't live in Storrs."

Aside from the magazine I stumbled across few signs of spring. Winds slapped hills, and the metal frame of my glasses burned cold. Near the ski-tow poison ivy clasped the trunks of ashes, rootlets jutting out stiffly, resembling bushy eyebrows. A rough shawl of snow rumpled off the ridge above the Ogushwitz meadow. While boulders tied the hill into knots, fallen trees wrinkled across the slope, snagging line and cable. Without a dress of leaves the forest looked worn and tired. Cankers opened ragged sores, and blisters burst oozing from branches. Lichens pocked bark with age spots, and fungi sloughed off trunks like eczema. Tops of trees dangled down, broken into whisks, and shattered limbs stuck upward in forks. Along the path panes of marbled ice covered depressions while throws of oak leaves buckled through the woods, mottled with damp.

That afternoon I walked the corn fields west of Unnamed Pond. The fragrance of old manure warmed the day. A flock of geese beat low over the woods and planed into a field, air pushing the horseshoes of white feathers on their tails into canters. A turkey scooted across a furrow and vanished between blackberry canes. White-throated sparrows switched whistling through alders. Pokeweed sprawled atop low mounds of rubble, the broken stems dried and white, appearing blasted not by cold but by heat. At the edge of woods paperbark birches bent over, rolling groundward in sweeping curtseys. That night rain and snow stuttered across eastern Connecticut. Early the next morning I drove Eliza to a soccer tournament at the Maybelle B. Avery School in Somers. The sky was doughy, and along the Willimantic River ice clung to the shoreline like pastry to the lip of a pie pan. In Somers gloves of ice grasped scrub, bending limbs into wheels so that bushes seemed to bound through sunlight, tossing blue and yellow sparks into the air.

Foolishness blooms through all seasons. When I returned from Somers, Josh met me in the kitchen. Recently controversy over cloning had spotted newspapers like hives, giving every prattler in the nation vapors. For his part Josh thought cloning might save humanity from the "crepitus bombastus of political mountebanks and the rending nitrosity of night-walking, talon-sharpening spiritual comedians." Precedent for cloning was hallowed. If the Ancient of Days could accomplish it, Josh noted, then chefs in the medical factory should do the same, cloning females, say, from cutlets sliced from males. Once this was accomplished couples would enjoy the same sex drive, and divorce would end. No longer would husbands and wives argue over movies at the video store. Courtship rituals would be simplified. The standard greeting "haven't I seen you somewhere before" would sound absurd and molder away. Because populations would think and act similarly all happenings would be coincidental, and the word *coincidence* would become archaic. Indeed as people embraced the old adage "know thyself," and in a landscape of clones a person could embrace no one other than the self, communication would become intuitive and words themselves would vanish. Because differentiating one self from another would be impossible, discrimination would disappear overnight. The number one song on the Hit Parade would always be "I'm My Own Grandpa." Cloned with the same strengths and weaknesses, people would be truly equal, and democracy would flourish. "Because self-love determines behavior," Josh stated, "peace would spread like measles." Not only armies but governments would disappear. "Paradise would be now and forever." "As generations of me and my rib cage dozed under palms," Josh hymned, "Aurora would swathe our sensibilities with balm. Snakes would sparkle like doves amid a symphony of mosses, and angels would dance through clouds, music trickling tremulous from their wings."

The old gray mare ain't what she used to be, the farmer said to the insurance adjuster, after lightning struck his horse. As months gallop past, doings of days change. Josh, however, remains constant, mocking the platitudinous and reminding people that life isn't simple. "Don't forget," he said at the kitchen door, "the red blackberry is green." The mail is almost as constant as Josh. In March I receive more strange letters than during any other month of the year. Because of weather, people spend a goodly portion of the month in houses. The longer they remain inactive inside, the more they imagine the active and the out-of-doors. As a result they write crank letters. On March 16, I received a letter written on the stationery of the Iowa State Senate. "You have an important letter," the secretary of the English department said when I walked into the office that morning. "The letter is official, and I didn't want to put it in your box and risk losing it," she said, handing me the letter. Printed on the bottom left corner of the envelope and at the top of the stationery itself was a picture of the Iowa Statehouse. Above the building a banner waved. Printed on the banner was "OUR LIBERTIES WE PRIZE AND OUR RIGHTS WE WILL MAINTAIN."

"Dear Professor Pickelring," Ralph Ames, senator from the 31st district began. "Greetings from the State of Iowa on behalf of its citizens. I am writing to invite you to participate in a very special celebration here at the State Capitol April 15, 1997. On that day, the Iowa General Assembly will be holding its annual joint session to honor Iowa citizens who exceed the norm. This year we will honor Mrs. Neoscaleeta Pemberton of The Carts for Wienie Dogs Foundation (TCFWDF) for her fundraising efforts to provide sweatshirts and Billy Bob Halloween costumes for afflicted little dogs of the Wienie breed. In addition and in conjunction with the Iowa Arts Council, we are honoring the Rev. Ephram Zender, President and Founder of the Remain Intact ORGANization (RIO), for his creative efforts in forming the group's motto: 'Circumcision—the unkindest cut of all,' which grew out of his work with the IAC's Mottoes-in-the-Schools program of which our state is justly proud. Because Mrs. Pemberton is also a member of RIO, I understand that this will be the first time in the two-year history of the award that we will so honor an organization twice in a sense. We would like you to address the session and present awards to Mrs. Pemberton and the Rev. Zender, who will receive a plaque and an all-expenses-paid trip to Kansas City to attend a volunteers' conference at the Raphael Hotel. Please be in touch with my assistant for further information. We look forward to hearing your remarks, although I call attention to the attached document and caution you to remember the decorum required by such an event."

The letter was the work of a friend. Each March as snow melts and creeks overflow banks, my friend bounds out of winter, her good humor sweeping high seriousness off its ponderous foundations. Attached to the invitation was a letter written to the senator from Mrs. Pemberton herself on March 10. "Thank you for your letter asking me to recommend someone to speak at the special ceremonies at the Statehouse in April. Through my work with the Foundation, I have been in touch with a Professor Sam Pickelring. Although I do not know him personally, I have made inquiries and believe that—given the proper security arrangements by doorkeepers and guards—he could be allowed to participate on a limited and closely monitored basis. For several years I've been writing to him although I had heard about him for a lot longer (now he says that most of that stuff is not true and was supposed to be expunged from the record after he paid the bribes). As far as I know, he won't steal too much from anyone at the Statehouse, but you should know that I suspect he is a Free Mason. There was that talk a few years ago, but he swears it was all the transsexual's fault."

At this point decorum demands that I skip to the end of Mrs. Pemberton's recommendation. Reputation is fragile, and as readers of my books forever confuse the true with the fabricated, the line between the two being nonexistent, at least in my writings, discretion seems the better clone of cowardice. Be that as it may, Mrs. Pemberton, or Neoscaleeta, as I now address her, concluded her letter to the senator, saying, "I'm looking forward to the gala events at the Statehouse. Rev. Zender and I will meet you at your office at 9:30 if he can get away early from his NoCirc of Iowa Meeting. This may be difficult as the group is having its annual 'Joy of Uncircumcising!' conference with guest speakers discussing restorative procedures."

The next day I received a letter from a Virginian. In February the man had sent me a folk tale. Enclosed in the letter was yet another tale, or "dramatic sunbeam," as he called it. The tale was exuberant, and when composing it, my correspondent, I suspect, suffered from lemon fever, or had been slurping, as blue bloods put it, giggle soup. According to the story, however, a tapeworm plagued a prominent Tidewater Republican for a decade. Doctors from all over the South tried to rid the man of the unwanted resident, or squatter, as Democrats inelegantly dubbed the worm. One physician tried to blast the worm out by making the man eat two bushels of black-eyed peas. Instead of

swelling bilious, though, the worm thrived. He thought New
Year's Eve had arrived, and cramming his head up the man's
esophagus, demanded stewed tomatoes. A fisherman from Orvis
tied flies shaped like corn on the cob and sweet potatoes and
then cast them into the man's stomach. No matter how the fisherman skipped the flies through the bowels, the worm refused to
bite. Unfortunately as the fisherman was reeling in a fly shaped
like an artichoke, one of the spines speared the man's epiglottis.
Extracting the lure was difficult, and the fisherman had to saw
through the barb, in the process rupturing a sinus.

Urged by the governor of the state, professors at the Medical
College of Virginia sponsored a seminar devoted to separating
man from worm. Happily the seminar fashioned a solution. One
blistering July day a relay team of physicians chased the man
around his house until he began to sweat like a butcher. After he
"ran dry," doctors forced the man to lie on his side along the
ground. Next the doctors chained the man down then forced him
to eat seven country hams. Although the man begged for water,
the doctors refused him "even a drop." Near the man's backside
the physicians placed a tub brimming with iced tea. Over the
man's bottom, the doctors hung a thick rope tied into a hangman's
noose. While the man ate ham, the physicians lurked just out of
sight behind the curve of his buttocks, all the while, however,
studying "the fundament like foxes watching the entrance to the
burrow of a groundhog." The ham made the worm thirsty. From
the tea fragrances of lemon and sugar wafted cool and so tempting that the worm tossed caution "to the winds" and poked his
head out of the man. As soon as the worm's head dipped into the
tub, the doctors cinched the rope tightly around his neck then
tied the other end of the rope to a Farmall tractor.

Pulling the worm out was difficult and took thirty-eight minutes and fourteen seconds, according to the account published
in *The New England Journal of Medicine*. "Forty-two feet long
with a neck as thick as a culvert and a mouth resembling that of
a snapping turtle, the tapeworm weighed three hundred and
ninety-two pounds, twelve ounces." After the worm had been

weighed and photographed, the team of doctors standing beside it holding the rope, the manager of a carnival bought the worm and displayed it in an aquarium, claiming it was a monster from twenty thousand leagues under the sea. Although a popular exhibit, the worm proved too expensive for country sideshows, a thirty-seven-and-a-half-pound bag of chicken feed, for example, furnishing only two days of meals.

Eventually an Episcopal minister purchased the worm. Declaring the worm to be a demon he had cast out of the womb of a virgin, the minister made a respectable living exhibiting the creature throughout the church's southern dioceses. Late one Halloween night, however, the worm escaped from a tank at the Tennessee State Fair in Nashville. Hungry, it crawled into the vegetable pavilion where, alas, it choked to death trying to swallow what was billed as "The World's Largest Pumpkin." The following morning a buyer for Brooks Brothers purchased the carcass and shipped it by rail to New York in a refrigerator car. After a boulevardier met the train, a fashion designer oversaw both skinning the worm and tanning the hide. Shortly thereafter Brooks Brothers advertised a line of "Stylish New Alligator Belts." Indirectly the worm also brought wealth to the man who'd acted the part of innkeeper for years. Before the extraction the man was barrel-chested. Afterward he was "thin as a grub." Removal of the worm so reduced the man's girth that he received a "mountain of money" for appearing in Before and After advertisements promoting the magical dietary properties of "Dr. Pei Loo's Celestial Stomach Balm and Chinese Fat Extractor."

Like March weather itself my correspondent's letter was a trifle raw. Despite wandering corn fields, I spent much of the month in the library, hunting neither birds nor plants but searching for story, concocting paragraphs describing spring days in Carthage. Rarely does winter chill the pages of my Carthage. The third Saturday in May was workday at the Pillow of Heaven Cemetery. Early that morning families from the Tabernacle of Love gathered in the graveyard. Using shovels, brooms, and hoes, they swept and cut grass from walkways, mounded graves, set fallen stones upright, and planted flowers, starting new beds of periwinkle and setting small pots containing white pansies at the heads of graves. In a low spot far down the slope of Battery Hill, Proverbs Goforth planted a grove of weeping willows. Before lunch much of the conversation was religious. To the surprise of the congregation Orpheus Goforth turned up at ten o'clock. Orpheus knew more about fiddling than about praying. In fact he brought his fiddle and during lunch played "Short'ning Bread." Before lunch he and Loppie Groat mounded graves.

While they worked Loppie catechized Orpheus, asking him, among other things, if he knew where Jesus was buried. The question stumped Orpheus. Still, when Loppie said *Bethlehem,* Orpheus was not at a loss for words. "Shucks," Orpheus said, "I knew He was buried somewhere in Pennsylvania." "I might not know more about theology than a virgin does about dog liver," Orpheus continued, leaning on his shovel. "But I can tell you I'm rowing the fast boat to Glory."

The yellow and blue speckling petals of the pansies made Hoben Donkin ponder heredity. "Do you believe in heredity?" Hoben asked Hink Ruunt as they arranged flowers on the grave of Pony Boguski. "You bet," Hink answered. "I ain't seen it done, but I understand it's an everyday thing in New York City. I'd hate to see it catch on around here, but I wouldn't be surprised if there weren't a couple of cases in Nashville, especially out toward that fancy-pants Belle Meade section." His carnival happening to be performing in Carthage at the time, Hollis Hunnewell helped at the cemetery and drummed up business. Not only did Hollis sell patent medicine and exhibit marvels of nature at the carnival, but he also staged short plays, old favorites such as "Red Hand," "Rip Van Winkle," "Meg Merrilies," and "The Fat Man's Club." Accompanying Hollis to the graveyard was the carnival's lead man, a one-armed actor named Caesar Julius Jelks. Vardis Grawling was more inquisitive than a lawyer, and just being in the company of an actor titillated her. When Vardis saw that Caesar had only one arm, her curiosity practically barked, and she almost dislocated her jaw asking questions. For a while Caesar tolerated the inquisition. But after being turned through two score wrenching questions, he couldn't stand the rack any longer and said, "One final question. I will answer only one more question." "Well, what should it be?" Vardis said coyly, before leaning forward and demanding, "What happened to your arm?" "It was bit off," Caesar said and walked away.

Before he became an actor, Caesar was an inventor. According to Hollis, years earlier Caesar invented a flypaper, one stronger even, he said, than "Steers Chemical Ipecac and Professor Goethe's Matchless Sanative." Unfortunately, as Caesar was hanging a strip of the paper on the clothesline in his back yard, he trod on the opening to a yellow jacket's nest. Hornets swarmed out of the hole. In the rush to avoid being stung, Caesar threw his right arm above his head, in the process slapping it against the flypaper. The paper stuck so tightly to his skin that doctors at Vanderbilt Medical School couldn't pry it loose, and they advised him to seek treatment at the fairgrounds. "A mule team at the state fair might be able to rip it off," the head of the medical school told Caesar. "The prescription was successful," Hollis declared, "but the arm died." The glue held tight. Instead of peeling the paper off, the mules tore out Caesar's arm "fingers and root." "The paper was mighty good," Hollis concluded. After the mule pull Caesar threw the paper and his arm into the trash behind the Homecrafts building. Stuck to the paper the next morning along with the arm, Hollis stated, "were three possums, a prize beagle dog, a bucket of maggots, six Bibles, a baby's hand, and four rat tails."

Families brought baskets of food to the workday, and for lunch people ate fried chicken, potato salad, deviled eggs, and fudge cake. Although children and some ladies drank lemonade bought at Barrow's store, most people drank spring water provided by Dapper Tuttlebee. Dapper brought the water in Mason jars, covering the tops with foil to keep flies out. The water was extraordinarily popular, the only complaint coming from Orpheus who reckoned "the water contained a little too much spring." Nevertheless after finishing a jar, Orpheus played the old favorite "The Still House on the Green." During lunch itself Slubey Garts preached a short sermon, urging parishioners to donate to the Sunday school fund, reminding them that shrouds did not have pockets. "He who goes down," Slubey said, "never comes up."

The drink made people thoughtful. After lunch the congregation wandered graves and visited old acquaintances. People's minds ran naturally to the element that made the spring water intoxicating, and Turlow Gutheridge told a story about Hiram Povey. When he was young, Hiram dug borax in California. "Did you ever suffer from a burning thirst?" Turlow once asked him in Ankerrow's Café. "Oh, yes," Hiram said. "One time when I was traveling to Barstow, I drank a quart of furniture polish." "Good Lord!" Turlow exclaimed. "Didn't you have any water with you?" "Water?" Hiram said, looking scornful. "What's water got to do with anything? A man suffering from a parched throat doesn't think much about personal cleanliness."

Clevanna Farquarhson strolled over to the grave of Royce, her first husband. When Clevanna started wiping her eyes with a handkerchief, Slubey hurried to her side. "We shouldn't weep," Slubey said. "Royce is only sleeping." "For God's sakes, don't talk so loud," Clevanna whispered. "You might wake the bastard. A passel of son-of-a-bitching spring onions, not grief, caused these here tears." Royce was an unblushing vagabond, so low, Turlow said that "he had to climb a stepladder to get into hell." Still, after lunch the graves of scoundrels attracted more attention that those housing the sanctified. "Flies," Turlow said, "aren't afraid to tickle dead lions." A locksmith by training, Lloyd Griffer used his skills to pick and steal. Even worse, he was a bully. He hated Frank Emberley, for example, who thrashed him after seeing him beat a sick horse. The day after Emberley drowned in an accident at the tannery, Lloyd strolled into the Widow Emberley's yard and with a hoe chopped the head off Sweetkins, little Betsy Emberley's pet kitten. Not long after, Lloyd himself died. One night he tried to steal Davy Crockett, Ben Meadows's Jersey bull. The next morning Ben found Lloyd gored and stomped to death in the pasture, a rope halter twenty yards from the body. The inscription on Lloyd's tombstone was ambivalent, stating, "His Sun Set at Noon. Praise Be to God." "The hanged dog don't bother sheep," Proverbs Goforth said, wrapping his tongue like a slingshot around a wad of tobacco then flinging it hard against the gravestone. "Do you reckon Lloyd's in hell?" Loppie Groat asked. "Is a pig's ass pork?" Proverbs answered. "He's probably enjoying it, though. Buzzards like rotten meat."

Not all after-lunch remarks were critical. After graduating from Carthage High School, Pervis Holland attended Sewanee then the University of Virginia Law School. For years Pervis served on the Federal Court of Appeals in Cincinnati. When he retired, he returned to Carthage and devoted himself to education, serving three terms as head of the Smith County School Board. Some people thought Pervis the most intelligent man in Carthage. According to story when a neighbor sowed nails on Pervis's land, Pervis planted hammers. Next spring when the hammers ripened, they smashed the nails into the ground. On Pervis's death at eighty-six, his wife Lucille had an old-fashioned inscription carved on his stone. "Oh ye young, ye gay, ye proud, / You must die and wear the shroud, / Time will rob you of your bloom, / Death will drag you to your tomb." The verse rankled Carthaginians. who thought Pervis deserved a more dignified inscription. "Lucille always had less sense than a Siamese catfish," Turlow said. "Beef at the heels and at the brain," Proverbs added, referring unkindly to Lucille's size. Not surprisingly, shortly after lunch or maybe during dessert, someone etched a new inscription on the back of Pervis's stone. "At This Man's Funeral A Library Was Buried."

When the university closed for spring vacation, students left town. For my part I abandoned books and for nine days roamed Storrs. Years ago when I drifted from organized religion, I hoped that amid Nature I would discover, if not religious truth, at least the stuff of spiritual nourishment. Although impressions of field and wood have made days blossom, I have only stumbled upon common-sensical revelation. Beyond the green wood lurks no deity, and the sky, no matter how domed and cerulean, is not the temple of the numinous. Seeing more in a flower than the flower itself distorts what truths and beauties exist. To know a thing as itself is enough, however. Indeed it is more than people are generally capable of. Forever hoping for, then imposing meaning, people force fiber out of form and so elevate things that life is reduced to a blur. On Palm Sunday I walked for six hours. For a while I regretted the day's having lost religious meaning. But then I realized that the absence of high meaning enabled my walk to be significant, at least significant enough for word and line.

I spent the vacation exploring hills beyond the university's sewerage treatment plant. Once a dump, the land was broken. Moisture seeped out of bruised slopes. Before running into gullies and draining into wetlands, water collected in red pools, chemicals blooming on the surface like pansies. Sweet fern grew brown and scraggly atop mounds of asphalt. Strewn across a trench heaps of sidewalk buckled like the remnants of blasted buildings. A thick pipe jutted out of a pile of gravel, its mouth five inches in diameter and resembling a cannon barrel. A door to a cabinet sank into the ground. Fifty-six inches tall and twenty-three wide, the door made a fine shelter for snakes. In March only a small black cricket lurked underneath. In ample summer snakes would coil like roots, not only beneath the door but throughout the dump, under slabs of plywood, sheets of tar paper, wooden gates, and broken stiles and pallets.

I climbed a brush pile and sat on a stump. While the handle of a shovel leaned against a log, chairs collapsed out of form, rust burning slowly through metal backs and water pulling plugs from wooden seats and legs. Under a board at my feet a ball of caution tape frayed into black and yellow splinters. A grapevine wrapped around a NO PARKING sign, and coils of black hose dried hard and brittle. Near a slab of sidewalk twenty-three blue pipes exploded from a pool of water, resembling a sculpture standing in a giant bird bath. Each pipe was four feet long.

Attached to the ends of eleven of the pipes were hunks of concrete shaped like muffins. Amid the concrete, stones shined like hard candy, and the muffins themselves rose, almost as if baking soda had been pumped into them through the pipes. A curved pink lecture table sank into wetlands. If four such tables were placed end to end, they would form a circle. The table was two and a half feet wide, and while the outer edge of the table, the side facing the lecture hall, measured nine feet, three inches, the inner curve, near the lecturer, was five and a half feet long. Reaching the table was difficult. Alders surrounded it, and I picked my way through a lumberyard of scraps, including, among other things, lengths of stairs, from the steps of which boards had fallen into the mud, forming an irregular path.

According to an old Armenian tale Noah was a convivial guy. On the day he finished the ark, Noah visited his closest neighbor. After eating apricots and drinking a pitcher of pomegranate wine, Noah told the man about the flood. "You and your family can join me on the ark," Noah said, "and we'll ride out the high water together." Instead of replying the man scanned the heavens. The sky was gray, and a dark cloud hung over Mt. Ararat, but a seam of light ran so brightly along the eastern horizon that the dark seemed on the verge of lifting like a curtain. "Thanks for the invitation, Brother Noah," the man said. "There is a bit of rain about, but I don't think it will amount to much. I reckon I'll just hunker down here until the sun comes back out."

Occasionally appearances deceive. Much as Noah's neighbor misjudged the weather, so instead of finding the dump inhospitable, life thrived amid the disturbed landscape. On the ridge above the dump a red-tailed hawk perched in a white oak, his tail shuttering like a Venetian blind. A pair of flickers skipped along the edge of the woods while a flock of robins hurried through olives, their movements quick as laughter but their flights low and chortling. While the songs of cardinals sped swift as arrows, those of blue jays bubbled then broke. Beyond the dump a woodpecker thumped a tree, and calls of red-winged blackbirds rose muffled out of wetlands. Crows mobbed a barred owl in the woods, driving him from a maple and harrying him as he blundered above the dump.

As I walked across a hillside, mourning doves clattered into the air. Late one afternoon four buzzards rose over the dump, the long primaries at the tips of their wings scraping the air like fingers digging into water, tilting and ruddering through currents. Under a ridge a fox enlarged the burrow of a groundhog. The fox hunted along the ridge, leaving droppings along the top, usually next to trees. Between a half and three-quarters inches in diameter, the droppings were smaller than those of coyotes. Strings of hair wound through the droppings, and exoskeletons of beetles glistened like slivers of candy. The droppings had fermented, and here and there small white grubs curled contentedly.

Bulldozers having shaved trees from the dump, saplings erupted in bristles, in the damp, alders, female catkins drooping like the feet of ballerinas, rolling above each ankle a thick white sock. Next to the alders rose thickets of gray or field birch, the white bark tinged with green and branches clawing upward out of gray eyes in the bark. Atop barrows of rubble olive trees grew in webs, the light twigs waving in the light like loose radii. Winter smashed the middles out of many olives, either snapping branches or pinning them to the ground, much as big moths break the hubs of webs.

Brown shafts of mullein stuck out of heaps of gravel. Nearby rosettes of new plants opened along the ground, their leaves resembling wrinkled shammy cloths. Burrs spun around burdock in constellations, spines on the fruits collecting enough of the gray light to glow. Under a rocky chin phragmites grew unkempt and streaked with yellow like an old man's beard. Below an olive a tuft of dandelions bloomed in a bouquet. In wetlands skunk cabbage screwed red and orange upward out of mud. Along the ridge near the fox den boutonnières of wintergreen and rattlesnake plantain clung to the ground, their leaves green and white, exotic against the bare soil. Although March did not bring me face to face with a deity or appoint my days with spirituality, I did see anew. For the first time I noticed horsetails, scouring and variegated scouring rush growing in the damp above the dump, the cone of the latter a bud with a needle tip and the sheath toothed black and white. Such a sight fills the dark sky, as Slubey Garts would put it, "with sweet carolings."

This year Easter ended March. Early Easter Sunday light shone clear and silver. I hid thirty-six eggs in the yard then wandered about until the children woke. A pair of song sparrows scratched the ground under a bird feeder. Atop the feeder perched a brown-headed cowbird, the first of the season. Peonies pushed through the dry grass by the driveway, the tips fat with red. Three crocus bloomed by the woodpile, one yellow and two blue. At the edge of the wood, catkins dangled in tassels from hazelnut. Flower buds on spicebush were swollen, but I saw no sign of bloodroot or dutchman's breeches. Winter had peeled bark from the dead oak by the porch, and locks of grass hung out of an old flicker nest. This year the birds would nest elsewhere. April was in the air as well as on the ground, however, and I knew I would find the nest.

Vicki cooked a leg of lamb for lunch. Before we ate, I read the 114th Psalm, the Easter Psalm. "The mountains," David declared, "skipped like rams, and the little hills like lambs." When I read "which turned the rock into a standing water, the flint into a fountain of waters," Eliza said, "that's spring." The following afternoon snow started falling. The next morning was the first of April. At seven o'clock sixteen inches of snow were on the ground, and I trudged around the yard. Two downy woodpeckers squawked in the woods, and doves huddled on branches like students waiting for a lecture to begin. Palms of snow pressed the yews flat, but I noticed that cornelian cherries were blooming. Each year soon after the cherries bloom, spicebush blossoms, and colors riot through days. I pushed through a drift, and snow reached my thigh. The world was quiet, the sort of place that transforms tongues into pens. Suddenly I wanted to scroll days back to the beginning of March, "that reassuring stable month," as Eliza described it.

Zone 5

Gardening Advice
from Mertensia Corydalis

Q: Our family tries to be ecologically correct. We're talking about getting a live Christmas tree this year and planting it after the holidays. Any tips?
— Vanya, Cherry Grove

A: Dear Vanya: Most cut trees come from tree farms rather than primeval forests, but if you need a fir tree on your property, then go ahead with the live specimen. There are a couple of problems, the main one being the arid atmosphere inside your house, so you should not have the live tree indoors more than a day or two, which minimizes the decorative value. The other big problem is that conifers should ideally be planted in the spring, giving them a long growing season to get established, so there's some risk involved. Either way, I could never bring myself to buy an artificial tree. The scent of pine evokes the memory of a college summer spent on a hemlock taxonomy project in Quebec, the heady aroma of paper mills, and the amber-eyed Gilles, a barely literate but otherwise diversely skilled conifer-removal technician.

Q: Every year I try to keep my poinsettias going after the holidays. They invariably drop their leaves and never recover. I would like to get them to rebloom.
—VRONSKY, MOKBA STATION

A: Dear Vronsky, When it comes to poinsettias I'm afraid I just don't get it. It's not that attractive a plant and just not worth the trouble required to keep one going all year, not to mention what is needed to make it repeat blooming. I have seen awestruck crowds in shopping malls admiring twelve-foot-tall pyramids of potted red poinsettias as if they were witnessing Mary in the birthing lounge at Bethlehem General, huffing and puffing the Savior into the world. Let me hasten to add, however, that any poinsettia brought to my house as a gift (it's the thought that counts, they say) is appreciated for the splash of color it offers, and I am warming up to some of the delicate pastel shades. If you just have to have it, put out one big, lavish plant rather than half a dozen dinky supermarket specimens dotted here and there around the house. You don't need to decorate every nook and cranny, you know. Poinsettias need plenty of sun to keep growing and most coffee tables don't offer that. The potting medium they are sold in is usually an impenetrable mass, making them difficult to water properly. Feel free to tinker with them.

Q: While working on my lawn this morning, I unearthed a whole gaggle of white larvae. I got out my old Big Book of Bugs, *which I've had since child-hood, and identified the larvae as the Australian witchiti grub. (Did you know that the natives there eat them!) Am I going to have to have the whole lawn fumigated and new sod laid?*

—Kingsley, Hamford

A: "Kingsley," just how are these Australian witty-titty grubs supposed to have turned up on your lawn? I think what you have there are the grubs of Japanese beetles, and I'm not very happy about that, because in no time flat the beetles will be over here eating my roses. Go get some milky spore at the garden center. This is a bacteria that will do in the grubs eventually. It is hardly necessary to lay all new sod, but no advice I might give you would be heeded anyway. By the way, it's about time you added a grown-up book on insects to your garden library, particularly one that narrows the topic down to, say, North America. And your Masterpiece Theatre pseudonyms do not fool me for a moment. I'm making an exception this one time, but if I see one more lawn-care question in my mailbag, I shall toss it out unread.

Next time . . . a knot garden how-to . . .
espalier your medlar

No Strings Attached

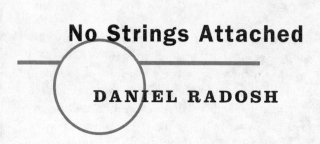

DANIEL RADOSH

"Howdy was so successful that Mr. Smith commissioned a stand-in, whom he called Double Doody, and a third puppet with no strings attached who posed for photos. He was called Photo Doody."
—from the *New York Times* obituary of Howdy Doody creator "Buffalo Bob" Smith

There are some stories you can't tell at the time. Too many reputations are at stake. But now I'm the only one left. Me? You've probably never heard my name. You'd know my face in a second, though. I was called Photo Doody.

Howdy was my big brother, and whatever happened, I never forgot that. Between us was Double Doody—or Double Trouble, as they called him in the tabloids. Both were strong personalities, so I played the role of peacemaker: massaging egos, negotiating truces and always, always putting on a happy front for the public.

We all worked for Mr. Smith. (We never called him Bob or Buffalo Bob off camera. It was always Mr. Smith, and it couldn't hurt to follow up with a "sir.") But Howdy was the star. People loved him, and on TV he was lovable. What didn't come across on the screen was his complexity. Howdy Doody was, I believe, the most complicated puppet who ever lived—and, yes, I'm including Alf. Howdy was a visionary whose ideas couldn't always be shoehorned into easy entertainment. I still recall his reaction when Mr. Smith nixed his modern-dance interpretation of *Eugene Onegin* in favor of another "Iggly Wiggly Spaghetti" sing-along. "They're always jerking my strings!" he cried. And it was true.

Yet Howdy's self-importance sometimes made him insensitive. Fishing for gratitude once, I remarked what a pain some of those still photographers could be—believe me, I felt for the Princess. Howdy just snorted, "Try lip-synching sometime." I learned to shrug off his imperiousness, but poor Double Doody took it hard. Howdy never showed any appreciation for Double's work, sweating before the Peanut Gallery so Howdy could hit the links with Bogey and the original Rat Pack. Yes, Double resented Howdy, plain and simple.

The common belief is that Mr. Smith named him Double Doody because he did double duty for Howdy. In fact, Mr. Smith originally christened him Stand-In Doody, a moniker that generated much snickering among the potty minded. "Double" came about from those Fridays after taping, when the crew would convene across the street at Marionette's, a dive bar that catered to "dummies." This was before the days when people of ventriloquism mingled with mainstream society. Every week, Stand-In would be the first through the door. "Whiskey, Mac!" he'd roar to the bartender. "Double, Doody?" the knowing Mac would ask.

Double could slam 'em back. He had that Irish sap in him. He was a bitter drunk, but a funny one. We'd laugh ourselves silly at his impressions of Chief Thunderthud, Princess Summerfall Winterspring and Benito Mussolini. Then we'd giggle when, sloshed, he'd stumble out to pick up a whore on Tenth Avenue, warbling his familiar, sardonic refrain:

It's Howdy Doody time
It's Howdy Doody time
It only costs a dime
To get your booty shined.

Howdy loathed Double's coarse behavior, but the more he tried to curb it, the more fiercely Double lashed back. As Howdy's fame and Double's shame grew in tandem, my attempts at conciliation became more and more futile.

Double's worst rupture with Howdy took place in '48, when Howdy was running for president of all the boys and girls. Walter Winchell ran into Double at a pub one night at the tail end of the election, when it was beginning to look like Howdy had a shot. The next day, Winchell famously reported that Double had said to him, "I don't know about the girls, but he'd sure like to be president of the boys." Howdy's poll numbers dropped precipitously, and the editors of the *Chicago Daily Tribune* scrambled to change their front-page headline—DOODY DEFEATS TRUMAN—though in hindsight they didn't scramble enough.

Finally, I gave up trying to mend fences, partly because I had my own falling-out with Double. Ah yes, it was over a woman. Neither of us ever lacked for female companionship. Groupies flocked to the puppet scene in a way that makes the NBA look like a kiddie show. But Double didn't believe in true love, and when I told him I had met my soul mate, my Lamb Chop, he scoffed in a way I could never forgive. "Do you have to get a woody for every slab of meat you see?" he hissed cruelly.

By the end, Double's boozing lost its charm. One night at Marionette's, Clarabell the Clown snuck up on Double and got off an epic blast with his seltzer bottle. We all laughed except for Double, who spat, "Anyone ever tell you you got a girlie name?" and smashed his fist into the clown's solar plexus, dropping him to the sawdust. Back then no one understood the disease that is alcoholism.

Shortly after that, I left the show. I suspect that Howdy and Double both ached to follow me, but they could never break free. They were bound too tightly by their strings.

Ferret-Face

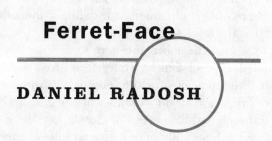

DANIEL RADOSH

A cursory search finds only two Web sites devoted to pet slugs. This is as it should be. Slugs are disgusting animals to keep inside a house, and I would be shocked to discover any more than two slug owners proud enough to post home pages about their deviant pet habits.

Why then are there so many ferret pages? And why are they all so obsessively enthusiastic? I mean, we're talking about the most foul, unappealing house pets since, well, slugs.

According to Ferret Central, the two most-accessed pages of the Ferret FAQ are: "What are ferrets? Do they make good pets?" and, "Are ferrets legal where I live?" Obviously, the FAQ's response to the former is all lies, or no one would bother to check out the latter.

What are ferrets? Ferrets are rodents.

OK, I'm kidding. And boy, do ferret fanciers hate it when people make the rodent mistake. "I am not a rodent!" screams one ferret's home page. (It is common for ferret owners to write in their animals' voices. How annoying is that?) "I am related to . . . weasels." Yup, that's much more attractive.

Are ferrets legal where I live? Real pets are legal everywhere. Ferrets, however, are banned by many cities, towns, counties, and even a few states. In these places, ferrets are classified as wild animals. This should tip people off to the fact that these creatures might not make ideal companions. Instead, ferret lovers—like militiamen stockpiling automatic weapons—hold that the law itself is unjust.

To answer the above question, Katie Fritz has painstakingly compiled a list of United States ferret-free zones—thirty-nine in all. "My apologies for the long delay in updating this list," writes Fritz. "I'm afraid a number of 'life changes' have kept me out of touch and largely out of circulation till now." Um, don't you need to have a life in order to have life changes?

Do ferrets make good pets? The big claim about ferrets is that they are awfully cute. There's no arguing with that. Not because it's true, mind you, but because ferret owners will stubbornly insist on it, despite glaring evidence to the contrary. Ferret web sites are littered with allegedly adorable JPEGs. In every single one, the object of admiration is, to any objective eye, mind-bogglingly un-cute—typically resembling a mole rat that's been stretched out on a torture rack. And yes, I'm including "Doofus, the Ferret King" and "Pixxel asleep with her head on her own tummy."

The sites detail all the cute things that ferrets do—which frequently involve socks. "Ripple . . . loved to pull socks right off your feet and hide them under the water bed," remembers "The Weasels of Wyrdhaven" page. And if you're wondering who still owns a water bed in this day and age, it's the same people who have ferrets.

In addition to water beds, think renaissance faires, how-to-speak-Klingon books and Tori Amos. Or think Geri L. Neemidge, who writes, "In my spare time I play with computers, and I enjoy dressing in silly costumes at Mensa regional gatherings."

"The traditional view of a ferreter," explains "The Hunting Ferret" page, "is that of a furtive poacher, out on a dark night, with one or more vicious, bloodthirsty ferrets secreted about his person, probably in his trousers." The contemporary view, on the other hand, is that of a hapless stoner, in on a dark night, watching "Space: Above and Beyond" with one or more vicious, bloodthirsty ferrets secreted about his person, probably in his trousers.

Maybe vicious and bloodthirsty isn't the best description of a ferret. Vicious, bloodthirsty, and fetid is more like it. "Some people think we smell bad," counters "Bosht." "But I've trained my humans to wash my bedding often, and that keeps me pretty sweet smelling." That's the ferreters' party line, and they stick to it even if they can't resist telling *stories* about their pets' too-cute but none-too-sanitary habits. "Tootsie likes to go trash-can diving." "Kodo loves to dig and dive in fresh litter." Fresh, with ferrets, being a relative term.

As for that "one or more," ferret freaks always have more. "Six ferrets are as easy to care for as one," they'll tell you. Or, "Ten ferrets share our house with us." Any problems this might cause are easily solved. "Today I brought home my 70-centimeter-tall pachira and put it on the table in the living room. Late in the evening, I found it overturned, all the soil on the table and the floor, and several of the roots severed," writes Urban Fredriksson in his *ferret diary*. "Well, I've got too many plants anyway, and why not let my ferrets do the weeding?"

"The Ferret Stroller is basically a (human) baby stroller that I ferret-proofed," writes Roger Poore. "This idea came to me when I decided that five ferrets were just too much to carry around when we go out." Laugh if you want. He could have said, "Well, I go out too much anyway."

Then there's Bill Sebok. His fourth ferret wasn't getting along with the first three—Bridgett was "biting at the other ferrets' faces." Sebok's brilliant solution was to add another beast to his collection. "We were hoping that a younger ferret would be a friend and companion for Bridgett." The result: Bridgett "instantly discovered how to bite and shake Jasmine's neck."

Let's talk about biting. Ferreters swear that ferrets don't bite . . . any more than they smell. In the same breath, however, they'll say something like: "He was scared and tended to show it by biting." "She would bite hard." "I picked him up, and the first thing he did was bite me. I knew he wanted to go home with me." "When we found her she was marked down to $25 because of her 'viciousness.'" "She would rest in my winter coat pocket, where she would gnaw on my little finger. Needless to say, we fell in love with her too."

Needless to say, biting is never inherent in the ferret's personality. "Vanna bit anyone who got near her, so she was given a 'Will Bite' sticker at the shelter . . . I knew this little bundle of white fluff wasn't a biter at heart, so I began to handle her every week. She improved a little over time, but after biting me and another club member very hard one Saturday night, I decided to take her home to give her more time with people." As opposed to, for instance, not sticking one's hands in her cage anymore.

It is hardly uncommon for ferret freaks not to realize just how unpleasant their own stories make these animals sound. One of the first things anyone browsing through a ferret web site learns is that these creatures are not the healthiest on God's green Earth. Vivid (meant to be heart-wrenching) descriptions of what it takes to nurse a ferret through an exotic disease are the least of it. One ferreter also posts his late pet's necropsy report, and another invites us to download a photo of her charge afflicted with adrenal disease. This picture shows a matted, scrawny animal—in other words, one that is indistinguishable from a healthy ferret. And if you absolutely must look at a bloody ferret, cut open and sprawled out on the operating table, there's always "Pathology of the Ferret"—Doofus the Ferret King like you've never seen him before.

Have I mentioned yet how awfully cute ferrets are? No matter how disgusted ordinary people are when confronted with a ferret in the flesh, ferret freaks will continue to be won over by the animals they call "critters," "fuzzies," and "carpet sharks."

"Having ferrets for company, as well as talking about them, always cheers me up tremendously," says Gier Friestad. "No need for cable TV in a house with ferrets!" cheers Lars Eriskssol. On the other hand, no need for air-freshener in a house with cable TV.

They just won't stop. "Ever wonder what a ferret sounds like?" asks John Rosloot. Sure—what it sounds like as it hits the pavement from a five-story drop, maybe. But no. This sound file is of Cassie "dooking" and "power-sniffing." Isn't it cute?

Maybe you'd rather see ferrets in art history, or a French ferret folk ballad, or a disastrously un-interactive ferret racing game, or amateurish cartoons of ferrets as *Star Trek* characters. Or maybe by now you're reconsidering that necropsy report.

Barnes Ennobled

DANIEL RADOSH

Unsettled by flagging sales and heavy book returns, publishing executives in search of oracles have begun turning to the dominant chains like Barnes & Noble and Borders for guidance about a broad range of issues—from dust-jacket colors and punchy titles, to authors' sales histories and forecasts of customer demand—that could determine a manuscript's destiny.

—*New York Times*

3 November

DEAR MAX,
Thank you for sending along the manuscript of George Eliot's latest tome, *The Mill on the Floss*. While it may be an excellent novel, as Mr. Eliot's usually are, I can't say for certain, because frankly I didn't make it past the title, and neither, I promise you, will book buyers. Our records show that no book with the word "floss" in the title has ever sold more than seven copies, despite a

major advertising campaign for *Floss Your Way to Better Gums.* The biggest success we could find was the children's book *Flossy Bunny's Baby Brother,* a consistent catalog best-seller. Perhaps if your new book were published with a cheery animal-theme cover, engaging illustrations and, let's say, 550 fewer pages, it might have a shot. Otherwise, "floss" really has to go. And don't even get me started on "mill."

> DARIUS WIGBY
> VICE PRESIDENT FOR MARKETING
> AND PROMOTION
> THE CORNER BOOKCHAIN, INC.

7 November

DEAR ANDRE,
While there is certainly a market for this treatise by Mary Wollstonecraft, I can only assume that *A Vindication of the Rights of Woman* is a working title. What are you really going to call it? I know *Girl Power!* is taken, but you'll think of something. Also, our research shows that the best way to sell a book like this is with a cover that demonstrates that the author's feminist agenda is informed by her unique personal perspective. Is she willing to pose naked?

> DARIUS WIGBY
> VICE PRESIDENT FOR SALES
> AND DISTRIBUTION
> THE CORNER BOOKCHAIN, INC.
> A SUBSIDIARY OF TIME WARNER

12 November

DEAR GARY,
Re: *The House of the Seven Gables*. The results from market research are in, and responses ranged from "What's a gable?" to "Why seven?" to "The seven what?" Still, there's no denying that home improvement is a hot category. See if you can get a blurb from Martha.

> DARIUS WIGBY
> VICE PRESIDENT FOR CONTENT
> THE CORNER BOOKCHAIN, INC.
> A SUBSIDIARY OF TIME WARNER/ABC

19 November

DEAR PHYLLIS,
Everyone here is delighted with *The Catcher in the Rye*, but we are underwhelmed by the proposed jacket design. Put simply, maroon and yellow do not sell except with reference titles (and even there we encourage maroon and gold). What's more, the version you sent us is missing its illustration. Please forward this just as soon as it's ready.

> DARIUS WIGBY
> THE CORNER BOOKCHAIN, INC.
> VICE PRESIDENT FOR HUMINT AND RECON
> A SUBSIDIARY OF TIME
> WARNER/ABC/RAYTHEON

28 November

DEAR ROGER,
I think we have a winner with this slim volume by Jonathan Swift, but I am surprised by your choice of a title. As you must know, there is nothing modest about

this proposal. It would hardly be worth buying if there were! If Mr. Swift expects to be taken seriously, his title must be at least as bold as his ideas. My suggestion—
Eat Brats: The Most Controversial Proposal of Our Time.

> Darius Wigby
> Vice President for Commodity Futures
> The Corner Bookchain, Inc.
> A Subsidiary of Time Warner/
> Disney/Raytheon-Wackenhut

2 December

Dear Barney,
I am disturbed and offended by your latest manuscript, the so-called novel *Lolita*. Such a thing has no place in decent American bookstores. I mean, there's hardly any sex in it at all! The one or two hot scenes in the early chapters are utterly misleading, as the remainder of the book devolves into some sort of psychological journey— and a rather wordy one at that. Yes, the book will sell, but will customers be getting their money's worth? That, after all, is what this business is about.

> Darius Wigby
> Chief Financial Officer
> Olde Corner Bookchain, Inc.
> A Subsidiary of the Travelers Group

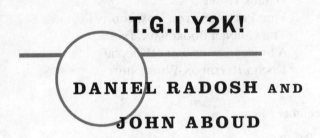

T.G.I.Y2K!

DANIEL RADOSH AND
JOHN ABOUD

For New Agers, Y2K is being greeted as something
of a godsend. People will join together to "empower"
their neighborhoods.

—*New York Times*

SEPTEMBER 1999

End Times? Just the beginning! The coming crisis is a chance
to move away from technological dependence toward human
interdependence. Everyone can pitch in: Midwives and natural
healers will be needed at hospitals. Car mechanics can retrain
themselves to fix bicycles or to become midwives and natural
healers. Teenagers at Phish concerts can be conscripted as
organic gardeners. Elders have skills that mechanized society
has forgotten—sewing, glassblowing, bootblacking and entertaining children without television.

Host a local action group to reweave community resilience
with positive visioning. Offer jerky snacks and assure guests
their defecation will be composted.

Possible Pep Talk

Hi! I'm [your name/dharma name]. Now that we've learned about the urgent need to stockpile tahini paste, let's share our feelings. I, for one, felt [extreme emotion] when I heard there'd be no more [television/Wayne Dyer videos/Fresh Samantha smoothies]. But then I realized, hey, I'll finally get to [write/build/shellac] that [non-linear fable/eco-sensitive home extension/mytho-poetic artwork] I've always wanted to. And think how it will bring us citizens of [city/county/ashram] together! How's everyone else coping? [Open up the room for reflection and learning. Allow for tears, but always respect the talking stick.]

OCTOBER 1999

One of the great challenges confronting us is how to build a new communication system after the telephones explode. Explore hand-cranked radios, crystal singing bowls, and patchouli smoke signals. Whichever medium you adopt, don't forget the most powerful communications device of all: your smile.

Empowering Children

Prepare your kids without frightening them. Suggested discussion starter: *Little House on the Prairie*. Offer statements like, "It must be neat to live in that shack," and, "Doesn't butter churning look fun?"

NOVEMBER 1999

Y2K preparedness must respect differences and celebrate diversity. For instance, encourage your local synagogue to declare itself YJewK compliant. Homosexual meeting places can double as Y2Gay discussion forums. (Some may prefer a Bi2K group; they're not fooling anybody.)

Possible Pep Talk

Hi! I hope everybody's feeling good about the abundant world we're making. I know [neighbor] has had great success creating aromatherapy hurricane candles. Stay grounded in your joy, and ignore the rumors that [neighbor resistant to reweaving community resilience] has traded his [crystal singing bowls/mytho-poetic artwork] for [guns/ammunition/lots of ammunition].

Empowering Children

Discussion starter: *The Road Warrior.* "You can sure make cool clothing out of old tires!"

DECEMBER 1999

You don't want to be having surgery in January 2000, so check into the hospital immediately to remove any unnecessary organs (appendix, tonsils, redundant kidney or lung). Don't forget to compost!

By now, windmills should be providing your power. They also make great turrets.

Possible Pep Talk

Listen. None of us are happy that [noncollaborative neighbor] stopped sharing his [canned goods/can opener/ammunition]. But remember our friends who are [elderly/infirm]. They need our protection. And they'll pay for it—dearly.

NEW YEAR'S EVE 1999

Check on your neighbors' preparations. Have they converted their cash to gold? Are they keeping their gold safely at home rather than in a bank? Where exactly are they keeping the gold?

Does the dog linger near there? What kind of herbs from your organic garden will render a dog unconscious?

Bring together your community's diverse groups for a final meeting. Note which groups have developed distinct and incompatible cultures. Prepare to lay siege to them.

Empowering Children

Discussion starter: *Quest for Fire*. "If you listen closely, those grunts are really a form of language."

•• NEWS QUIZ ••

3/11/99 "NOTHING BUT CASH"

Devise a pair of words to fill in the two blanks—one word each—as Thomas Rogers, president of NBC cable, describes his shift away from the old network economic model: "Our goal over time is to turn viewers into _____ and _____."

"Hunters and gatherers."
—M.G. Lord, Marshall Efron,
Jon Delfin, Joe Shaw

"Dharma and Greg."—Jon Hotchkiss

"Readers and writers. (He was promptly fired.)"
—Paul Tullis

"Cash and checks."—Steve Lyle

"Imbeciles and quick."—Tamar Haspel

"Malcontents and loners. ('We're going to steal the Internet's thunder!')"—Doug Strauss

"Gays and lesbians. (Turns out Falwell was right all along.)"—Tim Carvell

• RANDY'S WRAP UP •

It's a little too easy to disdain TV, although please do, especially that *Animal Medical Center* where, just the other night I saw some kind of vomiting Chihuahua, which, let me tell you, after a long day working for some big jerk at the . . . no, wait, I lie: it wasn't *Animal Medical Center,* it was *20–20,* and it wasn't a Chihuahua, it was Barbara Walters, and she wasn't vomiting, that was me. But the point stands: TV is like tap water or take-out pizza; it's not really good, but it's so conveniently available that we dully consume it instead of making the effort to go out for really good pizza or some truly magnificent water from, like, a solid gold tap. And yet, if you ask people about their actual number one recreational activity, it's watching TV. And if you ask them their imaginary number one recreational activity, it's stripping naked and firing out the window at passing cars with that actress from that show, you know, the pretty one. So perhaps it's a little facile to blame all our problems on some sap from NBC cable, when the fault, my friends, is some whole other sap entirely. If you write me, I'll send you his name.

ACE AWARD-WINNING ANSWER

"Our goal over time is to turn viewers into *buyers* and *customers.*"

Tired of relying on ad revenues from so called "popular" shows, NBC, the first broadcast network to own part of a home shopping channel, is expanding its efforts to sell souvenirs. The network did well hawking a music CD, a tie-in to its miniseries "The 60s," and expects to sell viewers a lot more stuff once it ties together TV shows, home shopping, and the Internet. "We've made it clear that figuring out ways to drive sales of product through our broadcast platform is a key ingredient we see in the overall mix," said Rogers. "And that means one thing—an anatomically enhanced Tom Brokaw Action Figure," he did not add.

NEW FURBY/NEW DOLE EXTRA

A new version of the annoying yet popular toy, and a new presidential candidate from the awkward yet enduring political family are aggressively courting acclaim.

Some comparisons:

- Oft-Cited Personality Trait:
  New Furby: spunky playmate
  Elizabeth Dole: thin-skinned perfectionist

- Core Belief:
  Furby: provide cuddly animatronic fun
  Dole: cut taxes, build antimissile system

- Positions on Other Major Issues:
  Furby: undisclosed
  Dole: undisclosed, but promises "We're going to be laying out positions on all of these issues."

- Handicap for Presidential Candidate:

    Furby: overly programmed

    Dole: same thing

- Slogan:

    Furby: "Collect them all for phenomenal Furby fun!"

    Dole: "Let's make this a crusade!" (antecedent unclear)

- Nickname:

    Furby: pretty much just "Furby"

    Dole: Miss 3-by-5 Index Card (as a Duke undergrad)

- Hair:

    Furby: three "wild" fur designs in all new wildlife colors and patterns

    Dole: can't tell from newspaper, but former aide Alex Castellanos says: "She's a tough lady; she's as hard as her hairdo."

- Recent Innovation:

    Furby: "deep sleep" lets new Furby go to sleep quicker and stay asleep until turned completely upside down

    Dole: same thing (unconfirmed rumor only)

COMMON DENOMINATOR:

crummy TV shows, crummy snacks

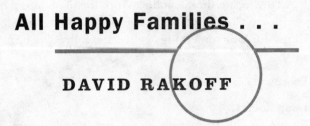

All Happy Families . . .

DAVID RAKOFF

Every time you buy one of our products you become a part of our company family, and we love our family.

Please let us hear from you and we will let you know what's new. We hope you enjoy.

> *Thank you.*
> *Robert Ehrlichs*

—from the package of Robert's American
Gourmet Gingko Biloba Rings®

January 3, 1999

Dear Robert:
I was so glad to read on the back of the package that you love your family. I love family, too. And I love your chips! I've been eating the Robert's American Gourmet® St. John's Wort Tortilla Chips for just under two weeks now—it's my New Year's resolution to explore more natural avenues to happiness; I had a kind of bad breakup in December, but I'm not gonna let it get me down, right? That's just not the Ehrlichs' family style, am I

right? I'm also using that St. John's wort lip balm. Do you know it? I call it my Happy Grease.

> Well, *bro'* (ha ha!), I'll be seeing you.
> David Rakoff

P.S. How come the St. John's Wort Tortilla Chips package doesn't have your address like the Gingko Biloba Rings do? Got something against sad folks? (ha ha)

February 12, 1999

Dear Robert:
Sitting in the front seat of my car, watching my ex-girlfriend Marion's house, and I just wanted to drop you a line to let you know how incredibly grateful I am for your friendship and your chips. You've put the "home" in "homeopathy" for me, Robert, and I'll never forget it.

> Patrol car. Gotta go.
> David

February 27, 1999

Dear Robert:
Did you get the sweater? Let me know if it didn't arrive and I'll "go postal" at the post office (ha ha. Just kidding. I don't even have a gun anymore). Just to let you know that I'm up to four packages a day now. That's twenty-six servings at 140 calories each (60 from fat), 3,640 calories per day, in case you're compiling data or something. I feel great, but I'm breaking out a little bit.

I'm going to start the Chewy Choosers Chip Crunchers Club. With T-shirts and a baseball team!

> Best,
> David Rakoff

P.S. The sweater is not for Valentine's Day. It's just a gift, OK? I love you, but like a brother, man. I'm not even gay, but if you want, we can explore taking it to another level later. Just something to think about.

March 16, 1999

Dude:

My therapist, Janice Baker, C.S.W., is bugging my ass to get back on the psychotropic meds. I just told her what my bro' Rob thought of the psychopharmacology industry, namely, that they were a bunch of blood-sucking pill pushers narcotizing us into feeling nothing! She seems really "concerned" with my "cycling," her overreactive way of referring to my standing outside the Honduran consulate in my underpants.

    She wants to meet you. She's right about one thing, and that's how much you mean to me. My sessions are Wednesdays at ten-thirty, so let me know when you can come.

            Later.
            Dave

April 9, 1999

R:

The health food store has asked me to observe a thirty-foot "circle of friendship preservation" from its premises. Apparently I was making Miranda, the girl who works there, "nervous." I wrote to you about her, remember? She's the one who looks like my ex, Marion. Frankly, I think the jury is still out on whether she actually *is* my ex. Marion + Miranda = Mirandarion . . . you do the math.

    Anyway, who cares? I saw a mouse by their salad bar once. Plus, they don't have anything I need, case in

point that lip balm bullshit, which I quit taking. They
should call it bullshit balm, 'cause that's what it is,
Robert (bullshit!). I called the manufacturers and told
them where to put their greasy snake oil sticks.

D

May 28, 1999

Rob-o!

Thought you'd be "amused" at the enclosed "letter"
from my insurance company:

> *"Dear Mr. Rakoff: Regarding your recent submission
> of receipts in the amount of $387.45. We regret to
> inform you that snack foods are not covered under your
> plan and so we will be unable to reimburse you for your
> out-of-pocket expenses."*

Snack foods? I'm happier than I've ever been yea ver-
ily for I AM THE GODHEAD MADE MANIFEST IN
THIS TIME OF KINGS APPROACHING. YAHWEH
ALLAH GAUTAMA BUDDHA AND I WILL HEAP
CONTUMELY UPON THE INFIDELS IN THE LAKE
OF FIRE.

Stay real, man. You're the only one I can count on.

D

Christmas Freud

DAVID RAKOFF

I am the Ghost of Christmas Subconscious. I am the anti-Santa. I am Christmas Freud. People tell me what they wish for. I tell them the ways their wishes are unhealthy, or wished for in error.

My impersonation merely involves me sitting in a chair, either writing or reading the *Times* or *The Interpretation of Dreams* every Saturday and Sunday from late November until Christmas. I sit in a mock study facing Madison Avenue at Sixty-first Street. My study has the requisite chair and couch. It is also equipped with a motorized track on which a video camera–wielding baby carriage travels back and forth, a slide projector, a large revolving black-and-white spiral, two hanging torsos, and about ten video monitors that play Freud-related text and images: trains entering tunnels, archetypal mothers, title cards that read "I DREAMED," etc.

When I sit down in the chair for the first time, I am horrified at the humiliation of this and I have no idea how I'm going to get through four weekends of sitting here on display. This role raises unprecedented performance questions for me. For starters, should I act as though I had no idea there were people outside my window? I opt for covering my embarrassment with a kind of Olympian humorlessness. If they want twinkles, that's Santa's department.

I am gnawed at by two fears: one, that I'm being upstaged by Linda Evans's wig in the "Blondes of the twentieth Century" window next door, and two, that a car—a taxi most likely—will suddenly lose control, come barreling through my window, and kill me. An ignoble end, to be sure. A life given in the service of retail.

Sometimes, for no clear reason, entire crowds make the collective decision not to breach a respectful six-foot distance from the window. Other times, they crowd in, attempting to read what I'm writing over my shoulder. I thank god for my illegible scrawl.

Easily half the people do not have any idea who I'm supposed to be. They wave, as if Freud were Garfield. Others snap photos. The waves are the kind of tiny juvenile hand crunches one gives to something either impossibly young and tiny or adorably fluffy. *"Oh, look, it's Freud. Isn't he just the cutest thing you ever saw? Awww, I just want to bundle him up and take him home!"*

There are also the folks who are more concerned with whether or not I'm real—this I find particularly laughable since where on earth would they make mannequins that look so Jewish?

My friend David came up yesterday and was writing down what people were saying outside:

> *"Hey, he really looks like him, only younger."*
> *"Wait a sec. That's a real guy."*
> *"He just turned the page. Is he allowed to do that?"*
> *"Who is that, Professor Higgins?"*

If psychoanalysis was late nineteenth-century secular Judaism's way of constructing spiritual meaning in a post-religious world, and retail is the late twentieth century's way of constructing meaning in a post-religious world, what does it mean that I'm impersonating the father of psychoanalysis in a store window to commemorate a religious holiday?

In the window, I fantasize about starting an entire Christmas Freud movement. Christmas Freuden everywhere, providing grown-ups and children alike with the greatest gift of all: insight. In department stores across America, people leave display window couches, snifflingly and meaningfully whispering, "Thank you, Christmas Freud," shaking his hand fervently, their holiday angst, if not dispelled, at least brought into starker relief. Christmas Freud on the cover of *Cigar Aficionado* magazine; Christmas Freud appearing on *Friends;* people grumbling that, here it is not even Thanksgiving and already stores are running ads with Christmas Freud's visage asking the question, *"What do women want . . . for Christmas?"*

If it caught on, all the stores would have to compete. Bergdorf Goodman would leap into action with a C. G. Jung window—a near-perfect simulation of a bear cave, while the Melanie Klein window at Niketown would have them lined up six deep, and neighborhood groups would object to the saliva and constant bell-ringing in Baby Gap's B. F. Skinner window.

There is an unspeakably handsome man outside the window right now, writing something down. I hope it is his phone number. How do I indicate to the woman in the fur coat, in benevolent Christmas Freud fashion, of course, to get the hell out of the way? Then again, how does one cruise someone through a department store window? Should I press my own number up against the glass? Like some polar bear in the zoo holding up a sign reading *"Help, I'm being held prisoner!"* I feel like a birthday clown at a party for potentially violent grown-ups.

One day, I come up to the store for a photo-op for a news story about the holiday windows of New York. It is my second birthday. I am paired with a little girl named Sasha. By strange coincidence, it's her birthday, as well. She is turning ten. She is strikingly beautiful and appears in the Howard Stern movie. She is to be my patient for the photographers; it's all somewhat Alice Liddell and Charles Dodgson.

In true psychoanalytic fashion, I make her lie down and face away from me. I explain to her a little about Freud, and we play a word association game. I say *"center,"* she responds, *"of attention."* I ask her her dreams and aspirations for this, the coming eleventh year of her life. *"To make another feature and to have my role on* One Life to Live *continue."* She sells every word she says to me, smiling with both sets of teeth, her gem-like eyes glittering. She might as well be saying *"Crunchy!"* the entire time. But she is charming. I experience extreme counter-transference.

I read a bit from *The Interpretation of Dreams* to her.

"Is this boring?" I ask.

"Oh no, it's relaxing. I've been working since five o'clock this morning. Keep going."

Even though her eyes are closed, she senses the light from the news cameras on her. She curls toward it like a plant and clutches her dolly in a startlingly un-childlike manner. The glass of the window fairly fogs up.

I've decided to start seeing patients. I'm simply not man enough to sit exposed in a window doing nothing; it's too humiliating and too boring. My patients are all people I know. Perhaps it is because the window faces away from both the street and myself that the sessions are strangely intimate and genuine. But it's more than that. The window is, surprisingly enough, very cozy. More like a children's hideaway than a fishbowl. Patients seem to relax immediately upon lying down.

S. begins the session laughing at the artifice, and ends it crying on the sofa talking about an extramarital affair. Christmas Freud is prepared and hands her a handkerchief.

K. has near-crippling tendonitis and wears huge padded orthopedic boots. The people watching think it's a fashion statement. She wears a dress from Loehmann's, but I treat her anyway.

H., a journalist, likes to talk with children, and write about them. Perhaps that is why his shirt is irregularly buttoned.

B. is a woman who only entered counseling once, briefly, to decide which of the two men she was seeing she would choose. When she made her selection, she terminated therapy. I have distaste for her glacial pragmatism. I am also amazed, as a day when I am no longer in therapy seems as distant and fictive as a future of jet packs and Smell-o-Vision.

I. is not happy in his relationship. His boyfriend stands outside the window in the gray drizzle for the entire session, his face a mask of dejection. He knows exactly what we are talking about, although he cannot hear a thing we're saying.

In fact, the real transgression, in this age of tell-all television, is not that therapy, no matter how sham, is being conducted in a store window. It is that its particulars remain private and confidential.

I'm told that a woman outside the window wondered aloud if I was an actual therapist. I suppose there must be one in this town who would jeopardize his or her credibility in that way. *"I've scheduled our next session for the window at Barney's, I hope that's OK . . . huh . . . you seem really resistant. Do you want to talk about it?"*

A journalist is doing a story on the windows for the *Times*. He asks me if this is a dream come true. *"Well, it is a dream. It's logical,"* I reply. *"One of my parents is a psychiatrist and the other is a department store window."* He doesn't laugh at my joke, but it's half true. One of my parents *is* a psychiatrist, and the other is an M.D. who also does psychotherapy. I've been in therapy myself for many, many years. The difference between seeing a shrink and being a shrink is not only less pronounced than I imagined it might be, it feels intoxicating. When my own therapist says to me, *"I have a fantasy of coming by the window and being treated by you,"* I think, *Of course you do.* I feel finally and blissfully triumphant.

My father tells me a dream he had in which I have essentially analyzed and exposed him. It's the only indication I've gotten from him so far that he is anything other than amused at what is basically a mockery of what he does. In a certain sense, I'm not just aping my father and my mother, but their father, in a way—the man who spawned their profession. And when I sit there with a patient on my couch, my pipe in my mouth, listening, it feels so . . . perfect. Like any psychiatrist's kid, I know enough from growing up, and from my own years on the couch, to ask open-ended questions, to let the silences play themselves out or not, to say gently, *"Our time is up,"* after forty-five minutes. The charade feels real, the conclusion of an equation years in the making. And more than that; it is different from being in a play. The words I speak are my own.

Even the media coverage for this escapade is extensive and strange. People from newspapers and television are asking me these deep questions about the holiday, the nature of alienation at this time of year, the subtextual meaning of gifts, things like that, as though I actually *was* Freud. It's disconcerting because with very little effort, I could be drunk with the power. But it also points out the O. Henry *Gift of the Magi* quality of it all. The media is so desperate for any departure from the usual holiday drivel they have to churn out, they come flocking. And yet, the public doesn't particularly want to read about the holiday in the first place. It's like trying to jazz up a meal nobody wanted to eat anyway.

I get a call from the store that Allen Ginsberg might be in the Beats window on Sunday and, if he wants to, would I speak with him. *"I have no sway over Mr. Ginsberg, but if he has something he'd like to talk about, I'm certainly available,"* I reply. Not entirely true—I'm pretty well booked.

The whole Allen Ginsberg thing depresses me a bit. Then again, if he can see it as some cosmic joke, why can't I? I feel indignant and very territorial. *Impostors only! No real ones in the window!* Anyway, it's moot, he doesn't show.

There is a street fair outside that seems to have brought a decidedly scarier type of spectator. They are like a crowd at a carnival sideshow and I'm the Dog-faced Boy. A grown woman sticks her tongue out at me. Later, during a session, a man in his fifties presses his nose up against the window, getting grease on the glass, presses his ear up to hear and screams inaudible things at me. Today may well be the day some group of thick-necks say, *"Man, that Freud guy's a fag. Let's beat the crap out of him!"*

When I leave after each stint, I put up a little glass sign that reads "Freud will be back soon." It's like a warning. The postmodern version of "Christ is coming. Repent!" "Freud will be back soon, whether you like it or not." "Freud will be back soon, stop deceiving yourselves." In the affluent downtown neighborhood in Toronto in which I was raised, someone had spraypainted on a wall, "Mao lives!," to which someone else had added, "Here?"

My window is a haven in midtown. I can sit here, unmindful of the crush in the aisles of the store, the hour badly spent over gifts thoughtlessly and desperately bought. As I sit here, I hear the songs that play for the blondes display, one window over. Doris Day singing "My Secret Love," Mae West singing "My Old Flame," Marlene Dietrich's rendition of "Falling in Love Again." As I listen, I feel that they're really referring to *my* window, to Freud. Every time they come up on the repeating tape loop, I find them almost unutterably poignant, with all their talk of clandestine love, erotic fixation, and painfully hidden romantic agenda. But, they might also just as easily be referring to this time of year, with the aching sadness and loneliness that seems to imbue everything. Where is that perfect object, that old flame, that secret love that eludes us? Unfindable. Unpurchasable.

This is my final weekend as Christmas Freud, and I am starting to feel bereft in anticipation of having to take down my shingle.

I started off as a monkey on display, and have wound up uncomfortably caught between joking and deadly serious. A persona that seems laughable at times, fated for me at others. I know this will fade, but for now, I want nothing more than to continue to sit in my chair, someone on the couch, and to ask them, with real concern, *"So tell me. How is everything?"*

El Niño Has a Headache

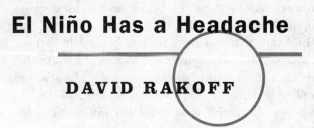

DAVID RAKOFF

I. EL NIÑO HAS A HEADACHE

"Mr. Niño's gonna be late . . . headache," says one of his functionaries, a compact squall of warm Gulf Coast rain. I am sitting in the Bar Marmont, drinking one of the blueberry vodka infusions for which the bar is justifiably famous. Blueberries whose extra-mild New England winter was due, in large part, to the efforts of my delayed interviewee.

Indeed, the entire bar is filled with the evidence of El Niño's influence. The grain bases of the spirits, the Costa Rican hardwood marquetry, the bamboo of the basket holding my shrimp dumplings (ordered because they were out of the gravlax, due to the dearth of Pacific salmon), even the windswept hair of my suspiciously thin, pillow-lipped, neurasthenic waitress can all be traced back to El Niño.

No wonder El Niño has a headache. On his third worldwide tour this decade alone, El Niño has become Chairman of the Board of the Climate business. His global reach has transcended his rather modest beginnings as a meteorological bit player to the point where nowadays, when people say "weather," what they mean is El Niño.

"Nino," says Hollywood mogul and *eminence grise* Lew Wasserman (who pronounces Niño's name to rhyme with "Reno"), "is a force of nature. He is responsible for everything. Literally. Your opening weekend grosses bottom out because of unexpectedly nice weather? Nino. A plane goes down in Southeast Asia because of brush fires caused by years-long drought? Nino."

El Niño finally arrives, trailing behind him three or four sycophants and a thirty-five-foot wall of sea water that washes away the couple sitting at the next table. Our waitress looks very pissed. "Duke her," El Niño says to one of the hangers-on, who peels off a crisp hundred-dollar bill and hands it to the waitress, busy pulling minnows from her hair.

II. EL NIÑO HAS A TANTRUM

We're on La Brea, looking for Noguchi lamps. "My decorator got me hooked and I love their organic forms." He calls his assistant from his HUMV, outfitted with NASA-level amounts of communications hardware, for the address of the store. He is solicitous on the phone, apologetic for making a purchase, for feeling entitled to this small, unnecessary expenditure. Paradoxically shy behavior from someone who, it is said, has just become the most expensive network of interconnected natural disasters in history.

"Yeah, when the figure came on the news, I had tons of joke messages on my machine . . . you know, Tom Cruise asking to borrow some cash. But, it's really not about the money for me. It's about my personal journey. I mean, *I* didn't even know I could do this."

It is true, second only to John-John and Caroline, there are few whose growth has been as scrutinized or as public. Niño's occasional acting out belies an inner sensitivity—a sensitivity that loves Noguchi—that is all too easy to forget. "It's nice to be the subject of almost every dinner conversation. I won't lie, I like the attention. I mean, who wouldn't? But it comes with a price. I get blamed for just about everything going."

I bring up some of the rumors that hound him: the drought and forest fires in much of Southeast Asia; 300,000 starving in Papua New Guinea; the gerbils. Describing Niño to himself as some kind of überweather makes him bristle and, for the first time in our brief acquaintance, lose his cool.

"You know, I gave the Weather Channel the best numbers they ever had, and then they're all, 'Oh, too rough, man.' So, I'm like, OK, how about fewer hurricanes on the Atlantic coast this year, fewer tornadoes in the Midwest, how about fishermen up in Alaska pulling fresh pompano and orange roughie up into their nets? And then, it's like, 'Oh, Niño's lost his edge!' and I'm like, why don't all you motherf—s in New York and Boston come complain about my edge when your utility bills go down to almost nothing this winter."

Chastened by his own outburst, he drives us out to Malibu for lunch. "I like the ocean. It's where I come from. It relaxes me," El Niño says. The view from the outdoor restaurant is magnificent, the sun brilliant, the Pacific lapidary, each white-cap applauding my lunch date. His irritability now gone, El Niño takes justifiable, proprietary pride in our surroundings.

He picks at his seared tuna over Asian greens. "Asian greens," he muses, "I thought I got rid of all those." He lets out a bark of laughter that dislodges a large mansion from the cliffs above us, sending it crashing down to the highway where it crushes a schoolbus full of children. El Niño does not notice, restored as he is by the sea.

III. EL NIÑO HAS A MOMENT

We meet again at the Bar Marmont, before I catch my flight back East. I worry a little because El Niño's high spirits on this day produce thermals strong enough to cause no fewer than three crashes at LAX. He is feeling on top and exuberant; interviewing ghost writers for his memoirs, weighing offers from heavy industry for a global-warming-as-natural-phenomenon campaign. Even, perhaps, putting off his imminent disappearance for a while. "Who knows?" he quips. "Meteorologists can't really figure me out. Neither can I, I'm completely mysterious."

That he is. The ceiling of the bar is festooned with butterflies. El Niño looks up, charmed (only natural that he should appreciate a particularly skillful *nature mort*). He begins to sing softly to himself: *"Only a dark cocoon before I get my gorgeous wings and fly away, only a phase, these dark cafe days."*

Suddenly becoming conscious of my presence, he laughs, a little sheepish. "That's one of my favorite Joni Mitchell songs. You know, she used to live just up the road in Laurel Canyon. *Blue* totally changed my life."

The Noguchi-loving Joni fan falls silent for a moment and the only sound is the faraway doppler of a DC-10 going down.

In New England Everyone Calls You Dave

DAVID RAKOFF

I do not go outdoors. Not more than I have to. As far as I'm concerned, the whole point of living in New York City is indoors. You want greenery? Order the spinach.

Paradoxically, I am being sent by an outdoor adventure magazine to climb a mountain on Christmas Day with a man named Larry Davis. Larry has climbed Mount Monadnock in southwestern New Hampshire every day for the last five-plus years. I will join him on ascent number 2,065.

The trip up to New Hampshire will involve a tiny plane from Boston. I tear my medicine cabinet apart like Billie Holliday and still only uncover one Xanax. The hiking boots the magazine sent me to buy—large, ungainly potato-like things that I have been trying to break in for the past four days—cut into my feet and draw blood as if they were lined with cheese graters. I have come to hate these Timberlands with a fervor I usually reserve for people. Just think, the shoes I wouldn't be caught dead in might actually turn out to be the shoes I am caught dead in.

It bears mentioning here that Monadnock is not Everest. It

is 3,000 feet high and the most climbed mountain in the world. It's not even a real mountain.

I do not let this sway me from my worrying.

I have other reasons for concern. My status as an adult perpetually teeters on the verge of being exposed as a sham and revoked. Plus, I am only playing at reporter here. I have up to this point relied upon my relentlessly jokey, glib, runny-mouthed logorrhea and the unwarranted good graces of magazine editors who just let me make stuff up. I have never been sent anywhere on someone else's dime, and it takes all my strength not to call my editor and tell him that the jig is finally up, that I cannot do this piece. It seems too bad that the jig has to be up so far from my home in New York with its excitement, bright lights, and major teaching hospitals. The central drama of my life is about being a fraud, alas. That's a complete lie, really. The central drama of my life is actually about being lonely, and thin, but fraudulence gets a fair amount of play.

At the connecting airline at the Boston airport, I sit, the only dark-haired person among the broad-faced butter eaters, wondering if my outdoors journalist drag—flannel shirt, jeans, most hated boots of Satan's workshop, down jacket—is fooling anyone.

Across the aisle of the waiting area sits a fourteen-year-old girl, her face a somnolent mask of misery and hatred for the parents who sit nearby. Is my fakery as apparent as her anguish? She is outfitted in the teen Goth uniform: black jeans held together with safety pins, a torn black tank top, a black shirt over that. She has a tattoo of a small blue tear at the corner of her right eye—which should prove very helpful at job interviews in ten years' time. She could be a poster child for adolescent self-loathing, aside from the jarring fact that she is reading *Chicken Soup for the Teenage Soul*.

A brief flight and half a Xanax later, I land in New Hampshire, horrified to learn that the place where I'll be staying is a bed and breakfast, *not* a hotel. My heart sinks. That means there is probably neither television nor phone in my room. And I have very little patience for what is generally labeled "charming." In particular, "Country Charm." I have an intense dislike of flowered wallpaper; ditto jam of all sorts. The former is in all-too-abundant evidence when I enter, and the latter, I'm sure, lies in ominous wait somewhere in the cheery kitchen. There is a knotty pine bar off the entrance hall with a settee with several embroidered pillows: "I'd rather be golfing." "On the eighth day, God created golf." "Golfers have sex in some humorous, golf-related manner," etc.

The proprietress is the kind of tall, stalwart woman of a certain age that used to be called "handsome." She is approximately nine feet tall, her eyes blue, resolute, her faithful dog, Charlie, at her side. She smiles at me warmly and introduces herself as Annie, extending a hand the size of a frying pan. "You must be Dave," she says. (In New England, everyone calls you Dave regardless of however many times you might introduce yourself as David. I am reminded of those fanatically religious homophobes who stand on the steps of St. Patrick's Cathedral during Gay Pride, holding signs that say "Adam and Eve, not Adam and Steve!" I have always wanted to go up to them and say, "Well of course not Adam and Steve. *Never* Adam and Steve. It's Adam and *Steven*.")

"You're in room three," she continues. "Why don't you go into the dining room and have some lunch and then we'll talk some. Come on, Charlie Dog." In spite of myself, I am charmed. She puts on a dark green slicker and knee-high Wellingtons and is out the door, presumably to chop the ice off the pond, deliver a calf, or simply just raise a barn.

I eat a club sandwich and drink some coffee to try to eradicate my Xanax buzz. I'm trying to appear legitimate, masculine, adult. Like I deserve to be there.

Larry Davis stops by the inn. I shake his hand in a hearty, hail-fellow-well-met way. As my reward, he gives me dispensation to climb the next day in my twenty-dollar plastic Payless shoes.

★ ★ ★

I realize I have done almost no research for this trip so I walk into downtown Jaffrey to check things out. This seems to me to smack of journalistic realness, a kind of topography-as-destiny-New-Journalism-Joan-Didion opening, perhaps.

I am taking notes by speaking into a little tape recorder. Perhaps that is what attracts attention. Or perhaps it is that there is not another living creature out at five P.M. on Christmas Eve, because a car passes and immediately circles back. The driver rolls down his window and asks me if I want a lift. I don't, but, How nice, I think. He drives on.

I am charmed by the congeniality of this interchange; how friendly, how uncreepy. I speak too soon. He circles back. He hands me a rectangular package in tartan wrapping paper. "Take this. It's the most watched video in the world," he says. *This man is giving me a copy of* Forrest Gump? "It's the life of Jesus." I beg off politely, claiming Judaic immunity. He drives on.

(Here's an interrupting thought: If your therapist calls to reschedule your appointment—as mine did just at the moment I finished writing this part of the story—and you make him laugh [as always], and if, in wrapping up, you say, "Well, I'll see you on Wednesday at twelve-thirty then," and he responds, "I'm looking forward to it," is that bad?)

I return to the inn, now wreathed in the kind of Christmas-in-New-England-Warm-Hearthed-Cheery verisimilitude that Ralph Lauren would burn down a synagogue to achieve. Nat King Cole's Christmas album plays at tooth-loosening decibels. I go upstairs and continue reading the new Truman Capote biography.

The inn starts to fill up with families and couples who have come for Christmas Eve dinner. Alone, Jewish, and awash in unkind thoughts about Christmas and the countryside as I am, I stay out of sight for the most part. I can hear general revelry and prandial merriment coming from the dining room.

Finally, I head directly into the Bar of Golf Pillows. Annie is there with a couple. "Merry Christmas, Dave," she greets me. A retired airline pilot sits at the bar enjoying a decidedly un–New England cocktail with an orange slice, maraschino cherry, and pineapple spear crowding the glass. The bartender is a woman in a sweater knit with a portrait of a family of snowpeople. The wife of the couple also wears a sweater knit with a smiling, holly-festooned teddy bear. The husband presents Annie with a very well-rendered framed watercolor of a largemouth bass. It's really very good, and I say so. "Well, we'll put it here to keep you company," says Annie, propping the frame up on the bar stool next to mine. I make sure to look at it attentively, my face frozen into the Art Appreciation rictus, until Annie and the couple go into the dining room. Uncricking my neck, I order a steak and a red wine.

"Are you the Writer?" the bartender asks me.

The Writer. Finally. Despite the fact, or precisely because this is just what I wanted, I reply, my voice far too bright, "Oh god, no. I'm a complete idiot."

She doesn't entirely know how to take this. She gives me the careful half smile one levels at a very large, possibly erratic dog.

The pilot is the anti-me. A man so utterly comfortable with himself that he can drink a cocktail with no fewer than three different pieces of fruit in it and still seem the very picture of adulthood. He talks awhile about fixing up houses. It's what he does in his retirement. His voice is velvet soft and Atticus Finch authoritative, but there's a sad whiff of mortality—a smell of old leaves underneath everything he speaks of. It's a bit like watching *This Old House* hosted by Baudelaire.

The pilot leaves fairly early in the evening. I hope he has somewhere to go. Then again, I think, I don't have anywhere to go, why am I so concerned with the imagined loneliness of a total stranger? Then again *again,* I actually am somewhere. I am sitting in a bar of a New England inn on Christmas Eve. I am the Writer, eating a steak, drinking alone, talking to the bartender. And, even though I loathe animals, I lazily toss bits of popcorn to Charlie as he sits at the foot of my bar stool.

It's just me and the bartender and my faithful dog. Plus my date the largemouth bass, whom I've been ignoring. I fairly drip with authenticity now. I have let go of my paranoia about being scrutinized. I feel completely comfortable. So comfortable, in fact, that, inexplicably, I find myself asking the bartender if there's either a synagogue or a gay bar in Jaffrey. I clearly feel the need to out myself to her in every possible way. Why stop there, I wonder, and not just go ahead and ask if there's a Canadian consulate nearby?

She keeps refilling my wine glass as we talk. She cuts me an enormous piece of baklava. More popcorn for the dog. I have a mountain to climb in the morning, damnit.

My reverie is undone by the strange series of glottal kecks and surds coming from below. I look down to Charlie Dog, whose neck is arching forward and back in an ominously regular, reverse peristaltic fashion. I find the words, as my voice Dopplers up to a fairly effeminate and vaguely hysterical pitch: "I think this dog might be getting sick. . . . This dog is getting sick. The dogissick. . . . OHMIGODTHEDOGISSICK!!!"

Charlie vomits out a small viscous puddle for which, from my quick and queasy perusal, I am largely responsible. The bartender cleans it up without a second glance.

Thoroughly unmasked, I settle up for dinner and take myself upstairs to sleep. And to all a good night.

The climb hardly bears mentioning. It was fairly awful; cold, slippery, kind of arduous in the middle of an ice storm. Although kind of monochromatically silvery pale and glamorous at the top.

We are climbing with two of Larry's friends. It's three men and a baby. But what's striking is how ready they are to include me as one of the guys. "I gave Patty her Christmas present last night," Larry tells us. "My tongue still hurts."

Later, he asks us: "Hey, what's the difference between oral sex and anal sex? Oral sex'll make your whole day and anal sex'll make your whole week."

I am amazed. This is not really much of a joke at all, more of an observation, I think, and I find its relaxed, surprisingly positive attitude toward anal penetration a complete eye-opener.

"I don't get it," says one friend.

"It'll make your hole weak. Your H-O-L-E W-E-A-K. Get it?"

Oh. Good thing I didn't call forth a hearty "I'll say it will!"

A lot of the talk focuses on "1028s." (*"Think we'll see any 1028s?" "She was a real 1028." "All we need is some 1028s to make this a perfect Christmas."*) 1028 is code for babes.

I realize that everything about me, my inappropriate footwear, my effete lexicon, my unfamiliarity with such natural phenomena as trees, rock, and ice, are met with great equanimity and good grace. They're friendly. It becomes quite clear to me that the only one casting strange glances of disapproval my way is me.

At the summit, I made Larry take my picture a number of times. When the film comes back, I will look at the photos of myself, scanning them for evidence. Looking for the face of an adult. The face of a man who climbs mountains. The face of a Dave.

On the nightclub door:
All Exits Are Final.—M.O'D.

The Million Millionaires March

MICHAEL RUBINER

WASHINGTON, D.C.—They came by Audi. They came by BMW. They came by limousine and by private helicopter. On a damp, drizzly fall day, tens of thousands of men and women from across the country converged on the Mall today for the first-ever Million Millionaires March. It was a day of repentance, healing, and resurrection—a day of sharing in the joy and the struggle that are part of being a millionaire in late-twentieth-century America.

"I came here to meet other people who also have a lot of money and are uncertain about how to spend it," Todd Eberhard, a Chicago hedge-fund manager, said, summing up the feelings of many here.

"We're a community in crisis," said Patricia Kuhn, a retiree from Boca Raton, Florida. "The old money looks down on the new money. Barney's is in Chapter Eleven. We're out golfing when we should be home with our kids."

From a podium set up at the foot of the Mall, speaker after speaker hammered home the themes of unity, pride, and responsibility. "Look around you: We are one million strong," Barry Siegel, the chairman of the President's Task Force on Millionaires, said to enthusiastic applause. "A million people times a million dollars—that makes a gazillion dollars."

"I know there are times when it's hard," said Reverend Bertram Potter, of Christ Church in Grosse Pointe, Michigan. "Some days, you want to say the heck with the Nasdaq and the museum benefits and the kidnapping insurance. But you've got to reach deep down inside yourself and find the strength to go on making money."

The millionaires overcame many hardships to be here. Some passed up important business meetings or long-anticipated wine tastings. Others had to fly on commercial airlines. But not even the dull gray sogginess of the day could dim their enthusiasm. "If we put all our money together, I'll bet we could buy a controlling interest in the sun and make it shine," one millionaire joked, braving a smile as he hugged his Hugo Boss jacket tightly across his chest.

The rally brought together a diverse group of millionaires from around the country. Some made their millions on Wall Street, others in technology, still others in the garment industry. Throughout a day of soul-searching, prayer, and celebration, they spoke of shared concerns like the volatility of world markets, Harvard's early admissions policy, and the nagging sense that, as one put it, "Paris has lost it."

For many, the day was one of spiritual awakening. William J. DeVry, a millionaire insurance executive from Atlanta, flew here in his Gulfstream, along with three of his golfing partners who are also millionaires. "We were jabbering all the way up," Mr. DeVry said, "sharing our experiences as millionaires. One of the guys talked about some problems he was having with a contractor who was renovating his house, and when he was through, there wasn't a dry eye in that plane. And that includes the pilot."

Others viewed the rally as a message of hope for future generations of millionaires. E. Bradley Hargrove, a millionaire from Sedona, Arizona, came here with his ten-year-old son, E. Bradley Jr., who is also a millionaire. "I wanted to show my son what this tax bracket is all about," said Mr. Hargrove. "It's not just about the Austin-Healey in the driveway and the second house with the heated bathroom tiles. It's also about caring."

But almost all agreed that the rally will have an impact only if people go home to their boardrooms and their country clubs and continue to organize and mobilize. "We have to spread the message to other millionaires in our community," said Tom Mannerling of New Canaan, Connecticut. "We have to tell them, 'You're a millionaire. This is the hand that life dealt you. What you do with it is up to you.'"

Wing Tsu

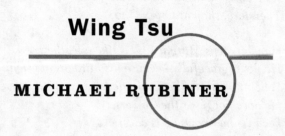

MICHAEL RUBINER

Scholars have long speculated that Lao Tsu, the revered sixth-century B.C. Chinese philosopher and author of the *Tao Te Ching*, had a younger brother, but they never suspected that he was one of ancient China's most brilliant ad men. Now, a recently discovered cache of scrolls, notebooks, and storyboards reveals that Wing Tsu was nearly as important a figure in the commercial sector as his brother was in the realm of philosophy.

Wing's career choice greatly displeased his family, who had hoped that, like his brother, he would go into academic life. Instead, he opted to major in marketing, and soon afterward found work at a small ad agency. The writing of his early campaigns hewed to the rather formal style of the era.

> *Nothing good can come of boasting,*
> *Nothing noble can come of greed.*
> *But feeling clean has ten thousand rewards.*
> *Therefore, buy Zeal.*

What is a sane man?
One who sells at market price.
What is a crazy man?
One who will give you five pounds of free bean curd
If he can't beat your best deal.
Therefore, shop at Crazy Cho's.

He who owns Mutual Life is like a feather.
He floats gracefully because his burdens are light.
When he falls to the earth, he lands gently.
He does not resist the universe,
because he knows he is covered.

What is the way of the sage?
It is the way of listening.
What is the way of the Big Bubble?
It is the way of chewing.

As Wing gained more confidence, he began to experiment with new modes of expression. For example, he was one of the pioneers of attack advertising.

The competition says they'll get your package there faster.
Yet he who hurries often stumbles,
And forgets to watch for bandits along the road.
We take it slow,
and thus always arrive on time.

Ours will make your dishes sparkle;
Theirs will leave a film.
Ours costs only pennies per wash;
Theirs will cause great financial hardship.
Thus, ours is the way of Virtue.
Theirs the way of Disgrace.

In later years, Wing moved up to a larger, more prestigious agency, where he worked on "glamour" accounts like perfume and cigarettes. During this period, he developed a new style— shorter, punchier, and more inventive—that would permanently alter the course of advertising.

Come on down
To Tranquility country.
Come on down
To Emperor Lights.

Skin like porcelain;
She casts off selfishness.
Maybe tonight—
Passion.

You'd look more Virtuous in a pair of Ranchers.

Just let go.

As Wing was reaching the top of his profession, he began to grow disillusioned. He became convinced that he'd frittered his life away on a spiritually empty enterprise, and was filled with remorse for having spurned his family's advice. Though he continued to work, his tone became increasingly sour.

Be young,
Have fun;
It will not last.

Style?
We have it.
Luxury?
Right here, my friend.
Performance?

Look no further . . .
Well—have you found happiness yet?

Jade—because you're nothing.

In his final years, Wing renounced commercial advertising and dedicated himself to writing public service announcements and political messages. This work, he noted in his diary, restored his sense of self-worth and inner harmony. What follows are among his last known campaigns.

The sage is not seduced by easy money.
He does not stand on street corners
Or roam the land with flashy youths.
The sage honors his parents—
He stays in school.

When a ruler is cruel,
He takes everything he can.
When a ruler is wise
He lets the people give freely.
Therefore, vote no on Proposition 11.

T. S. Eliot Interactive

MICHAEL RUBINER

Let us go then

> *Click on one*
> you and I
> the three of us
> just the men

> *Click on one*
> When the evening is spread out against the sky
> When the morning is spread out against the sky
> Around noon

Like a patient etherized upon a table;
Let us go,

> *Click on one*
> through certain half-deserted streets
> through the souks of Marrakech
> through the fourth dimension

The muttering retreats
Of restless nights

> *Click on one*
> in one-night cheap hotels

in the Sultan's Palace
in Foo Ching's opium den

Click on one
And sawdust restaurants with oyster-shells
And a State Dinner for the Russian Ambassador
And a Brooklyn steakhouse that's a reputed mob
    hangout

Streets that follow

Click on one
like a tedious argument of insidious intent
to a secret passageway, where the Prince and his
    monkey are hiding out
to an abandoned building, sometime in the post-
    apocalyptic future, where a gun battle is raging

To lead you to an overwhelming question. . . .
Oh, do not ask,

Click on one:
"What is it?"
"Where are the jewels?"
"Have you ever flown one of these babies before?"

Let us go and make our visit

In the room the

Click on one
women
K.G.B. agents
androids

come and go
Talking of

> *Click on one*
> Michelangelo
> Detective Jack Lowry
> Spork
> Sir Gowanus
> Abu

I grow old . . . I grow old . . .
I shall

> *Click on one*
> wear the bottoms of my trousers rolled
> launch a nuclear strike
> enter the Cave of Doom
> invade Carthage
> go back for the boy

Shall I part my hair behind? Do I dare to

> *Click on one*
> eat a peach?
> use the flame thrower?
> use the harpoon?
> use the immobilizing ray?

I have heard the mermaids singing, each to each
I do not think that they will

> *Click on one*
> sing to me
> blow up Santiago's underwater laboratory
> find the Seventh Scroll
> rescue Princess Naftiya
> return to the present
> save the inhabitants of Zoltar 5

We have lingered in the chambers of the sea

By sea-girls wreathed with seaweed red and brown
Till human voices wake us, and we

> *Click on one*
> drown
> go to another poem
> end session

Buy Me

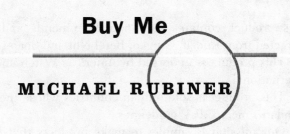

MICHAEL RUBINER

No animals have been used in the testing or manufacture of this product.

This product contains no trans-fatty acids, saturated fats or partially hydrogenated oils.

This product is rbGH-free.

One percent of our profits is donated to organizations that protect the rain forest.

Our packaging is made from 100 percent recycled paperboard and post-consumer recycled plastic.

This product is an excellent source of fiber and complex carbohydrates.

All of our ingredients are organically grown in soil that has been nurtured for at least three years without synthetic pesticides or herbicides.

We run a nonhierarchical, nonauthoritarian company.

★ ★ ★

Our packaging is tuna- and dolphin-safe.

This product does not in any way diminish the earth's topsoil.

513

All of our employees enjoy comprehensive health care benefits and free day care.

One percent of our profits goes toward establishing literacy programs for Salvadoran migrant workers.

This product contains rich natural minerals and nutrients extracted from Kudzu, Gingko, Betel Nut and Soapwort.

This product is endorsed by Americas Watch and Amnesty International.

This product is sold only in countries whose fuel emission standards meet E.P.A. guidelines.

Our mission is simple: to make products that honor and sustain our natural world.

The Coltsfoot Leaves, Burdock Root and Babassu Oil utilized in this product have been gathered through sustainable environmental practices by native peoples.

This is an official product of Farm Aid.

One percent of our profits goes toward lobbying Congress to ban private automobiles from major urban areas.

This product is PABA-free.

Our employees are encouraged to refrain from using shampoo and dishwashing liquid.

We own and operate the largest laboratory-rat sanctuary in North America.

There is absolutely no fat in this product.

This product contains Mandrake Root and Calendula, which the native peoples of Papua, New Guinea, have used for centuries to cleanse and purify the colonic tract.

This product is phosphate-free, dye-free, noncorrosive and nonabrasive.

Bob Geldof gives out this product for Christmas.

The Trout Excretions, Sand and Watermelon Compost contained in this product can provide a healthier skin tone and increased mobility.

Our mission is simple: to promote sustainable environmental practices, support the survival of indigenous peoples and cleanse and purify the colonic tract.

This fat-free product is distributed only at stores whose parent corporations support equality in the workplace, gender- and race-neutral language and a retrial for Leonard Peltier.

Our employees come to work only when they feel like it.

One percent of our profits goes toward lobbying the Federal Government to convert private golf courses to low-income housing.

This is an official product of the Sting World Tour.

Our mission is simple: to achieve total wellness and world peace through the healing agents contained in Bee Juice, Coconut Hair and Papaya Mold, all of which are also excellent colon-flushers.

In accordance with the religious practices of indigenous cultures, all of the ingredients used in this product have been approved by tribal shamans.

We encourage our employees to come to work naked.

Our packaging can be used in a variety of casseroles. See side panel for recipes.

We welcome the underprivileged to come live in our factory.

Every year, we convert our profits into the currency of a different developing nation, charter a fleet of gliders and scatter the currency over that nation's most impoverished areas.

Our employees live in biodegradable grass huts and survive by foraging for fiber on the savannah.

We're actually losing money on this product, but we hope we're at least making a difference.

This product is Pareve for Passover.

Our mission is simple: this planet allows us to bring you this product, and we, in turn, must respect the planet's integrity. That's a covenant we take seriously. If you are interested in adopting a laboratory rat, we have a wide selection of species and colors to choose from. Send for your free catalogue (printed on recycled recycling bins). For thousands of millenniums, indigenous peoples have known about the colon-cleansing qualities of Jojoba Cheese and Fig Warts. By reducing your intake of fat, sodium and nitrates and adopting an all-fiber diet, you can play an important part in bringing down infant mortality rates in the sub-Sahara. Every year, scores of delicate ecosystems are destroyed in order to build golf courses for overweight, alcohol-dependent members of the power elite. Feel free to write to us for more information. Or better yet, come live with us.

Rejected Celebrity Cab Announcements

BILL SCHEFT

[In 1997, all New York City taxicabs were equipped with pre-recorded announcements from various celebrities reminding passengers to buckle their seatbelts and ask the driver for a receipt. Some well-known Gotham-associated personalities—Mayor Giuliani, Judd Hirsch, Dr. Ruth, Joe Torre, Jackie Mason, Adam West—got the gig. Others auditioned and were never heard from again. Until now.]

Hi, this is Ron Pallilo. You may remember me as Horshack from the hit television series, *Welcome Back, Kaplan*. I'm an actor, but the role I'm always playing is that of a safe passenger. That's why when I'm not on the stage, I like to—.

"Hey, Pallilo, table six needs ice water!"

Right there, Mr. Ronasi. . . . Before I remind you to buckle your seat belts, may I tell you about tonight's specials?

This is Don Imus. Look, you never know when one of these hideous, fundamentalist, turban-wearing, curry-drenched weasels might start having sex with a goat in the front seat and wind up driving on the sidewalk, so remember to buckle your seat belt. And remember I'm not a racist, I'm a satirist. Big difference. Huge difference. Like the difference between regular store-bought salsa and salsa from the Auto Body Express. Hang on and my brother Fred will take your order.

Hi, I'm Shosanna Lowenstein, former girlfriend of Jerry Seinfeld. What is the deal with guys who can't commit? Why do they call it a commitment? Do I look like a mental institution? And why do they call it cradle-robbing when you not only don't own a cradle, but haven't slept in one in, like, over five years? And why would anyone rob a cradle? Are they valuable?

Is that Bendel's? Let me out here.

This is Jimmy Breslin. Carmella Entonces stood on the platform at Fifty-first Street, waiting for anything uptown. It was 4:00 A.M., and she had once again cleaned what seemed like every office in the Citicorp building. Once again, she had made less than what the lowest Citicorp suit clears during his second latte. Once again, she had walked the dark three blocks, down darker stairs, fueled by that rare mixture of exhaustion and pride that drives the single two-job working mother in the slice of fair territory between destitution and hope. Here on the platform at Fifty-first Street. If everything broke right for her, and it would be the first time since Christmas 1969, when she was seven, Carmella Entonces would make it home to 1021 Grand Concourse and have an hour to herself, an hour of peace, before her five children, ages four to nineteen, were up sniffing for breakfast. This morning, she would get her hour, but there would be only four children.

Some people never get to ride in a cab.

Hello, I'm Michael Feinstein. You know, before he died, whenever I would leave Ira Gershwin's apartment, on Seventy-second and Lex, he would say, "Check your seat for any personal belongings you may have left behind." And we'd always laugh. His words live on today, although I'm sure he hates the acoustics in here.

My name is John Gotti, Jr. Listen, pal, if you are going to run a successful plumbing-supply business, which is the business I took over from my father, the plumbing-supply business, you should be concerned with safety. Even if you are not in the plumbing-supply business, you should be concerned with safety. I'm not saying I'm not in the plumbing-supply business, because I am, I'm just saying that you, you, hey, over here, you should be concerned with your safety. Especially you, *capece?* This is not a threat. If this was a threat, you'd need more than that seat belt.

By the way, we never had this conversation.

Hello, this is Salman Rushdie. People often ask me, "Hey, what's it like having a million-dollar death threat hanging over your head for the last ten years?" And I tell them it's like getting in a cab and not buckling your seat belt, putz.

Yeah, like I'm going to get into a cab in New York. Right. Oh, if anyone wants to kill me, I'll be in seat G-118 at *Ragtime* tomorrow night, and then a late supper downtown at Nader, the Persian restaurant on Park and Twenty-ninth. Ask for Mr. Verses.

This is Linda Tripp. Check, one. Check, one-two. Check. Check. Can you hear me, Ken? Check. Check, one. This is Linda Tripp. Hello, hello? Check. *It's raining men . . . Hallelujah, it's raining men. . . .* Check, one-two. Hello, Ken? How are the levels? Are the levels OK? OK? OK? *Once I had a secret love. . . .* Ken? Ken? Ken? Ken? *Ken't buy me love -ove, love -ove. . . .* Check, check one-two. Abel, Baker, Charlie, Don't forget to buckle your—check, check-one, check. This is Linda Tripp. Hello?

You are Jay McInerney. You get in a cab. You think about buckling your seat belt. You think about asking the driver to take you down to The Tunnel and trying to score some blow and at least one model. You remember it's the late nineties, there's no more Tunnel, no more blow, so you ask for a receipt instead. You wish to God you could stop talking in the second person.

Look, the only reason I'm doing this is because my dog thought it would be good for my career. So, I listened. Then I find out everybody's making money off this except me. Schmuck. But I'll be a good sport. Buckle up. . . . Oh yeah. This is David Berkowitz.

This is Leona Helmsley. Don't forget to demand a receipt, and then send it to me. Now shut up and drive.

Conspir-U.S.-cy History

BILL SCHEFT

First of all, I am not going to fall for your tricks. I will not be lured out of my ironclad ideological hole and into your mind-bending snare. But I need the money, so I'll fill your space.

The entire history of the United States never happened. Never happened spontaneously, that is. It was all staged. All an elaborate 222-year ruse to distract you and me (well, you, not me) while an unseen force from the Unknown Galaxy makes untold riches pulling the marionette strings on its earthly ally.

By the way, if you're paying attention, 222 is one third of 666.

You'd love to know what I know. I have all the data, and all the documentation, but I refuse to feed your "lawyers" and "experts" who will spin my logic in the centrifuge of so-called "rational thought." Whose rational thought? Yours? THE MEDIA'S? What, and leave show business?

However, for the sake of discourse and because, like I said, I need the money, I will indulge you slightly. Ask yourself these questions, and let yourself see, if you dare, the pattern that emerges:

- Why on the *original* Declaration of Independence—
the one nobody can seem to find anymore—does the
flourish under John Hancock's signature look like a Nike
swoosh?
- Why did John Hancock die without life insurance?
- Why were **the French** so nice to us during the revolution
and so rude since?
- Is it just a coincidence that the last thing eyewitnesses
heard Alexander Hamilton say to Aaron Burr was, "Now,
you're sure this will get me on the ten?"
- We all know tobacco was America's first cash crop. How
come everyone in **France** still smokes and no one gets
sick?
- Why, in the middle of a battle, does Francis (pronounced
France-iss) Scott Key write a song he knows is not nearly
as good as "America the Beautiful"? (And we're not even
talking about the Ray Charles version.)
- How come there's a first draft of the shooting script for
Gone with the Wind registered with the Writers' Guild
and dated April 1859?
- Why does the Statue of Liberty (a gift from **France**) have
its torch perfectly aligned with Neptune? Or do you think
it's just cute that "immigrants" are now called "aliens"?
- How come the Native Americans in California, who'd
lived on the land for centuries, never found gold, but
some idiot from New Jersey with a pick and a pan did?
- Why was a man fitting Walt Disney's description seen
sneaking into an ice wagon near Anaheim in 1884, seventeen years before he was "born."
- How come the first airplane flight didn't take place until
1903, over three thousand years *after* the first kosher
meal?
- Why do sequels traditionally fail, yet World War II made
much more money than World War I?
- And while we're on the subject, how come every vaca-
tioning foreign tourist left Hawaii on December 6, 1941,

despite the fact that the cheaper air fare required a Saturday night stay?

- Why would a guy trying to prove he wasn't a spy keep the name Alger Hiss?
- How come the Korean War lasted four years, but *M*A*S*H* lasted eight?
- If there really was a cold war, as reported, why do you suppose that of the six men who each knew one number of the combination of the safe that contained the recipe for Coca-Cola, three of them spoke Russian? And all of them spoke **French**?
- And why, in the list of ingredients on a can of Coke, is nerve gas never included?
- Am I the only one who, when he saw the "moon landing," noticed the Paramount water tower in the corner of "outer space"?
- Why was the Gulf War so conveniently scheduled during February sweeps?
- How come Linda Tripp has the exact same jowls as Nixon?
- Why is soccer popular everywhere else in the world but the United States?
- Why is Jerry Lewis popular in **France**?
- What country won this year's World Cup?

This was too easy. And now, if you'll excuse me, I have to deactivate the land mines the Department of the Interior planted under my living room rug while I wrote this.

(By the way, you didn't hear any of this from me.)

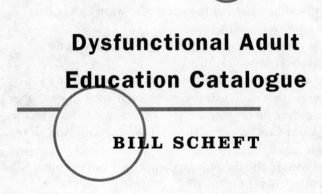

Dysfunctional Adult Education Catalogue

BILL SCHEFT

MAKING YOUR COMBOVER WORK

Why should guys in Congress have all the luck? Why waste hundreds of dollars on remedies that work? It's your hair—play with it!

Starting your part too high? How about a little lower? Say, your armpit. This is just one of countless techniques of follicle chicanery at the fingertips of world-renowned combover maven, **Martin Reznick**. Reznick has toured the country (on non-windy days) helping hundreds turn male-pattern baldness into male-pattern badness. Seats are limited. Don't let your hair be stranded!

(Course fee $59. Special eighteen-tooth styling rake, $10.)

ADVANCED SELF-ABSORPTION— GATEWAY TO FREEDOM

Where is the incentive to getting in touch with your feelings if you're going to feel lousy once you get in touch? You've tried everything—shrinks, meditation, motivational tapes—how about grandiosity and delusional entitlement? Under the self-involved tutelage of **Missy Bornstein,** owner/operator/founding diva of The Narcissus Institute, you will come to believe, glee-fully, that it *is* all about you. Learn how to live in a future founded on unreal expectations, how to make everyone else extras in the movie of your life, and how to bask in a world where your only responsibility is assigning blame.

(Course fee $99, special 50 percent discount if you say "Why should I have to pay $99?" 100 percent off if you say to Missy Bornstein, "I had no idea Sharon Stone was teaching this course.")

RIGHTEOUS ANGER—POISON OR ANTIDOTE?

What's better than being right? Am I right? Well, in this one-time-only-this-month seminar, celebrated Euro-crackpot **Dr. Sven Issacssonlund** will go one better as he extols the virtues of being angry about being right. For too long, justifiable rage has been the haven of megalomaniacs and the criminally insane. Turns out, it's available to anyone with the discipline and tenacity to hang on to otherwise petty, long-forgotten resentments. Help pay Dr. Issacssonlund's legal fees as he demonstrates techniques in Selective Visualization that will enable the most diligent student to rocket past the righteous anger—all the way to Self-Pity and Victimization.

(Course fee $39. Bonus offer: $59 for this course, and next month's seminar: "Self-Pity and Victimization: Everybody Can Be Wrong.")

PIPE DOWN! CRACK IN MODERATION

Finally, a cheap high, and it's immediately condemned as hope-lessly addictive and potentially fatal. Well, that's just the opinion of the medical community, and we all know what spoilsports they can be. "Don't knock it till you've tried it, once a week." That's the credo of your vial-melier, **Edgar "Bic" Willis,** who will show you how to score some product, then some willpower.

(Course fee: Free. Supplies: $10–$5000. No cops.)

EARN UNTOLD $$$$$–AS A BEARD

If you're a single woman and willing to admit that all the good men are married or gay, you are more than ready to cash in on the fastest-growing second job market in the country—escort for closeted homosexuals. You know the stats: Over thirty and unattached, the odds are overwhelmingly against a trip down the aisle, but they've never been better for a free trip to the theater—or the deposit button on your ATM machine! All you need is a couple of nice outfits and our two-hour seminar co-lectured by **Shauna Wishner** (thirty minutes of "Do's") and **Ariel Euridice** (an hour and a half of "Don'ts"). The money you make your very first month helping others live a lie will afford you an upscale sham life of your own. It's nobody's business, but it could be your livelihood.

(Course fee: $69. "Priceless" makeup and hair tips from Ariel: $20.)

QUADRUPLE YOUR INCOME–BECOME A RIGHT-WING BLOND ON TV

Sitting at home with no real opinions on important issues? Shame on you. You could be making the nightly cable rounds as a female conservative political analyst. Here's the beauty part: You need not be a conservative. You need not be a real blond. The only requirement: You must be ditsy, or at the very least, willing to be ditsy. Why? The liberal guys who run television dig that. Like, duh. In fact, if you can say "duh" to any pointed question on policy, agenda, or constitutional law, you're as good as in. Your instructor, self-acclaimed right-wing blowhard **Marissa "Bicky" Harrington,** will empty her fanny pack of insight based on almost two years of experience as a clueless gadfly. She'll help you start a phony conservative newsletter for some fast sham legitimacy. She'll teach you the hair flip, the "tcch" sound and that pained, bored expression when the panel goes nuts with the polysyllabic words. There's not much more. Oh yeah, you're pro-life. Remember that.

(*Course fee: $99. Additional one-hour intensive tutorial to learn a vague Eastern European accent: $500.*)

PUSHING YOUR PARENTS' BUTTONS

Sorry, Mom and Dad, game over.

You've patiently waited until they're well into their sixties, now it's time to turn the tables. What if one day, *you* were suddenly the manipulator, the guilt inducer, the steady, toxic drumbeat of negativity? Sounds like fun? You bet!

Why be passive, when after one two-hour class, you can be passive-aggressive?

Dr. John Duris, in addition to being one of the country's leading authorities on transference and the family dynamic, has been driving his parents nuts since he took his first undergraduate psych course. Author of the best-selling book, *You Two Won't Be Happy Until I Die Before You,* Dr. Duris will show you not only how to uninstall the buttons your folks put in at birth, but rewire them back to the source. Pound away at abandonment issues until they run from the room. Constantly hark back to slights and scars two decades old! Don't have any? Make some up! Your parents wouldn't dare contest your version of the facts. Not after what they've put you through. Don't let yourself be neglected for another second, even if you haven't been. Take the first step. Get Dad to pay for this class.

(*Course fee: $99. Optional last will rewrite kit: $39.*)

TEASING THE AMISH

Pennsylvania Dutch country is breathtaking and serene, but what kind of vacation is that unless you can blow off some steam? The Amish are peace loving, deeply spiritual people who live in a much simpler time—they're asking for it. Our most popular course is back, and our most popular instructor, **Carmine Ciccarelli** (author of *Thou Suck,* Vol. I–VI) has cooked up five hundred more of his patented Amish taunts. We'll give you only one: "Hey, what about a battery-operated vibrator? Anything wrong with that, Jebeddiah, you black-hatted hump?" You'll have to sign up for the rest.

(*Course fee: $29. First fifty to enroll receive Ciccarelli's patented "Amish Wooden Condom."*)

STALKING IN THE NEW MILLENNIUM

Still making calls at two o'clock in the morning and hanging up? Still sending threatening letters through, hah, regular mail? Stop trying to live out your psychosexual fantasies in the 1980s and become stalk-of-the-art. Your instructor, **Damien Fisk,** has the knowledge, computer skills, and a full range of low-cost, hi-tech surveillance devices to put you in the action, yet far enough away to not violate a restraining order. Damien stakes his two-thousand-page FBI file and twenty years of mind-game experience harassing ex-girlfriends, ex-bosses, and ex-shrinks on your complete satisfaction. Don't reject this offer! Damien hates rejection. . . .

(*Course fee: $99. Smokers welcome.*)

BABY-TALK YOUR WAY THROUGH AN IRS AUDIT

They're trained to deal with embezzlers, racketeers, thieves, liars, and con artists. But IRS agents have no timetable for infantilism. Why should an audit be stressful for you when it can be annoying and uncomfortable for the feds? **Dr. Jeremy Bratz,** who pioneered his method of regressive adaptation in the best-selling book, *Baby Talk Your Way Through Med School,* and the follow-up works, *Baby Talk Your Way In AND Out of an Extramarital Affair,* and *Baby Talk Your Way Back onto the Best-Seller List,* has applied the technique to its practical zenith. Have you ever explored pursing your lips and saying "Can't Unca Sam do better?" or "Make mean Mr. FICA go 'way   ." over and over again? How about stomping your feet, covering your ears, and "la la la-ing" during the capital gains schedule? After Dr. Bratz's ten-minute all-inclusive lecture and the accompanying six hours of practice tapes, the government will do anything to get you off its fiscal back.

(*Course fee: $99. Tapes: $199, with special 50 percent discount if you hold your breath for three minutes.*)

YOU'RE NOT IN DENIAL ENOUGH!

Susan Brophy, who taught last semester's third-most-popular seminar, "Clutter? What Clutter? I Don't See Any Clutter," is back with an expanded approach to erasing all of life's problems. Like Ms. Brophy, the route to bliss is comprehensive, but simple: twenty-four-hour-a-day denial. After a weekend of research, Ms. Brophy uncovered a startling fact: People tend to say "I didn't do it" and "It's not my fault" only when they mean it! In just forty-five minutes, you realize those phrases are always there for you, and other gems, such as "I never said that," "You never said that," "You must be mistaken," "I've never seen you before," and "So what?" And we're not even talking about that bellwether classic: not saying anything and walking away!

It's all here. If you don't believe the answers are all here, you're just not being honest with yourself. And that's a great start!

(*Course fee: $59, $39 if you say you're signing up "for a friend."*)

FOOD POISONING—NATURE'S DIET

You've tried everything else, how about a piece of two-day-old, out-of-town sushi? Get that weight off and keep it off—food-poison yourself once a week. You'll look great, after the first twenty-four hours, and, as an added bonus, you'll have others feeling sorry for you. Self-appointed "nut-tritionist," **Dr. Wayne Weil (not his real name)** will customize an eating plan based on one or all of his Four Basic Boot Groups—expired dairy, tainted meat, spoiled fruits and vegetables, and rancid grains. Remember, it's not an eating disorder if it looks like bad luck.

(Course fee: $59. "Just call me 'Wyatt Earp'" T-shirts, $15. Available in medium only. Sorry.)

(Available next semester)

TAE-BO FENG-SHUI

Register early and get in on this brand-new ancient Chinese martial art of interior design! Using only your hands and feet, trash a hotel room, your boss's office, or your in-laws' china cabinet in the name of balance and harmony.

(Course fee: $2,500. Includes $2,441 security deposit.)

Gardening Advice
from Mertensia Corydalis

Q: *Dear Miss Corydalis: We're so relieved that you are back. We heard rumors that you had been lost in a ballooning accident. Our zucchini vines are suddenly turning mushy, the leaves wilting and dying. Help!*

— NELSON AND BOB, MT. ASHFORD

A: Dear Nelson and Bob: The ballooning mishap has been greatly exaggerated. There was a sudden down draft and I lost a very nice hat to the prevailing winds, but we recovered our altitude quickly. On your zucchini: I want all of you out there to close your eyes and conjure up the flavor of zucchini in your mind. Now try to describe it. Can't do it, can you? Now, why did you plant a vegetable that has no flavor, reaches behemoth proportions if not plucked off the vine in its infancy, and which, in the end, no one wants? You will find yourself collecting recipes for zucchini muffins and chocolate zucchini cake, sending your partner off to the office with loaves of zucchini bread to give away. But to answer your question, the vines are being destroyed from the inside by the larvae of the squash vine borer. You might save some of the plants by applying a *Bacillus thuringiensis kurstaki* dust, which is a bacteria that destroys the larvae, but not you or good insects like ladybugs. More effective is to purchase a hypodermic syringe and inject a solution of the Btk into the stalk of the vine (but do you really want to face a pharmacist with this cock-and-bull story?).

Or, you can do nothing. Just yank out the plants, sneak them into the rubbish bin (don't spread the problem to your compost pile), and your friends and colleagues will stop avoiding you all summer.

Q: Dear Mertensia: I'd appreciate advice to a beginning composter.

—DANIELLE, ITALIAN VILLAGE

A: Welcome to our fold, Danielle! Good compost is like rocket fuel when applied to your plants. There is never enough of it, and you will find yourself rationing it, giving a little extra to your favorites. Don't bother with tedious recipes for layering brown and green vegetation. You are not making a pousse café. Just toss in leaves, garden tidyings, the salad ingredients you bought to start your new diet, now decomposing in the fridge as you revert to your usual fare of frozen lasagna. Bin or rough pile, no matter, time is on your side. Dig out from the bottom, throwing back big chunks. Eventually everything organic will compost, as will you. As will I.

Q: *We have planted a redwood tree in our growing collection of specimens. Do you have any cultural advice?*

—BUNNY, BIRWYCK

A: Dear Bunny: You have caught Miss Corydalis with her knickers down with this question, I've always considered the sequoia to be the domain of the Supreme Being and the California forestry department. I don't believe the redwood has been native to this part of the country and its climate and soil conditions in any recent geological epoch. However, consider where it grows, in the Pacific Northwest. I assume it requires rich, moist soil, relatively mild winters, and if you want it to grow straight and tall, full sun with no competition from surrounding trees. Plant it and jump back. In four or five hundred years, you will really have something there.

Next time . . . make a hypertufa
trough for your alpines

The All-Purpose
Concession Speech

BILL SCHEFT

First of all, this is not a concession speech. I don't like the word *concession*. I prefer *confirmation*. I'm here to confirm that we did not win. The people have spoken. Fine. I just wish they had spoken before I went $500,000 into debt kissing ass. And let me tell you something about kissing ass: It ain't kissing ass if you win. If you win, it's brilliantly targeted campaigning.

Apparently, I overestimated the people. Thought they were a little brighter, a little more savvy, a little less content with their aimless, misbegotten lives. The people are the real losers. And you know something? I suspected they were losers before I even got into this race. But sometimes, I think with my heart, not my head. If that's a crime, throw me in jail and let me make some guy a nice girlfriend.

In my six months of active campaigning (who's around from Memorial Day to Labor Day that really matters?), I learned many things. I learned that chicken can be prepared 147 different ways, all dry. I learned that it's good to remember your wife's name when you're introducing her in front of 500 women. I learned that when voters say they care about the issues, they really mean "Do you have any free stuff, like a T-shirt or a baseball cap?" I learned that the president can get sex from an unpaid worker, but I can't get a volunteer to wash my car. And I learned that if you borrow money from the mob, the interest is fifteen points a week, every week, and they don't want to hear anything about the federal government being late with matching funds.

I know a lot of people will say my performance in last week's debate was the turning point. First of all, nobody told me you had to dress up. Informal debate. That's what they said. I mean, it was a clean jogging suit. And OK, maybe I could have come up with a better rebuttal than "Hey, whatever. . . ." But it got a nice laugh the first time, so I went with it.

My opponent ran an admirable campaign. He didn't kill anybody. Not to my knowledge. There are still a lot of things we do not know about him. And you'd think you'd discover something about a guy after going through his garbage for nine months. Well, he's your problem now.

You know what my problem is? Jealousy. People have always been jealous of me. I am no better than you. And if I am, I don't let on. I'm very considerate that way. Can I help it if I'm a visionary, and you get shamelessly bamboozled by a haircut with a Stepford wife on his arm, and a tobacco lobbyist in each pocket? And by you, I mean the voters. I don't mean you, my staff. You just didn't work hard enough.

I would be remiss if I did not mention the unflagging support and optimism of my campaign manager. Hal, what can I say? Could you have possibly been more wrong about the sixth precinct? All night, I'm hearing, "Don't worry. The sixth precinct hasn't come in yet. They love you in the sixth precinct." You know that category "others," the candidates that they don't even bother to name? Well, "others" beat me in the sixth precinct. And Hal, that little secret between us about how you might be gay? Well, I might have told somebody. Oh, I'm sorry. Is this microphone on?

By the way, it's now a cash bar. Drinks are $10 each; $20 if you want ice. Knock yourself out.

•• NEWS QUIZ ••

3/8/99 "DEATH SENTENCE?"

Under pressure from the Federal Trade Commission, R. J. Reynolds will add a single sentence to each print ad for Winston. Saying what?

"Banned in California, but now qualifies as assisted-suicide device in Oregon."—Daniel Radosh

"Due to interference from the Federal Trade Commission, R. J. Reynolds regrets to announce that it will no longer include a free toy in every pack of Winstons."—Tim Carvell

"No cartoon camels were used in the marketing of this product."—Matt Sullivan

"These fine tobacco products can be comfortably smoked through a tracheotomy hole."
—Larry Amaros

"Smoke up: Delaware needs a new capitol building!"
—James Poniewozik

"Paid for by the Committee to Elect George W. Bush."—Ellen Macleay

"See you in court."   —Mary Anne Townsend

• RANDY'S WRAP UP •

After smoking a pack of Camels a day for a dozen years, I gave it up in 1985. I still miss it. Cigarettes stimulate thought, distract from woe, and require playing with matches. Cigarettes promote intimacy: What could be sexier than sharing a smoke, passing that small fire from hand to hand? Cigarettes impose form on your day; they are a means of demarcation: You smoke one after something and before something else. And they look so cool. I'd be smoking right now if it weren't for the part about the hideous respiratory illness and coughing away my life in a painful and protracted demise.

I intend to resume the habit as a delight of old age; my first Social Security check will just about cover the cost of a carton. Smoking will offer a reliable indoor pleasure that I can enjoy seated, much to be desired in my decripitude. And malignancy develops slowly. With a little luck, by the time I contract a fatal disease, I'll already be dead. You'd think instead of messing around with Winston, RJR would produce a brand they can market to old folks. Call it Golden One Hundreds. Use the slogan: Hey, Granny, feeling lucky?

DELIGHTFUL DOUBLE NEGATIVE ANSWER

"No additives in our tobacco does not mean a safer cigarette."

Winston's "no bull" ads proclaim that the cigarettes are 100 percent tobacco with no additives. RJR was shocked—shocked!—to learn that some might interpret this as a health claim. In the eighteen months since the campaign began, Winston's market share rose from 4.86 percent to 4.93 percent.

SUNDAY'S SERMONS IN REVIEW EXTRA

All preached yesterday in New York; none actually heard by News Quiz.

- "Better Than Evian" (Rev. Sharon Blackburn, Plymouth Church of the Pilgrims, Congregational)— promotional fee paid by Perrier. At last, sacred product placement.

- "Thirsty?!" (Rev. Dr. Dale D. Hansen, St. Luke's, Lutheran)—What would Jesus drink? Or the Rev. Sharon Blackburn?

- "Are There Any Rats in Your Cellar?" (Rev. Dr. Thomas K. Tewell, Fifth Avenue Presbyterian Church)—Either that's a metaphor, or the church has started a pest removal side line.

- "The Divine Maitre d' . . . " (Dr. J. Barrie Shepherd, First Presbyterian)—Would you ask the divine wine steward what goes with rats? And send over a bottle of Perrier.

COMMON DENOMINATOR:

winsomely toxic products

Front Row Center with
Thaddeus Bristol

DAVID SEDARIS

Trite Christmas: Scottsfield's young
hams offer the blandest of holiday fare

The approach of Christmas signifies three things: bad movies, unforgivable television, and even worse theater. I'm talking bone-crushing theater, the type our ancient ancestors used to oppress their enemies before the invention of the stretching rack. We're talking torture on a par with the Scottsfield Dinner Theater's 1994 revival of *Come Blow Your Horn*, a production that violated every tenet of the Human Rights Accord. To those of you who enjoy the comfort of a nice set of thumbscrews, allow me to recommend any of the crucifying holiday plays and pageants currently eliciting screams of mercy from within the confines of our local elementary and middle schools. I will, no doubt, be taken to task for criticizing the work of children but, as any pathologist will agree, if there's a cancer it's best to treat it as early as possible.

If you happened to stand over four feet tall, the agony awaiting you at Sacred Heart Elementary began the moment you took your seat. These were mean little chairs corralled into a "theater" haunted by the lingering stench of industrial-strength lasagna. My question is not why they chose to stage the production in a poorly disguised cafeteria, but why they chose to stage it at all. "The Story of the First Christmas" is an overrated clunker of a holiday pageant, best left to those looking to cure their chronic insomnia. Although the program listed no director, the apathetic staging suggested the limp, partially paralyzed hand of Sister Mary Elizabeth Bronson, who should have been excommunicated after last season's disastrous Thanksgiving program. Here again the first- through third-grade actors graced the stage with an enthusiasm most children reserve for a smallpox vaccination. One could hardly blame them for their lack of vitality, as the stingy, uninspired script consists, not of springy dialogue, but rather of a deadening series of pronouncements.

Mary to Joseph: "I am tired."
Joseph to Mary: "We will rest here for the night."

There's no fire, no give and take, and the audience soon grows weary of this passionless relationship.

In the role of Mary, six-year-old Shannon Burke just barely manages to pass herself off as a virgin. A cloying, preening stage presence, her performance seemed based on nothing but an annoying proclivity toward lifting her skirt and, on rare occasions, opening her eyes. As Joseph, second-grade student Douglas Trazzare needed to be reminded that, although his character did not technically impregnate the virgin mother, he should behave as though he were capable of doing so. Thrown into the mix were a handful of inattentive shepherds and a trio of gift-bearing seven-year-olds who could probably give the Three Stooges a run for their money. As for the lighting, Sacred Heart Elementary chose to rely on nothing more than the flashbulbs ignited by the obnoxious stage mothers and fathers who had created those zombies staggering back and forth across the linoleum-floored dining hall. Under certain circumstances parental pride is understandable but it has no place in the theater, where it tends to encourage a child to believe in a talent that, more often than not, simply fails to exist. In order for a pageant to work, it needs to appeal to everyone, regardless of their relationship to the actors onstage. This production found me on the side of the yawning cafeteria workers.

Pointing to the oversized crate that served as a manger, one particularly insufficient wise man proclaimed, "A child is bored."

Yes, well, so was this adult.

Ten-year-old Charles St. Claire showed great promise with last year's "Silent Falls the Snow." Now he's returned to the holiday well and, finding it empty, presents us with the rusty bucket titled "A Reindeer's Gift," currently running at Scottsfield Elementary. The story's sentimentality is matched only by its predictability and the dialogue fills the auditorium like an unrefrigerated boxcar of month-old steaks. The plot, if I may use that word so loosely, involves a boy named Jeremy (Billy Squires) who waits beside the family hearth for . . . guess who! When Santa eventually arrives, he chows down a few cookies and presents our hero with a stack of high-tech treasures. But Jeremy doesn't want gadgetry, he wants a reindeer. Strong-armed into submission, Santa agrees to leave behind his old warhorse Blitzen (played by a lumbering, disobedient Great Dane the program lists as "Marmaduke II"). Left alone with his rowdy charge, Jeremy struggles with his pea-sized conscience, finally realizing that "Maybe it's wrong to keep a reindeer cooped up in the storage space above my stepfather's den." What follows is a tearful good-bye lasting roughly the same length of time it takes a giant redwood to grow from seed to full maturity. By the time the boy returns the reindeer to Santa's custody, we no longer care whether the animal lives or dies. I was just happy he was hustled offstage before his digestive system could process and void the eighteen pounds of popcorn it took to keep the great beast from wandering off before his cue. At the risk of spoiling things for any of our retarded theatergoers, allow me to reveal that the entire Santa-reindeer encounter was nothing more than a dream. Our hero awakes full of Christmas spunk, a lesson is learned, blah, blah, blah.

The only bright spot in the entire evening was the presence of Kevin "Tubby" Matchwell, the eleven-year-old porker who tackled the role of Santa with a beguiling authenticity. The false beard tended to muffle his speech, but they could hear his chafing thighs all the way to the North Pole. Still, though, the overwrought production tended to mirror the typical holiday meal in that even the Butterball can't save the day when it's packed with too much stuffing.

Once again, the sadists at the Jane Snow-Hernandez Middle School have taken up their burning pokers in an attempt to prod *A Christmas Carol* into some form of submission. I might have overlooked the shoddy production values and dry, leaden pacing, but these are sixth-graders we're talking about and they should have known better. There's really no point in adapting this Dickensian stinker unless you're capable of looking beyond the novel's dime-store morality and getting to what little theatrical meat the story has to offer. The point is to eviscerate the gooey center but here it's served up as the entrée, and a foul pudding it is. Most of the blame goes to the director, eleven-year-old Becky Micheals, who seems to have picked up her staging secrets from the school's crossing guard. She tends to clump her actors, moving them only in groups of five or more. A strong proponent of trendy, racially mixed casting, Micheals gives us a black Tiny Tim, leaving the audience to wonder, "What, is this kid supposed to be adopted?" It's a distracting move, wrongheaded and pointless. The role was played by young Lamar Williams, who, if nothing else, managed to sustain a decent limp. The program notes that he recently lost his right foot to diabetes, but was that reason enough to cast him? As Tiny Tim, the boy spends his stage time essentially trawling for sympathy, stealing focus from even the brightly lit EXIT sign. Bob Cratchit, played here by the aptly named Benjamin Trite, seems to have picked up his Cockney accent from watching a few videotaped episodes of "Hee-Haw," and Hershel Fleishman's Scrooge was almost as lame as Tiny Tim.

The set was not without its charm but Jodi Lennon's abysmal costumes should hopefully mark the end of a short and unremarkable career. I was gagging from the smell of spray-painted sneakers and if I see one more top hat made from an oatmeal canister, I swear I'm going to pull out a gun.

The problem with all of these shows stems partially from their maddening eagerness to please. With smiles stretched tight as bungee cords, these hopeless amateurs pranced and gamboled across our local stages, hiding behind their youth and begging, practically demanding, we forgive their egregious mistakes. The English language was chewed into a paste, missed opportunities came and went, and the sets were changed so slowly you'd think the stagehands were encumbered by full-body casts. While billing themselves as holiday entertainment, none of these productions came close to capturing the spirit of Christmas. This glaring irony seemed to escape the throngs of ticketholders, who ate these undercooked turkeys right down to the bone. Here were audiences that chuckled at every technical snafu and applauded riotously each time a new character wandered out onto the stage. With the close of every curtain they leapt to their feet in one ovation after another, leaving me wedged into my doll-sized chair and wondering, "Is it just them, or am I missing something?"

Life is the process of spending everything you have.—M.O'D.

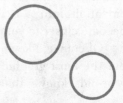

Humor Thy Father

STEPHEN SHERRILL

It's gotten so that you can't even watch the evening news with your family anymore. First it was the Starr report, and now each day brings us closer to hearings on the same tawdry subject matter. Before it's all over, millions of us will face the same dilemma: What about the parents? What do you tell them when they ask about Monica and Bill?

First, you should know that it's perfectly natural to feel uneasy talking about unconventional sex with your parents. I'll never forget the first time (last week) one of my parents asked me, "Son, what's a [vulgarism for oral sex]"? No child is prepared for that question. I hadn't expected to talk about that with my parents for years—perhaps ever.

Yet discussing this unfortunate situation doesn't have to be traumatic. In fact, with care and patience you can turn this sordid affair into a real learning opportunity and a chance to become closer to your parents.

Of course, like any responsible child, you should try to filter out the most graphic material. But anybody with two seventy-year-olds knows that's easier said than done—parents often enjoy watching news and other public-affairs programming, and the Starr documents are found in many of their favorite publications.

Likewise, watch what you say. Often, it may seem as though parents aren't listening—when they appear to have fallen asleep in their chair, for instance—but they take in more than you think. Especially avoid joking about the scandal in their presence, as you might find them innocently repeating your words at a dinner party without knowing what they mean.

Eventually, though, you have to accept that parents are going to pick up bits and pieces one way or another. If nothing else, they'll hear things about it from parents whose children aren't as vigilant as you. After all, you can't just keep them locked up in the house all day long.

Parents have a natural curiosity. So don't be surprised when they turn from their book clubs, volunteer work, or mall walking and begin asking those first awkward questions about raunchy sex in the Oval Office. When this happens, the most important thing is to be prepared. Parents are quite intuitive: they can tell when you're sickened or revolted. Avoid reactions like shuddering or groaning or staring at them with your mouth open, and do your best to remain calm and relaxed. When discussing dirty, smutty sex with my parents, I found sipping ginger ale, nibbling saltines, and sitting with my head between my legs while taking deep breaths all to be helpful.

And just because they're asking questions doesn't mean that they're ready for the answers. Don't give them more information than they're capable of processing. But also take the questions seriously—their elderly innocence is like an inborn lie detector. Be truthful, without being specific. An example:

PARENT: What's all this I keep hearing about a cigar?
YOU: Uh, wow, O.K., well, [Parent], the President was with Monica and he, uh, had a cigar.
PARENT: Did he smoke it?
YOU: No, Monica was just . . . holding it for him.

PARENT: Why was she holding it for him?

YOU: It's what two people do when they love each other. I have to go now. Goodbye.

Keep in mind that your parents will look to you for cues on what to think of these lewd, illicit sex acts. Assure them that these filthy, obscene activities aren't shameful—at least not *completely* shameful.

Finally, while creating an environment in which parents can question and explore, be sure to maintain control of the dialogue. If you do find it becoming too involved, pretend like you can't breathe, and start coughing violently. Their natural protective impulses will be triggered, and by the time they've fetched you some water and you've done the "I'm O.K., I'm O.K.," they'll probably have forgotten all about it and be on to something else.

If that fails, another method—which works best on older parents—is to say that you have no idea what they're talking about and they must have been dreaming. That should buy you a little time, anyway (in my case, four days). Of course, every family is different. With some, the coughing bit doesn't work, but telling them it's all just a new TV sitcom might do the trick. With others, a simple "I can't have this discussion—it's just too gross" will suffice.

The point is, when phrases like "to completion" and "the President indicated that Ms. Lewinsky should perform oral sex while he talked on the phone, and she obliged" are commonplace, we're clearly living in different times. We can't expect our parents to maintain their innocence forever. But if you handle this difficult stage with a little patience, a strong stomach, and a lot of love you'll find that your parents won't just be your parents. They'll be your best friends.

Khmer Roué

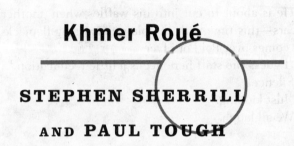

STEPHEN SHERRILL
AND PAUL TOUGH

Pol Pot has a problem. It is 11 A.M. on a warm, lazy California morning and he's having breakfast poolside at the Beverly Hills Hotel. The problem is that he ordered the flapjacks, and the waitress has just brought him the Belgian waffles. He looks down at the plate. His shoulders tighten. The waitress stutters an apology.

But then something unexpected happens: Pol Pot relaxes. He takes a breath. "It's O.K.," he tells the waitress. "I'll eat the waffles." As she walks away, the former leader of Cambodia chuckles. "There was a time," he admits, looking around for the syrup, "when I would have sent the waffles back. But things are different now."

Different, indeed. When Pol Pot ruled Cambodia, his staff knew better than to disappoint him. But in 1979, after four years of primitivist agrarian reform, he was driven from power and spent the next two decades waging a guerrilla war in the jungle of northern Cambodia, a period in his life that he now describes as "difficult." Earlier this year, word around the jungle was that Pol Pot was burned out, bitter. For too long, he'd stayed out of view, and, fame being the fickle mistress she is, his name had dropped off the front pages. But now, suddenly, Pol Pot is back.

He is about to cut into his waffles when another waitress appears—this time with the plate of missing flapjacks. A stern look comes over Pol Pot's face.

"I guess the staff here needs a little reeducation."

Silence.

"Just kidding."

We all laugh.

Pol Pot was born in 1928, in a little town he calls "Nowheresville, Cambodia." It's a long way from the Santa Monica Freeway, where right now we're driving to the gym in his Subaru Outback. The air-conditioning, which is on full blast, has mussed his hair, and he's checking himself out in the rearview mirror. Despite his sixty-nine years, his round, clean-shaven face is tanned and smooth. He's wearing a plain white T and a pair of faded—but not too faded—combat pants. A beige linen jacket is draped over the back seat. He smells good. Satisfied, he pushes the mirror back into place.

Though Pol Pot has always kept quiet on the subject of his early life, driving seems to have put him in the mood to talk: "After college, my parents wanted me to get a steady job, but I just kicked around—odd jobs, hitchhiking, this and that. But I always had the revolution bug, and I finally realized that the only thing I was really good at was forced collectivization. The rest is, you know, history."

So how did his parents feel when he finally made it?

"They were my biggest fans," he says. "But, no matter how big I got, they never let me forget where I came from. In Phnom Penh, I might be Supreme Revolutionary Commander, but when I came home it was always just Pol."

A passenger in the next car recognizes him and waves excitedly. Pol Pot seems flustered and speeds up. "It's weird, you know? Six months ago, I could go anywhere and no one cared," he says. "Now everybody wants a piece of me. I mean, I'm glad the phone's ringing again, but I'm not really sure I trust it."

As we near Brentwood, a hand-painted sign on an overpass catches his eye. It reads "O.J.'s House," with an arrow pointing to the right. Pol Pot shakes his head. "Murderer" he says.

At the Odyssey Gym, in Santa Monica, Pol Pot is known as Mr. Pot, as in "Hi, I'm Scott, Mr. Pot's personal trainer." Since turning single again a few years ago, he's become a self-described "health nut." "Don't get me wrong," he says, climbing off a Lifecycle. "I'm still a big fan of radical primitivist agrarian reform. But one morning I woke up and it hit me: I'd been so busy thinking about the masses that I hadn't been taking very good care of Pol Pot."

At the moment, Scott seems to be doing a fairly good job of looking after the aging socialist leader. "Let's do ten minutes on the treadmill, Mr. Pot," he says, "and remember to breathe." Scott hands him a bottle of water, and Pol Pot muses aloud: "Anlong Veng, my remote jungle hideout, used to be a real people place. Now it's all about who's up, who's down—not who's doing the best job of seizing control of the means of production. I just don't think I want to play that game anymore. I'm playing a different game now—the game of life."

A few minutes later, Scott reappears, to turn down the treadmill. "Warm down—*very* important," Pol Pot says, running a towel over his hair. The sunlight is shining through the front window, warming Pol Pot's face, which breaks into a bright, satisfied smile. The most sought-after man in Southeast Asia looks out at the world. The treadmill slows to a stop. Pol Pot has finally stopped running. Pol Pot is happy at last.

Taking the A Train
to Early Retirement

STEPHEN SHERRILL
AND PAUL TOUGH

New Yorkers celebrated Gov. George Pataki's announcement last week of discounted daily, weekly and monthly subway and bus passes. But perhaps we haven't celebrated quite enough. Let's do the math.

First, if you buy 10 rides on your Metrocard, you get an 11th ride free. Used carefully, this feature effectively cuts the cost of a subway ride to $1.36 from $1.50. If that were the entire discount, it would be a good deal. But let's look a little further.

There's also a $63 pass, which gives the bearer unlimited rides for a month. More savings, or less? Well, it depends on how you use the subway. And this is where things get complicated.

If you ride the subway only once a month and walk back home, that ride will cost you $63. Very little savings there. But do that twice a month and it brings your cost down to $31.50 a ride. Still pricey, but you've just saved $31.50. How? By riding the subway more. Watch the way it works.

If you ride the subway back and forth to work each weekday, say 22 days a month, that's 44 rides for $63, which works out to $1.43 a ride. Still not a huge discount, but, over time, you'll save $3 a month, or $36 a year. That's real money. That's real savings. But you can do better.

Say you ride the subway 80 times a month: back and forth to work each day, out on the town 16 evenings—dinner, drinks, a Broadway show, it doesn't really matter—and about 5 trips each weekend. You're looking at a subway ride for 79 cents—the sort of fare your parents are always reminiscing about. It's like getting a real old-fashioned egg cream for a nickel.

Take 252 rides a month and you'll find that you can get anywhere in the Big Apple for just two bits. Pretty flinty, huh? Well, stand clear of the closing doors, because you're not done yet. A thousand rides a month gets you to a per-ride fare of just 6 cents. Not bad—but still about 5 cents too much. What? That's right: if you merely take 6,300 rides a month, or about 210 rides a day, your fare works out to a shocking 1 cent per ride.

Two hundred ten subway rides a day might seem daunting, but it's actually quite easy. The committed but frugal straphanger would merely travel the lines of the subway one stop at a time, exiting and immediately re-entering—for just one penny, mind you!—at every single stop. Assuming that trains arrive every six minutes (of course, we can't guarantee that but, hey, this is New York, what are you going to do?) that's 10 rides an hour. True, the rider would have to keep this up 21 hours a day, 30 days a month, but let us just reiterate: subway rides for a penny. When's the last time you found a penny and said to yourself, hey, maybe I'll go to Brighton Beach?

Paying full fare, those 6,300 rides would cost $9,450. Instead, you're paying just $63—a savings of $9,387 a month, or a whopping $112,644 a year. If you've got $112,644 a year that for some reason you don't need, then maybe you'd feel more comfortable traveling downtown in your Lear Jet. But if you're like most New Yorkers, this isn't a deal you can afford to pass by. Never pay retail, always take the Queensboro, and never pay more than a penny for a subway ride. Thank you, Governor.

Gardening Advice from
Mertensia Corydalis

Q: This past spring, my husband planted moon-flower seeds. Summer is slipping through my fingers. Evenings I lie under the stars, the earth my com-forter, and watch the luminescent flowers slowly unfurl themselves, only to be spent by sunrise. [Note: The reader then launched into a lengthy, bitter account of the husband leaving her for another man, which Miss C. has edited out.] Will the moonflowers return next spring?

—Patricia, New Portugal

A: My poor Patricia. I suspect you are an artist or liter-ary type, as no one else fancies his childhood so wretched, his affairs of the heart so tragic, his sex life so varied, or his constipation so intractable that others will not only desire that he share these experiences, but will gladly pay admission to the sharing, as well. Get up, take a bath, and get into a proper bed, prefer-ably with a new love. Moonflowers are annuals. They will not return next spring.

Q: There is a strip between my house and the neigh-bor's which is nearly covered with thick moss. I would like to sow grass seed there so I could make

*that part of the weekly mowing. What's the best
product to use to keep the moss from coming back?*
— STEVE, GRANDVIEW

A: Why anyone would want to expand the dreadful
task of lawn mowing is beyond me. Apparently, nature
has found a most hospitable location to give you the
gift of a soft, velvety, green path. And a nearly mainte-
nance-free path, I might add. Just a gentle raking to
remove any autumn leaves is all that is required. Make
a special trip to the library and find a picture of the
Saiho-Ji Moss Temple garden in Kyoto. You will thank
Providence that a thousand years ago no one shopped
for a product to get that moss under control and fired
up the Lawnboy. I am making this one exception to my
total ban on lawn-care questions.

*Q: Please suggest some varieties of cucumber that
are not seedy and bitter.*
— LOTTE, GALLOWAY

A: A common variety is the lemon cucumber. If picked
fairly small, it might answer your requirements. Tran,
my garden assistant, introduced me to the Asian
cucumber, which is a slim fruit. It is crisp and mild
tasting and unlike the English hothouse variety, which
I used to prefer, does not wilt readily. Which brings me
to some news. I noticed the sylphid Miss Vong was getting plump about the middle. Yesterday she made us a
little tea, with a snack of julienned cucumber dressed
with a bit of nuoc mam, wrapped in moistened rice
papers. It seems that a young Mr. Troung, hoping to

qualify for residency status, seduced Miss Vong. Mr. Troung is in detention, and Miss Vong, suffice it to say, is distraught. Her brother Tran is set on slitting Mr. Troung stem to stern with a grafting knife, gutting him like a Tet festival suckling pig. The fate of all three seems to be in the tiny fist of Miss Vong's "surprise." In a future column I will write about the cornichon.

This column has turned out to have an Oriental theme. So, since no one in the Far East has an interest in vast expanses of lawn (except for a few plastic toy manufacturers in Singapore), we will pass on the lawn-care questions.

Next time . . . sundials, armillaries
and astrolabes . . . cardoons

Life's already a gamble; gambling makes it a long shot.—M.O'D.

A Few Notes on Sex Education

BOB SMITH

There exists a widespread folk myth that humans should learn about sex from their parents. The reticence most parents have about discussing sex with their children almost ensures confusion. Although it's possible parents may not be shirking their responsibility in refraining from teaching sexual education, it may be a genetically programmed strategy to allow children and parents to survive adolescence. For example, my relationship with my father nearly ended when he tried to teach me how to drive. I can't imagine our relationship having survived his instructing me how to operate my penis. Imagine the stress of a first date, as you clumsily explore intimacy, your father in the backseat coaching: *Just put your arm around her! No, no, like this—here, lemme show you how.*

While talking about sex with your parents is difficult for straight teenagers, it's even more trying for gay teenagers. It takes considerable maturity, when your parents are attempting to tell you the facts of life, to interrupt and inform them of the facts of *your* life. Since our society regards producing a gay child as an event rarer than being abducted by extraterrestrials, it's not surprising that most parents of gay children are unprepared to give them guidance. Instead of giving their gay children the benefit of their own experience, they unintentionally make the mistake of giving advice based upon a heterosexual model of same-sex relationships. The results can be disastrous. Heterosexual men frequently keep their male friends happy for years by golfing with them once a week and then buying them a few beers afterward—behavior that may not be enough to sustain a relationship with the principal dancer of the Miami City Ballet. Of course, a gay son could ask his mother about keeping a man happy, but it's doubtful whether even the most ardent gay activists would—or should—feel comfortable talking about oral sex with Mom.

Lesbian daughters find themselves in a similar predicament. Their mothers may suggest that the best way to sustain a relationship with another woman is to "stay in touch," a turn of phrase that can mean something completely different to a woman who has the hots for a lanky blond lawyer named Jean. It's also not advisable for a lesbian daughter to try to use her father's method of keeping a woman happy: Agree to whatever she says and then do what you want anyway.

Since most parents are reluctant to talk about sex, schools have tried to fill the gap. In America, when we decide to ignore a subject, our favorite form of denial is to teach it incompetently. Familiarity without true understanding is not only the basis of our families but of our educational system as well. When it comes to sex, Americans have been reluctant to spell it out since the time of *The Scarlet Letter.*

Our schools teach only the most basic principles of human reproduction: naming and identifying the sexual organs and a simple explanation of how the sperm fertilizes the ovum. If mathematics was taught in the same cursory manner as human sexuality, when children learned to count they would be considered masters of the subject. The teaching of human sexuality in our schools can also be compared to how they teach music— most students of the oboe become proficient enough to use the equipment, but they never develop the ability to give anyone else pleasure. Part of the problem is the reserved textbooks used to teach human sexuality. Due to the puritanical nature of our school boards and a fear of offending conservatives, most textbooks on sexual education are simultaneously explicit and vague—a writing style most frequently employed by daily horoscopes.

Our educational programs are only explicit when they try to scare teenagers off sex, alcohol, and drugs by arousing their fear of death. As a means of dissuasion, it doesn't take into account that what most young people fear more than death is embarrassment because only a handful of people have returned from the other side to write New Age best-sellers about death, but we've all experienced embarrassment. Depending upon the circumstances, a film showing drunken relatives at a family gathering can actually be more horrifying than a film showing drunken cheerleaders killed in a car accident. Just as a five-hour film of nothing but a baby crying constantly on a nonstop flight between New York and Los Angeles would be a major deterrent to teenage pregnancy.

The opponents of sex education believe that if we keep our teenagers ignorant about a topic, then they won't become interested; a theory that has proven itself by the lack of interest shown by teenagers in other subjects missing from the curriculum, such as playing loud music, eating French fries, and the use of pimple creams.

In many school systems, the teaching of safe sex has even been a source of controversy. Schools should obviously give extensive and explicit information about safe sex and the transmission of AIDS, but right-wing extremists have suggested that homosexuals want to teach about safe sex because they're trying to recruit children into the "homosexual lifestyle." If anyone is trying to recruit, it's the militant conservatives who are trying to draw children into their own unnatural lifestyle in which people who are different are evil, and creating fear is considered a form of affection.

If the goal of conservatives is to discourage young people from having sex, they should change their strategy and push to make comprehensive sexual education compulsory. Our educational system has proved that if a subject is taught in a boring enough manner, Americans will make every effort to avoid it for the rest of their lives. If homosexuality was taught in the same manner as trigonometry, even most gay people would have no use for it after graduation.

There are many proven educational techniques that could be used to make Sex Ed unpopular. Dissecting the sex lives of most Americans could become as repugnant a classroom experience as dissecting a frog. Children could be drilled relentlessly in the spelling of sexual vocabulary, such as orgasm, cunnilingus, fellatio, clitoris. Teachers could encourage science fair projects in human sexuality, therefore making any kids interested in sex seem like total geeks. Boredom could be induced by dismal graphs of orgasms per capita and pie charts illustrating the conflicting percentages of the population who are straight, gay, bisexual, and transgender. Furthermore, textbooks on human reproduction could be made voluminously heavy—ensuring that they would only leave the lockers of aspiring shot putters.

Second only to AIDS, our educational system needs to address the subject of another frequently incurable sexually transmitted disease: Bitterness, the Glib Reaper. Bitterness has reached epidemic proportions among gay and straight alike. Optimism alone won't guard you against this scourge of modern life because it takes only one sharp remark to tear a hole in your protection. What are the symptoms of Bitterness? A burning sensation occurs whenever you think of your ex's name. If you start uncontrollably dripping with sarcasm, seek help immediately.

The test for Bitterness is simple, quick, and accurate. The doctor merely asks, "Are you seeing anyone?" and then waits for your response. The difference between being tested for HIV and being tested for Bitterness is that with HIV, if you're negative, it's good news. With Bitterness, if you're negative—you're infected.

American teenagers urgently need a program to show them the horrifying consequences of Bitterness. One way to do this would be to bring the bitter into classrooms to give a presentation which would then be followed by a short question-and-answer period. Invite a single woman in her late thirties, give her three wine spritzers, and then get her started on her last boyfriend. Pair her testimony with a twenty-six-year-old straight man with a comb-over, smiling to express every emotion but happiness, talking as an expert on the nature of women, his expertise based upon two brief, failed relationships. Follow him with a gay man, a cigarette dangling from his hand like a smoldering piece of jewelry, exuding acrimony as if it were a designer cologne. End the program with a dejected lesbian who "is working through" her rage about breaking up with her last girlfriend with a series of chiropractic adjustments. Ninety relentless minutes of despair, broken promises, and crushed hopes should be enough to turn most young people off sex for years.

Another subject that isn't being adequately addressed by our schools is whether or not to have sex on the first date. From my experience, it's usually better to wait. Sex on the first date is like dinner on the first date—years later you can never remember what you had. To help teenagers make informed decisions, we need to provide them with good reasons not to have sex on a first date:

Number One: If you need immediate gratification on a first date, order dessert. Always remember: It's easier to not finish a piece of cake than it is to not finish a blow job. If you feel guilty after eating a piece of mud pie, you can always work it off on the StairMaster—which is much cheaper and easier than trying to burn off your sexual guilt with your therapist, the StareMaster.

Number Two: Before sleeping with someone, consider trying to find out if you're sexually compatible by thinking about them while masturbating. Remember: If you can't make a relationship work in a fantasy, then it will never work in reality.

The purpose of sex education should be to prepare us for real-life problems. For example, I've often heard well-meaning people say that "too many of our young people feel pressured to have sex for the wrong reasons," presupposing a utopian world where all adult sexual activity occurs without vacillation or doubt. What must be made clear to young people is the desirability of waiting until they establish a loving relationship and *then* having sex for the wrong reasons.

From my experience of being in a relationship for eight years, I think it would be healthy to admit that everyone will, at some point in their lives, have sex for the wrong reasons. There will come a time, with even the most devoted couples, when one partner will initiate sex and the other partner will think, *Oh, I just want to go to sleep. Well, I'd better do IT—it's been a while—and if we don't he'll be in such a bad mood tomorrow.* What educators need to address and thoroughly explain are the differences among consenting sex: consenting to have sex for an inadequate reason, consenting to have sex for a reason that's reasonable but unappealing, and the much rarer and more desirable instances of consenting to sex when the person, time, and place are right.

What it comes down to is this. There are just two things that every student of human sexuality should always remember: Most people don't know sex from a hole in the ground, and the more you know, the better off you'll get.

The Last Supper, or The Dead Waiter

JON STEWART

The lack of information and interpretation concerning the life and times of Jesus Christ has, for years, frustrated scholars, theologians and lovers of information and interpretation. To date, the only notable published material on the subject is Franz Shecter's thorough yet ambiguous dissertation, "That Guy from the Thing." So little is known of Jesus because, as Shecter asserts, "He died a long time ago."

This virtual blackout has recently been lifted, in light of an astonishing discovery in the Sinai Peninsula. A German tourist in Israel, searching for the keys to his luggage, stumbled upon an ancient city buried beneath two thousand years of desert sand and a Starbucks. A month's excavation later, this man, still wearing the same pants and shirt he originally traveled in, found what is to date the only written account pertaining to the existence of Jesus Christ. The manuscript contains explicit reference to a dinner party Jesus had with twelve male friends. It is an eyewitness account penned by Avram the Waiter, who served the Christ party at the then-popular Jerusalem eatery, Jerry's. The conventional wisdom concerning the manuscript was that it proved Shecter's Crucifixion hypothesis of a "bachelor party gone awry." Although when Shecter reread the document, this time with his glasses on, grave doubts arose. Now you can decide for yourself as the ancient memoir has finally been translated from its original Spanglish.

THE MANUSCRIPT OF "AVRAM THE WAITER"

So much for things being slow during Passover. It was April of 33 and as usual Jerry's was jammed. Jerry's was the "in" spot of the moment. Ever since Pilate started coming here the place has been packed with gawkers and wannabes. Personally, I could care less. You're a person; I'm a person. Doesn't matter if you're Augustus or Barabbas. You treat me with respect, you get good service. Anyway, I'm at the end of an eight-hour double, slopping kishke to drunken centurions, and in walks Jesus with his flock of hangers-on. "Here comes trouble," I say to Moishe the barback. We'd all seen Jesus and his little bunch of frat boys around town and believe me, *not impressed*. The Greeks invented a lot of great things—namely naked wrestling—but fraternities, or any other platonic male organization for that matter, weren't one of them.

So Luke, he's the skinny one with the greasy hair—oops, that's all of them—Luke says to me with a snotty attitude, "Table for thirteen . . . I believe it's under *Christ*." So I check the book. "Well, I can't find your reservation and besides, it looks like there's only eight of you here," I say to him. I'm telling him the truth, by the way, not just being pissy. They didn't have a reservation and even if they did, I can't seat them if the whole party hasn't shown. Sorry, but it's not my rule. "They're coming. They'll be here. They got a little hung up. Holiday traffic," Luke says. You're kidding! Hung up in traffic? Well, that changes everything . . . please. Anyway, the guy's just checking out the scene, not even looking me in the eye. So all I say is, and Moishe will back me up on this, "You're welcome to hang out in the bar and wait for them . . . But I'm afraid—" and boom, he's on me. "Wait in the bar? You want *us* to wait in the bar. We're not waiting in the bar, little man." The way he was carrying on you'd have thought I asked him to bathe. (P.S. If Jesus is right and there is an afterlife, I hope they've got soap.)

"Let me ask you something. What year is it?" Luke says. I know what he's going for but I play dumb. "What do you mean?" I ask innocently. You should have seen me, all wide-eyed and sheepish. Elijah caught my performance and said he was going to throw me a graduation party because it was obvious I no longer needed acting classes. "33 A.D.," Luke says. I just let it hang there. "*Anno Domini?*. . . Year of *the Lord*," he says, giving the head nod over in Christ's direction. "You got me?" he says. So I turn to him real cool and go, "Well last time *I* checked *my* calendar it was still 3706." And then I snap my fingers and go back to marrying ketchups. Luke's jaw about hit the floor. Moishe turns and says, "Bathsheba one, Luke zero." It was really funny, but I wasn't just being a bitch. A lot of the folks at Jerry's did still use the Hebrew calendar. And besides, with that attitude those boys weren't getting any special treatment from me. Jesus slips his tunic over his head just like the rest of us; I don't care who his father is.

I do have to admit I was a little scared. Some of these apostles are pretty rough trade, the blue-collar Nazareth crowd. And I think the others work out. They were pissed. Luke was yelling at me, saying if they don't get their table right away, Jesus is going to turn all our Château Lafite-Rothschild into low-grade zinfandel. "Do it!" I say. It's not like it's my wine.

Jesus' boys are in a bit of a frenzy, giving me the third degree. "What's your name?" "We want to talk to the manager!" "Fine," I say, "talk to the manager. Get me fired." I'm an artisan/poet. I'm putting up a night of spoken word in three weeks. I don't need to take shit from cult members. I should have gotten the Etruscan bouncer, Vito the Unreasonable. He'd have thrown them out on their apostles. So just as I'm about to hurl some sea salt in Peter's face, Jesus pipes up. "Boys," he says. "Please. The wise builder doesn't build on sand, but the foolish builder can't build on rock." I had no idea what he was talking about, but suddenly, the angry mob's all kittens and puppies. It's "Right, Rabbi." "Sorry, Rabbi." "Couldn't have put it better myself, Teacher." Please! They're so affected. Jesus could've said, "Hey, look at me, I've got a banana up my ass!" and they would've acted like they just heard the word of God.

Finally, everybody shows up. It's nine o'clock. It's my last table, and the kitchen wants to close. So lucky me has to try and wrangle their order. It ain't easy. Matthew "has" to sit next to Jesus but John is having none of it, because his birthday's Monday and Jesus promised. Simon's blowing into his hand and pretending he farted. Mark and James are pouting because I carded them. Thomas wants a Caesar salad but doesn't believe it when I tell him you can hardly taste the anchovies in the dressing. Paul says he's lactose intolerant and claims if there's sour cream in his borscht, it's coming out of my tip. Judas sits glowering because no one will split an appetizer with him, and the rest of them just giggle at my ASK ME ABOUT OUR KUGEL! button. The way they all behaved, I should have made them order off the children's menu.

If my ex-roommate hadn't just screwed me on last month's rent, believe me, I would've walked. I needed the shekels, but obviously none of these guys had ever waited tables. One of them actually snapped his fingers at me for a water refill. Not even to drink. He wanted to wash Jesus' feet! That's right, feet. Right at the table! It was enough to make Caligula nauseous. The only bev they ordered, one glass of house red. They all *split* it. Hello! Misers, party of thirteen.

At this point I think they saw I was getting pissed and realized I would be handling their food. If you think that kind of thing doesn't happen in good restaurants all the time, you're kidding yourself. We had a bartender, Isaac, who had a special drink recipe for rude customers. I'll give you a hint: The magic ingredient is yak piss. You think I'm lying? He's a Bedouin and believe me those people could give a shit.

After I got them settled down, everyone ordered the lamb,
except John, who'd had lamb for lunch. You'd have thought we
were feeding the lions the way they attacked that thing. I hope
Jesus is planning some commandments on table manners.
Anyway, we got through dinner but you can be sure I had
Carlos prepare a fatty cut, even though they asked for lean.

As far as Jesus goes, we'd all heard about the miracles he
performs, but he actually seemed pretty normal. I've had
friends who get a little success and immediately turn into ass-
holes, but he was cool about it. My friend's sister caught him
when he did two nights in Thebes. She said it was OK. He bent
some spoons and guessed that one guy in the audience was
thinking about changing jobs, but she said he was better when
he was still with the Lepers. Jesus definitely did no miracles at
this dinner, although one of the waiters who got his autograph
said it cleared up his sinuses.

No real pearls of wisdom either. Once, right before dessert,
Jesus said to no one in particular, "Why do people park on a
driveway and drive on a parkway?" It was *kind of* funny. Truth-
fully, Jesus spent most of the time asking people whether or not
a beard would make him look smarter. There was a bit of a scuf-
fle when Paul liked the idea but Judas thought it was trendy. I
say cut the hair. Please. You're not a musician and it's very B.C.

Personally, when I found out one of those guys had betrayed
Jesus, it didn't surprise me a bit. You can ask David son of Phil. I
told him that night, "I would *not* trust these guys if I were Jesus."
It's so obvious they're not really his friends. They're just hanging
around him because he's famous. You should have seen them
scatter when I brought the bill. "Can you cover me, Jesus?" "I'll
get you next time, Jesus." "I gotta go drain the staff, Jesus!" I
don't know how Jesus puts up with it. Poor guy probably had to
walk on water just to get some peace and quiet.

Not that it kept me up nights. Let's face it. Messiahs come
and go. Just last week I had a creep on table five who claimed
that if I followed him, I would enjoy eternal joy in a place called
Utah. He said I could have as many wives as I wanted but not

caffeine. Get real. Me? Choose women over coffee? Please. Still, I *was* sorry to hear what happened to Jesus. He was a good tipper.

Editor's note: After this piece was published it was brought to our attention that Avram's manuscript is not the only document pertaining to the life and times of Jesus Christ. A work titled "The New Testament" was sent to our offices along with a large number of other pertinent volumes. We regret this oversight. Also, upon great scholarly review, Avram's manuscript was found to be written in Magic Marker, an implement not discovered until the early nineteen hundred and fifties. Again, our regrets.

Pen Pals

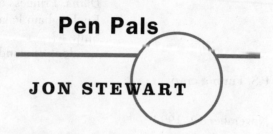

JON STEWART

October 3, 1994

Dear Mother Teresa,

Hi. You don't know me but my name is Diana and I'm your biggest fan. I've never written a letter like this before so don't think I'm crazy but I think you're the coolest. The more I hear about you the more I think we're like sisters or something, where one of the sisters is this really beautiful princess and the other isn't.

I want to know everything about you. Where do you live? I know you spend a lot of time in India, which is really weird because I live in England and India used to be one of our colonies. Do you spend summers there? I hear it's really hot. Do you drink tea? Iced tea? Have you ever been to Monaco? It's totally fun.

I'm married, are you? You're probably too busy what with the lepers and everything. I think it's kind of fun to be married. Well I guess I should be going, Cindy Crawford is coming to meet my kids and then we have to go to an Elton John concert—yuccck! Anyway, I would love to meet you for a drink or coffee, whatever, my treat! Please write back or call me soon. You can call collect (but don't make it a habit . . . ha-ha).

Your friend (hopefully),

Her Royal Highness
Diana, Princess of Wales
Buckingham Palace
Suite #3
London, England

P.S. I'm not crazy.

November 12, 1994

Dear Mother of All Big Snobs,

Braaaaaay!! Braaaaaaay!! Do you know what that sound is? It's the sound an ass makes, which is what I feel like after writing you with an offer of friendship and never hearing back. I really thought you were different but I guess you're just too big and important to write. I could have any friend I want including any of the surviving Beatles and I chose you. But I guess that doesn't matter to a bigshot like you huh?

Maybe all those people on TV who say such nice things about you don't really know you or maybe if I had some stupid disease like leprosy or hemophilia you'd find it in your supposedly big heart to answer my letter. I hate you. Actually I don't even care enough to hate you. You could row to England, then walk to London, then crawl to the palace and beg me to be your friend and I wouldn't. I have a good mind to tell my husband THE FUTURE KING about this but I'm afraid he would bomb you and your stupid country bumpkin charity house.

Your ex-friend,

Princess Diana
London, England

P.S. Some people pay up to 100,000 pounds for a simple picture of me in my workout tights. Beat that!!!

November 11, 1994

Dear Supporter,

Thank you for your interest in Mother Teresa's Charities of Hope foundation. As you know the Living Saint's schedule is quite busy so we will not be able to schedule the requested meeting.

The Charities of Hope foundation provides for the basic care of thousands of indigents in the Calcutta region. We have enclosed literature concerning the good works of the Living Saint and the Charities of Hope foundation. We very much appreciate any support you can give.

> God bless you,
>
> Sisters of Charity
> Charities of Hope
> Calcutta, India

November 14, 1994

Dearest friend Mother Teresa,

I just got your letter and I am soooo sorry for the terrible things I said to you in my last letter which you probably just got. I forgot how very slow the mail is in Third World regions. Please, please, please forgive me. I beg forgiveness even though friends like us don't usually have to do that, it's just understood.

I know this sounds crazy but I feel like we've known each other for years or in another lifetime or something. Like I was this beautiful Egyptian princess and you were my super great Egyptian servant/friend who I could confide in. I've enclosed a picture of myself (I'm the one standing in the carriage!). I know I look so fat but I don't care. The pale man with the big ears to my right is my husband, Prince Charles (Charles the turd I call him). Does he seem dull and devoid of any passion in the picture? He is in real life. I've had more passionate evenings with the Energizer Bunny if you know what I mean!! Normally I would be clearer with what I mean but I'm not because friends like us have an unspoken bond of understanding that means I don't have to be clear or specific.

Please send me a picture of yourself and I will put it on one of my dressers in one of the houses I use more frequently than the other ones.

Thank you in advance,

Your Dear Soulmate,
Diana
England

P.S. Sometimes I want to kill myself.

January 4, 1995

Dear Mr. (Miss) Mrs. <u>Diana,</u>

Thank you for your interest in Mother Teresa. We regret that we do not send pictures of the Living Saint to her admirers. We have enclosed literature on Mother Teresa's Charities of Hope foundation. Thank you again for your interest.

Sisters of Charity
Charities of Hope
Calcutta

One Year Later

January 10, 1996

Hey Girlfriend,

I know it's been a week since my last letter but things have been crazy here. Miss me? Anyway I'll get right to the point. Free at last, free at last. Thank God Almighty . . . Free at last!!! The divorce came through days ago and I couldn't be more pleased. Well . . . I'm 25 million pounds pleased at least. By the way, how many Royals does it take to screw in a lightbulb? . . . Give up? . . . nine!! Prince William to screw it in and the other eight to go fuck themselves.

Your guidance has meant so much to me. I couldn't have had the strength without you. I feel reborn. I've been a Lady so long I've forgotten how to be a woman . . . (not counting the rugby squad I wrote about in my letters of July 17–21).

How are you? How's that thing going in India? Any new men? You're so pretty but you always play it down. I wish you'd let me make you over as I requested in my letters of May 12, 1994, August 5, 1994, and March 22, 1995. Now that I'm single again I'm not taking no for an answer. Some of my lesser girlfriends and I are discussing plans for an all-girls Mexican Fiesta in Cabo. If I'm not mistaken there's a margarita there with your name on it. By the way you never answered my question of June 19, 1995—salt or no salt?

Missing you terribly,

Di-Di
Kensington Palace
England

P.S. What has sixteen legs, inbred genetic defects and a giant stick up its ass? Give up?! . . . The Royal Family!!!!!

August 11, 1997

Hey You,

You little scamp!! I hadn't heard from you in ages and I thought maybe you hadn't liked the matching swim-suits I had made for us ... and I was actually quite upset about it, until watching the telly one day I find out you've been in hospital. Do you think so little of me that you didn't want to burden me with your troubles? After all we've been through? Well, I've enclosed a get well card, including a bit of philosophy concerning friendship. I don't want to give it away but it's a drawing of two naked imps holding hands with the caption "Friendship is being there for the tough times." I believe this has been the credo for our relationship and have personalized the imps by hand to drive the point home. (I'm the imp with the full chest and you're the one with wrinkles.) I only hope you take this message to heart as I am quite disappointed with your lack of candor about your health. I've also included brownies in this care package. You really should be careful of the food down there. After my unfortunate run-in with an intestinal parasite off the coast of Fiji I've learned the value of hygienic food preparation.

On a more upbeat note, I've met someone!! He's rich and dashing and here's the best part . . . He's a darkie!!! I think you'll agree that forbidden fruit tastes the sweet-est . . . and won't that burn the Queen Mother's Royal Ass!!!

Luv,

D.

P.S. Don't worry about the sex. We're being safe.

October 1, 1997

Dear Earl Charles Spencer,

We were all greatly saddened to hear of Princess Diana's untimely passing. As you begin the processes of healing and determining the Princess's final wishes, please keep in mind the Charities of Hope foundation. We know you have wisely begun a foundation in Diana's name, to continue with her good works. As you may know, our late beloved Mother Teresa and the Princess were great friends and constant correspondents. Perhaps it is fate that we continue, in their absence, the relationship they had so energetically forged. Also, to reassure you, it would be a legal write-off.

God Bless You,
Sisters of Charity
Charities of Hope
Calcutta

·· NEWS QUIZ ··

3/1/99 "CHAT AND ARGUE CHOO CHOO"

Next month, hoping to reestablish cordial relations, more than 140 congressmen will board a chartered Amtrak train bound for Hershey, Pennsylvania. What will they do when they get there?

"The same thing everyone does after getting off an Amtrak train: attempt to wash that vague uriney smell out of their clothes."—Tim Carvell

"Let Mary Bono out of the bathroom."
                                    —Michael Gerber

"I'm not sure, but if Bob Barr is going, I'll bet he doesn't touch any "Special Dark" chocolate."
                                    —Rich Harrington

"Chocolate-covered prostitutes."—I. C. Graham

"Hershey? Train? Congressmen? Is it just me, or is it a little homoerotic in here?"—Larry Schnur

"Bang on drums and try to get the talking stick away from a weepy Tom Delay."—Molly Gabel

• RANDY'S WRAP UP •

Beyond a preschool visit to a local dairy, my first assembly line was at the Hershey's chocolate factory, and it was perfect—incredibly loud, with a cocoa aroma as thick as a fist. There were ordinary items—candy bars and kisses—in infinite multiples, and ordinary objects in gigantic versions—mixing bowls, ladles, boxes. But you'll never see it.

Hershey no longer runs a factory tour. Instead it has a visitors center—Candytown or The Chocolate Work Shoppe, or Fattyland, something like that—pathetic, fake, Disneyfied. It's the same at most factories. Fear of libel suits has superseded pride in the product.

One delightful exception, should you like your kids to see something made, and an easy drive from Hershey is Mack Truck in Macungie, Pennsylvania. While it's an assembly plant, not a manufacturing plant, they do start with a pile of parts in the morning and roll fifty of those big boys out the door by the end of the day. You get to see people building something that's not idiotic, a great treat for one who's worked in TV.

It's interesting that the dem-rep safari is at the site of a pseudo-experience rather than the real thing. But if you're trying to inspire artificial amity, that's not such a bad choice.

RANDY'S RECANTATION

Several of you chided me for calling the travelers "congressmen," omitting the women representatives. Quite right. My mistake.

TOUCHY-FEELY ANSWER

They're going to pretend that Sam Waterson is Lincoln.

As they did in 1997, the representatives are attending a retreat. Leaders of both parties are expected, including Dennis Hastert and Richard Gephardt. Among the speakers will be historian Doris Kearns Goodwin and John Hume who, along with David Trimble, won the Nobel Peace Prize last year for his work in Northern Ireland. Waterson, supported by a troupe of actors and historians, will present selections from *The Great Emancipator.*

The Pew Charitable Trust is providing $700,000 to underwrite the event.

MONTH OF JUNK EXTRA

I received thirty-five unsolicited E-mails in February, not a huge number, but it's a short month, and I use a local service provider. Most of this trash, nineteen pieces, proffered business opportunities—dubious investments, credit card schemes, home employment. Eleven involved retail sales (dental care, computers, divorce lawyers, on-line auctions); four announced some sort of performance; one was an ancient chain-letter scam.

Each investment scheme began with a lie. Ask to be removed from the list and you learn that the return address is bogus. I suppose I'll never get my money back. Or earn enough to buy that solid gold hat.

A few highlights:

• From: clinical14b@gmc.edu

Subject: CBSNews:1st Aphrodisiac Drug Apr

"The announcement of this scientific breakthrough has set off a media firestorm."

If this is an investment opportunity, it's unconvincing. If it's a personal suggestion, it's impertinent—like I'm not doing fine with Nyquil and Kahlua cocktails.

• From: marketwatchernow1999sb@he.com.br

Subject: RE: "STRONG BUY" HI-TECH MEDICAL

"PDCID has announced priority production of their proprietary Hypo-Sterile 2000, which renders medical contaminants harmless."

Tempting. But my money's tied up with Rumplestiltskin's process, which renders straw into gold.

• From: aoolw@prodigy.net

Subject: Earn 2–4k Per Week from Home!!

"What have you done with your dreams?"

My dreams rarely involve becoming a travel agent, but they frequently include an enormous cartoon swan.

• From: Laura.Hunter@Cwix.Com

Subject: Next Networking Events@Cheetah, Limelight

"After Work Networking Events for Young Professionals"

It's difficult to decide which word in the above phrase is the least attractive.

• From: DrwBior1@aol.com

Subject: A Bit About Your Family's History

"Do you know WHO your ancestors are and WHAT they did?"

I already employ a system for addressing these questions; it's called psychotherapy.

COMMON DENOMINATORS

the dangers of an underfunded rail system
the joys of erotically applied chocolate

I Am a Tip-Top Starlet

GARRY TRUDEAU

When the huge *Evita* production company blew into Budapest last month to rent its ancient architecture, Madonna, the film's star, was much too busy staying in character to meet with the local press. Finally, on the eve of her departure, good manners prevailed, and the pop diva submitted to an interview with the Budapest newspaper *Blikk*. The questions were posed in Hungarian, then translated into English for Madonna, whose replies were then translated back into Hungarian for the paper's exclusive. Shortly thereafter, at the request of *USA Today*, Madonna's comments were then retranslated from Hungarian back into English for the benefit of that paper's readers. To say that something was lost in the process is to be wildly ungrateful for all that was gained. "I am a woman and not a test-mouse!" reads a typical quote. *USA Today*, presumably pressed for space, published only a few of these gems, leaving the rest to the imagination, whence has sprung the following complete transcript:

BLIKK: Madonna, Budapest says hello with arms that are spread-eagled. Did you have a visit here that was agreeable? Are you in good odor? You are the biggest fan of our young people who hear your musical productions and like to move their bodies in response.

MADONNA: Thank you for saying these compliments [*holds up hands*]. Please stop with taking sensationalist photographs until I have removed my garments for all to see [*laughs*]. This is a joke I have made.

BLIKK: Madonna, let's cut toward the hunt: Are you a bold hussy-woman that feasts on men who are tops?

MADONNA: Yes, yes, this is certainly something that brings to the surface my longings. In America it is not considered to be mentally ill when a woman advances on her prey in a discothèque setting with hardy cocktails present. And there is a more normal attitude toward leather play-toys that also makes my day.

BLIKK: Is this how you met Carlos, your love-servant who is reputed? Did you know he was heaven-sent right off the stick? Or were you dating many other people in your bed at the same time?

MADONNA: No, he was the only one I was dating in my bed then, so it is a scientific fact that the baby was made in my womb using him. But as regards these questions, enough! I am a woman and not a test-mouse! Carlos is an everyday person who is in the orbit of a star who is being muscle-trained by him, not a sex machine.

BLIKK: May we talk about your other "baby," your movie, then? Please do not be denying that the similarities between you and the real Evita are grounded in basis. Power, money, tasty food, Grammys—all these elements are afoot.

MADONNA: What is up in the air with you? Evita never was winning a Grammy!

BLIKK: Perhaps not. But as to your film, in trying to bring your reputation along a rocky road, can you make people forget the bad explosions of *Who's That Girl?* and *Shanghai Surprise?*

MADONNA: I am a tip-top starlet. That is my job that I am paid to do.

BLIKK: O.K., here's a question from left space: What was your book *Slut* about?

MADONNA: It was called *Sex,* my book.

BLIKK: Not in Hungary. Here it was called *Slut.* How did it come to publish? Were you lovemaking with a man-about-town printer? Do you prefer making suggestive literature to fast-selling CDs?

MADONNA: These are different facets to my career highway. I am preferring only to become respected all over the map as a 100 percent artist.

BLIKK: There is much interest in you from this geographic region, so I must ask this final questions: How many Hungarian men have you dated in bed? Are they No. 1? How are they comparing to Argentine men, who are famous for being tip-top as well?

MADONNA: Well, to avoid aggravating global tension, I would say it's a tie [*laughs*]. No, no, I am serious now. See here, I am working like a canine all the way around the clock! I have been too busy even to try the goulash that makes your country one for the record books.

BLIKK: Thank you for your candid chitchat.

MADONNA: No problem, friend who is a girl.

To Our Valued Customers

GARRY TRUDEAU

Dear Readers:

It's April again, which means Jan and I have just returned to Mill Valley from another buying trek through the Annapurna, an ordeal that has left us spent but elated. As always, you, our valued catalog customers, were never far from our thoughts—especially the evening we lingered over jasmine tea with a Mahayana Buddhist monk at the Four Winds Monastery, perched precariously above a roaring tributary of the Ganges. As we sipped to the rhythmic whirl of prayer wheels, I in my all-cotton, breathable Sahib Gear™ Punting Pants, Jan in her wind-resistant Amelia Earhart Aviator's Bra, we couldn't help noticing the elegant saffron robe that enveloped our host. The rustic fabric, simple and unfussy, draped beautifully—perfect, as Jan remarked to his holiness, for curtains.

Well, one thing led to another, and before you knew it, we'd bought the monastery and put the monks to work weaving our new Katmandu Cottage Curtains (see page 32; also available in cranberry and moss). We're proud to have brought a traditionally indolent people into the new economy, giving them dignity and a chance to con-tribute to their country's nascent GNP. And because we've taught the monks to scrupulously detoxify their dyes before dumping them upstream from the tiny, unspoiled Nepalese villages (whose honey-skinned chil-dren are so to die for that Jan and I actually adopted one), your purchase of our hand-stitched window dress-ing will help save the planet for future generations.

You can find this and other new offerings in our Simpler Times Furnishings Collection, which still features best sellers like our woven bamboo Margaret Mead Litter Chairs; our World War I Turkish Cavalry Helmets (wonderful as planters); and our Lord Kitchener Lawn Furniture, made entirely of distressed, vintage cricket paddles. A new favorite of Jan's dad, who's very particu-lar when it comes to comfort, is our hand-rubbed rhino-skin Royal Bengalese Club Chair. Sink into this over-stuffed beauty, and try not to imagine yourself in the highest echelons of the Raj, ordering a vodka tonic or dispatching 1,000 Gurkhas to certain death in the Khyber Pass.

The excitement over our new home furnishings spills over into the latest additions to Sahib Gear™, our tra-ditional theme-wear collection for anyone born too late to experience colonial rule, steamer travel, first-edition Fitzgerald, freshly ironed linen and servants who were like members of the family. Since you can't go back to Paris in the '20s or Havana in the '40s or even Brooklyn in the '50s, we bring it to you, with all the quality jodh-purs, dusters, spats, boaters, corsets, spurs, poodle skirts, pince-nez and butcher's smocks you've come to expect from us—but at a fraction of the price you might pay at an ordinary costume shop.

Why do we go to so much trouble? Because here at J. Entitlements we believe that you, our valued customers, deserve a life—even if it's not your own. Toward that goal, we now offer Enhanced Living®, a total life-style ensemble inspired by the visual and sartorial motifs of leading bygone eras. Simply choose a historical period or figure, and one of our life-style engineers will refurbish your entire house and wardrobe with the corresponding furniture, objets, garments, fragrances and bedding. We'll even panel your library with our famous Books-by-the-Yard, with customized, hand-tooled leather spines of the classic works with which you wish to be identified. (Call our 800 number for available titles.)

Finally, to complete your life-style package, we still offer our Papa Hemingway Trophy Wife to preferred gentlemen customers. Exclusive to us, each of our hand-picked replacement spouses has been raised under Jan's watchful eye at our own private boarding school, situated in the rolling countryside of lovely Sonoma Valley. Why take a chance on that stunning Lufthansa flight attendant who may or may not have a prescription-drug problem? Choose from over ten popular archetypes, from Coquettish to Contemporary Bold. (Because of the normal cycles of anorexia, Trophy Wives may vary slightly in size and appearance, so please allow us to select one for you.)

Sometimes when Jan and I are raft-drifting down the languid Orinoco, where the only sound is the mesh lining in Jan's flight vest wicking moisture away from her skin, we'll gaze up into the indigo Venezuelan night and thank the stars for our large, loyal customer base. Without you, there wouldn't be a J. Entitlements—and we'd be just two more lawyers without lives!

Well, that's all for now. See you in the Casbah or Key West or the Côte d'Azur!

Best Regards,

Roger and Jan

Getting Over Getting Stoned

GARRY TRUDEAU

> "Zero! Zero! Zero!"
> —Bob Dole, describing the amount
> of tolerance a Dole Administration
> would have toward drug use

It was a stirring call to arms. The G.O.P. Candidate may have sounded like a panicky swabbie alerting the bridge about incoming Japanese fighters, but as wedge issues go, the war on drugs definitely has juice. If the Democrats wanted to take credit for the cascade of positive economic indicators, then they'd have to step up to the new negative drug numbers as well. Smartly reasoned, if you overlooked one tiny detail: a lot of Republicans are under fifty.

Why this is a problem was dramatically illustrated when, on the eve of the G.O.P. convention, family values keynoter Susan Molinari, thirty-eight, was outed as a former pot user. "Mustang Susan," as she was soon dubbed, quickly trotted out the "youthful-experimentation" defense, an option not available to vice-presidential short-lister Connie Mack, whose shot at the ticket can't have been helped by news that he was still lighting up in his thirties.

Does Dole really want to start down this road? When he excoriates the White House gang who never grew up, who never did anything, he adds, by implication, "except get high." He means to ask voters, How can you expect people who never respected our drug laws to enforce them now? But as Molinari's untimely admission so vividly demonstrates, this is a dangerous game.

By now, eighty million Americans have tried marijuana. That's a lot of people using a substance we all say we abhor. Before we can get any traction on controlling pot (which accounts for most of the rise in teen drug use), the generation that popularized the stuff has got to finally come clean about what made it so alluring in the first place—and then square that with current marijuana policy. A good start might be for every middle-aged public official in America to take the following oath:

Let it be known that I, an educated, middle-class baby boomer, do declare that I have knowingly utilized a delta-9-THC delivery system (hereinafter referred to as "TOKING UP") for the purpose of inducing intoxication. My actions cannot be described as "experimental," as their outcome (hereinafter referred to as "GETTING STONED") was known to me in advance.

I further acknowledge that my memories of TOKING UP are fondly held, particularly as they cross-reference with memories of concurrent sexual activity. It is even possible that I once believed GETTING STONED to be a beneficial experience, teaching tolerance, since it rendered all co-users equally attractive and all rock bands equally talented. I may also have believed that GETTING STONED engendered profound INSIGHTS, which I may have, at least once, attempted to record with a Day-Glo marker on the back of an empty doughnut box (in Molinari's world, this would be known as a "LAB REPORT").

In the alternative, if I did *not* enjoy GETTING STONED, I admit that my cessation reflected a simple preference for abstinence, rather than any deep moral concerns or a sudden new respect for our nation's drug laws. Moreover, I am not willing to describe my earlier actions, which I knew to be illegal, as "youthful indiscretions" unless I am also prepared to characterize similarly other nonviolent offenses, such as fraud or burglary.

I acknowledge that in the unlikely event that I never tried TOKING UP, I probably attended parties where TOKING UP took place, an activity currently considered criminal in several states.

I further concede that small marijuana transactions were at one time so commonplace that I may have even forgotten being involved in one. In the event that I did sell a friend a single JOINT, I accept that that activity renders me a former DRUG TRAFFICKER, guilty of an offense that is now punishable by several years in prison.

I concede that I once did not view marijuana as dangerous, knowing that it is not physically addictive or lethal. (A fatal dosage would be three-quarters of a ton smoked over a fifteen-minute period.) Accordingly, I believed marijuana laws to be draconian, a view once shared by Jimmy Carter, Dan Quayle and Richard Nixon's marijuana commission, all of whom favored decriminalization. It was only after my appetite for recreational drugs had abated, and I had produced children whom I did not believe capable of "handling" marijuana as responsibly as I had, that I came to oppose decriminalization. I acknowledge that it was this fear, and not new medical evidence, that caused me to subsequently support mandatory sentencing for other people's children caught emulating the actions of my generation.

To summarize, at one time I possessed, consumed and probably distributed marijuana—activities for which I may feel embarrassment but not guilt. I concede that there is nothing in my actions to distinguish them from the charges on which nearly 4 million Americans have been arrested since 1982.

Finally, I admit that this has not caused me to lose a moment of sleep, except insofar as it has pertained to my career.

Manifesto

JOHN UPDIKE

I've never been soft on foreigners, but this here arrest of Mr. Hugh Grant for trying to make a friend in Los Angeles has got me so darn mad I've gone and joined the local militia. Armed Citizens of Cranberry Corners doesn't have much of a ring, some say, but we like the acronym ACCC. Sounds like a Uzi automatic mowing down a bunch of pests from the vice squad, doesn't it?

I mean, is a man's brand-new white BMW his castle, or not? So, the windows were getting steamed? It's not as if he was parking at a bus stop or next to a fire hydrant. It was 1:30 A.M., on Hawthorne Avenue. "Engaging in a lewd act?" Come on, officers Terry Bennyworth and Ernest Caldera, of the understandably notorious LAPD. How you think you got here, to the surface of the planet Earth? A lewd act, every one of us.

That is, excepting for these test-tube or intra-vitro babies that are in the papers all the time, and don't you think the government won't be poking its nose and its microscopic tweezers in there, splicing a tax-compliance gene into the poor little helpless thing's DNA?

You could have knocked me over with a feather when Dan Rather, or maybe Diane Sawyer, explained that there was a crime called "soliciting for sex." And another called "sexual harassment." Where was I when the government passed these outrageously unconstitutional laws, product of a clear conspiracy to bring heterosexuality into disgrace and create a secret oligarchy of Ivy-league eunuchs? Out in the cranberry bogs, that's where I was, tending to business in my hip waders, floating the harvest to shore.

We've been such patsies, up to now. We've been so damn *good*. The wetlands bleeding hearts and their Department of Interior musclemen always after us about breaking up the nests of the fan-tailed egrets. Then the clean-water freaks in their armored helicopters crabbing about our gelatinous insecticides drifting out to sea and smothering the mackerel. Yeah, yeah, we said. We'll comply. We'll toe the line. God forbid a single fan-tailed egret or ugly spiny-finned mackerel should make a little sacrifice so millions and millions of loyal Americans can celebrate Thanksgiving properly, with the traditional fare.

They make you feel *ashamed,* of doing a day's honest work and trying to bring something positive, something edible, into people's lives. Be a teenage mother on welfare or a former draft dodger, they fall all over you, they build ramps all over the post office for you, they even elect you president. But go out there under the broiling sun, armed with just a wooden cranberry rake, and do daily battle with the fruit-eating water mites, they treat you like a criminal. Regulation this, regulation that, and seven layers of taxation besides.

Now, it's like there were two *mes*—the old oppressed me, the patsy me, a guy about two feet tall and shrinking, and then the post-LA (lewd act) me, with the fog lifted from my brain and my head seven feet off the ground. This afternoon, on our secret parade ground, we have bazooka practice and then dressage, in case underhanded government tactics revive the cavalry.

I feel strong. I feel clean. If I ever feel a twinge of trepidation, like during one of our free-form mine-planting sessions, all I have to do to get my blood boiling again is to think of that poor young Englishman being booked, staring out at the camera hollow-eyed from being up past his bedtime and rudely pulled out of what he thought was his own BMW by minions of the law Bennyworth and Caldera and still trying to digest the sushi and saki he had consumed a few hours before at the trendy Matsuhisa restaurant with his *Nine Months* director Chris Columbus.

Chris Columbus! What an irony!! If this is what freedom means, the real Chris Columbus could have stayed in Genoa. I've got Hugh Grant's mug shot tattooed on my right forearm, where I can see it. On the other forearm, Divine Marie Brown, looking bored. She knows the drill, we know the drill, but poor Mr. Grant? He thought he was visiting a free country, where soliciting for sex was a normal human act.

They do anything to put a crimp into that pretty boy's sheepish grin, we'll be ready. Cranberry Corners as you've known it will cease to exist.

Life is an endless gym class with involuntary perfect attendance.—M.O'D.

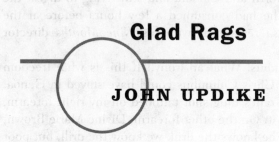

Glad Rags

JOHN UPDIKE

To those of us who were alive and sartorially active at the time, it was saddening to read in *Vanity Fair* recently the allegation, by "New York socialite" Susan Rosenstiel, that in 1958 J. Edgar Hoover was parading around in a Plaza Hotel suite wearing women's clothes: "He was wearing a fluffy black dress, very fluffy, with flounces, and lace stockings and high heels, and a black curly wig." I was saddened to think that future generations, trying to grasp the peculiar splendor and excitement of high-echelon cross-dressing during Eisenhower's second term, will imagine that dowdy bit of black fluff, with its fussy flounces and matching wig, to have been *très à la mode*, when the truth is we all considered J. Edgar something of a frump.

Ike, for instance, dear Ike with his infallible instincts, would never have let himself be caught in lace stockings, even though he did have the legs for them. I remember, within a month of St. Laurent's 1958 collection for Dior, Ike coming out in a stunning cobalt-blue wool trapeze, with white open-backed heels and a false chignon. That very day, if memory serves, he had sent five thousand marines to Lebanon, and not a hair was out of place. It was with this outfit—or was it a belted A-line from the previous year?—that he sported a flowered silk neck cloth, when scarves were still thought to be strictly for babushkas. He was very conservative as to hemlines, however; when St. Laurent lifted skirts to the knee in 1959, the president waited three months for Congress to decide the issue and then, losing all patience, switched to Balenciaga with a stroke of his pen. Thenceforth, to the very end of his administration, he stuck with long-waisted day dresses in neutral duns and beiges.

John Foster Dulles, on the other hand, favored a slinky-pajama look, and pastel pants suits with a touch of glimmer in the fabric. Oodles of bangles, upswept blond wigs, and pom-pommed mules. For all his staunch anti-Communism, he was oddly partial to red, though I believe on good authority that Sherman Adams at least once took Foster aside and made the point that bright colors did not become a big-boned frame. Sherman, though he was undone by vicuna, lingers in my mind's eye as a creature of whimsical ostrich-feather boas and enchantments in lightly starched lemon voile. Neil McElroy, the secretary of defense, vied with Senator Dirksen for the title of Most Quietly Elegant; at a time when bell-shaped skirts and full-sleeved blouses were controlling the silhouette, McElroy denounced Pentagon cost run-ups in a shimmering jade-green sheath, side slit to the thigh and topped by a cloth-buttoned brocade linen bodice with shoelace shoulder straps. Foster Dulles's brother Allen also preferred the slim look—tailored suits of pencil-striped wool, the jackets sharply cinched at the waist, with wide lapels piquantly emphasizing the bosom of a padded corselette.

That terrible weekend after *Sputnik,* to rally our spirits Ike commandeered a ballroom at the Mayflower and sent down the directive: *Glad rags only.* My God, what floods of organdy and tulle, ruffles and ruchings and appliquéd beadwork! Present-day Washington, with its dreary cutbacks, has no concept of our kind of style. Of course, the U.S. had half the world's refrigerators then, and the national debt was peanuts. I went up to Allen, who in the spirit of the occasion had forsaken his pin-stripes for a so-called "corolla" gown by Capucci of dusty-rose taffeta, with a real rose stuck in his silver-dusted wig, and asked him, "My goodness, what ever are we going to do about the Soviets and this terrible Cold War!"

Eavesdropping as he always was, J. Edgar came up to us in some perfectly inappropriate, pathetic little frock of cocoa crêpe gathered in front to a ribbon bowknot. That winsome bulldog-puppy face of his was crowned by a grotesque paste tiara, and the spike heels of his patent-leather pumps kept sticking in the parquet floor.

Allen suavely elbowed him aside and spoke *sotto voce* to me. "Mr. Under-Secretary"—I was always being Under-Secretary of something or other in those giddy years—"not to worry, though the Commies have the rocket power for now. Our top-secret reconnaissance flights, I can inform you, have come back with photographs of Khrushchev in an evening dress of gold-threaded silk chiffon and of Mikoyan in a two-piece, low-backed outfit of velvet and shirred georgette. If this is the game they want to play, we'll outspend the bastards right into the ground!"

From: Corporate Communications at CRT301

CorpCorp Strengthens Diversity Commitment

COLLEEN WERTHMANN

June 23, 1998

Dear Associate:

Marketing and distributing our brands and products to diverse groups of consumers with ever-changing tastes and values provides a continuing challenge for us. Children under five, religious ascetics, and the terminally ill have proven to us, time after time, that we must be more effective, more creative, and more innovative than our competitors in persuading consumers to prefer and buy our brands. As the new millennium dawns, we need to stick our fingers up our competitors' nostrils and twist, good and hard, until their faces are all contorted and they stand on the desperate tiptoe of the free market. Naturally, we will carry clean hankies.

As a worldwide leader in the entertainment and beverage industries, it is more critical than ever that we, as a company, are able to attract and retain the best possible drones—er, talent. This mandate is summarized in the opening paragraph of the "Letter to Our Shareholders"

MIRTH OF A NATION

in last year's annual report, which, in case you neglected to memorize it, goes: "The CorpCorp Company Ltd.'s purpose is to create long-term growth for our share-holders, by serving our communities and constituencies with integrity; by recruiting, guiding, and developing the highest quality of people with the highest standards; and by making and marketing competitively superior products to consumers throughout the world."

This statement clearly explains the "who, what and where" of our company's business focus. The "who," of course, are people—of every kind (more about that later). The "what" are products, specifically our brands and labels. And the "where" is *the world in its entirety.* Mwah-hah-hah-hah-hah-HAAAAAAAH!!!

In each of these factors, diversity is an integral element, especially in the various constituencies we serve, the array of brands and labels we sell, and the numerous countries and communities in which we do business.

Did we reach 250 words with that last paragraph?

To help ensure that CorpCorp takes full advantage of available talent in all sectors of the workforce, a Diversity Accountability Committee has been established. We have been asked to lead this committee because we have strong personal beliefs in the added value of human diversity to our businesses and a strong commitment to leveraging that diversity for our competitive advantage.

In addition to the three of us who will serve as co-chairmen (what a drag—how did we ever get roped into it?), the committee will include the following people:

- Tom Janacek, vice president of Human Resources Development, Studio Division
- Richard Kristiansen, director, Bottling Services, Embalming Services/Special Projects, Americas

- Elaine DiGiacomo, senior vice president of Human Resources, Vineyard, and Estate Wines Group
- Cast-Iron PopBot, director of Industrial Relations, Americas
- Mbuti Lars Cheng-Paramahansa-Velazquez-Truong-McKeever, vice president of Diversity, Corporate
- Keith Mosley, vice president of Organizational Development, The CorpCorp Grappa and Absinthe Group
- White Noise, vice president of Human Resources, Corporate

The purpose of the Diversity Accountability Committee is to put a process into place for measuring and reporting business unit progress in advancing diversity at all levels of our organization. Each business unit will define diversity according to its own business needs and will set its objectives accordingly. Those who fail to meet Diversity Objectives will be shot, execution-style, at 500 Park Avenue. A light meal will be served beforehand. Should you be slated for termination, please contact Sheri Wilson at ext. 7354 in Accountability to choose from several menu options.

As its name implies, the committee will hold all business units accountable for creating and maintaining an environment that provides equal opportunity for all types of people—men and women of all races, ethnicities, cultures, ages, physical and mental abilities, religions, and sexual orientations. Additionally, the committee will focus on continuing the Company's efforts to ensure that the highest standards of integrity and performance are "fairly" applied to all employment candidates and employees, whether ugly, boring, or stupid.

It is our expectation that everyone in our company will be receptive to new ideas about business processes and methods of working that are direct outcomes of enhancing diversity within our ranks. Further, it is our intent to use our diverse talents to gain every competitive advantage in the marketplace and among diverse consumer groups. This includes [but, naturally, is not limited to] illegal headlocks, biting, and kicking.

In the coming months, our committee members will focus primarily on managers' efforts to increase and leverage employee diversity in their business units. This process will involve the outsourcing of levers, crowbars, wedges, and other leveraging tools. All employees at every level of our organization are encouraged to support the committee's work, and take over on lunch breaks, bathroom breaks, etc. It is our hope that the pursuit of workforce diversity, like our CorpCorp Values, will become a regular part of our vocabulary, decision-making, and our pursuit of making lots, and lots, and LOTS of money.

G. F. Warren III	Irving Thomson	Bill Prince
President	Vice Chairman	President/COO
CorpCorp	and CFO	CorpCorp
Estate &	The CorpCorp	Studios, Inc.
Vineyards	Company, Ltd.	Wines Company

The distant voice lesson is not distant enough.—M.O'D.

A NOTE ABOUT THE EDITOR

The editor, Michael J. Rosen (born 1967, Cedar Rapids, raised Presbyterian, no fan of asparagus or cod, married 1992, two children, one kind and one homely, both loud, with big, red tongues), would like to make a small point with regard to his name. Specifically, he would like to insist that his name be spelled, from here on out, in all cases and all contexts, in ALL CAPS. As it is on the cover, it shall be in all other instances: newspaper articles, profiles in magazines thick and odorous, Christmas gift lists, notes scrawled on envelopes. Why? Because the editor is overly tired of all this feigned humility by his fellow editors and authors—"e. e. cummings" this and "bell hooks" that. Both of these writers, like all writers and editors, had or have egos the size of clipper ships—the act of writing and thinking someone would have any interest whatsoever in reading it necessitates it—so attempting to cover these egos up with all the faux humility is not only disingenuous, it's nauseating. This editor, for one, is sick about it. Look at this editor. He is sick! Sick about it! Thus, the editor requests that he be referred to, in all cases, in all caps, thus more accurately reflecting the high regard in which he holds himself. To illustrate:

Incorrect (in more than one respect): "Michael J. Rosen is perhaps the oddest-looking writer-editor since Thomas Dryden."

Correct (in all respects): "MICHAEL J. ROSEN is much too handsome to be a writer-editor. One would expect him to be modeling, or perhaps playing second base for the Yankees."

Please adopt the new style immediately, and do not waver or slink or fudge. E-mail friends about the wonderful book MICHAEL J. ROSEN has edited. Write to relatives about how if MICHAEL J. ROSEN does not receive some kind of award, or statue? at least a talk show? for his efforts herein, then there is no justice. HAIL MICHAEL J. ROSEN! Even when *thinking* about MICHAEL J. ROSEN, think of his name in all caps. Say it aloud in all caps. MICHAEL J. ROSEN! Say it with your feet spread apart and your hands on your hips. MICHAEL J. ROSEN! No, louder. Louder, I say! MICHAEL J. ROSEN! Use your diaphragm! MICHAEL J. ROSEN! Now bigger!

MICHAEL J. ROSEN!

MICHAEL J. ROSEN!

A NOTE ABOUT THE TYPE

The text of this book was set in Garamond, a font the provenance of which has long been shrouded in mystery. No one, including the editor, knows anything about its history or creator. Even so, the makers of this book, like you, know what they like. They like that it is a stately font, and is compact, and looks great in ALL CAPS, better in SMALL CAPS, and divine when T R A C K E D O U T. And though ambiguity surrounds this font, readers can safely assume certain things. It was likely invented hundreds of years ago, in Europe, by someone named Something Something Garamond—like, say, the Count of Garamond. Or the Vice-Count of Garamond. The Duke of Garamond. The Duke of Earl of Garamond. (Really, does it matter?) Whatever his name, you can bet on one thing: this Garamond fellow was extremely popular. See, back in the day, those who invented fonts were *incredibly huge stars*. For instance, accompanying the advent of a new typeface, there would be a massive, gala opening, held in Milan, Tokyo or Los Angeles—or all three simultaneously, as was regularly the case with Baskerville in his prime—at which all kinds of wonderful and glittery people would strut around, walk to and fro in burgundy tights and shiny shirts with puffy shoulders, drinking mead and eating whole turkeys on sticks. On the runway they would ignore the Rivers rats and instead talk to Geena Davis, cooing about the font being a groundbreaking font, a watershed font, the fontmaker's best work yet, while sometimes muttering about the poor dubbing in the chase scene, or the woeful miscasting—but always!—of Winona Ryder.

Index

AL FRANKEN

Contributors' Notes

BONNIE ABBOTT, a native of Ohio, grew up on a hobby farm and graduated from The Ohio State and Franklin universities in English and Business, respectively. She currently resides in Columbus with her daughter Kirsten and two nutsy dogs, Floyd and Gracie.

JOHN ABOUD lives and works in New York City. He wishes everyone would concentrate less on the "exotic" and more on the "dancing."

HENRY ALFORD is the author of *Big Kiss* and *Municipal Bondage*.

KURT ANDERSEN is the author of *Turn of the Century*, a novel, and a writer for *The New Yorker*. He lives in New York City.

DAVID M. BADER is the author *of How to Be an Extremely Reform Jew* and *Haikus for Jews*. He is not even distantly related to Supreme Court Justice Ruth Bader Ginsburg, though he insists on referring to her as Aunt Ruth.

DAVE BARRY is a humor columnist for the *Miami Herald* and the author of several books, most recently *Dave Barry Turns 50* and a novel *Big Trouble*.

ROY BLOUNT JR.'s books include *Be Sweet: A Conditional Love Story, First Hubby, Crackers, Not Exactly What I Had in Mind*, and *Roy Blount's Book of Southern Humor!*

ZEV BOROW is a contributing editor at *Spin* and a regular contributor to *McSweeney's*, *New York* and other periodicals. He thinks love is a wonderful thing; freedom, too.

DAVID BOUCHIER, resident essayist at National Public Radio station WSHU in Fairfield, Connecticut, writes a weekly humor column in the regional edition of the Sunday *New York Times*.

CHRISTOPHER BUCKLEY lives in Washington, D.C., with his wife, daughter, son and dog, Duck. He is the author of several books including *Little Green Men*, *Wry Martinis*, and *Thank You for Smoking*.

FRANK CAMMUSO is the political cartoonist for the Syracuse newspapers. He and Hart Seely are the authors of a forthcoming book to be published by Random House.

RANDY COHEN has written for *The New Yorker* and *Late Night with David Letterman*. He currently writes "The Ethicist" for the *New York Times Magazine*, and "The News Quiz" for *Slate*.

RICH COHEN is the author of *Tough Jews, A Chronicle of Brooklyn Gangsters* published by Vintage Books.

CATHY CRIMMINS has chronicled the baby boomers' slow and torturous crawl through life in such books as *When My Parents Were My Age, They Were Old, Or Who Are You Calling Middle-Aged?*, and *Curse of the Mommy: Pregnant Thoughts and Postpartum Impressions of a Reluctant Mom*. Her articles have appeared widely, including publications such as the *Village Voice, Redbook, Hysteria, Working Woman*, and *Funny Times*.

PRUDENCE CROWTHER is a sometime writer who lives in New York City.

DAVE EGGERS, editor of *McSweeney's*, was also editor of *Might* magazine. His new book is entitled *Heartbreaking Work of a Staggering Genius: A Sentimental Anti-Memoir*.

MICHAEL FELDMAN is the Michael Feldman of *Michael Feldman's Whad'ya Know?* heard nationally on public radio.

AL FRANKEN is the author of *Rush Limbaugh Is a Big Fat Idiot; Why Not Me? The Making and Unmaking of the Franken Presidency;* and *I'm Good Enough, I'm Smart Enough, and Doggone It, People Like Me!*

BILL FRANZEN was born in 1952, in Minneapolis, and now lives in Connecticut with his wife and two children. His stories have appeared in *The New Yorker, Harper's, National Lampoon, GQ,* and *George. Hearing from Wayne,* a collection of stories, was first published in 1988 by Knopf.

IAN FRAZIER writes essays and books, including *Coyote v. Acme,* winner of The 1997 Thurber Prize for American Humor. He lives in New Jersey.

FRANK GANNON has contributed to *The New Yorker, GQ, Harper's* and other national magazines. He is the author of three books and is presently composing a book about Ireland for Warner Books.

VERONICA GENG's collected works, *Love Trouble,* was published in 1999 by Houghton Mifflin and received The Thurber Prize for American Humor Special Citation. She was an editor at *The New Yorker* for many years.

CHRIS HARRIS is a writer for *The Late Show with David Letterman.* He is the author of the travel guide parody *Don't Go Europe!* and a contributing editor to *Might* magazine.

PAUL HELLMAN is a consultant, speaker, and columnist. His work has appeared in the *New York Times,* the *Wall Street Journal,* public radio's *Marketplace,* and regularly on the back page of *Management Review.* His forthcoming book is about office anxieties.

DAVID IVES is the author of *All in the Timing: 14 Plays,* published by Vintage Books.

JAY JENNINGS was born in Little Rock, Arkansas and lives in Tarrytown, New York. His humor and journalism have appeared in *Sports Illustrated, Vogue,* the *New York Times,* the *Los Angeles Times,* and the anthology *The Best of Bad Hemingway.* He is also the editor of *Tennis and the Meaning of Life: A Literary Anthology of the Game.*

GARRISON KEILLOR is the host of National Public Radio's *Prairie Home Companion,* and *The Writer's Almanac.* He has authored several books, including *Me: by Jimmy (Big Boy) Valente, Wobegon Boy, Lake Wobegon Days,* and *Leaving Home.*

CHRIS KELLY is head writer at *Politically Incorrect with Bill Maher.*

JOSH KORNBLUTH is an author and monologist, whose works include *Red Diaper Baby* and *Ben Franklin Unplugged.*

FRAN LEBOWITZ is best known for her two books *Social Studies* and *Metropolitan Life.*

FRANZ LIDZ is a senior writer at *Sports Illustrated,* an essayist for the *New York Times,* author of the memoir *Unstrung Heroes,* and adored by all who have ever met him.

SANDRA TSING LOH is a writer/performer whose critically-acclaimed off-Broadway solo shows include *Aliens in America* and *Bad Sex with Bud Kemp.* Her books include *Depth Takes a Holiday: Essays From Lesser Now,* which was named by the *Los Angeles Times* as one of the 100 best books of 1997. Her short story "My Father's Chinese Wives" won a 1995 Pushcart Prize, and is included in Ira Glass's *This American Life.*

MERRILL MARKOE has four Emmies for her writing on *Late Night with David Letterman* in the 1980s, and has published three books of humorous essays in the 1990s. She currently lives with the four most incredible dogs in the continental United States.

PATRICIA MARX is thrilled to be included in this anthology. She writes for film, television, books and magazines.

DANIEL MENAKER, an editor of fiction for twenty-six years at *The New Yorker,* currently serves as vice president and senior literary editor at Random House. He has contributed to almost every major magazine, and has written two collections of stories and one novel.

HOWARD MOHR is the author of *How to Tell a Tornado, A Minnesota Book of Days (And a Few Nights),* and *How to Talk Minnesotan (A Visitor's Guide).* In collaboration with songwriter Drew Jansen, Howard has written two musicals based on *How to Talk Minnesotan*; to date, they have enjoyed three years of (alternating) continuous performance at the Plymouth Playhouse in the Twin Cities.

MARK O'DONNELL's plays include *That's It, Folks!, Fables for Friends,* and *Strangers on Earth.* Knopf has published two collections of his stories and his novels *Getting Over Homer* and *Let Nothing You Dismay.* His humor, cartoons and poetry have appeared in *The New Yorker, Spy, The Atlantic,* and *Esquire.*

P. J. O'ROURKE was born in Toledo, Ohio in 1947. He attended Miami University in Oxford, Ohio, and the Johns Hopkins University in Baltimore. The author of several books—most recently *Eat the Rich*—he lives in New Hampshire and Washington, D.C.

SAM PICKERING JR. teaches English at the University of Connecticut. He has written eleven books of familiar essays, the two most recent being *A Little Fling* and *Deprived of Unhappiness.*

DANIEL RADOSH is a freelance writer in New York City.

DAVID RAKOFF has written for the *New York Times, The New York Times Magazine, Outside, GQ, Gourmet,* and *Condé Nast Traveler,* and he has been a sporadically frequent contributor to

Public Radio International's *This American Life*. He has appeared as an actor on *Cosby, As the World Turns,* and *Late Night with Conan O'Brien.* He lives in New York.

MICHAEL RUBINER has written for *The New Yorker,* the *New York Times, Rolling Stone,* and *GQ.* He has also written and produced television shows for Nickelodeon and MTV.

STEVE RUSHIN, author of the travel memoir *Road Swing,* is a senior writer at *Sports Illustrated.*

BILL SCHEFT is the former head monologue writer for *Late Night with David Letterman.* He has contributed pieces to *The New Yorker, George,* and the *New York Times.*

DAVID SEDARIS is a playwright and a regular commentator for National Public Radio. His works include *Naked, Holidays on Ice,* and *Barrel Fever.*

HART SEELY is a reporter with the *Syracuse Post-Standard* newspaper. He has a wife and three kids.

STEPHEN SHERRILL has written for *The New Yorker,* the *New York Times, GQ,* and *Esquire,* and is a former staff writer for *Late Show with David Letterman.* He lives in New York.

BOB SMITH tours extensively, performing across the country, and has written for numerous television shows and performers including *Roseanne* and the *MTV Video Music Awards.* He is the author of the book *Openly Bob.*

JON STEWART is the author of *Naked Pictures of Famous People* and host of Comedy Central's "The Daily Show."

PAUL TOUGH is the editor of *Saturday Night,* a Canadian monthly, and a contributing editor of *Harper's* and of the public-radio program *This American Life.*

GARRY TRUDEAU is the creator of *Doonesbury* and a contributing essayist for *Time.*

JOHN UPDIKE is the author of many novels, essay and story collections, children's books, and volumes of poetry. His most recent collection of prose, from which his contributions here are taken, is *More Matter*.

COLLEEN WERTHMANN is a writer and performer living in New York City. She is at work on her third solo show, *She Hates Her Supervisor*, excerpted here. Her previous shows are *Catholic School Girls Rule* and *Fire in the Hole*. She is a contributor to *McSweeney*'s and *Slate*'s "The News Quiz."

Acknowledgments

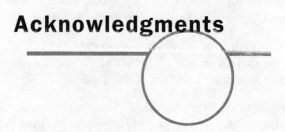

While many people provided invaluable counsel and support during the creation of this book, particular thanks are extended to Jay Rishel, my colleague at The Thurber House, and to one fine reader, Charlie Cole.

Several pieces in *Mirth of a Nation* appear here for the first time. Others are reprinted with specific thanks to the editors and authors listed below, or as otherwise specified.

"Zone 5: Gardening Advice by Mertensia Corydalis" appears here for the first time, courtesy of Bonnie Thomas Abbott.

"You'll Never Groom Dogs in this Town Again!" originally appeared in Henry Alford's collection, *Municipal Bondage* (Random House). "The Young Man and the Sea" originally appeared in *New York* magazine. "Cafe Manhattan" and "How to be Difficult" originally appeared in the *New York Times Magazine*.

"The Yanni Files" by Kurt Andersen originally appeared in the *New York Times*.

"A Prayer for Bill Clinton," © copyright 1998 by David M. Bader was first published in the *New York Post*.

"*Parlez-Vous Francais?,*," "An Aesthetically Challenged American in Paris (Part II)," and "Independence Day," by Dave Barry originally appeared in *Tropic* magazine.

"You Could Look Me Up . . . Sometime" by Roy Blount, Jr., originally appeared in *Men's Journal.* His essay, "I Go to Golf School," originally appeared in *Travel & Leisure Golf.*

"A Graceland for Adolf" by Zev Borow originally appeared on *McSweeney's* Web site. "Upcoming House Votes" appears here for the first time, courtesy of the author.

"The Bane of Every Vacation: Souvenirs," "A Year-Round Tan for the Asking," "Lapses of Photographic Memories," and "Let's Hear it for Cheerleaders," by David Bouchier all aired originally on National Public Radio Station WSHU in Fairfield, Connecticut.

"As I Was Saying to Henry Kissinger . . ." by Christopher Buckley originally appeared in *Forbes FYI* magazine. "Memo from Coach" originally appeared in *The New Yorker*.

"The News Quiz" episodes, wrap-ups, and extras, by Randy Cohen originally appeared on *Slate*, an online magazine.

"God Help Me," which first appeared in *The New Yorker,* and "Autumn of the Matriarch," which first appeared in *Spy,* are reprinted here courtesy of the author, Rich Cohen.

"Future Schlock" by Cathy Crimmins first appeared in her book *When My Parents Were My Age They Were Old, Or, Who Are You Calling Middle-Aged?*

"What We Told the Kids" and "Un Caballo In Maschera" appear here courtesy of Prudence Crowther.

"Submission Guidelines," "A Note about the Type," and "A Note about the Editor," were created specifically for this volume by Dave Eggers.

"The Midwest: Where Is It?" appears here courtesy of Michael Feldman.

"Index," by Al Franken is reprinted from *Rush Limbaugh Is a Big Fat Idiot* copyright © 1996 by Al Franken, Inc. Used by permission of Delacorte Press, a division of Random House, Inc.

"Come Stay with Us" originally appeared in Bill Franzen's book, *Hearing from Wayne* (1998). "Desert Surprise" and "Return Saddam's Limo. . . Now!" first appeared in *The New Yorker*. All appear here courtesy of the author.

"Laws Concerning Food and Drink; Household Principles; Lamentations of the Father," by Ian Frazier, copyright © 1997 by The Atlantic Company, appears here courtesy of the author.

Frank Gannon's contributions each appeared previously and are reprinted courtesy of the author: "Yankee Come Home," the *New York Times Magazine*; "Authors with the Most," and "Long Day's Journey Into Abs," *The New Yorker*; "Flowers of Evil: Ask Charles Baudelaire," *The Atlantic*.

Excerpts from *Love Trouble: New and Collected Work* by Veronica Geng copyright © 1999 by The Estate of Veronica Geng. "A Good Man Is Hard to Keep: The Correspondence of Flannery O'Connor and S. J. Perelman" copyright © 1995 by Veronica Geng and Garrison Keillor. Reprinted by permission of Houghton Mifflin Company. All rights reserved.

"Design Intervention" by Chris Harris originally appeared in *Might* magazine. All "Clarifications" originally appeared in *Might* magazine with these exceptions: "Kevin Johnson Injury/ Historical Midwest Destination" originally appeared in *ESPN: The Magazine*; "Supermodel/Mideast Nation" originally appeared on *The Late Show with David Letterman*, "Person/Pasta Dish" originally appeared in *Don't Go Europe!* "Why Are Kids So Dumb?" and "Green Men" are printed here for the first time. All contributions by Chris Harris appear courtesy of the author.

"Into the Giga Jungle" copyright © 1998 Paul Hellman, was originally published in the *New York Times*. "Too Late to Become a Gondolier?" copyright © 1999 Paul Hellman, "Eating Your Desk" copyright © 1998 Paul Hellman, and "Me and My Delusions" copyright © 1997 Paul Hellman appear here courtesy of the author.

Four contributions by David Ives appear courtesy of the author. "The Life of Rocks," "Degas, *C'est Moi*," and "Chicken à la Descartes," were first published in the *New York Times Magazine*. "You Say Tomato, I Say Tomorrow" originally appeared in *Spy* magazine.

"More Mergers" by Jay Jennings originally appeared in the *New York Times*. His piece "Love Bug" originally appeared in *Vogue*, while "Even More Memoirs by Even More McCourts" appears here for the first time. All are courtesy of the author.

"Rejected Polls" by Chris Kelly appears courtesy of the author.

"Driving Mister Crazy," by Josh Kornbluth appeared first in *San Francisco Magazine*, and appears here courtesy of the author. "Red Diaper Baby" from *Red Diaper Baby: Three Comic Monologues* © copyright 1996 by Josh Kornbluth, is published by Mercury House, San Francisco, California, and reprinted by permission. Lyric excerpts on p. 293 of "Oh, How I Hate to Get Up in the Morning" by Irving Berlin copyright © 1918 by Irving Berlin Music Company. Copyright renewed. International copyright secured. Used by permission. All rights reserved.

"Money" copyright © 1997 by Fran Lebowitz originally appeared in *Vanity Fair*, July 1997. Reprinted by permission of William Morris Agency, Inc., on behalf of the author.

"Trout," "Jumpin' Jiminy," and "Space Travel Food," by Franz Lidz appear courtesy of the author. "Piscopo Agnostics" by Franz Lidz and Steven Rushin, originally appeared in *The New York Times*.

"11th Hour Bride" and "The Way of the Ear" by Sandra Tsing Loh originally appeared in *Buzz* magazine.

"Phone Hex," which originally appeared in *Buzz*, "Birthdays: So Now What," and "I Network with Angels," which originally appeared in *New Woman*, are included here courtesy of the author, Merrill Markoe.

"How and Why Book of Magnets" and "Joyce Maynard Looking Back" by Patricia Marx originally appeared in *National Lampoon*. "Things That Are Confusing" originally appeared in *Spy* magazine. "Bad Numbers" originally appeared in *Salon* magazine.

"Sunken Treasure" by Daniel Menaker originally appeared in *The New Yorker*.

"One Guy's TV," "Gambling in Schools," "OJ: The Trial of the Next Century," and "After This Word from Motel 3" by Howard Mohr appear here courtesy of the author.

"I Confess," and "The Last Publicist on Earth" by Mark O'Donnell appear here courtesy of the author. His other pieces previously appeared as follows: "My Genetic Memories," *The New Yorker*; "Diary of a Genius," the *New York Times Magazine*; "Millennial Maxims," *7 Days*; "TV Guide, Soon" *Forbes FYI*.

"Memoir Essay" by P.J. O'Rourke originally appeared in *The New York Times Book Review*.

"March," © copyright 1998 by Sam Pickering, Jr., originally appeared in *Deprived of Unhappiness*, Ohio University Press.

"No Strings Attached" and "Barnes Ennobled" by Daniel Radosh originally appeared in *GQ*. "Ferret-Face" originally appeared in *Stim*, an online magazine. "T.G.I.Y2K!" by Daniel Radosh and John Aboud appear courtesy of the authors.

David Rakoff's four contributions appear courtesy of the author. Each appeared previously as follows: "El Niño Has a Headache," in *Outside*; "All Happy Families," in *GQ*; "In New England

of Famous People published by Rob Weisbach Books, a division of William Morrow and Company, Inc.

"I Am a Tip-Top Starlet," "To Our Valued Customers," and "Getting Over Getting Stoned" by Garry Trudeau originally appeared in *Time* magazine.

"Glad Rags" and "Manifesto" by John Updike are from his collection *More Matter*, copyright © 1999 by John Updike, published by Alfred A. Knopf.

"From: Corporate Communications at CRT301" by Colleen Werthmann appears courtesy of the author.